Leg over Leg

Volume Two

Letter from the General Editor

The Library of Arabic Literature is a new series offering Arabic editions and English translations of key works of classical and pre-modern Arabic literature, as well as anthologies and thematic readers. Our books are edited and translated by distinguished scholars of Arabic and Islamic studies, and are published in parallel-text format with Arabic and English on facing pages. The Library of Arabic Literature will include texts from the pre-Islamic era to the cusp of the modern period, and will encompass a wide range of genres, including poetry, poetics, fiction, religion, philosophy, law, science, history and historiography.

Supported by a grant from the New York University Abu Dhabi Institute, and established in partnership with NYU Press, the Library of Arabic Literature will produce authoritative Arabic editions and modern, lucid English translations, with the goal of introducing the Arabic literary heritage to scholars and students, as well as to a general audience of readers.

Philip F. Kennedy
General Editor, Library of Arabic Literature

كتاب

الساق على الساق

في ما هو الفارياق

فارس الشدياق

المجلد الثاني

LIBRARY OF
المكتبة
ARABIC
العربية
LITERATURE

Leg over Leg

or

The Turtle in the Tree

concerning

The Fāriyāq

What Manner of Creature Might He Be

by

Fāris al-Shidyāq

Volume Two

Edited and translated by

HUMPHREY DAVIES

NEW YORK UNIVERSITY PRESS

New York and London

NEW YORK UNIVERSITY PRESS
New York and London

Library of Congress Cataloging-in-Publication Data

Shidyaq, Ahmad Faris, 1804?-1887.
Leg over leg or, : The turtle in the tree / Faris al-Shidyaq ; edited and translated by Humphrey Davies.
volumes cm
Bilingual edition In English and Arabic on facing pages.
Includes bibliographical references and index.
ISBN 978-0-8147-6984-3 (cl : alk. paper) -- ISBN 978-0-8147-4524-3 (e-book) -- ISBN 978-0-8147-4541-0 (e-book) 1. Shidyaq, Ahmad Faris, 1804?-1887. 2. Shidyaq, Ahmad Faris, 1804?-1887--Travel--Middle East. 3. Arabic language--Lexicography. 4. Middle East--Description and travel. I. Davies, Humphrey T. (Humphrey Taman) translator, editor. II. Shidyaq, Ahmad Faris, 1804?-1887. Saq ʿala al-saq. III. Shidyaq, Ahmad Faris, 1804?-1887. Saq ʿala al-saq. English. IV. Title. V. Title: Turtle in the tree.
PJ7862.H48S213 2013
892.7'8503--dc23
2013007540
CIP

New York University Press books are printed on acid-free paper, and their binding materials are chosen for strength and durability.

Series design by Titus Nemeth.

Typeset in Tasmeem, using DecoType Naskh and Emiri.

Typesetting and digitization by Stuart Brown.

Manufactured in the United States of America

Table of Contents

Letter from the General Editor iii

LEG OVER LEG, VOLUME TWO 1
Contents of the Book 4
Chapter 1: Rolling a Boulder 8
Chapter 2: A Salutation and a Conversation 38
Chapter 3: The Extraction of the Fāriyāq from Alexandria, by Sail 62
Chapter 4: A Throne to Gain Which Man Must Make Moan 84
Chapter 5: A Description of Cairo 104
Chapter 6: Nothing 114
Chapter 7: A Description of Cairo 116
Chapter 8: Notice that the Description of Cairo is Ended 122
Chapter 9: That to Which I Have Alluded 134
Chapter 10: A Doctor 142
Chapter 11: The Fulfillment of What He Promised Us 150
Chapter 12: Poems for Princes 160
Chapter 13: A *Maqāmah* to Make You Sit 174
Chapter 14: An Explanation of the Obscure Words in the Preceding *Maqāmah* and Their Meanings 186
Chapter 15: Right There! ☞ 292
Chapter 16: Right Here! 294
Chapter 17: Elegy for a Donkey 370
Chapter 18: Various Forms of Sickness 382
Chapter 19: The Circle of the Universe and the Center of This Book 390
Chapter 20: Miracles and Supernatural Acts 400

Notes 409
Glossary 433
Index 436
About the NYU Abu Dhabi Institute 444
About the Typefaces 445
About the Editor-Translator 446

الساق على الساق

المجلّد الثاني

Leg Over Leg

Volume Two

كتاب

الساق على الساق فى ما هو الفارياق

او

ايام وشهور واعوام فى عجم العرب والاعجام

تاليف العبد الفقير الى ربه الرزاق

فارس بن يوسف الشدياق

Leg over Leg

or

The Turtle in the Tree

concerning

The Fāriyāq

What Manner of Creature Might He Be

otherwise entitled

Days, Months, and Years

spent in

Critical Examination

of

The Arabs

and

Their Non-Arab Peers

by

The Humble Dependent on His Lord the Provider

Fāris ibn Yūsuf al-Shidyāq

فهرست الكتاب

	الكتاب الثانى	٦
الفصل الاول	فى دحرجة جلمود *	٨
الفصل الثانى	فى سلام وكلام *	٣٨
الفصل الثالث	فى انقلاع الفارياق من الاسكندرية *	٦٢
الفصل الرابع	فى منصّة دونها غصّة *	٨٤
الفصل الخامس	فى وصف مصر *	١٠٤
الفصل السادس	فى لا شى *	١١٤
الفصل السابع	فى وصف مصر *	١١٦
الفصل الثامن	فى اشعار انه انتهى وصف مصر *	١٢٢
الفصل التاسع	فيما اشرت اليه *	١٣٤
الفصل العاشر	فى طبيب *	١٤٢
الفصل الحادى عشر	فى انجاز ما وعدنا به *	١٥٠
الفصل الثانى عشر	فى ابيات سَرِيّة *	١٦٠
الفصل الثالث عشر	فى مقامة مقعدة *	١٧٤
الفصل الرابع عشر	فى تفسير ما غمض من الفاظ هذه المقامة ومعانيها *	١٨٦
الفصل الخامس عشر	فى ذلك الموضع * ☜	٢٩٢
الفصل السادس عشر	فى ذلك الموضع بعينه *	٢٩٤
الفصل السابع عشر	فى رثآء حمار *	٣٧٠
الفصل الثامن عشر	فى الوان مختلفة من المرض *	٣٨٢
الفصل التاسع عشر	فى دائرة هذا الكون ومركز هذا الكتاب *	٣٩٠
الفصل العشرون	فى معجزات وكرامات *	٤٠٠

Contents of the Book

Book Two 6

Chapter 1: Rolling a Boulder 8

Chapter 2: A Salutation and a Conversation 38

Chapter 3: The Extraction of the Fāriyāq from Alexandria, by Sail 62

Chapter 4: A Throne to Gain Which Man Must Make Moan 84

Chapter 5: A Description of Cairo 104

Chapter 6: Nothing 114

Chapter 7: A Description of Cairo 116

Chapter 8: Notice that the Description of Cairo is Ended 122

Chapter 9: That to Which I Have Alluded 134

Chapter 10: A Doctor 142

Chapter 11: The Fulfillment of What He Promised Us 150

Chapter 12: Poems for Princes 160

Chapter 13: A *Maqāmah* to Make You Sit 174

Chapter 14: An Explanation of the Obscure Words in the Preceding *Maqāmah* and Their Meanings 186

Chapter 15: Right There! ☞ 292

Chapter 16: Right Here! 294

Chapter 17: Elegy for a Donkey 370

Chapter 18: Various Forms of Sickness 382

Chapter 19: The Circle of the Universe and the Center of This Book 390

Chapter 20: Miracles and Supernatural Acts 400

الكتاب الثاني

Book Two

الفصل الاول

فى دحرجة جلمود

قد القيت عنى والحمد لله الكتاب الاول وارحت يافوخى من حمله * وما كدت ١،١،٢
اصدق ان اصل الى الثانى فانى لقيت منه الدُوار * ولا سيما حين خضت البحر مشيّعا للفارياق تفضّلا وتكرما * اذ لم يكن مفروضا علىّ ان ارافقه فى كل مكان * وقد مضى علىَّ حينٌ بعد وصوله الى الاسكندرية والتقامه الحصاة من
الارض ولسان قلمى يتمطّق * وثغر دواتى مطبق * حتى عاد الىّ نشاطى فاستانفتُ ٢،١،٢
الانشآ ورايت ان ابتدى هذا الكتاب الثانى بشى ثقيل ليكون عند الناس اكثر اعتبارا * واطول اذكارا * وكما انى ابتدات الكتاب الاول بما يدل على المامى بشى من العلويات ان كنت لمّا تنسَ ما مرَّ بك * استحسنت الان ان آخذ فى شى من السفليات لاجل المطابقة * هذا ولما كان الجرم من الجواهر المنيعة المفيدة راق لى ان ادحرج منه هنا جلمودا من اعلى قنة افكارى الى اسفل حضيض المسامع * فان وقفت تنظر الى تصوّبه من دون ان تتعرض له وتحاول توقيفه مرّ بك كما تمرّ السعادة علىّ * اى من غير ان يصيبك منه شى * والّا اى ان استسهلت حبسه عن منحدره كرّ عليك ودفعك تحته * والعياذ بالله مما ورآ هذا الدفع * فانظر اليه ها هو متحرك للسقوط * ها هو متصوب * فالحذر الحذر * قف بعيدا واسمع من دويّه ما يقول * ان من نظر بعين المعقول الى هذه الدنيا والى ما اختلف فيها أئتلف من

Chapter 1

Rolling a Boulder

I have cast from me, thank God, Book One, and relieved my pate of its burden. I scarcely believed I'd ever get to the second book, the first made me feel so dizzy, especially when I set out upon the waves to pay the Fāriyāq a respectful and honorable farewell. Anyway, I'm under no obligation to follow him wherever he *goes*, and for a while, after he reached Alexandria and swallowed the pebbles off its ground, my pen just sat there smacking its lips, my inkwell *closed*. 2.1.1

Then my energy returned and I started writing again, thinking it best that I commence Book Two with something weighty, so that it should be given greater *consideration* and remain for longer a matter of *cogitation*, and, just as I commenced Book One with something to demonstrate my thorough knowledge of certain high matters—and I'm assuming you haven't already forgotten what you read earlier—I thought it would be a good idea now to start with certain low matters, to keep things symmetrical. In addition, given that plain rock must be counted among the precious stones that are both hard to obtain and beneficial, it occurred to me that I should roll a boulder of that material down from the topmost peak of my thoughts to the lowest bottoms of men's ears. Now, then, if you stand and watch its progress without getting in its way or trying to stop it, it will pass you by just as happiness has me, which is to say, without touching you. Otherwise (if you think it a simple matter to bar its descent), it will pass over you and thrust you under it, and God protect us from the consequences of such a thrust! Observe: here it is, shifting in preparation for its fall, and now it's on its way. Beware then, and beware! Stand at a distance and hear the message in its thunder: "Who looks on this world with the eye of reason—on the diversity and convergence of its 2.1.2

الاحوال والاطوار* والجواهر والاعراض * والاوطار والاغراض * والعادات والمذاهب * والمراتب والمناصب * وجد ان كل شي يمرّ عليه منها يفوق كنهَه ادراكُه ويفوت تامّله * وان حواسّنا وان تكن قد اَلِفت اشيآء لم تغادر الالفة عليها محلاّ للتعجّب منها * الا ان تلكم الاشيآء لا تنفك فى نفس الامر عن كونها معجبة محيّرة * ومن تبصّر فى ادنى ما يكون منها حقّ التبصّر راى نفسه كمن قد اهمل ادآ

٣،١،٢ فرض تعيّن عليه * انظر مثلا الى اختلاف ضروب النبات فى الارض فكم فيه من الازهار البديعة الصنعة العجيبة الكِيْنة * من دون ان نعلم لها منفعة خصوصية * والى اختلاف انواع الحيوان من دبابات وهوامّ وحشرات وغيرها * فان منها ما هو حسن الشكل ولا فائدة منه ومنها ما هو قبيحُه والحاجة اليه ماسّة * وانظر فى السماء الى هذه النجوم درارِئها كوكب دِرّىءُ ويضمّ متوقّد متلالئ *

وخُنَّسها — الخنَّس الكواكب كلها او السيَّارة او النجوم الخمسة الخ *

وبَيانِيّاتها — الكواكب البيانيات التى لا تنزل الشمس بها ولا القمر *

وتوائمها — توائم النجوم واللولو ما تشابك منها *

وبروجها — معروف *

وتِنّينها — التنين بياض خفى فى السمآ يكون جسده فى ستة بروج وذنبه فى البرج السابع الخ *

وَمجرّتها — باب السمآ او شَرَجها *

ورُجُمها — النجوم التى يرمى بها *

واَعْلاطها — اَعْلاط الكواكب الدرارى التى لا اسمآء لها *

واِناثها — الاناث صغار النجوم *

وخُسّانها — النجوم لا تغرب كالجدى والقطب وبنات نعش والفرقدين *

states and *conditions*, of what's *essential* and what *incidental*, of objects and *ambitions*, of customs and schools of thought, of ranks and *dispositions*—will find that the quintessence of all that passes before him is beyond his comprehension and moves too fast for his discernment and that, while our senses may have become familiar with certain things, that very familiarity leaves us no room for wonder. Those same things never cease, all the same, to be amazing and puzzling and any who subjects even the least of them to proper scrutiny will realize that his failure to pay them due attention is equivalent to the omission of the performance of a religious obligation.

"Observe, for example, the different types of plants there are on Earth— 2.1.3
how many flowers of which we cannot say, brilliantly constructed and amazingly formed though they be, that they serve a specific purpose. And look at the different types of animals—reptiles, vermin, insects, and others: some are beautiful to look at but have no use and some are ugly to look at but are most urgently needed. And look at the heavens, at all their stars—

their *darāri'*,	a star that is *dirrī'* or *durrī'* is "a star that burns and flashes"
their *khunnas*,	"the *khunnas* are all stars, or the planets, or 'the Five Stars,'"[1] etc.
their *bayāniyyāt*,	"those stars that neither the sun nor the moon takes down with them at their setting"
their *tawā'im*	[literally, "twins"] "with reference to either pearls or stars, those that are conjoined"
their *burūj*	[literally, "the Houses" (of the zodiac)] "too well known to require definition"
their *Tinnīn*,	[literally, "the Dragon," i.e., Draco]; "the Dragon is an obscure whiteness in the sky whose body lies in six constellations of the zodiac while its tail is in the seventh," etc.
their *Mijarrah*,	["the Milky Way"] "the gateway of the sky or its anus"[2]
their *rujum*,	["shooting stars"] "the stars used for stoning"[3]
their *aʿlāṭ*,	"the *aʿlāṭ* stars are the bright ones (*al-darāri'*) that have no names"
their *ināth*,	[literally, "the females"] "the *ināth* are small stars"
their *khussān*,	"the stars that never set, such as Capricorn, the Pole Star, Ursa Minor and Ursa Major, and the Two Calves"[4]

وأَنْوائها النوء النجم مال للغروب او سقوط النجم فى المغرب مع الفجر وطلوع آخر يقابله من ساعته فى المشرق *

٤،١،٢ التى يرجع البصر عنها وهو كليل * والى اختلاف سحَن الناس وروسهم * فانك لا تكاد ترى سحنة بشر تشبه سحنة آخر غيره * ولا تجد بين رؤسهم اى عقولهم راسا يشبه غيره * فمن عباد الله هولآء من اختار المخالطة والمقارفة * والمحاشرة والمزاحمة * والمضاغطة والمصادمة * والمباراة والمعاجمة * والملاهسة والمداحمة * والمجاحسة والمداغمة * والمزاعمة والمداهمة * والمساومة والمزاهمة * على اختلاف فيها * وذلك كالتجار والنسآ * ومنهم من قابلهم بضد ذلك فاختار العزلة والانفراد كالنساك والزهاد * ومنهم من جعل دابه التهافت على المين والافترآ * والغلو والاطرآ * كالشعرآ والمستاجرين لمدح الملوك فيما يطبعونه من هذه الوقائع الاخبارية * ومنهم من قابلهم بضده فآثر الصدق والتحرّى * والتحقيق والتروى * والقول الفصل والمطابقة بين الماضى والحاضر والاتى *

٥،١،٢ وذلك كاهل الفلسفة والحكمة والرياضة * ومنهم من يعمل النهار كله ويكدّ بكلتا يديه وكلتا رجليه وربما لم ينطق بكلمة واحدة * وذلك كاصحاب الصنائع الشاقّة * ومنهم من لا يحرك يده ولا رجله ولا كتفه ولا راسه وانما ينطق فى بعض ايام الاسبوع بكلمات ثم يقضى سائر الايام مستريحا متنعما * مترّفها متترّفا * وذلك كالخطبآ والوعّاظ والمرشدين الى الدين * ومنهم من يفتك ويبطش ويجرح ويقتل كالجند * ومنهم من يعالج ويداوى ويشفى ويحيى كالأُساة واوليآء الله تعالى اهل الكرامات والمعجزات * ومنهم من يُستاجَر للتطليق * ومنهم للتحليل * ومنهم للايلاد * ومنهم للالحاد * ومنهم للتفريق * ومنهم للتاليف بين الآحاد * ومنهم من يتكوّى فى بيته فلا يكاد يخرج منه الّا لضرورة * ومنهم من يصعد

and their *anwā'* — "a *naw'* [singular] is a star that inclines toward its setting point or sets in the west at dawn while, at the same time, another rises opposite it in the east"

—stars so dazzling that the eye turns from them in exhaustion.

"Observe too the differences among people's countenances and heads, for you see scarcely one human face that resembles another or find among their heads, meaning their minds, one that is like another. There are mortals who have chosen propinquity and mixing, jostling and crowding, pressing together and colliding, vying with and trying one another, pushing and shoving, battling and butting, competing and blackening each other's names, bargaining and chaffering, and so on, according to their different persuasions; examples are traders and women. Others provide a contrary model, having chosen isolation and withdrawal; examples are ascetics and hermits. Yet others have made it their business to fall over one another to tell lies and *blather*, exaggerate and *flatter*, such as poets and the hirelings who sing the praises of kings in all those gazettes that they print,[5] while yet others again confront the latter with the opposite, preferring truth-telling and investigation, enquiry and careful consideration, definitive decisions and the comparison of past, present, and future; examples are the great philosophers, physicians, and scientists. 2.1.4

"Some work all day long, toiling with both hands and both feet, quite possibly without uttering a single word; examples are those involved in arduous industries. Others move neither hand nor foot nor shoulder nor head and pronounce only a few words on certain days of the week, the rest of which they spend coddled in comfort, lolling in luxury's lap; examples are preachers, homilists, and religious guides. Some murder, batter, wound, and kill, such as soldiers, while others treat, medicate, cure, and revive, like nurses and the Friends of God Almighty, men of extraordinary spiritual feats and miracles.[6] One man is hired to bring about divorces,[7] another as a 'legitimizer,'[8] one for impregnation and another for inhumation, one to put asunder and another to make peace between persons. Some lurk in their houses and hardly ever leave them unless obliged to do so, while others climb mountains and lateen yards, trees, and *pulpits* or descend into valleys, drains, and *cesspits*. 2.1.5

الجبال والادقال * والمنابر والاشجار* ومنهم من يهبط الاودية والبواليع والمراحيض * ومنهم من يسهر الليالى فى تاليف كتاب * ومنهم من لا يذوق النوم حتى يحرقه * ومنهم من يسود ومن يُساد * ومنهم من يقود او يقاد * ومع هذا التنافى والتباين فمآل مساعيهم وحركاتها كلها الى شى واحد * وهو ادخال الانسان خنابتيه غداة كل يوم فى رائحة كريهة قبل ان يستنشق روائح الازهار* ويتمتّع بمتوع النهار* واعجب من جميع ما مّر بك من هذه الاحوال حالتا اصحابنا ٦,١,٢
السوقيين والخرجيين * فان حرفتهم لما كانت لا تتوقف الا على استعمال اداتين فقط * اى المخيّلة والقَسْم دون افتقار الى آلة اخرى * وكان مورد اقوالهم * ومصدر جدالهم * ومبنى انتحالهم * وجلّ راس مالهم * قولهم يحتمل ان يكون هذا الشى من باب المجاز الاسنادى او اللغوى * او من مجاز المجاز او الكناية * او من حمل النظير على النظير * او النقيض على النقيض * او من باب ذكر اللازم وارادة الملزوم او بالعكس * او من قبيل ذكر البعض وارادة الكل او بالعكس * او من نوع اسلوب الحكيم * او من باب التهكم * او من طاقة التلميح * او من كوّة الالتفات * او من خرق الحشو* او من خرت الادماج * او من خصاص الاكتفاء * او من شقّ الاحتباك * او من سَمّ عكس التشبيه * او من خلل سوق المعلوم مساق غيره * او من فتحات التجريد * او من فرجة الاستطراد * او من ثقوب التورية * لم يكن من اللائق بهم ان يخلطوا هذه الآوّات وتلك اللوّات بشى

من العَرّادات — العرّادة شى اصغر من المنجنيق * ٧,١,٢

والدَبّابات — الدبّابة آلة تتخذ للحروب فتدفع فى اصل الحصن فينقبون وهم فى جوفها *

والدَرّاجات — الدبّابة تعمل لحرب الحصار تدخل تحتها الرجال *

Some stay up all night writing books, while others can't sleep a wink till they've burned one. Some rule and others are ruled. Some lead and others are led. And yet, for all that contradiction and contrast, all their efforts and actions bring them to the same end, which is that, when a person gets up each morning, he sticks his nostrils into a foul smell before sniffing the scent of *flowers* and enjoying the pleasures of the daylight *hours*."

Stranger, though, than any of the situations you have just passed in review is that of our friends the Market-men and the Bag-men. Given that their trade depends on the employment of just two tools, namely surmise and assertion, and has no need of any others, and that the wellspring of their statements and source of any *tirade*, the basis of their claims and greater part of their *stock-in-trade* is to say,[9] "It is likely that this thing to which you refer falls under the rubric either of the trope attributive or the trope lexical, or the trope tropical or the expression periphrastic, or it may be that it belongs to the category of referring like to like, or opposite to opposite, or under that of 'expressing the intrinsic while intending the extrinsic' (or the reverse), or belongs to the type known as 'mentioning the part while intending the whole' (or the reverse), or to the category known as 'the method of the sage,'[10] or is to be approached via the door of irony, or the aperture of allusion, or the peephole of person-switching,[11] or the rent of redundancy, or the casement of carefully crafted composition, or the inlet of implication, or the tear in 'tight weaving,'[12] or the spiracle of the quasi-paradoxical simile, or the knot-hole of the substitution of what is known for what is not, or the toe rings of the generalization of the attribute, or the eyelet of the appositional aside, or the portholes of punning," it is inappropriate for them to mix in among all these "ors" and "ifs" any of the following: 2.1.6

ʿarrādāt,	"*ʿarrādah* [singular] is a thing smaller than a *manjanīq*" 2.1.7
or *dabbābāt,*	"the *dabbābah* [singular] is an engine of war that is pushed to the base of the [besieged] fortress, after which the men inside make a breach"
or *darrājāt,*	"a *dabbābah* made for siege warfare, which men get underneath"

المنجنيقات	المنجنيق آلة ترمى بها الحجارة كالمنجنوق معربة والمنجليق المنجنيق *
والنَفّاطات	النفّاطة اداة من نحاس يرمى فيها بالنفط *
والخَطّار	المنجنيق والذى يطعن بالرمح *
والسَبَطانات	السَبطانة قناة جوفآ يرمى بها الطير *
والضَبْر	جلد يغشى خشبا فيها رجال تقرّب الى الحصون للقتال *
والقَفْع	جُنّة من خشب يدخل تحته الرجال يمشون به فى الحرب الى الحصون *
والجُلاهق	الذى يرمى به ونحوه البراقيل والبنادق *
والحَسَك	اداة للحرب من حديد او قصب فيلقى حول العسكر تعمل على مثال الحسك المعروف * ٨,١,٢
والقُرْدُمانىّ	قبآ محشو يتخذ للحرب وسلاح كانت الاكاسرة تدّخرها فى خزائنهم والدروع الغليظة *
والتِجْفاف	آلة للحرب يلبسه الفرس والانسان *
واليَلَب	التِرسة او الدروع من الجلود *
والسَرْد	اسم جامع للدروع *
والدَرَق	التروس من جلود بلا خشب ولا عَقَب ونحوه الحَجَف *
والحَرْشَف	الرجّالة وما يزيّن به سلاح *
والعَتَلات	العَتَلة العصا الضخمة من حديد لها راس مفلطح يهدم بها الحائط *
والمِنْسَفات	المِنسفة آلة يقلع بها البنآ *

or *manjīqāt*,	"the *manjanīq* is a machine with which stones are thrown; also spelled *manjanūq*—an Arabized word[13]—and *manjalīq*"
or *naffāṭāt*,	"the *naffāṭah* [singular] is a copper device with which bitumen is thrown"
or the *khaṭṭār*,	"the *khaṭṭār* is the [same as the] *manjanīq*"; it also means "a man who thrusts much with his spear"
or *sabaṭānāt*,	"the *sabaṭānah* [singular] is a hollow reed through which projectiles are blown"
or the *ḍabr*,	"the *ḍabr* is a leather-covered wooden structure containing men who approach fortresses in order to fight"
or the *qaf*ʿ,	"protective structures made of wood beneath which men get and which they move up to fortresses in war"
or *julāhiq*,	"balls that are thrown"; similar are *barāqīl* and *banādiq*
or *ḥasak*,	"devices of iron or reed for use in war that are thrown down around the soldiers and that work like common caltrops"[14] 2.1.8
or the *qurdumānī*,	"a padded outer garment used in war; also a weapon the Caesars kept in their storehouses; also thick shields"[15]
or the *tijfāf*,	"a device for war worn by horse and man alike"[16]
or *yalab*,	"shields and coats of armor made of leather"
or *sard*,	"a general term for armor"
or *daraq*,	"shields made of leather without wood or sinews; similar are *ḥajaf*"
or *ḥarshaf*,	"foot soldiers; ornaments for weapons"
or *ʿatalāt*,	"the *ʿatalah* [singular] is an enormous iron pole with a blunt head with which walls are demolished"
or *minsafāt*,	"the *minsafah* [singular] is an instrument for uprooting built structures"

والفَلَق مقطرة السجّان وهى خشبة فيها خروق على قدر سعة الساق *

والخَنازِر الخَنْزرة فاس عظيمة يكسّر بها الحجارة * ٩،١،٢

والعَذْرآ شى من حديد يعذب به الانسان لاقرار بامر ونحوه *

والمقاطِر المقطرة خشبة فيها خروق على قدر سعة ارجل المحبوسين *

والمراديس المِرْداس آلة يدكّ بها الحائط والارض *

والدَهَق خشبتان يغمز بهما الساق *

والصاقور الفاس العظيمة *

والمَلاطِس المِلْطس المِعْول الغليظ *

والمَقارِيص المقراص السكين المعقرب الراس *

والملاوظ المِلْوَظ عصا يضرب بها *

والمقامع المِقمعة خشبة يضرب بها الانسان على راسه * ١٠،١،٢

والمقافع المقفعة خشبة يضرب بها الاصابع *

والحَدَأة الفاس ذات الراسين *

والمِنقار حديدة كالفاس *

والمَهامِز المِهْمزة المقرعة او العصا *

والعَرافيص العِرْفاص السوط يعاقب به السلطان *

والمخافق المخفقة الدِرَّة او سوط من خشب *

ولا بالرماح الطاعنات والسيوف الباترات والنبال الصاردات والنصال المدميات والمقادع المولمات والمقارع المضنيات والصُلُب المهلكات والخوازيق النافذات والاغلال المصلصلات والنيران المتاججات والغارات والغزوات

or the *falaq*,	"the jailor's pillory, consisting of a length of wood with holes the size of the shanks"	
or *khanāzir*,	"the *khanzarah* [singular] is a large axe used for breaking stones"	2.1.9
or the *ʿadhrāʾ*,	"a thing made of iron with which people are tortured to make them confess, etc."[17]	
or *maqāṭir*,	"the *miqṭarah* [singular] is a piece of wood with holes the size of the prisoners' legs"	
or *marādīs*,	"the *mirdās* [singular] is an instrument with which a wall, or the ground, is pummeled"	
or the *dahaq*,	"two pieces of wood with which the shanks are squeezed"	
or the *ṣāqūr*,	"a large axe"	
or *malāṭis*,	"the *milṭas* [singular] is a large *miʿwal* "	
or *maqārīṣ*,	"the *miqrāṣ* [singular] is a knife with a curved blade"	
or *malāwiẓ*,	"the *milwaẓ* [singular] is a stick for beating"	
or *maqāmiʿ*,	"the *miqmaʿah* [singular] is a piece of wood with which people are beaten on their heads"	2.1.10
or *maqāfiʿ*,	"the *miqfaʿah* [singular] is a piece of wood with which the fingers are beaten"	
or the *ḥadaʾah*,	"a double-headed axe"	
or the *minqār*,	"the metal blade of the axe"	
or *mahāmiz*,	"the *mihmazah* [singular] is the same as the whip (*miqraʿah*) or the stick (*ʿaṣā*)"	
or *ʿarāfīṣ*,	"the *ʿirfāṣ* [singular] is the whip with which the secular power metes out punishment"	
or *makhāfiq*	"the *mikhfaqah* [singular] is the whip, or a lash made of wood"	

or lacerating lances or severing swords or shooting shafts or blood-letting blades or stinging sticks or weakening whips or crucifying crosses or impaling posts or chinking chains or flaming fires or invasions or raids or murderous onslaughts or surprise attacks or looting or rapine or the bereavement of mothers or feuds or grudges or, last but not least, the rough treatment of women during intercourse.

والنكايات والكبسات والاستلابات والافتضاضات والاثكالات والعداوات والمشاحنات وآخر الجميع بالركاكات * فكم لعمرى من دم سفكوا * وجند اهلكوا * ١١،١،٢
وعرض هتكوا * وحرمة انتهكوا * وذى اهل ربكوا * وعزب همكوا * ونسآ ايّموا * واولاد يتّموا * وبيوت خرّبوا * واموال نهبوا * ومصون اذالوا * وحرز نالوا * ومستور فضحوا * وحرام اباحوا * فهل فعل ذلك من قبلهم سَدَنة *

الاَنْصاب — الانصاب حجارة كانت حول الكعبة تنصب فيهلّ عليها ويذبح لغير الله تعالى *

والكَعَبات — الكعبات او ذو الكعبات بيت كان لربيعة كانوا يطوفون فيه *

والرَبَّة — كَعْبة لمَذْحِج *

وبُسّ — بيت لغطفان بناها ظالم بن اسعد لما راى قريشا يطوفون بالكعبة ويسعون بين الصفا والمروة فذرع البيت واخذ حجرا من الصفا وحجرا من المروة فرجع الى قومه فبنى بيتا على قدر البيت ووضع الحجرين فقال هذان الصفا والمروة واجتزأ به عن الحج فاغار زهير بن جناب الكلبى فقتل ظالما وهدم بنآءه *

وعَبَدة مَرْحَب — صنم كان بحضرموت *

والعَبْعَب — صنم *

والغَبْغَب — صنم *

ويَغُوث — صنم كان لمَذْحِج *

والبَجَّة والسَّجَّة — صنمان *

وسَعْد — صنم كان لبنى مِلْكان *

ووَدّ — صنم ويضم * ١٢،١،٢

Dear God, how much blood they have shed! How many a soldier they have destroyed! How many a virgin's honor they have defiled! How many a time they have violated the sanctity of the home, thrown men into confusion before their families, tormented bachelors, made wives into widows and sons into orphans, reduced houses to ruins, pillaged wealth, ripped veils from the faces of decent women, made off with treasure chests, ravished that which was protected, and violated sanctuaries! Were such things done by those who, before them, were custodians of 2.1.11

al-Anṣāb,	"al-Anṣāb were stones that formerly stood around the Kaaba [of Mecca] at which they used to celebrate and make sacrifice to other than God Almighty"
or al-Kaʿabāt,	"al-Kaʿabāt, or Dhū al-Kaʿabāt, was a holy house that belonged to the tribe of Rabīʿah which they used to circumambulate"
or al-Rabbah,	"a kaaba belonging to the tribe of Madhḥij"
or Buss,	"a holy house belonging to the tribe of Ghaṭafān built by Ẓālim ibn Asʿad when he saw Quraysh circumambulating the Kaaba of Mecca and running between al-Ṣafā and al-Marwah: he measured the holy house [of the Kaaba], took a stone from al-Ṣafā and a stone from al-Marwah, and then returned to his people, built a holy house of the same size as the house [of Mecca], set down the two stones, and said, 'These are al-Ṣafā and al-Marwah' and he set up his own pilgrimage to rival that of Mecca. Then Zuhayr ibn Janāb al-Kalbī raided [Ghaṭafān] and killed Ẓālim and demolished his house"
or ʿAbdat Marḥab,	"an idol that used to be in Ḥaḍramawt"
or al-ʿAbʿab,	"an idol"
or al-Ghabghab,	"an idol"
or Yaghūth,	"an idol belonging to the tribe of Madhḥij"
or al-Bajjah and al-Sajjah,	"two idols"
or Saʿd,	"an idol belonging to the Banū Milkān"
or Wadd,	"an idol; also spelled Wudd" 2.1.12

وآزَر صنم *
وباجَر صنم عبدته الأَزْد ويكسر *
وجِهار صنم كان لهَوازِن *
والدَوّار صنم ويضم *
والدار صنم سمّى به عبد الدار أبو بطن *
وسُعَير صنم *
والأُقَيصِر صنم *
وكَثْرَى صنم لجديس وطسم كسره نهشل بن الرئيس ولحق بالنبى صلعم فاسلم *
والضِمار صنم عبده العباس بن مرداس و رهطه *
ونَسْر صنم كان لذى الكِلاع بارض حمير * ١٣،١،٢
والشمس صنم قديم *
وعُميانِس صنم لِخَولان كانوا يقسمون له من انعامهم وحروثهم *
والفلْس صنم لطيّئ *
وجُرَيْش صنم كان فى الجاهلية *
والخَلَصة صنم كان فى بيت يدعى الكعبة اليمانية لخثعم
وعَوْض صنم لبكر بن وائل *
وِاساف صنم وضعه عمرو[1] بن لُحَىّ على الصفا *
ونائلة صنم آخر وضعه على المروة وكان يذبح عليهما (فى قول) *
والمحَرِّق صنم لبكر بن وائل *

---

[1] كذا في القاموس وفي ١٨٥٥: عمر.

or Āzar,	"an idol"
or Bājar,	"an idol worshipped by the tribe of al-Azd; also pronounced Bājir"
or Jihār,	"an idol of the tribe of Hawāzin"
or al-Dawwār,	"an idol; also pronounced al-Duwwār"
or al-Dār,	"an idol, after whom ʿAbd al-Dār, the founder of a clan [of the tribe of Quraysh], was named"
or Suʿayr,	"an idol"
or al-Uqayṣir,	"an idol"
or Kathrā,	"an idol belonging to Jadīs and Ṭasm[18] that was broken to pieces by Nahshal ibn al-Raʾīs, who then attached himself to the Prophet, may God bless him and grant him peace"
or al-Ḍimār,	"an idol worshipped by al-ʿAbbās ibn Mirdās[19] and his company"
or Nasr,	"an idol of the Dhū l-Kilāʿ tribe in the land of Himyar" 2.1.13
or Shams,	"an ancient idol"
or ʿUmyānis,	"an idol belonging to the tribe of Khawlān by whom they would swear against their flocks and their crops"
or al-Fils,	"an idol belonging to the tribe of Ṭayyiʾ"
or Juraysh,	"an idol of the Days of Barbarism"
or al-Khalaṣah,	"an idol that was in a holy house called 'the Yemeni Kaaba' belonging to the tribe of Khathʿam"
or ʿAwḍ,	"an idol belonging to the tribe of Bakr ibn Wāʾil"
or Isāf,	"an idol set up by ʿAmr ibn Luḥayy[20] at al-Ṣafā"
or Nāʾilah,	"another idol that he set up at al-Marwah; sacrifices were made both to it and the preceding" (according to one definition)
or al-Muḥarriqah,	"an idol belonging to the tribe of Bakr ibn Wāʾil"

والشارِق صنم فى الجاهلية * ١٤،١،٢

والبَعْل صنم كان لقوم الياس عم *

وسُواع[١] صنم عُبد فى زمن نوح عم فدفنه الطوفان فاستشاره ابليس فعُبد وصار لهذيل وحُج اليه *

والكُسْعة صنم *

والعَوْف صنم *

وذى الكَفّين صنم كان لدَوْس *

ومنَاف صنم *

ويَعُوق صنم لقوم نوح أو كان رجلا من صالحى زمانه فلما مات جزعوا عليه فاتاهم الشيطان فى صورة انسان فقال امثّله لكم فى محرابكم حتى تروه كلّما صلّيتم ففعلوا ذلك به وبسبعة من بعده من صالحيهم ثم تمادى بهم الامر الى ان اتخذوا تلك الامثلة اصناما يعبدونها *

والاَشْهَل صنم ومنه بنو عبد الاشهل لحىّ من العرب *

وهُبَل صنم كان فى الكعبة *

وياليَل صنم * ١٥،١،٢

والبَعِيم صنم والتمثال من الخشب والدمية من الصِبغ *

والاَسْحم صنم *

ونُهْم صنم لمُزَيْنة وبه سموا عبد نهم *

وعائم صنم *

١ كذا في القاموس وفي ١٨٥٥: سَواع.

or al-Shāriq,	“an idol of the Days of Barbarism”	2.1.14
or al-Baʿl,	“an idol that belonged to the people of Ilyās, peace be upon him[21]”	
or Suwāʿ,	“an idol worshipped in the days of Nūḥ, peace be upon him; it was submerged by the Flood, then Satan made it reappear, and it was worshipped and came to belong to the tribe of Hudhayl and pilgrimage was made to it”	
or al-Kusʿah,	“an idol”	
or al-ʿAwf,	“an idol”	
or Dhū al-Kaffayn,	“an idol belonging to the tribe of Daws”	
or Manāf,	“an idol”	
or Yaʿūq,	“an idol belonging to the people of Nūḥ, or a righteous man of his time who died, and when they mourned for him, Satan came to them in the shape of a person and told them, ‘I shall make you a representation of him in your sanctum so that you shall see him whenever you pray’; so they did that with him and with seven of their righteous men after him, and in the end things reached a point at which they took these representations as idols and worshipped them”	
or al-Ashhal,	“an idol who gave his name to the tribe of Banū ʿAbd al-Ashhal Luḥayy, of the Arabs”	
or Hubal,	“an idol that was in the Kaaba”	
or Yālīl,	“an idol”	2.1.15
or al-Baʿīm,	“an idol; also a statue made of wood and a doll made of condiment”	
or al-Asḥam,	“an idol”	
or Nuhm,	“an idol belonging to the tribe of Muzaynah, whence the name ʿAbd Nuhm”	
or ʿĀʾim,	“an idol”	

والضَيْزَن صنم *

والمَدان صنم *

والجَبْهة صنم *

واللات صنم لثقيف سمّى بالذى كان يلتّ عنده السويق بالسمن ثم خفف وهو فى حديث عروة الرَبّة *

وذى الشَرَى صنم لدَوْس *

والعُزّى صنم او سَمُرَة عبدتها غطفان اول من اتخذها ظالم بن اسعد فوق ذات عِرق الى البستان بتسعة اميال بنى عليها بيتا وسماه بُسّا وكانوا يسمعون فيها الصوت فبعث اليها رسول الله صلّعم خالد بن الوليد فهدم البيت واحرق السمرة * ١٦،١،٢

ومَناة صنم *

والإلاهة الحية والاصنام والهلال والشمس ويثلث كالاليهة *

والطاغوت اللات والعزّى والكاهن والشيطان وكل راس ضلال والاصنام وكل ما عُبد من دون الله *

والزُوْن الصنم وما يتخذ ويعبد — والموضع تجمع فيه الاصنام وتنصب وتزيّن *

والجِبْت الصنم والكاهن والساحر والسحر والذى لا خير فيه وكل ما عُبد من دون الله تعالى *

اوعَبَدة الشمس والقمر وزحل والمشترى والمريخ والزهرة وعطارد وفُرْدود والفرقد والذِيخ والكَتَد والعَوائذ والحَضار والاحور والزُبْرة والاَظفار والعُذْر والمعَرّة والاَعْيار والنَثْرة والجَوْزآ والبِرْجِيس والتِياسَيْن والمَيْسان والسُنَيْق والشرَطَين

or al-Ḍayzan,	“an idol”	
or al-Madān,	“an idol”	
or al-Jabhah,	“an idol”	
or al-Lāt,	“an idol” belonging to the tribe of Thaqīf “named after a man in whose house parched barley meal used to be moistened (*yulattu*) with clarified butter; then the word was shortened”; it is to be found in ʿUrwah's hadith “al-Rabbah”[22]	
or Dhū al-Sharā,	“an idol belonging to the tribe of Daws”	
or al-ʿUzzā,	“an idol, or a gum-acacia tree, that was worshipped by [the tribe of] Ghaṭafān, the first to adopt it as an idol being Ẓālim ibn Asʿad; at the top of Dhāt ʿIrq,[23] nine miles from al-Bustān. He built a holy house over it and called it Buss, and they used to hear a voice inside. The Prophet (God grant him blessings and peace) sent Khālid ibn al-Walīd, and he knocked down the house and burned the tree”	2.1.16
or Manāh,	“an idol”	
or al-Ilāhah,	[literally, “the Goddess,” means] “the serpent, or idols, or the crescent moon, or the sun; also pronounced al-Alāhah, al-Ulāhah, al-Ilayhah, al-Alayhah, and al-Ulayhah”	
or al-Ṭāghūt,	“the idols al-Lāt and al-ʿUzzā, or a soothsayer, or Satan, or any leader in error, or any idol, or anything that is worshipped to the exclusion of God”	
or a *zūn*,	“any idol or anything that is taken as an object of worship; also a place in which idols are gathered, erected, and adorned”	
or a *jibt*,	“any idol, or a soothsayer or magician, or magic, or anything in which there is no good, or anything that is worshipped to the exclusion of God Almighty”	

or by those who worshipped the sun or the moon or Saturn or Jupiter or Venus or Mars or Mercury or *Furdūd*,[24] Pherkad, Edasich, *al-Katad*, *al-ʿAwāʾidh*, Hadar, *al-Aḥwal*, *al-Zubrah*, *al-Aẓhār*, Aludra, *al-Maʿarrah*, *al-Aʿyār*, *al-Nathrah*, Gemini, *al-Birjīs*, *al-Tiyāsān*, Almeissan, *al-Sunnayq*,

والفارِطَيْن والاثافى والعَيُّوق والعَوْهقَين والصَرْفة والطَرْفة والابيض والضِباع
والهَقْعة والهَنْعة والرِدْف والمَعْلَف والناقة والنَسَقين والسِماكين وسُهَيل والشَوْلة
والعوَكَلين والمِرزَمين والسُلَّم والبُطَيْن والقدر والحيّة والتحايى والخَراتَيْن والخِبآ وسُهى
١٧،١،٢ والشاة والعوّآء وكُوَى * فكان يجب عليهم ان يجمعوا رايهم على امر واحد
ويقولوا من حيث ان حرفتنا لا تحتاج بحمد الله الى قياس وعدد لحرفة الطبيعيين
والمهندسين والرياضيين * فانهم ايّان طلب المناقش منهم دليلا بادروا حالا الى
البرهان بالمقادير والمساحة والحساب * فانصبوا انفسهم وانفس سائليهم * كان
حقا علينا ان ننهج منهاجا مريحا يقرّبنا ومُعاملينا الى الغرض المقصود * وهو ان
نيسّر اسباب تعلّم هذه الحرفة لكل مضطر اليها منهم * فمن شآ بعد ذلك ان يلبس
قبآ او جبّة مع سراويلات من تحتها او تُبّان فليصنعها هو باى لون اعجبه وباى
شكل راق له * اذ ليس من الرشد ان يعترض الانسان انسانا آخر فى كيفية لبسه
١٨،١،٢ او فى ذوقه ومنامه * لان ابن ادم من يوم يستهل بالبكآء الى ان يبلغ اربع عشرة
سنة يعيش مستغنيا عنا غير مفتقر الى ما رسمنا به عليه * اذ الغريزة تهديه الى
ما يلائمه ويصلح له * الا ترى ان الطفل اذا خُلِّى وطبعه لم يلبس الكتّان الرفيع فى
الشتآء وان كان مطرّزا * ولا الفرو فى القيظ وان كان مزركشا * وانه متى جاع
طلب الاكل * ومتى نعس نام * وان طرّبته بجميع آلات الطرب والانغام * ومتى
ظمى شرب * ومتى تعب استراح فهو فى غنًى عنا من اصل الفطرة * حتى انه
يمكنه بحول الله تعالى ان يعيش مائة وعشرين عاما وشهرا من دون رؤية وجه احد
١٩،١،٢ منا او مشاهدة تاجه وحلّته الفاخرة وخاتمه النفيس وعصاه المفضّضة * فلندَعِ
الناس اذًا فى دعتهم وسلامتهم وشغلهم * ولا نتطفّل عليهم ولا نكلّفهم ما
لا طاقة لهم به * اذ لو شاء الله ان يحوج الطفل الينا لاوحى اليه ان يسال ابويه

Sheratan, *al-Fāriṭān*, Alsafi, *al-ʿAyyūq*, *al-ʿAwhaqān*, *al-Ṣarfah*, Alterf, *al-Abyaḍ*, *al-Ḍibāʿ*, Heka, Alhena, *al-Ridf*, *al-Maʿlaf*, *al-Nāqah*, Nusakan, *al-Simākān*, *Shuhayl*, Shaula, *al-ʿAwkalān*, *al-Mirzamān*, *al-Sullam*, Botein, *al-Qadr*, *al-Ḥayyah*, *al-Taḥāyā*, *al-Kharatān*, Alchibah, *Suhā*, *al-Shāh*, Auva, and *Kuwayy*?

They would have done better to have reached a consensus and said, "Given that our trade requires, thank God, neither measuring nor counting—unlike that of practitioners of the natural sciences, engineers, and mathematicians, who, whenever asked for proof by an opponent in debate, immediately set about providing it through the use of quantities, areas, and arithmetic, exhausting themselves and their questioners alike—we should pursue a more restful path that will bring us and those with whom we deal closer to the desired end, which is to facilitate the learning of this trade by any who is obliged to practice it. Thereafter, anyone who wishes to wear an outer garment or robe, with drawers underneath or with wrestlers' breeches, can make them himself of any color he pleases and of any shape he likes, for it makes no sense for one person to raise objections to how another, just like him, may dress or to his taste or to how he sleeps." 2.1.17

From the day of his first cry till he reaches his fourteenth year, the human lives quite independently of us and without any need for what we plan for him. Instinct guides him to what is appropriate to and good for him. Do you not see how a child, if left to his own devices and nature, will not wear thin linen in winter even if it be embroidered, or furs in the heat of summer even if they be edged with brocade? How, when he feels hunger, he asks for food and, when he gets sleepy, sleeps, even if you seek to distract him with all the music and songs known to man? How, when he gets thirsty, he drinks and, when he gets tired, he rests? In other words, he is in no need of us because of his natural inborn disposition. He could even live, through the strength of the Almighty, for a hundred and twenty years, plus a month, without looking on the face of any one of us or setting eyes on our crowns and gorgeous robes, our signet rings of precious metal, our silvered sticks. 2.1.18

Let us then leave people, unmolested, to their humble pursuits and to their work and not stick our noses into their business or charge them with tasks beyond their ability to perform. If God had wanted to make the child dependent on us, he would have inspired him to ask his parents, from the moment that he started to grow and flourish, their names and station and 2.1.19

من وقت ترعرعه عن اسمائنا ومقامنا * وعما نحن عليه من المماحكة والجدال * والقيل والقال * والتشاحن والتشاجر * والتناقر والتنافر * والتلاعن والتهاتر * والتدابر والتهاجر* واحسن من تركه على هذه الحالة ما اذا عُنينا بتاديبه وتربيته وتهذيبه وتعليمه صنعة تنفعه فى تحصيل معيشته ومعيشة والديه * كالقراة والخطّ والحساب والادب والطب والتصوير * وما اذا نصحنا له ان يسعى فى خير نفسه وخير ابويه ومعارفه وجنسه وكل من صدق عليه انه انسان بقطع النظر عن هيئات اللباس وتفاوت الالوان والبلاد * لان اللبيب الرشيد لا ينظر الى الانسان الا لكونه متصفا بالانسانية مثله * ومن اعتبر الامور الطارئة عليه كالالوان والطعام والزىّ فانه يتباعد عن مركز البشرية كثيرا * وانما يتم حسن صنيعنا هذا كله ما صنعناه حسبةً لوجه الله تعالى * غير طالبى الجزآ والهدايا * ولا النذور والعطايا * لان كثيرا من الاطبآ يداوون المعسرين مجّانا * فترى احدهم يغادر طعامه وفراشه ويذهب الى مريض محموم او به جُدَرى او طاعون احتسابا عند الله * اذ الناس كلهم عيال على الله * واحبّهم الى الله انفعهم لعياله *
٢٠،١،٢ هذا ما كان ينبغى ان يقولوه * وهذا ما اقوله انا * تامل فى خرجى اقبل يطوف البحار والامصار * ويجول فى الجبال والقفار* ويعرّض نفسه ونفس من ينحاز اليه للسبّ والقذف والعداوة والمشاحنة * وما ذلك الا ليقول للناس انه اعرف منهم باحوالهم * واذا سُئل عن دوآء لعين رمدت * او ساق قرحت * او أُدرة انتفخت * او اصبع دميت * او اذا قيل له ما ترى فى من كثرت عياله * وقلّ ماله * وعضّه زمانه * وجار عليه سلطانه * فُنى بالجوع * وحُرم الهجوع * واصبح يمشى والناس ينظرون جَهْوته * ويتجنبون خلطته * ولا يستعملونه ولا يستخدمونه * لما تقرر فى عقولهم من ان الفقير لا يحسن عملا * وقد اصبحت

about the matters over which we wrangle and debate—all the back and forth, the mutual wretchedness and recrimination, the sniping and snippiness, the vilification and reviling, the contradicting and cutting. Better than letting him go down that path, we should concern ourselves with teaching him manners and morality, with refining him and teaching him skills that will help him to earn a living and provide for himself and his parents—such as reading, penmanship, arithmetic, letters, medicine, and painting—and in advising him to exert himself for his own good and that of his parents, his acquaintances, his community, and everyone to whom the term "human" may be applied, without regard for the styles of people's dress or differences of color or country. The wise and well-guided man sees in others only their common humanity, and any who pays attention to incidental matters such as colors, food, and costume distances himself greatly from what is central to humanity. And all that we do in this regard will be good only if we do it for the sake of God Almighty, not as seekers after rewards or gifts, offerings and donations, but like those many physicians who treat the hard-up for free and whom you'll see leaving their food and beds and going to a patient with a fever, or leprosy, or the plague, in anticipation of only heavenly reward. All people are God's children, and the person God loves best is he who is of greatest benefit to His children.

This is what they should have said and is what I say now. Take a Bag-man. **2.1.20**
He has undertaken to make the circuit of the world's seas and *metropolises*, to roam its mountains and *wildernesses*, to expose himself and his allies to insult and abuse, hostility and hatred, all so that he can tell people that he knows better than they do what they are about. If you ask him for medication for a rheumy eye or an ulcerated *leg*, a swollen scrotal hernia or a finger that's *bled*, or if he's asked, "What say you to one whose litter has *grown* while his wealth has *flown*, whom Fortune has put to the *test* and whom by his government's been *oppressed*, so that he's afflicted with *hunger* and condemned to *insomnia* and now, wherever he walks, people, seeing his podex is *bare*, refuse to acknowledge that he's *there*, and will not do business with him or employ him, thinking in their minds that a poor man cannot do a job well; to one whose children have started to weep and wince with *pain* and whose wife has begun to ask for mercy and *complain*, though none spare a thought for the youth she's lost in raising her children?" or if someone says to him, "Have you any refuge for a guest who's a *stranger* and has none to take his

اولاده يبكون ويتضورون * وامراته تشكو وتسترحم ولا راحم لها لكون شبابها قد ذهب فى تربية اولادها * او قيل له هل عندك من ماوى لضيف عرير* ما له من نصير* قال ما جئتكم لهذا وانما قدمت اليكم لانظر فى انوالكم التى تنسجون عليها بضاعتكم وفى الوانها التى لا تشاكل ما عندى فى الخرج من اللون الناصع * وما ان يهمّنى النظر فيما فيه راحتكم وانما الراحة فيما به تعبكم * ولو تعطّلت جميع معاملكم لاقتصاركم على لونى الذى ابرزه لكم راموزا وعنوانا واستوجبتم بذلك لوم
التجار والحرّاث والحكام لم يكن علىّ فى ذلك من شى * وهذا سوقى يضع احدى ٢١,١,٢
عينيه على فم جاره والاخرى على عينيه * ثم يغلّ يديه ورجليه * ويقول له اليوم يجب عليك ان تتنحّس(١) * لان شيخ السوق اصبح متخما يشكو وجعا فى معدته وامعائه واضراسه وهو نحس * فينبغى ان نجانسه ونمسك معه * لا يحل لك لليوم ان تنظر* لان الشيخ المشار اليه اضرّ به طوال السهر البارحة مع ندمآئه ونديماته فغدا وباحدى عينيه الكريمتين رمد او عمش * لا يحل لك اليوم ان تعمل بيديك * ولا ان تحرك رجليك * ولا ان تسمع باذنيك * او تستنشق بمنخريك لان السوق اليوم لم تقم والبياعات لم تنفق * ثم هو اذا قيل له افلا تصلح بين زيد وزوجته فقد خاصمته بالامس بعد ان جآت من حانوتك العالى وتماسكا بالشعور * وحلفت المراة لتمنينَّه بحيزبون او لتشكونه الى احد اصحابك الضواطرة الكبار * او ان عمرا التاجر قد حُبس مذ يومين لكونه دان بعض الامرآء ولم يمكن له ان يحاكمه ويستوفى منه حقه * ففلّسه القاضى واركبه حمارا فى الاسواق ووجهه الى دبر الحمار* او ان فلانا قد مرض ولزم فراشه لانه ناقش بعض خدّام الامير فنكل به الامير ضربا بالعصى على رجليه وصفعاً بالنعال على القذال * فغدا لا حراك به وقد ورمت رجلاه وانتفخ قفاه * لم يكن منه الا قوله ما دام السوق وشيخه

(١) التنحّس ترك اكل اللحم *

side against *danger*?" he'll say, "I didn't come to you to provide such things. I came only to inspect the looms on which you weave your goods, and their colors, which cannot rival the brilliant colors that I have in my saddlebag. It is no concern of mine to look into what might bring you ease; my ease lies in your troubles. If all your workshops fall idle because you're incapable of producing these colors of mine that I have displayed to you in the shape of samples and specimens and you thus earn the reproof of your merchants, plowmen, and physicians, that is of no importance to me."

And here's your Market-man, one eye trained on his neighbor's mouth, **2.1.21**
the other on his eyes, who then binds him hand and foot and tells him, "Today you have to be 'distressed'(1) for the Market Boss awoke with indigestion, complaining of pains—in other words, 'distress'—in his stomach, guts, and molars. We must therefore be as he is and abstain along with him"; or "Today you aren't allowed to use your eyes because staying up late last night with his boon companions (male and female) has laid the aforesaid boss low, and he woke up with pus or rheum in one of his noble peepers"; or "Today you aren't allowed to work with your hands or to move your feet, and you mustn't listen with your ears or breathe with your nostrils because no market was held today, and no sales were made." If someone then says to him, "Can you not make peace between Zayd and his wife, for yesterday she wouldn't do his bidding after she came back from your most honored store, and they fell to tugging at each other's hair, and the wife swore she'd make him wish she were an old hag, or would complain of him to one of her friends among the big-time traders?" or "The merchant ʿAmr has been in prison these last two days because he lent money to one of the emirs and couldn't obtain a judgment against him or recover what he is owed, and the judge bankrupted him and had him mounted on a donkey and paraded through the marketplaces, facing the donkey's rump," or "So and so has fallen ill and taken to his bed because he got into an argument with one of the emir's servants, so the emir punished him by beating him with sticks on his feet and slapping him with slippers on the back of his neck, and the next day he couldn't move, and his feet swelled up, and his nape was all puffy," all he'll say is, "So long as the market and its boss are safe and sound, the rest of the world is too. Business is going well, and the market's up and *running*, bellies are full, mouths are *munching*, stomachs are digesting, molars are *crunching*,

(1) "To be distressed" (*tatanaḥḥas*) means here "to abstain from eating meat."

سالمين فالدنيا كلها سالمة * والمصالح مستتبّة والسوق مرفوعة وقائمة * والبطون ملأى والافواه لاقمه * والاضراس خاضمه * والمعَد هاضمه * والايدى غانمه * والافراح دائمه * والخيرات متراكمه * والرؤسآ حارمه * والعناية عاصمه * والقادمات بالنذور متزاحمه * والوقوف شاملة عامه * وثغور الامانى باسمه * والسلامة خاتمه * الى السوق * الى السوق * فهو حرز العلوق * وذخر الحقوق * فى الصندوق * فى الصندوق * فهو اولى من الصَبوح والغَبوق * وقد ٢٢،١،٢
طالما والله امتلأ هذا الصندوق ذهبا وجواهرثم افرغ على تهاتر وترّهات ومباحث فارغة وامور سخيفة * فقد بلغنا ان بعض ضواطرة السوق انفق فى مدة ستّ سنين قضاها بالبحث والجدال على شكل قُبَّعة كذا وكذا بدرة من المال * وتفصيل ذلك انه نظر نفسه ذات يوم فى المرآة وكان قد تعلّم مبادى الهندسة والهيئة * فراى راسه مدوّرا كالبطيخة * فراق له ان يتخذ قبّعة مدورة على هيئة راسه * لان المدوّر يلائم المدوّر كما تقرر فى الاصول * فرآه بعض مزامليه من سوق آخر وكان اعظم منه قدرا ووجاهة واوفرعلما * فسخرمنه وقال له مَن وسوس اليك ياابن قُبَعة(١) * حتى لبست هذه القُبَّعة * مع ان شكل راسك مخروط * فقال له قد ضللت بل هواكثر استدارة من راسك كما يشهد لى بذلك شيخ السوق * قال كذبت بل هو مخروط وان كنتَ كثير العَنَس اليه وانى اهدى من شيخك واقوم طريقا * قال كفرت وعميت عن معرفة نفسك فانّى لك ان تعرف غيرك * قال تبدَّعت بل انت عَمِه كَمِه وقد حمقت وسفهت فى عدم قبولك النصح * فاليوم ترى الناس المدوّر من المخروط * والسارط من المسروط * ثم لجّ بينهما العناد وتقابضا ٢٣،١،٢
بالازياق والجيوب والاقلاع * ثم بالجمم ثم بالاعراض * فمزق كل منهما عرض صاحبه اى عدوّه * ثم صاحا واستغاثا وتشاكيا لدى الحاكم وتباهلا وتهاترا *

(١) ابن قُبَعة وقابعاً وصف بالحمق *

hands are *snatching*, joys are *everlasting*, fortunes are *accumulating*, bosses are *prohibiting*, Providence is *protecting*, women bearing ex-votos in droves are *arriving*, pious bequests are all-*encompassing*, the mouths of the Fates are smiling, and all's well that ends well. To market! To market! There's the box of delights, there the trove of truths! Into the chest! Into the *chest*! Morning and evening, the *chest* is *best*!"

Many a time, I swear, has that chest been filled with gold and precious stones, only to be emptied again on confrontations, confabulations, pointless investigations, and foolish matters. We have been informed that one of the market traders spent a vast amount of money over a period of six years on study and debate concerning the shape of a certain hat. To be specific, he looked at himself one day in the mirror and, being somewhat acquainted with the principles of engineering and construction, noticed that his head was round, like a watermelon. It therefore seemed appropriate to him that he should adopt the use of a round hat of the same shape as his head, for round goes best with round, as good taste has long determined. One of his colleagues from another market, who was of higher standing and dignity and more learned than he, saw him and made mock of him, asking, "Who whispered in your ear, you featherbrain (*Ibn Quba'ah*),(1) that you should wear that bird's nest of a bonnet (*qubba'ah*) when your head in fact is conical?" "You are misled," he replied. "My head is, on the contrary, rounder than yours, as the Market Boss will testify." "You lie," said the other. "It truly is conical, as you should know since you keep looking at it in the mirror, and I am better guided and walk a straighter path than your boss." "You blaspheme," said the first, "and are blind to your own self; how then can you know others?" "And you," said the second, "are a godless innovator; nay, you are confounded and confused and have become stupid and silly in refusing to accept my advice. People today can tell the rounded from the *turned*, the con-man from the *burned*." 2.1.22

(1) *Ibn Quba'ah* [literally, "Son of a (certain) bird (smaller than a sparrow)"] and *Qābi'ā'* are epithets used to describe stupidity.

At this, obduracy seized them in its relentless grip, and they grabbed each other by their collars, their pockets, and their shepherd's sacks, and then by their long hair, and then by their reputations, each man tearing apart that of his friend, meaning his enemy. Next they screamed, appealed for help, and complained of each other before the ruler, each calling the other a fool and reviling him. When it became clear to the ruler that they were both acting 2.1.23

فلما ثبت للحاكم ان فعلهما فعل الشبازقة(١) راى ان مداواتهما بغرامة رابية * اولى من حصرهما فى الزاوية * فانصرف كل منهما وقد غرم كذا وكذا بدرة * ثم ان الضوطار الاول اتخذ له بعد ذلك قبَّعة بين بين * اى نصفها مدوّر ونصفها مخروط بحيث لا يقدر على تمييزها الا الجهبذ النحرير * والناقد الخبير * وآب الى حانوته كمن قفل من غزوة * او اسر الدِحْية * (رئيس الجند) او كذلك الديك الغالب * واول ما اطلّ على السوق امرجميع القبَّعيّين ان يخرجوا لملاقاته بالتقليس لا بالتلقيس(٢) * فخرجوا على تلك الحالة وهم يضجون ويقولون * اليوم عيد القبعه * اليوم يوم الفرقعه * ياإمّعة ياامّعة * فبصر بهم اعوان الحاكم فى ذلك الصقع فظنوا انهم خلعوا ربقة الطاعه * وشقّوا عصا الجماعه * فبادروهم بالات الأَزّ والبحز والبخز والبزّ والبغز والبهز والجرز والجلز والحزّ والحفز والخز والدغز والرزّ والرفز والزّزّ والشخز والشرز والشفز والشكز والضخز والضفز والطعز والعرز والقحز والقلز واللبز واللتز واللزّ واللكز واللقز واللمز واللهز والمحز والمرز والمهز والنحز والنخز والنغز والنكز والنهز والوخز والوكز والوقز والوهز والهبز والهرز والهمز والرهز * حتى جعلوهم عبرة للمعتبر * وفرّ الضوطار بقبعته وقد اوقع قومه فى الخزى ٢٤،١،٢

والعار مما اصاب الرجال من الرزء ولحق النسآ من الزيادة * ومع ذلك كله فلم يُجْده شيخ السوق المستعَزّ به شيا * بل ظل مكبّا على تعاطى الافيون لطول ارقه وتبييته * وقد سدّ اذنيه ببعض اوراق دفاتر السوق لئلا يسمع صراخ المستجيرين به او يوقظه احد من سباته * فهو راقد الى هذا اليوم اى يوم تدوين هذه الواقعة * فان افاق فللقارى ان يقيد ذلك فى اخر هذا الفصل فقد تركت له محلا *

انتهت دحرجة الجلمود والحمد لواجب الوجود *

(١) الشَبْزَق مَن يتخبطه الشيطان من المسّ *

(٢) التقليس استقبال الولاة عند قدومهم باصناف اللهو وان يضع الرجل يديه على صدره ويخضع * والتلقيس مبالغة لقسه اى عابه ولقّبه *

like lunatics (*shabāziqah*),(1) he decided it would make better sense to cure them with a heavy fine than to confine them in the pokey. Each then departed, after paying a fine of such and such a number of purses. Afterwards, the first trader adopted a hat that was half and half, that is, half round and half conical, and none but the most learned of scholars and most expert of examiners could tell which it really was, and he returned to his store like a conquering hero or one who'd captured a *diḥyah* (that's an army *general*), or even a prize-winning *cockerel*. The first thing he did when he reached the edge of the marketplace was to command all the hatters to come out and receive him—with entertainment and salaams (*taqlīs*), not with reproaches and slams (*talqīs*).(2) So they went forth accordingly, making noise and saying, "Today is the Feast of the *Hat*! Today the day of the firecracker! What a *twat*! What a *twat*!" and the ruler's henchmen, beholding them as they crowed, supposed them to have thrown off the yoke of *obedience* and abandoned their *allegiance*, so they set upon them with instruments that[25] hit, strike, smite, knock, belt, bat, clout, bang, slam, dash, bash, punch, jab, thwack, smack, clap, crack, swipe, whack, wham, whop, clump, bonk, clip, cut, swat, sock, slog, thump, pound, beat, maul, drub, thresh, spank, thrash, whip, slap, club, kick, stamp, stomp, push, shove, and fling, until they had made of them a warning for all who have eyes to see.

(1) ["like lunatics":] a *shabzaq* [plural *shabāziqah*] is one whom the Devil has afflicted with insanity.

(2) *Taqlīs* is receiving rulers on their arrival with various sorts of entertainment, and also a man's placing his hands on his breast and bowing. *Talqīs* is reproaching someone in an exaggerated fashion, i.e., denouncing him and calling him names.

The market trader then fled with his hat, having landed his people in ignominy and disgrace, which afflicted the men with grievous loss and brought the women even greater, despite all of which the Market Boss, who was so taken with him, thought the matter of no importance. In fact, he continued to devote himself to the taking of opium because of his endless insomnia and nightly brooding; he had stuffed his ears with pages from the market ledgers so that he wouldn't hear the screams of those who called on him for help and none should wake him from his stupor, and he's stayed flat on his back to this very day, which is to say, up to the day of the recording of this incident. If he awakes, it will be up to the reader to enter that fact at the end of this chapter, and I have left him space to do that. 2.1.24

Here ends the rolling of the boulder,
praise be to the Prime Mover.

الفصل الثانى

فى سلام وكلام

عمتَ صباحا يافارياق * كيف انت * وكيف رايت الاسكندرية * هل ١،٢،٢
تبيّنت نسآها من رجالها فان النسآ فى بلدكم لا يتبرقعن * وكيف وجدت مآكلها ومشاربها وملابسها وهوآها ومآها ومنازلها واكرام اهلها للغربآء * الم يزل براسك الدُوار* وعلى لسانك هجو الاسفار* قال اما موقع المدينة فانيق لكونه على البحر* وقد زادت بهجة بكثرة الغربآ فيها فترى روس ناس مغطاة بطراطير * واخرى بطرابيش * واخرى بكمام وغيرها بمقاعط * واخرى ببرانس وغيرها بعمائم * واخرى بأَصناع وغيرها بعصائب * واخرى بعَمارات وغيرها بمداميج * واخرى بِنصاف وغيرها بقبّعات * واخرى بقلانس وغيرها ببراطل * واخرى بسُبوب وغيرها باراصيص(١) * واخرى باراسيس وغيرها بخنابع * واخرى بقنابع وغيرها بدَنيّات واخرى بصواقع * وغيرها بصُمُد واخرى بصوامع * وغيرها بمشامذ واخرى بمشاوذ * وغيرها ببرانيط على شكل الشقيط والشبابيط والضفاريط والضماريط والقلاليط والعضاريط والعذافيط والعماريط
٢،٢،٢ والقماعيط * ومنهم من له سراويلات طويلة مفرسخة تكنس ما خلفه وما قدّامه * ومنهم من لا سراويلات له فبُعثُطه بادٍ والناس يتمسّحون بما امامه *

(١) الأُرصوصة قلنسوة كالبطيخة *

Chapter 2

A Salutation and a Conversation

"Good morning, Fāriyāq! How are you and how do you find Alexandria? Have you learned to tell its women from its men (for the women in your country do not veil their faces)? And how do you find its food and drink, its clothes, its air and water, its parks, and how its people honor strangers? Is your head still *swimming*, your tongue with disparagement of travel still *brimming*?" Replied he, "So far as the city's situation is concerned, it's elegant because it's on the sea, and the number of foreigners it contains adds to its brio: in it you see some people whose heads are covered with tall pointed hats and others with tarbushes, some with round caps and others with *maqāʿiṭ* turbans, some with burnooses and others with ordinary turbans, some with *aṣnāʿ* turbans and others with fillets, some with headgear of a generic nature[26] and others with *madāmīj* turbans, some with sailors' caps and others with hoods, some with caps and others with bonnets, some with further turbans and others with watermelon-shaped(1) and cantaloupe-shaped caps,[27] and others with head scarves large and small, some with judges' tun-caps[28] and others with antimacassars,[29] some with undercloths for turbans and others with head rags, some with the turban under the name *mishmadh* and others with the turban under the name *mishwadh*, and some with Frankish hats shaped like earthenware jars, or carp, or the creases between the cheek, nose, and eye, or the crevices between the same, or the children of the jinn, or armpit sinews, or white varan lizards, or disreputable demons, or babies' clouts. 2.2.1

(1) The *arṣūṣah* (plural *arāṣīṣ*) is a cap like a watermelon.

"Some of them have long saggy drawers that sweep the ground behind and before them and some have no drawers at all, so that their anuses are on display and the people pass their hands over what is in front of the latter.[30] 2.2.2

ومنهم من له تبّان * ومنه من له إتْب * ومنهم بوَثْر ومنهم بهِميان * ومنهم برجِلْ (السراويل الطاق) ومنهم بأنْدَرْوَرْد ومنهم بدِقْرارة او دُقْرور* ومنهم من يركب الحمير والبغال * وغيرهم على الخيل والجمال * والابل فى ازدحام * والناس فى التطام * فينبغى للسائر بينهم ان لا يفتر على الدعآ بقوله اللهم أجِر * اللهم احفظ * اللهم الطف * توكلت على الله * استعنت بالله * اعوذ بالله *

فاما براقع النسآء فهى وان كانت تخفى جمال بعضهن الا انها تريح العين ايضا من قبح سائرهن * غير ان تستّر القبيحات اكثر * لان المليحة لا يهون عليها اذا خرجت من قفصها ان تطير فى الاسواق من دون ان تمكّن الناظرين من رؤية ملامحها * لينظروا حسنها وجمالها ويكبّروا لافترارها * فيقولوا ما شا الله * تبارك الله * جل الله * الله الله * حتى اذا رجعت الى منزلها اعتقدت ان جميع اهل البلد قد شُغفوا بها حبا * فباتت تنتظر منهم الهدايا والصِلات * والاشعار والمواليات * فكلما غنّى مغنّ انصتت الى غنائه وسمعت اسمها يتشبَّب به * فاذا بكرت فى اليوم القابل الى الاسواق ورات الناس مكبّين على اشغالهم تعجبت من بقآئهم اصحآ قادرين على السعى والحركة * فزادت لهم فى كشف مسافرها * وقسامتها ومحاجرها * وفتنتهم باشاراتها وايمائها * ورأراتها وايبائها * ورمزها ولمزها * وهجلها وغمزها * وغنجها ودلالها * وتيهها وعجبها * وزهوها وشكلها * وتدعّبها وتصعيرها * ودعلجتها ودغنجتها * وتبغنجها ودهجتها *

Some of them have short breaches and some drawers without legs, some of them have drawstrings and some have belts, some have leggings (drawers made of one piece of material) and others have *underwear*,[31] some have boxers and others briefs. Some ride mules and *asses*, others dromedaries and *horses*. Camels are on every *side*, people *collide*. One moving among them must never slacken in his pious exclamations,[32] saying, 'God protect! God preserve! God be kind! I have put my trust in God! I seek God's help! I seek refuge with God!'

"As for women's face veils, if they conceal the beauty of some, at least they relieve the eye of the ugliness of the rest. It is, however, the ugly ones who most often cover their faces, for the pretty ones think it a pity, when they leave their cages, to fly through the markets without the onlookers being able to see their charms' *array*, behold their comeliness, and make much ado over the beauty on *display*, saying, 'As God wills![33] God be blessed! How mighty is God! O God, O God!' When such a one returns to her house, she believes that all the inhabitants of the city have fallen passionately in love with her and sits there expecting them to send her gifts and tokens of *esteem*, verses and sonnets with an amatory *theme*. Whenever anyone raises his voice in song, she cocks an attentive ear and believes she hears him rhapsodizing over her name, and if, then, she sets off early the following day to the marketplace and finds everyone busy with their work, she's amazed that they're still conscious and capable of effort and action. 2.2.3

"She therefore shows off more of her hidden charms, her elegance, and her forbidden fruits. She bewitches them with her gestures and nods, her eye-rolling and her gestures behind her back, her expressive looks and glances, her come-hither winks and cow eyes, her billings and cooings, her haughtiness and conceit, her vanity and coquetry, her playfulness and her turning aside of her cheek in pride, her comings and goings and goings and comings, her demurrals and her mincing walk, her glances to the side and her glances askance, her looks of surprise and swivelings of her eyes, her backward glances of spite or surprise and her angry looks, her peepings through her fingers against the sun to see[34] and her turnings to observe what lies behind her, her shading of her eyes against the sun to see and her peering through her fingers against the sun to see, her wantonness and her conceitedness, her staggering and swaying, her tottering and strutting, her bending and bowing, her coyness and bough-like curvaceousness, the trailing of her 2.2.4

وشزرها وخزرها * وشنَفها وحدقلتها * وشفونها وازلاقها * واستكفافها واستشفافها * واستيضاحها واستشرافها * وخلاعتها وخُيَلائها * وتمايلها وتهاديها * وتغدّنها وتعاطفها * وتثنّيها وتاوّدها * وتدكّلها وتخوّدها * وتذيّلها وتعيّلها * وتفتّلها وتقتّلها * وتذبلها وترفلها * وتبخترها وتخطلها * وتخنّتها وتدهكرها * وتبهكنها وتهذخرها * وتخلعها وتفككها * وميّحها وحَككها[1] * وتدأديها وتغطرفها * وتوذفها وتغضفها * ودألها ووهازتها * والّها وهَوادتها * وخيزلاها وخيزراها * وزأنباها وأُوَزّاها * ومُطيطآئها وكِرْدَحائها * وهَبَيّخَاها وعِجّيساها * وهِرِبْذاها وحَيَداها * وهبَصاها وجِيضّاها * وفَنْجلاها وهِبلّاها * وخِبقّاها ودِفِقّاها * وعَرْقلاها وهِمِقّاها * وعَمَيْثَليتّها وِقَمْطَراها * وسِبَطْراها * وتبدحها وترنحها * وخندفتها وخزرفتها * وخظرفتها وبادلتها * وبحدلتها وبهدلتها * وذحذحتها وحرقلتها * وحركلتها وهركلتها * ورابلتها ورهبلتها * وقهبلتها وكسملتها * وقندلتها وحنكلتها * وعردلتها وهيقلتها * وخذعلتها ودربلتها * وزيحلتها ووكوكتها * وكوكوتها * ووذوذتها * وذوذوتها زوزكتها * ورهوكتها وفرتكتها * ومكمكتها ورهدنتها * وكتكتها وبرقطتها * وقرمطتها وحرقصتها *

١ ١٨٥٥: وحَككّها.

skirts over the ground as she walks and her sweeping by, her turning of her face aside as she proceeds and her walking with a swinging gait, her stepping out manfully and her walking proudly in her clothes, her ambling and her rambling, her stepping like a pouting pigeon and her rolling gait, the swinging of her mighty buttocks and her sashaying, the insinuating wriggling of her shoulders, her pretty waddling and the way she walks as though she were short, her shaking of her shoulders, her sprinting and her haughtiness (especially in walking), her taking short steps and her sinuosity, her ponderousness and her modesty of deportment, her hastening and her willowiness, her slowness of motion and her looseness of motion, her slow stepping and her skipping from foot to foot, her stretching out her hands as she paces and her walking with short steps, her swaying and her slowness, her walking proudly like a high priest of the Parsees and her sudden startings off the road, her sprightly running and her bending as she walks, her languishing gait and her strutting, her galloping and her striding out, her stalking and her swaying from side to side, her nonchalant sauntering and her walking with the limbs held close to the body, her swaggering, her walking finely and loosely and her staggering as though intoxicated, her walking with her thighs far apart kicking up her feet and her walking with a swing, her striding fast and her rushing, her skelping and her stepping quick, her tripping quickly along with short steps and three other ways of walking, each with a difference of one letter, and her walking nicely, her limping and a fourth way of walking with yet another letter changed[35] and her walking making her steps close together, her gliding and her walking slowly, her shambling and a fifth way of walking, with further letters changed,[36] her walking with tiny steps[37] and her shuffling, her walking with conceit and her walking as though too weak to take long strides, her running with short steps and her walking fast, her disjointed walking and the moving of her buttocks and sides as she walks, the looseness of her joints as she walks and her walking with close steps, her walking with a rolling gait and her slowness and turning in walking, her walking fast with close steps and her close stepping, her walking with steps as close as closely written letters and her walking with steps as close as rapidly uttered words, her hopping like a shackled camel and her rolling walk, her walking with small hurried steps and her moving like a fast, well-gaited donkey, her easy pacing and her twisting and turning, her marching proudly (spelled two ways),[38] her walking arrogantly and her

وزهزمتها وحذلمتها * ودعرمتها وزهلقتها * وترهيئها وتعجّها * وتبهرسها وتهبرسها * وتغطرسها * وتهطرسها * وتكدسها وترهوكها * وتهالكها وتهكيلها * وتفركها وتومّزها * وتهيّمها وأُنُفها * ورَسَمها وزَوْفها * وزيَفها وهَوْجلها * وحَتَكانها وعَيكانها * وزَيكانها وزَوَكانها * ورفلانها وملدانها * وزيفانها وذالانها * ورَيسانها وكتفانها * وميسانها وتزابيها * وهَمَذانيّها وتثرطلها * وتعذلقها وتخزلجها * وحَقَطها ولَبَطها * وبفزّها وقفزها ونقزها مقبلة مدبرة * وزاد طمعها ايضا فى الهدايا * قال وقد نظمت فى البرقع بيتين ما اظن احدا سبقنى اليهما وهما *

لا يحسب الغِرُّ البراقع للنسا منعا لهن التمادى فى الهوى
ان السفينة انما تجرى اذا وُضع الشراع لها على حكم الهوا

فاما رجالها فان للترك سطوة على العرب وتجبرا * حتى ان العربى لا يحلّ له ان ينظر الى وجه تركى كما لا يحل له ان ينظر الى حُرَم غيره * واذا اتفق فى نوادر الدهر ان تركيا وعربيا تماشيا اخذ العربي بالسُنّة المفروضة * وهى ان يمشى عن يسار التركى محتشما خاشعا ناكسا متحاقرا متصاغرا متضائلا قافّا متقبضا متقبصا متقفصا متشمصا متحمصا متحرفصا مكتزّا متكاولا متازّحا متقرفعا متقرعفا مقرعفّا متقفّعا متكنبثا مقعنصرا متقوصرا مستزمرا معرنفطا مقرنفطا متجعثما متجعثنا مرزئمّا مرمئزّا مقمئنّا مكبئنّا متخبنلا متقاعسا مراعزا مكردَحا متضامّا متعصعصا متزازئا مقرنبعا مدنِقسا مطمرِسا مطرمسا متكرفسا منقفشا معقنفشا متحويا معرنزما متخشّلا آزِما لازبا كاتعا كانعا متشاجبا مُصعَنبا مُجرَنزا مجرمزّا متدخدخا * ٥,٢,٢
فاذا عطس التركى قال له العربى رحمك الله * واذا تنحنح قال حرسك الله *

tottering, her walking so fast that her shoulders shake and her cleavage rises and her moving like a wave, her walking as though falling onto a bed and her walking proudly like a horse, her walking like an effeminate man and her fast, agitated walking, her handsome way of walking and the same said another way,[39] the beauty of her walk and her walking like a dove dragging its wings and tail on the ground, her walking like a pouting pigeon and her floppy walking, her walking with close, fast steps, moving her shoulders, her swashbuckling and stepping like a crow, her nubile grace, her hastening as she sways and her running with close steps, her lion-like pacing and her hurrying, her swaying as she walks and her walking slowly with long steps, her walking finely and the way she drags her skirts behind her, her active way of walking and her racing, her nimbleness and her knock-kneed running, her starting like a scared gazelle and and her leaping, and her jumping up and down in place and her facing forward and facing backward—and all the time her appetite for presents grows. I have composed two lines[40] on the face veil that are, I believe, without precedent:

Only a fool would think to keep a girl
  From love's pursuit with nothing but a veil:
Not till the cloth's been set to the wind
  Is the ship in a state to sail.

"As for the city's men, the Turks boss the Arabs around like tyrants. The Arab is as much forbidden to look into the face of a Turk as he is into that of another man's wife. If by some quirk of fate a Turk and an Arab should walk together, the Arab will follow the custom that has been imposed, namely of walking on the Turk's left-hand side out of modesty and submission, head bent in self-derision, making himself as small and as thin as possible, shriveling, shrunken, unextended, drawing into himself, shrinking, cowering, tightly compressed, withered, making himself as short as possible, walking slowly and curled over himself, puckered, suckered, snookered, desiccated, tight as a miser, crouching, hugging himself to himself, making himself as small as possible, sucking in his sides and holding his buttocks tight, retracting and contracting, quaking and frozen in place, depressed, head and elbows pulled in, head bowed, aloof, dispirited, humiliated, regimented, intimidated, terrified, petrified, eyes downcast, recoiling and regressing, cringing, curled into a ball like a spider, debased [?],[41] twisted, coiled upon himself like an old 2.2.5

واذا مخط قال وقاك الله * واذا عثر عثر الآخر معه اجلالا له وقال نعشك الله لا
نعشنا * وقد سمعت ان الترك هنا عقدوا مجلس شورى استقر رايهم فيه لدى ٦،٢،٢
المذاكرة على ان يتخذوا لهم مركبا وطيئا من ظهور العرب فانهم جرّبوا سروج الخيل
وبراذع الجمال واكفها واقتاب الابل وبواصرها وحُصُرها وسائر انواع المحامل من

كِفْل	مركب للرجال *
وشِجار	مركب يتخذ للشيخ الكبير ومن منعته العلّة من الحركة *
وحِدْج	مركب للنسآ كالمحفّة *
وأَجْلح	هودج ما له راس مرتفع *
وحَوْف	شى كالهودج وليس به *
وقَرّ	مركب للرجال والهودج *
ومِحفّة	مركب للنسا *
وفرْفار	مركب من مراكب النسا *
وحَمْل	هودج *
وحِلال	مركب للنسآ *
وكَدْن	مركب لهن * ٧،٢،٢
وقَعْش	مركب كالهودج *
ومَحارة	شبه الهودج *
وقَعَدة	مركب لهن *
وكَتْر	الهودج الصغير *
وميثرة[١]	ج مواثر مراكب تتخذ من الحرير والديباج *

١ كذا في القاموس وفي ١٨٥٥: المئثرة.

snake, bent over in abjection, drawing back, cleaving, constricting himself and restricting himself, pulling back, holding back, compressing, repressing, and constringeing himself. If the Turk sneezes, the Arab tells him, 'God have mercy on you!' If he clears his throat, he tells him, 'God protect you!' If he blows his nose, he tells him, 'God guard you!' And if he trips, the other trips along with him out of respect and says, 'May God right you and not us!'

"I have heard that once the Turks here held a consultative assembly at 2.2.6
which, upon deliberation, they decided that they would use the backs of the Arabs as a comfortable conveyance, for they had tried horse saddles and camel saddles (both *bardhaʿah*s and *ikāf*s, as well as *qitbah*s and *bāṣar*s[42]) and their riding mats, and all other kinds of carrying devices, namely,

the *kifl,*	[a kind of saddlecloth] "a thing for men to ride on"
or the *shijār,*	"a conveyance for an old man or anyone whom illness prevents from moving"
or the *ḥidj,*	"a conveyance for women resembling the *miḥaffah*"
or the *ajlaḥ,*	"a camel litter that does not have a high peak"
or the *ḥawf,*	"something that resembles a litter but is not one"
or the *qarr,*	"a conveyance for men, or a *hawdaj*"
or the *miḥaffah,*	"a conveyance for women"
or the *farfār,*	"a conveyance for women"
or the *ḥaml* or *ḥiml,*	"a camel litter"
or the *ḥilāl,*	"a conveyance for women"
or the *kadn,*	"a conveyance for women" 2.2.7
or the *qaʿsh,*	"a conveyance like a camel litter"
or the *maḥārah,*	"something like a camel litter"
or the *qaʿadah,*	"a conveyance for women"
or the *katr,*	"a small camel litter"
or the *mītharah,*	"plural *mawāthir*: things that people ride on made of silk or brocade"

وِرِجازة مركب اصغرمن الهودج *

وعَرِيش كالهودج *

وعَبِيط مركب *

وحِزق مركب شبيه بالباصَر *

وبُلْبُلة هودج للحرائر *

وحِقّل هودج *

وتَوْأمة من مراكب النسآء توأمات *

وفَوْدج الهودج ومركب العروس *

ومن رَحْل وعجلة وعرش وشَرْجَع ومِزفّة ومِنصَّة وسرير ونعش فوجدوها كلها لا تصلح

لهم * ورايت مرة تركيا يقود جوقة من العرب بخيط من الكاغذ وهم كلهم يقودون ٨،٢،٢

له * استغفر الله مرادى ان اقول ينقادون له * ولم ادرِ ما سبب تكبّر هولآ الترك

هنا على العرب * مع ان النبى صلّعم كان عربيا * والقرآن انزل باللسان العربى *

والائمّة والخلفاء الراشدين * والعلماكانوا كلهم عربا * غير انى اظن ان اكثر الترك

يجهل ذلك فيحسبون ان النبى صلّعم كان يقول شويله بويله * او بقالم قبالم * او

غطالق قاپ خى دلها طغالق پاق يخ بلها

صفالق پاه خشت وكرد فصالق هاپ دركلها

دخا زاوشت قلدى نك خدا شاو زت قردلها

اشكلر هم كبى والله قلاقلها بلابلها

لا والله * ما هذا كان لسان النبى ولا لسان الصحابة والتابعين والائمة الراشدين

رضى الله عنهم اجمعين الى يوم الدين امين وبعده امين * فاما ماوها فما ٩،٢،٢

احسن راسه وانجعه * الا انه قذر الذنب تنجسه حيوانات الارض باجمعها *

or the *rijāzah*, "a conveyance smaller than a camel litter"
or the *ʿarīsh*, "something like a camel litter"
or the *ʿabīṭ*, "a conveyance"
or the *ḥizq*, "a thing people ride on resembling the *bāṣar*"
or the *bulbulah*, "a camel litter for noble people"
or the *ḥiql*, "a camel litter"
or the *taw'amah*, "a conveyance for women; plural *taw'amāt*"
or the *fawdaj*, "a camel litter; a conveyance for a bride"
or saddles, wheels, thrones, dead men's stretchers, bridal litters, podiums, beds, and biers, and found that none were good enough for them.

"Once I saw a Turk leading a band of Arabs with a thread of paper[43] while all of them were 'leading' him .... Whatever am I saying? I meant 'were being led *by* him.'[44] I have never been able to work out the reason for the sense of superiority felt by these Turks here with regard to the Arabs, when the Prophet (peace be upon him) was an Arab, the Qur'an was revealed in Arabic, and the imams, Rightly-guided Caliphs, and scholars of Islam were all Arabs. I think, though, that most Turks are unaware of these facts and believe that the Prophet (peace be upon him) used to say *şöyle böyle* ('thus and so') and *bakalım kapalım* ('let's see-bee')[45] and 2.2.8

Ghaṭālıq[46] *chāp khay dilhā*
Ṭughālıq pāq yakh balhā
Ṣafālıq pāh khusht wa-kurd
Faṣālıq hāp daraklahā
Dakhā zāwusht geldi nang
Khudā shawizt qardlahā
Eshekler hem gibi va-llāh
Qalāqiluhā balābiluhā

"Never, I swear, was the language of the Prophet so, nor that of the Companions or the generation that followed them or the Rightly-guided Imams, God be pleased with them all unto the Day of Resurrection, amen and again amen!

"As for the city's waters, what a fine and wholesome head is theirs! Though, on the other hand, what a filthy tail![47] All the animals of the earth and every fowl of the sky pollutes it; even the fish of the sea, when they catch 2.2.9

وطيور السمآء بجملتها * حتى ان سمك البحر اذا اصابته هيضة طفر الى راس هذا
الذنب فالقى فيه ما اثقله * فاما اكلها فالفول والعدس والحمص والزِنّ والدَوْسر ١٠،٢،٢
والقُرَيْنآ والخَرَفى والجُلبان والباقِلّى والخُنْبُل والدَجْر والخُلَّر والبُلْس والبِيقة والترمس
والخُرّم والشُبْرُم واللوبيآ وكل ما يحبنطى به البطن * وذلك ان اهلها لا يرون فى
الخمائص حسنا * حتى ان النسآ فيما بلغنى يتخذن معجونا من الجُعَل وياكلنه فى كل
غداة لكى يسمنَّ ويكون لهن عُكَن مطويات * واضرّما لاقيت فيها قَيْعَر قيعار * قدم ١١،٢،٢
اليها من بعض البلاد الحميرية وتعرف بجماعة من النصارى فيها * فصار يدخل ديارهم
ويسامرهم * فلما لم يجد عند احدهم كتابا اقام نفسه بينهم مقام العالم فقال انه يعرف
علم الفاعل والمفعول وحساب الجُمَّل * واتخذ له كتبا بعضها من غير ابتدآء وبعضها
بغير ختام وبعضها مخروم اوممحو * فكان اذا خاطبه احد فى شى عمد الى بعض هذه
الكتب ففتحه ونظر فيه ثم يقول * نعم ان هذا الشى هو من الاشيآ التى اختلف
فيها العلمآ * فان بعض مشايخنا فى الديار الحميرية يتهجاه كذا * وبعضهم فى الديار
الشامية كذا * ولمّا يستقرّ رايهم عليه فاذا استقرّ فلا بد من ان يخبرونى به * قال ١٢،٢،٢
الفارياق وقد سمعت مرة مَن استفزّه باعث من الشغل يساله عن الوقت * فقال
له ساعة وخمس دقائق اما الساعة فقد اشتق منها الساعى وعيسى * اما الساعى
فلكون السعى كله يتوقف على الساعات * اذ لا يمكن لاحد ان يعمل عملا خلوّا من
الوقت * فان جميع الافعال والحركات محصورة فى الزمان كانحصار— ثم ادار
نظره ليشبّهه بشى فراى كوزا لبعض الصبيان * فقال كانحصار المآ فى هذا الكُزّ *
ثم راى زنبيلا لصبىّ اخر فقال او كانحصار غدآ هذا الولد فى هذا الزِنّبيل * واما
عيسى فلكونه اشتمل على جميع المعارف والعلوم اشتمال الساعة على الدقائق *

a summer cholera, leap on top of this tail and vomit onto it whatever it is that's making them sick.

"The food they eat there is fava beans, lentils, chickpeas, darnel seed and darnel weed, water clover, *kharfā* vetch, *julbān* vetch, broad beans, the fruit of the *ghāf* tree, the black-eyed pea called *dajr*, *khullar* vetch, *buls* lentils, bitter vetch, lupine, the black-eyed peas called *khurram*, *shubrum*-lentils, black-eyed peas *tout court*, and everything else that makes the belly distend. This is because its people find nothing good in an empty stomach. It has even been reported to me that the women use a paste made of dung-beetles, eating some every morning so that they may grow fat and develop overlapping belly folds. 2.2.10

"The most noxious thing I came across there was Qayʿar Qayʿār.[48] He came to the city from the Himyaritic lands[49] and made the acquaintance of a group of Christians there, to whose houses he would repair, spending the evenings with them. Finding that they had no scribes among them, he appointed himself their scholar and said that he knew the science of 'subjects' and 'objects'[50] and of chronograms.[51] He got hold of a few books, some of which were missing their beginnings and some their ends, some of which were worm-eaten and some so faint as to be illegible, and if anyone asked him about anything, he'd turn to one of these, open it, gaze upon it, and then say, 'As I thought. This is one of those things over which scholars differ. Thus some of our shaykhs in the Himyaritic lands interpret it this way and some of them in the Damascene territories that, and they have yet to reach a consensus. When they do, they will certainly let me know.' 2.2.11

"Once," the Fāriyāq continued, "I heard someone who was bothered about some urgent business ask him the time, and the man told him, 'Such-and-such an hour and five minutes. Now, as to the word *sāʿah* ("hour"), from it are derived the words *sāʿī* ("errand boy"; literally "one who strives" or "makes effort") and *ʿĪsā*.[52] *Sāʿī* is so derived because all effort depends on the hours, for no-one can undertake any work outside the confines of time. All acts and motions are confined within time, just as . . .' and he looked about him for something to use as a comparison and caught sight of a tin mug belonging to some child and said, '. . . water is confined within this p'tch'r.'[53] Then he saw a palm-leaf basket belonging to some other child and said, 'Or like this child's lunch in this b'sk't. As for *ʿĪsā*, it is so derived because ʿĪsā contained within himself all knowledge and branches of learning as completely 2.2.12

ثم ان قولى خمس حقيقة معناه اربعة بعدها واحد او ثلثة قبلها اثنان ولك ان تعكس * وانما قالوا خمس دقائق ولم يقولوا خمسة طلبا للتخفيف والعجلة فى الكلام * فان بطول الالفاظ يضيع الوقت * وقولى دقائق هو جمع دقيقة وهو مشتق من الدقيق للطحين * اذ بينهما شبه ومناسبة بجامع النعومة * ثم ان هناك الفاظا كثيرة تدل على الوقت وهى المسآ والليل والصبح والضحى والظهر والعصر والدهر والابد والحين والاوان والزمن * اما الستّ الاولى ففيها فرق واما الاخيرة فلا * فاعترضه رجل من اولئك الكبرآ وقال قد رابنى يااستاذنا ما قلت * فان كلّا من جاريتى وستّها لها فرق * فضحك الشيخ من حماقته وقال له ان كلامى هنا فيما حواه الزمان لا فيما حواه المكان * فساله آخر قائلا اين جامع النعومة هذا الذى ذكرت ان فيه الدقيق * فضحك ايضا وقال اعلم ان لفظة جامع تسمَّى عندنا معاشر العلمآ اسم فاعل اى الذى يتولى فعل شى ايّا كان * لكنى طالما عزمت على ان اناقشهم فى هذه التسمية * لان من يموت او ينام مثلاً لا يصح ان يقال فيه انه فاعل الموت او النوم * فقولى جامع على القاعدة المعلومة عندنا هو اسم لمن جمع شيا * حتى ان الكنيسة يصح ان يطلق عليها لفظ الجامع لانها تجمع الناس * فلما قال ذلك اكفهرت وجوه السامعين * قال فسمعت بعضهم يجمجم قائلا * ما اظن الشيخ صحيح الاعتقاد بدين النصارى * فقد اصابت اساقفتنا فى حظرهم الناس ان يتبحّروا فى العلوم ولا سيما علم المنطق هذا الذى يذكره شيخنا * فقد قيل من تمنطق تزندق *
ثم انصرف عنه الجميع مدمدمين * وساله مرة قسيس عن اشتقاق الصلوة * ١٣،٢،٢
فقال هى مشتقة من الاصلآ لان المصلى يحرق الشيطان بدعائه * فقال له القسيس اذا كان ماوى الشيطان سقر مذ الوف سنين ولم يحترق فكيف تحرقه صلوة المصلّى * فتناول بعض الكتب ليقتبس منه جواب ذلك فاذا به يقول *

as the hour contains the minutes. Note too that, when I say "five," the real meaning is "four plus one" or "two plus three" or vice versa. They say *khams daqā'iq* ("five minutes") and not *khamsah daqā'iq* in pursuit of a more concise form and faster speech,[54] for the longer the words you use the more time you waste. The word *daqā'iq* ("minutes") that I just employed is the plural of *daqīqah,* which derives from the *daqīq* ("flour") that is milled, for they resemble and correspond to one another in that each is a "congregator of fineness" (*jāmiʿ al-nuʿūmah*).[55] There are many words that refer to time, namely *masā'* ("evening"), *layl* ("night"), *ṣubḥ* ("morning"), *ḍuḥā* ("forenoon"), *ẓuhr* ("noon"), *ʿaṣr* ("late afternoon"), *dahr* ("epoch"), *abad* ("eternity"), *ḥīn* ("point of time"), *awān* ("right time, season"), and *zaman* ("period"). The first six have "partings,"[56] the others do not.' Here, one of the important men who were present raised an objection, saying, 'I am confused, dear professor, by what you say. Both my slave girl and her mistress have partings!' The shaykh laughed at the man's foolishness and told him, 'My words here relate to the domain of time, not that of place.' Then another asked him, 'Where's this Nuʿūmah Mosque that you said has the flour in it?'[57] The man laughed again and said, 'To us scholars, the word *jāmiʿ* is known as an "active participle," meaning that it assumes the doing of something, whatever it might be (albeit for a long time I've had it in mind to discuss this terminology with them because someone who dies, or falls asleep, for example, cannot correctly be said to be "doing death" or "doing sleep"); when I used *jāmiʿ*, then, it was in accordance with the rule as recognized by us, namely as a noun descriptive of that which congregates a thing. It would be perfectly correct to apply the word *jāmiʿ* even to a church, because it congregates (*yajmaʿu*) the people.' When he said this, the faces of his listeners turned dark." The Fāriyāq resumed, "I then heard one of them muttering, 'I do not believe the shaykh holds a correct Christian belief. Our bishops were right to forbid people to delve deeply into the sciences, and especially this science of logic that our shaykh refers to. How rightly is it said, "He who practices logic practices unbelief!"' Then they all left him, muttering under their breath.

"And once a priest asked him about the etymology of the word *ṣalāh* 2.2.13
('prayer') and he said, 'It derives from the word *iṣlā'* ("burning") because the one who prays "burns" the Devil with his prayers.' The priest asked him, 'If the Devil has dwelt in hell fire these thousands of years without being burned up, how can prayer burn him?' so the man picked up one

قال احد علمآء الرهبان الاحتراق على نوعين * احتراق حسّى كمن يحترق بالنار * ومعنوىّ كمن يحترق بحبّ العذرة * ثم وقف وتاوّه قائلا * قد اخطأ سيدنا الراهب * لان العذرآ يجب مدّها * فقال القسيس وقد حنق عليه كيف يجب مدّها اذا لم تشأ * قال ويلى عليك انت الآخر لا تعرف المدّ والقصر فى الكلام واطفال الحارة فى بلادنا يعرفون ذلك * قال بلى ان اقتصار الكلام مع من يخطّى الرهبان مزية * ثم تولى من عنده مدمدما * قال الفارياق وقال لى مرة قد يظهر ١٤،٢،٢
لى ان حق استعمال دعا اذا اريد به معنى الصلوة ان يتعدّى بعلى * فيقال دعوت عليه كما يقال صليت عليه * قال فقلت له لا يلزم من كون فعل يوافق فعلا آخر فى معناه ان يوافقه فى التعدية * فغصّ بذلك ولم يفهمه * وشكا اليه مرة رجل من معارفه اسهالا آلمه * فقال له يغالطه او يسلّيه * احمد الله على ذلك ليتنى مثلك * قال كيف هو ان طال قتل واسال الجسم كله * فقال له انه منّة من الله * الم تسمع كل ملهوف يقول يارب سهل * فقال التاجر انا ما عنيت التسهيل بل الاسهال * فقال هما بمعنى واحد لان افعل وفعّل كلاهما ياتيان للتعدية * كما تقول انزلته ونزّلته * ولان كلاّ من التسهيل والاسهال فيه معنى السهولة * وكتب ١٥،٢،٢
مرة الى بعض المطارين العظام * المعروض ياسيدنا بعد تقبيل اردافكم الشريفة * وحمل نعالكم المنيفة اللطيفة * الظريفة النظيفة الرهيفة العفيفة الموصوفة المعروفة المخصوفة * قال فقلت له ما اردت بالارداف هنا * فقال هى فى عرف المطران بمعنى الراحة * ثم لم يلبث ان بعث اليه ذلك المطران ببركة وكتاب اطرا فيه على علمه وفضائله جدا فمما كتب اليه * قد قدم علىّ مكتوبكم الابنىّ وانا خارج عن الكنيسة فما قراته حتى دخلت الصومعة واولجت فيها * فلما اتيت على اخراه علمت

of the books to extract from it an answer and declared, 'A certain learned monk has said, "Burning is of two kinds: physical burning, as when someone is burned by fire, and figurative burning, as when someone is 'burned' by love as practiced by the tribe of 'Udhrah."' Then he paused and sighed, saying, 'Our Lord the monk was in error, because *'adhrā'* has to be stretched out at the end.'[58] The priest, enraged by the thought that the Virgin could be stretched out if she did not so desire, declared, 'Woe unto you! You're another who doesn't know the rules for the use of long and short vowels at the end of words, when the very children playing in the alleys in our country know them! Truly, it's a good idea to keep to a minimum one's conversations with those who accuse monks of error.' Then he turned and left him, muttering under his breath."

The Fāriyāq went on, "And once he told me, 'My studies have shown me that the proper way to use the verb *da'ā*, if one intends the meaning of "to pray," is to follow it with the preposition *'alā*. Thus one should say *da'awtu 'alayh,* just as one says *ṣallaytu 'alayh.*'[59] I told him, 'Just because two verbs have the same sense doesn't mean they should be followed by the same preposition,' but this was too much for him; he couldn't get his head around it. And once a man he knew complained to him that a bout of diarrhea was causing him pain, and he said to him—either to correct him or to amuse him—'Thank God for it! I wish I were like you.' 'How can that be?' said the first. 'If it goes on too long, it is fatal and carries the whole body off with it.' He replied, 'It is a blessing from God. Do you not hear how everyone who has a worry says, "Lord, make it pass easily"?' The merchant replied, 'I'm not worried about things passing easily, I'm worried about things passing through my bowels *too* easily.' 'It comes to the same thing,' the first told him, 'because verbs of the pattern *af'ala* and those of the pattern *fa''ala* both lend transitivity—one says either *anzaltuhu* ("I sent it down") or *nazzaltuhu* (ditto)—and because both *tashīl* and *ishāl* contain the sense of "ease."'"[60] 2.2.14

"And once he wrote to one of the great metropolitans, 'My request, Your Grace, after kissing your noble buttocks and raising your elevated, sophisticated, delectated, de-germinated, etiolated, uncontaminated, well-soled, much extolled, and often resoled slippers is . . .'—at which point I asked him, 'What do you mean here by "buttocks?"' and he replied, 'In the usage of the metropolitans, it means "hand."' In no time at all, the same metropolitan had sent him back his blessings and a letter praising him hugely for his learning 2.2.15

انك صاحب الفضول * مولف الفصول * جامع بين الفروع والاصول * طويل اللسان * قصير اليدان * (عن المحرمات) واسع الجبين * عميق الدين * عريض الصدر* مجوف الفكر* وكتب فى آخره * اطال الله بقاك * وقباك * وهنّاك ومنّاك * والسلام ختام *والختام سلام * والبركة الرسولية تشملكم اولا وثانيا الى عاشرا *فجعل يبدى هذا الكتاب لجميع معارفه وخصوصا لمن كانوا خرجوا من عنده مغضبين لتقريره عن لفظة الجامع * فلما وجدوها فى كلام المطران زال عنهم الاشكال والريب فى صحة استعمالها * وزاد الرجل عندهم وجاهة وجلالاً *

فاما سوالك عن كرم اهل هذه البلدة فانهم كانوا فى ظهور آبائهم على غاية من السماحة والجود * الا انهم لما برزوا الى عالم التجارة وخالطوا اصحاب هذى البرانيط اخذوا عنهم الحرص والبخل واللئامة والرَّثَع * بل برّزوا على مشايخهم * وانهم اذا ضمهم مجلس لم يكن منهم الا الحديث عن البيع والشرآ * فيقول احدهم قد جآنى اليوم جندىّ من الترك فى الصباح ليشترى شيا فتطيرت من صباحه واستفتاحه * اذ لا يخفى عنكم ان الجندى يستدين ولا يقضى دينه * واذا تكرم بنقد الثمن فما يعطى التاجر الا نصفه * فقلت له ما عندى مطلوبك ياافندى * وانما اردت تفخيمه بهذا اللقب ليتادب معى * فما كان منه الا ان دخل الحانوت وبعثر البضاعة كلها واخذ ما اراد منها وما لم يرد * ثم ولّى وهو يسبنى * فيقول آخر وانا ايضا جرى لى مع سيدة من نسآء الترك واقعة * وذلك انها بكرت علىّ اليوم وهى تنوء بحليّها * واقبلت باسمة الىّ وقالت هل عندك ياسيدى حرير مزركش* قلت وقد استبشرت عندى * فقالت ارنى المتاع فاريتها اياه * فتداركتنى بالخفّ وقالت امثلى يرى هذا * ارنى غير ذلك * فاريتها ما اعجبها فاخذته وقالت ابعث معى من يقبض الثمن * فبعثت غلامى فتبعها حتى دخلت ١٦،٢،٢

and virtues, of which the following is an excerpt:[61] 'Your sodomitical missive reached me when I was outside the church, and I could read it only after I'd entered my cell and penetrated it. When I came to the shittiest part of it, I realized that you were possessed of *excrements,* a creator of *pestilence,* a "congregator" of both the branches of knowledge and its roots, long of *tongue* and with 'ands too short (to do any *wrong*), with a broad little brow, deeply in *debt,* wide of waistcoat, of ideas *bereft.*' At the end of it he wrote, 'May God prolong your life and livery, grant you happiness, and awaken your hopes! In conclusion, our greetings, and a greeting for our conclusion. May the grace of the apostles embrace you, once, twice, and all the way up to ten!' The man made a habit of showing this letter off to all his acquaintances and especially those who had left him in anger over his interpretation of the word *jāmiʿ*. In view of the metropolitan's words, these were thenceforth relieved of all confusion and doubt as to the correctness of how to use it, and the man increased in dignity and venerability in their eyes.

"Turning now to your question concerning the hospitability of this town, in the days of their first forefathers they were exceedingly liberal and generous. However, when they started to excel in the world of commerce and to mix with the people of those Frankish hats that you wot of, they caught from them their reticence, miserliness, bad faith, and avarice; indeed, they've come to surpass their teachers. When they find themselves gathered together, the only talk they make is of buying and selling. One will say, 'Today, a Turkish trooper came to me in the morning to buy something, which I took as an evil omen for the morning and for the start of business, for, as you well know, troopers incur debts but don't pay them, and if they're gracious enough to provide the price in cash, they give the merchant only half. So I told him, "I don't have what you're looking for, effendi" (showing him the deference of this title solely in the hope that he would treat me politely). No sooner did he hear my words than he entered the store and threw the goods everywhere, taking what he wanted and what he didn't. Then he left, shouting insults.' Another will say, 'I too had a run-in with a Turkish lady. She sailed in early today, wallowing under the weight of her jewelry, approached me smiling, and said, "Have you, sir, any brocaded silk?" Taking a happy omen from her coming, I said, "I have." "Show me the goods," she said, so I showed them to her. Then she leaned forward and gave me a slap with her slipper, saying, "Is one such as I to be shown such stuff? Show me 2.2.16

دارا كبيرة وامرت حاجبها بضرب الغلام وايلامه * الا ان الحاجب لما كان من الترك وراى الغلام امرد لم يطاوعه قلبه على ضربه لكن انفذ فيه امر سيدته بما اوصل من الاذى والالم * وهكذا ينقضى نهارهم بالمكروه وليلهم بذكره * واظن ان التاجر يطرب بمجرد ذكر البيع والشرآ وان لم يكن فيه ربح * فاما ما جرى لى بعد ١٧،٢،٢
وصولى فانى نزلت عند خرجى من اصحاب صاحبى الاول * فتبوأت حجرة بالقرب من حجرته * فكنت اسمعه كل ليلة يضرب امراته بآلة فتبدى الانين والحنين * والرنين والخنين * فكان يهيجنى فعله الى البطش به * وكثيرا ما فكرت فى ان اقوم من فراشى لكنى خشيت ان يصيبنى ما اصاب ذاك الاعجمى المتطبب الذى جاور قوما من القبط * وانه سمع ذات ليلة صراخ امراة من جاراته فظن ان لدغتها عقرب وذلك لكثرة وجود العقارب فى بيوت مصر * فقام الى قنينة دوآ تابطها واقبل يجرى * فلما فتح الباب وجد رجلا على امراة يعالجها باصبعه كما هى عادة القوم * فلما راى الطبيب ذلك دهش فوقعت القنينة من يده وانكسرت * وكان ١٨،٢،٢

هذا الخرجى ابيض اللون ازرق العينين مع صغر واستدارة فيهما * دقيق ارنبة الانف[١] مع عوج فى قصبته * غليظ الشفتين * وانما تكلفت لوصفه لك ليبقى نموذجا عندك تقيس عليه جميع من تراه من الخرجيين وغيرهم * وكان قد اتخذ فوق سطح منزله هرما صغيرا مرصوفا من قنانى الخمر الفارغة * فكان سطحه اعلى سطوح الجيران * قال ثم عنّ له يوما ان يكلفنى انشآ خطبة فى مدح الخرج لكى اتلوها فى مخطب صغير كان قد استاجره * فلما فرغت منها عرضتها عليه فذهب بها الى قيعر قيعار * فقال له ما مرادك ان تصنع بهذه الاحجيّة الخرجية * قال يتلوها منشئها على الناس فما رايك فيها * قال هى حسنة الا ان عيبها هو ان لا يفهمها

---

١ ١٨٥٥: الالف.

something else," so I showed her something that she liked, and she took it, saying, "Send someone with me to collect the money," so I sent my young servant, who followed her till she entered a large house, where she ordered her steward to give the boy a sound drubbing. The steward, however, being a Turk and seeing that the lad was comely and smooth, couldn't find it in his heart to beat the boy, but implemented his mistress's command in a different way that nevertheless brought him both injury and pain.' Thus they pass their days in evil ways and their nights in going over them. I think merchants go into ecstasies simply at the mention of buying and selling, even if they aren't making a profit.

"As to what befell me after my arrival, I put up at the home of a Bag-man 2.2.17
who was the friend of my previous friend. I occupied a room close to his and each night would hear him beating his wife with some implement, while she produced moans and groans, sighs and nasal cries. His acts roused the desire in me to give him a hiding, and I often thought of getting out of bed but was afraid that it would be for me as it was for the Persian who practiced medicine and lived next door to a community of Copts: one night he heard one of his neighbor-women screaming. There being so many scorpions in the houses of Egypt, he thought one must have stung her, and, fetching a flask of medicine, placed it under his arm and set off in her direction at a run. When he opened the door, though, he found a man lying on top of the woman and treating her with his finger, after the custom of that people. When the doctor saw this, he was amazed, and the flask fell from his hand and was broken.

"This Bag-man had white skin and blue eyes that were both small and 2.2.18
round. His nose had a finely molded tip and went crooked at the bridge, and his lips were thick. I tell you these details only so that they can remain with you as a prototype against which to measure any other Bag-men or others you may see. On the roof of his house he had made a small, pyramid-shaped stack of empty bottles of alcohol, the roof being higher than those of his neighbors. One day it occurred to him to set me the task of composing a sermon in praise of saddlebags that I was to deliver at a small oratory he had hired. When I finished, I submitted it to him, and he took it to Qayʿar Qayʿār. 'What do you intend to do with this baggish rigmarole?' the latter asked him. 'I intend the one who composed it to deliver it to the people. What do you think of it?' 'It's good,' he said, 'but it does have one drawback, which is that nobody will understand it except him and me, and we've both already read

احد الا انا وهو * ونحن قد قراناها فلا موجب لاعادتها * فعدل عن ذلك *
قال واتفق لى وانا مقيم عنده انى خرجت فى عشية من عشايا الصيف البهيجة ١٩،٢،٢
امشى وحدى وبيدى نسخة الدفتر* ولما كان راسى قد حفل بالافكار فيما انا
عليه من فرقة الاهل والاحباب وذكر الوطن * والتغرّب عنه لغير سبب من
اسباب المعاش سوى لخصام سوقى وخرجى على قال وقيل* اوغلت فى المشى
فانتهيت الى ظاهر المدينة وكان يتبعنى رجل قد راى نسخة الدفتر فعرفها فاضمر
ليمنيننّى بداهية * فاقبل الىّ يكلّمنى ثم عطف بى يمنة ويسرة وهو يعللنى بالكلام
حتى انتهينا الى مكان خال * فتركنى هناك وقال لى ان علىّ ان اقضى هنا
مصلحة *فحاولت الرجوع الى مقرّى واذا بسرب عظيم من الكلاب جرت وهى
تنبحنى ودنت منى * فهوّلت عليها بالكتاب فهجمت علىّ هجمة السوقى على الخرجى *
ثم تحاصّوا جسمى وثيابى والكتاب فبعضهم عضّ * وبعضهم اَدْمَى * وبعضهم
جرّ * وبعضهم تهدّد فى المرة الثانية * فما كدت اتملّص من بين ايديهم الا وثوبى
وجلدى ممزق على ممزق * وقد مزّق الدفتر ايضا اوراقه وجلده * فلما رجعت
الى منزلى ورآنى الخرجى على هذه الحالة لم يكترث بشانى او انه لم يرنى من
فرط اشتغاله بالخرج * وانما علم انى رجعت خلوا من الدفتر فاعتقد انى اعطيته
لاحد * ففرح بذلك جدا ورغب فى ان يجعلنى عنده فى مصلحة خرجية *
لكن راى من الواجب ان يشاور صاحبه فمن ثم كتب اليه فى شانى * فابى ذاك
وقال لا بد من تسفيرى الى الجزيرة * لان النية استقرت على هذا من قبل *
وما حسن تغيير النيات * فعزم مضيفى على اجرآء ذلك وها انا منتظر السفينة *

it, so there's no call to have it read out again.' Consequently the man gave up the idea.

"It also happened that one delightful summer's evening when I was staying with him, I went out to take a walk on my own, a copy of the ledger in my hand. My head being filled with thoughts of how I was separated from my family and friends and with memories of my homeland and of how I had been exiled from it not for any reason linked to ordinary affairs but because of a feud between Market-man and Bag-man over polemical matters, I kept on walking until I ended up on the outskirts of the city, to which I had been followed by a man who, having seen the copy of the ledger and recognized it, had privately decided to bring a disaster down on my head. Now he approached me, spoke to me, and led me left and right, distracting me with talk, until we arrived at an empty wasteland, where he left me, telling me that he had to see to some business. I tried to return to where I was staying but suddenly found myself face to face with a huge pack of dogs that had run up, barking at me, and were closing in. I tried to scare them off with the book, but they attacked me like a Market-man attacking a Bag-man and divided my body, my clothes, and the book between them, as creditors might a debtor's possessions, some biting, some drawing blood, some dragging me, and some threatening to come back for more. I managed, barely, to escape their clutches, though my clothes and skin were torn to shreds, and the ledger too was ripped to pieces, both pages and binding. When I returned home and the Bag-man saw me in this state, he paid no attention to me or maybe didn't even see me, so preoccupied was he with the bag. When he discovered, however, that I had returned without the ledger, he imagined I must have given it away to someone, and this gave him such immense joy that he wanted to keep me with him in Alexandria for Bag-man business. However, he decided that he should consult his friend first and therefore wrote to him about me. The friend rejected his idea and said he had to send me on to the island, because this was what had been previously decided (though how sweet it can be when decisions are changed!). My host therefore decided to put the plan into action, and here I now am, awaiting the ship." **2.2.19**

الفصل الثالث

في انقلاع الفارياق من الاسكندرية

من نحس صاحبنا انه عند سفره الى تلك الجزيرة لم تكن خاصّية البُخار قد عُرفت عند الافرنج * فكان سفر البحر موكولا الى الريح ان شاءت هبّت وان شاءت لم تهب * كما قال الصاحب بن عباد ١،٣،٢

فانما هي ريح لست تضبطها   اذ لست انت سليمن بن داود

فمن ثم ركب الفارياق في سفينة ريحية من هذا النوع وكان في مدة السفر يتعلم بعض الفاظ من لغة اصحاب السفينة مما يختص بالتحية والسلام * من جملة ذلك دعآء يقولونه عند شرب الخمر على المائدة وهو قولهم طابت صحتك * الا ان لفظ الصحة عندهم يقرب من لفظ جهنم فكان يقول طابت جهنمك * فكانوا يضحكون منه وهو يسبّهم بقلبه ويقول * قاتل الله هولآء العلوج انهم يقيمون في بلادنا سنين ولا يحسنون النطق بلغتنا * فيلفظون السين اذا سبقها حركة زايا وحروف الحلق وغيرها محالة ونحن لا نضحك منهم * ٢،٣،٢ وقد سمعت ان بعض قسّيسيهم الذين لبثوا في بلادنا سنين رام مرة ان يخطب في القوم فلما صعد المنبر ارتج عليه ساعة الى ان قال * (ايها الكوم كد فات الوكت الان ولكني اهتب فيكم نهار الاهد الكابل ان شا الله) * ثم سار الى بعض معارفه من اهل الدراية والعلم والتمس منه ان ٣،٣،٢

Chapter 3

The Extraction of the Fāriyāq from Alexandria, by Sail[62]

A typical example of our friend's bad luck was that, at the time of his leaving for the island, the Franks had yet to discover the special properties of steam. Travel by sea was dependent on the wind, which blew if it felt like it and didn't if it didn't. As al-Ṣāḥib ibn al-ʿAbbād has said,[63] 2.3.1

'Tis but a wind you cannot control,
For you're not Sulaymān, son of Dā'ūd.

It follows that the Fāriyāq departed on a wind-propelled ship of that ilk.

In the course of his voyage, he learned some words of the language of the people of the ship related to greetings and salutes. One of these was a prayer that they utter when drinking wine at table, namely, "Good health to you!" Their word *health*, however, resembles their word *hell*, so he used to say, "Good hell to you!" and they'd laugh at him while he cursed them in his heart, saying, "God destroy these louts! They live in our country for years and still can't pronounce our language properly. They pronounce *s* with a vowel before it as *z*, and the palatal letters and others are a lost cause for them, despite which we don't laugh at them. 2.3.2

"I have heard that a priest who had lived in our country for years decided one day to preach to the people. When he ascended the pulpit, he stood there shaking for an hour before finally saying,[64] 'Good yolk, my lime is up but I shall peach to you next Fun Day, God willing.' Then he went to see an expert and learned acquaintance of his and implored him to write him a sermon that he could commit to memory or read out loud. The people came in great numbers to hear him, and, when the church was full to overflowing, 2.3.3

يكتب له خطبة يحفظها عن ظهر قلبه او يتلوها تلاوة * وحشد الناس اليه فلما غصت بهم الكنيسة صعد المنبر فقال * (بسم الله الرهمن) * ثم كأنّه انتبه من غفلته وعرف ان ذلك لا يرضى النصارى وان الكاتب انما كتب ذلك على طريقته * فاستدرك كلامه وقال * لا لا ما بدّيش اكول مسلما بيكول الاسلام بسم الله الرهمن الرهيم بل كما تكول النسارى بسم الاب والابن والروه الكدس * يااولادى المباركين الهادرين هنا لسماء هتبتى * وكبول نسيهتى وموهزتى * ان كنتم هدرتم وكلبكم مشكول بلزّات الآلم * اهبرونى هتى اكسر من هتابكم فلا يتدجّا اهد من تُوله ولا يتالّم * والا فهزى فرسة سنهت لى اليوم * ازكّر فيها النسآ والرجال تزكير من لا يكشى اللوم * وانزرهم يوم الهشر والهساب * يوم لا ينفا مال ولا اَسهاب * ولا سُهال ولا جواب * ايلموا رهمكم الله ان الدنيا زايله * ومتامهها باتله * وهالاتها هايله * ومهاليها سافله * فكونوا منها على هَزَر * ولا يُدلّكم ما آجب منها وما سرّ * اسرفوا اَنّها نَزَركم * ولا تالّكوا بها وَتَركم * افهسوا فيها كلبكم كبل ان تسندوا روسكم اَلَى المهدّة * ووازبوا الى السلوات فى الديك والشدة * كدموا للكنايس نزوركم ولوكليله * واستهينوا بالكدّيسين هال الفتيله * لتنكزوا من المِهَن والمسايب * وتتقسّوا من الكرنب والنوايب(١) اهترموا كسّيسيكم واساكفتكم ووكّروهم واكتدوا بهم * واركبوهم ولا هزُوهم ترشدوا بسايهم وركسهم ودابهم * ياايها النَّسارَى ان دينا هو الهكّ * وواده هو الاسدك * وكيره هو الاكدك وسُوكه هو الانفك * لا تكالتوا هولآء الكرجيّين * الزّين اندسّوا فيكم مزهين * يتربّون فى ادلالكم عن الزرات المستكيم * بما يزهرون لكم من الورا والكُلُك الهليم * الَا انهم هم الزياب الكاتفة المتردية بلباس الهملان * الجايلون فى كل كُتْر وسُك ينسبون الينا الزيك والبهتان * وهم ازيك من سلك تريكا *

(١) الكرنب مصحّفة عن الكرب *

he mounted the pulpit and declared, 'In the Name of God the Immersible!' Then it seems he noticed his mistake and realized that this wouldn't please the Christians and that the writer had written it according to his own tenets, so he corrected himself and said,

"'No, no! I ain't mean to say me Muslim man. Islam he say "In the Name of God the Immersible, the Inflatable." Contrarily, Kitchen People he say "In the Name of the Father, the Son, and the Holy Boast."

"'Blessed children lathered here today to spear my peach and listen to my insides, if you have lathered here while your farts are still fizzy with the Pleasures of This Knife, inform me, that I may submit you to my denture, and let none complain of its length or how it hurts. If not, then today's my inopportunity, as one who bears no importunity, to urge both women and men to bedrink themselves and to warn you of the Day of Insurrection and Beckoning—a day when neither honey nor blends will avail, nor indigestion nor regurgitation. Know, may God inflate you, that This World is ephemeral, its temptresses virginal, its mates undependable, its towering sights despicable. Stand on lard against it and let not its pleasures and temptations lead you into terror. Keep your lances from it averted. Hang not your ropes upon it. Examine your farts concerning it before you lay down your heads upon your holsters and sleep. Spray regularly when distressed or undressed. Coffer the churches your contributions, be they but spittle. Spray God's paints that they may help you and shave you from all piles and infibulations. Be of good fart if you would be freed from the cabbages of fate.(1) Respect your monsters and piss-offs, venerealize them, and wallow in their footsteps. Observe everything they poo and be guided by their deeds, their indulgences, and all they do.

(1) "'Cabbages' (*al-kurunb*) is a misspelling for 'ravages' (*al-karb*).

"'Good Kitchen People, our religion is the Roof! Its premises are the best licensed! Its dressings are the most humorous! Its market has the best rices! Have no intercourse with the fag-men, who have recently inserted themselves into you, pricking you into leaving the straight bath with the dignified and mild feces that they put on for you. They are naught but ravening poofs in clams' clothing cruising in every land and strand, accusing us of aberration and of spreading flies, when they are the most fly-blown of any who took a bath and the flightiest of any who ever cheated on a friend or led a companion down the primrose path.'

واكرب من كشّ سديكا * وكان رفيكا *) الى ان قال (ايها الكاركون فى بهار
الهتايا * تجنبوا ما يفدى بكم اليها فان آكبتها اَليكم بلايا و رزايا * الا فاسرموا ازبابها
سرما * وكاوموا اركابها اَزْما * واستاسلوا جزرها رهزا * واكلاوا مُكوّياتها تنالوا
ركزًا * الازباب الازباب * فاكاوا الازباب * حتى تهلسوا فى يوم الهساب *
من الكساس والازاب) * (اى اقطعوا الاسباب حتى تخلصوا فى يوم الحساب
من القصاص والعذاب) ومع ذلك فلم يصفعه احد من السامعين بل استمر ٤،٣،٢
الى آخر الخطبة على هذا النمط * الا ان امراة لبيبة كانت قد تزوجت مذ عهد
قريب لما سمعت الفقرة الاخيرة غضبت وقالت * الا لا بارك الله فى يوم راينا
فيه وجوه هولآ العجم فقد احتكروا خيراتنا وارزاقنا * وافسدوا بلادنا وسابقوا ناسنا
الى تحصيل ارزائهم من ارضنا * وعلّموا من عرفهم منا البخل والحرص والطيش
والسفاهة * وما لعمرى حصلوا على هذا الغنى الجزيل الّا لجشعهم وشحهم * فقد
سمعنا ان الرجل منهم اذا جلس على المائدة مع اولاده ياكل اللحم ويرمى بالعظام اليهم
ليتمشّشوها * ولكونهم حراميّن غبّانين فى البيع غشاشين * وقد بلغنى ان اخوانهم
فى بلادهم انجس منهم وافسق * وهذا النحس الان يغرى بعولتنا بارتكاب الفاحشة
لتخلو له الساحة فيفعل ما يشآ * فانى اعلم عين اليقين ان هولآ المنابريّين انما يقولون
بافواههم ما ليس فى قلوبهم * وانهم ليعلّمون الناس الزهد فى الدنيا والجَبّ وهم
احرص الثقلين عليها واقرم الخلق الى البعال * فما جزآوه الان الا قطع لسانه حتى
يعرف الم القطع * لعمرى ان الانسان لا يهون عليه احيانا ان يقلّم اظفاره لكونها
منه * ولذلك كانت اخواتنا نسآء الافرنج يربّين اظفارهن ويفتخرن بها مع انها لا
تلبث ان تنبت * فكيف يجوز قطع ما يعمّر به الكون * (طيّب الله انفاسك ياحديثة
عهد بالزواج وعتيقة نقد للاعلاج * ليت النسا كلهن مثلك وليتنى الثم شفتيك)

"Then he said,

"'O you who are clowning in a sea of pecker-dildoes, stay clear of all that may feed you to them, for the result will be disasters and calamities. Don't let them get up to their old tricks, but cut them off at the ass. Resist their fins resolutely. Pull them out by their boots directly. Strip off any ironing of theirs that makes you perspire and you will be granted retribution. The pricks! The pricks! Cut off your pricks, that you be saved on the Day of Beckoning from any stunts or tricks!'

"Despite all this, none of his listeners boxed his ears. On the contrary, 2.3.4
they sat quietly until the end of the sermon as given above. Then, however, a quick-witted woman who had just married, on hearing the last passage, grew angry and said, 'God curse the day we first set eyes on these non-Arabs. They have monopolized our resources and wealth and corrupted our lands and they compete with our own people in obtaining their sustenance from our own soil. They have taught those of us who have come to know them miserliness, stinginess, fickleness, and shamelessness. Never, I swear, would they have obtained these abundant riches were it not for their greed and avarice, for we hear that when one of their menfolk sits down at the table with his children, he eats the meat and throws them the bones to suck on, and because they are thieves and cheats, and swindle when they sell, and I've been told that their brethren in their own countries are even more disgusting and depraved than they. Now this wretch is inciting our husbands to commit an abomination so as to leave the field open to him to do as he wishes, for I know, without any doubt, that what these pulpiteers say with their mouths is not what is in the hearts. They teach people abstinence and emasculation in this world, while there isn't a human or a jinni who cares more about intercourse than they or is greedier for it. Let his reward now be to have his tongue cut off, so that he can know how much it hurts. Sometimes, I swear, one finds it hard to cut one's fingernails because they're a part of one, which is why our sisters, the women of the Franks, grow their nails and show them off. Those, though, are quick to grow back. How then can it be permitted to cut off the means by which life is generated?'" (Well said, you who are so new to marriage and so experienced in the criticism of such oafs! Would that all women might be like you and I might kiss your lips!)

ثم لما خرج القسيس من الكنيسة اذا بالناس جميعا اهرعوا لتقبيل يده وذيله * ٥،٣،٢
وشكروه على ما افادهم من المعانى البديعة بقطع النظر عن غيرها * لما تقرر فى
عقولهم من ان من خواص دين النصارى ان تكون كتبه ركيكة فاسدة ما امكن *
لان قوة الدين تقتضيه لتحصل المطابقة كما افاده المطران اتناسيوس التوتنجى الحلبى
البُشكانى الشلاّقى الشَوْلقى الِانقافى النشّافى المقسقسىّ اللَطّاعى النَطّاعى المُصنوى
الحُتفلى الاَرشمىّ التُرتمىّ القَدِيحى التخمّى الامّعى فى بعض مولفاته المسمىّ بالحكاكه فى
الركاكه * قال الفارياق واذ قد ابتلانى الله بعشرة هولآء اللئام فلا بد لى من مجاملتهم
ومخالقتهم الى ان يمنّ على بالنجاة منهم * قلت وحيث قد مرّ ما قاله الفارياق فى ٦،٣،٢
سفرته الاولى فلا موجب الان لاعادة ذكر شكواه هنا من الم البحر * وانما نقول انه
فى خلال معاناته ومقاساته حلف لا يركبنَّ بعدها فى شى من مراكب البحر * من

الجُفآ	السفينة الخالية ذكره صاحب القاموس فى المهموز *	
والمرْزاب	السفينة العظيمة او الطويلة *	
والزَنْبَرَ	ضرب من السفن *	
والبارجة	السفينة الكبيرة للقتال *	
والخليج	سفينة صغيرة دون العَدَوْلىّ *	
والطّرّاد	السفينة الصغيرة السريعة *	
والمُعبّدة	السفينة المقيّرة *	
والغامِد	السفينة المشحونة كالآمِد *	
والدَسْرآ	السفينة تدسر المآ بصدرها ج دُسُر *	
والزُرْزُور	المركب الضيّق *	
والزَنْبَرىّ	الضخم من السفن *	٧،٣،٢

"When the priest left the church, everyone rushed to kiss his hand and the hem of his garment, and all thanked him for the elegant figures of speech he had vouchsafed them, not to mention all the other wonderful things, for it had become an established fact to them that the books of the Christian religion should be written in as feeble and corrupt a style as possible, because 'the power of the religion requires it, so that everything be of one piece,' as stated by the Arabic-language-challenged,[65] Feed-sack-carrying, Sweetmeat-chasing, Marrow-slurping, Rag-sucking, Bone-gnawing, Finger-licking, Half-a-morsel-biting, Cauldron-watching, Drippings-drinking, Bottom-of-the-pot-scraping, Scourings-scarfing, Leftovers-off-polishing, Dinner-sponging Aleppine Metropolitan Atanāsiyūs al-Tutūnjī[66] in a work of his called *Al-Ḥakākah fī l-rakākah* (*The Leavings Pile Concerning Lame Style*).[67]" Said the Fāriyāq, "Since God had seen fit to afflict me with the company of such wretches, I had no choice but to compliment them and be cordial to them until such time as He grant that I be rescued from them." 2.3.5

I declare: since what the Fāriyāq had to say about his first voyage has already come and gone, there's no need to repeat here his complaints concerning the dolors of the sea. However, we will note that during his sufferings and afflictions, he did swear that he would never embark thereafter on any of the following sea-going vessels: 2.3.6

the *jufā'*,	"the empty hulk of a ship"; mentioned by the author of the *Qāmūs* under *j-f-'*
the *mirzāb*,	"any great, or tall, ship"
the *zabzab*,	"a sort of ship"
the *bārijah*,	"any large ship for fighting"
the *khalīj*,	"a small ship of less size than the *'adawlī*"
the *ṭarrād*,	"any small, fast ship"
the *mu'abbadah*,	"any tarred ship"
the *ghāmid*,	"any loaded ship; also *āmid*"
the *dasrā'*,	"any ship that plows through the water with its prow; plural *dusur*"
the *zurzūr*,	"any narrow ship"
the *zanbarī*,	"any huge ship" 2.3.7

والقُرْقور	السفينة الطويلة أو العظيمة *
والكار	سفن منحدرة فيها طعام *
والهُرْهور	ضرب من السفن *
والقادس	السفينة العظيمة *
والبُوصِىّ	ضرب من السفن *
والصَلْغة	السفينة الكبيرة *
والنُهْبُوغ	السفينة الطويلة السريعة الجرى البحرية ويقال لها الدونيج معرَّب *
وذات الرَّفِيف	سفن كان يعبر عليها وهى ان تنضَّد سفينتان او ثلث للملك *
والشُقْدُف	مركب م بالحجاز *
والحَرّاقة	ج حَرّاقات سفن فيها مرامى نيران * ٨،٣،٢
والزَوْرَق	السفينة الصغيرة *
والبُراكِيَّة	ضرب من السفن *
والعَدَوْلِيَّة	سفن منسوبة الى عَدَوْلَى ة بالبحرين او —
والجَرْم	زورق يمنى *
والخِنّ	السفينة الفارغة *
والشَوْنة	المركب المعدّ للجهاد فى البحر *
والتَلَوَّى	ضرب من السفن صغير ذكره فى ت ل و *
والجُفاية	السفينة الخالية ذكره فى ج ف ى *

the *qurqūr*,	"any long, or very large, ship"
kār,	"ships on the down run containing food"
the *hurhūr*,	"a kind of ship"
the *qādis*,	"any very large ship"
the *būṣī*,	"a kind of ship"
the *ṣalghah*,	"any big ship"
the *nuhbūgh*,	"any fast-moving ocean-going ship; also called *dūnīj*, a non-Arabic word"
dhāt al-rafīf,	[literally, "the planked," i.e., "boat bridges"] "ships used to cross over on, consisting of two or three ships set side by side, for the king"
the *shuqduf*,	"a boat; also a place in the Hejaz"
the *ḥarrāqah*,	"plural *ḥarrāqāt*; ships containing flame-throwers" 2.3.8
the *zawraq*,	"any small ship"
the *burrāqiyyah*,	"a kind of ship"
ʿadawliyyah,	"ships named after ʿAdawlā, a village in Bahrain; or . . . ."[68]
the *jarm*,	"a small Yemeni ship"
the *khinn*,	"the empty hulk of a ship"
the *shawnah*,	"any boat equipped for battle at sea"
the *talawwā*,	"a kind of ship (small)"; mentioned [by the author of the *Qāmūs*] under *t-l-w*
the *jufāyah*,	"any empty hulk"; mentioned [in the *Qāmūs*] under *j-f-y*

والخَليّة	السفينة العظيمة او التى تسير من غير أن يسيّرها ملاّح أو التى يتبعها زورق صغير *
والشَذا	ضرب من السفن *
الى الرِكْوة	الزورق الصغير *
والقارب	السفينة الصغيرة *
والرَمَث	خشب يضم بعضه الى بعض ويركب فى البحر *
والطَوْف	قِرَب ينفخ فيها ويشد بعضها الى بعض كهيئة السطح يركب عليها فى المآء ويحمل عليها *
والعامَة	عيدان مشدودة تركب فى البحر ويعبر عليها فى النهر ويقال لها ايضا العامّة *

وانه بعد وصوله الى مرسى الجزيرة اعدّ له فيه مكان حسن لتطهير انفاسه به مدة ٩،٣،٢ اربعين يوما * اذ قد جرت العادة عندهم بان من قدم اليهم من البلاد المشرقية وقد استنشق هواها فلا بد وان يُنثره فى المرسى قبل دخوله البلد * فاقام فيها ياكل ويشرب مع اثنين من اعيان الانكليز ممن ركبوا فى السفينة * وطاب له العيش معهما لانهما قد ساحا فى بلدان كثيرة من المشرق واخذا عن اهلها الكرم *

ثم بعد انقضآ المدة جآ الخرجى واخذه الى منزله بالمدينة * وكان المذكور قد فقد ١٠،٣،٢ زوجته من يوم نُوى تسفير الفارياق اليه * فلزم الحداد والتقشف * ولزمته الكابة والتاسّف * وآن لا ياكل غير لحم الخنزير اعلى الله شانك عن ذكره * وانما امر طباخه بان يتفنن فيه * فيوما كان يطبخ له راسه * ويوما رجليه * ويوما كبده * ويوما طحاله * حتى ياتى على جميع آرابه ثم يستانف من الراس * وانت خبير بان نصارى الشام يحاكون المسلمين فى كل شى ما خلا الامور الدينية *

the *khaliyyah*,	"any great ship, or one that sails without needing a navigator to sail it, or which is followed by a small boat"
the *shadhā*,	"a kind of ship"
and all the way down to	
the *rikwah*,	"any small boat"
the *qārib*,	"any small ship"
the *ramath*,	"pieces of wood fastened together on which one rides at sea"
the *ṭawf*,	"inflated water skins that are tied together to form a platform on which one rides on the water and on which loads are carried"
and the *ʿāmah*.	"tied sticks on which one rides at sea or crosses a river; also called *ghāmmah*"

On arriving at the island's harbor, fine quarters were made available to him in which to "purify his breath" for a period of forty days, for it has become the custom among them to distribute around the harbor, before they enter the country, anyone who comes to them from the lands of the Levant and has inhaled their airs. He stayed there then, eating and drinking with two English notables who had been on the ship, and found life with them pleasant, for they had traveled widely in the Levant and absorbed the habit of generosity from its inhabitants. 2.3.9

When the period was over, the Bag-man came and took him to his house in the city. This man had lost his wife on the very day that the Fāriyāq had made his decision to go to him and had given himself over to mourning and *squalor*, living in the clutches of melancholy and *dolor*. All he ate was pork (God elevate you above any pollution from the very notion!) and he had ordered his cook to produce it in every variety. One day the man would cook its head, another its feet, a third its liver, a fourth its spleen, and so on until he had covered all its parts; then he'd start over again with the head. You are well aware that the Christians of the Levant imitate the Muslims in all things other than those pertaining to religion, from which it follows that pork is an abomination to them. Thus, when the Fāriyāq sat down to table 2.3.10

فمن ثم كان لحم الخنزير عندهم منكرا * فلما جلس الفارياق على المائدة وجآ الطباخ بارب من هذا الحيوان الكريه ظن ان الخرجىّ يمازحه بارآته اياه شيا لم يعرفه * فامتنع ان ياكل منه طمعا فى ان ينال من غيره * واذا بالخرجى قضى فرض الغداء وشرع حالاً فى الصلوة والشكر للبارى تعالى على ما رزقه * فقال الفارياق فى نفسه قد اخطا والله صاحبى * فانه وضع الشكر فى غير موضعه اذ الثنآ على الخالق سبحانه لا جل فاحشة او اكل سحت لا يجوز * وفى اليوم الثانى جاء الطباخ بعضو آخر * فالتقمه وشكر عليه ايضا * فقال الفارياق للطباخ لمَ يشكر الله صاحبنا على اكل الخنزير * قال ولمَ لا وقد اوجب على نفسه ان يشكر له على كل حال وعلى كل شى كما ورد فى بعض كتب الدين * حتى انه كان يقضى هذا الفرض بعد ان يبيت مع زوجته * قال وهل شكر له على موتها * قال نعم فانه يعتقد انها الان فى حضن ابراهيم * قال اما انا فلو كان لى امراة لما اردت ان تكون فى حضن احد *

ثم ان دولة الخنزير اعتزت وعظمت * ومصارين الفارياق ضويت وذوت * ١١،٣،٢
فكان يقضى النهار كله على الخبز والجبن * ثم بلغه ان خبز المدينة يعجَن بالارجل ولكن بارجل الرجال لا النسآ فجعل يقلّل منه ما امكن * حتى اضرّ به الهزال * وصدئت اضراسه من قلة الاستعمال * فوقع منها اثنان من كل جانب واحدٌ * وهذا اول انصاف فعله الجوع على وجه الارض * اذ لو كانا وقعا من جانب واحد لثقل احد الجانبين وخفّ الآخر فلم تحصل الموازنة فى حركات الجسم * اما ١٢،٣،٢
المدينة فان القادم اليها من بلاد الشرق يستحسنها ويستعظمها * والقادم اليها من بلاد الافرنج يحتقرها ويستصغرها * واعظم ما حمل الفارياق فيها على العجب صنفان صنف القسيسين وصنف النسآء * اما القسيسون فلكثرتهم فانك ترى الاسواق والمنازه غاصّة بهم * ولهم على روسهم قبعات مثلثة الزوايا لا تشبه

and the cook brought out some part of that hated animal, he thought that the Bag-man was trying to trick him by producing for him something he was unfamiliar with, and he refused to take a bite, in the hope that he would be given something else. But the Bag-man kept right on going, finished his lunch, and launched immediately into prayer and thanks to the Almighty Creator for what He had provided. To himself, the Fāriyāq said, "I swear our friend is making a mistake. His thanks are misdirected, for to give thanks to the Creator, glory be to Him, for something immoral or for eating something forbidden is not allowed." The following day, the cook brought him another limb, and the man gobbled it up and thanked him once more. The Fāriyāq said to the cook, "Why does our friend thank God for eating pig?" and he replied, "Why not, when he has made it his duty to thank Him 'for every condition and every thing,' as it says in some book of religion? He even used to carry out the same rite each time he spent the night with his wife." "And did he thank Him for her death?" he asked. "Yes," the man replied, "for he believes she's now in the bosom of Ibrāhīm." "For my part," said the Fāriyāq, "if I had a wife, I wouldn't want to see her in any man's bosom."

Thereafter, the reign of the pig grew mightier and yet greater, and the 2.3.11
Fāriyāq's intestines grew lean and shriveled up, and he'd go the whole day on bread and cheese. Then he heard that the city's bread was kneaded by foot, but by the feet of men, not of women, so he took to eating as little of it as he could, until emaciation reduced him to a pitiful *state*, his molars become rusty so little he *ate*, and two of them fell out, one on each side—which was hunger's first act of evenhandedness on the face of this earth, since if both of them had fallen from the same side, one would have become heavier and the other lighter, and the movements of his body would have become unbalanced.

As to the city, one coming to it from the lands of the east will find it 2.3.12
handsome and *mighty* and one coming to it from the lands of the Franks will disdain it and regard it as *paltry*. Two classes of things most moved the Fāriyāq to wonder: the priests and the women. As for the priests, there are so many of them that you find the markets and parks swarming with them. They wear three-cornered hats on their heads that do not look like the hats of the Market-men of the Levant, and they wear drawers that are more like

قبعات السوقيين فى الشام * وسراويلهم اشبه بالتبابين فانها الى ركبهم فقط * وسيقانهم مغطاة بجوارب سود * والظاهر انها عظيمة لان جميع القسيسين فى هذه الجزيرة معلّفون سمان * وقد جرت العادة عندهم ايضا بان القسيسين واهل الفضل والكمال من غيرهم يحلقون شواربهم ولحاهم * وانما يجب على القسيسين خاصة ان يلبسوا سراويلات قصيرة مزنّقة حتى يمكن للناظر ان يتبيّن ما ورآها *

١٣،٣،٢ فاما النسآ فلاختلاف زيّهن عن سائر نسآ البلاد المشرقية والافرنجية * ولان كثيرا منهنّ لهن شوارب ولحًى صغيرة ولا يحلقنها ولا ينتفنها * وقد سمعت ان كثيرا من الافرنج يحبّون النسآ المتذكّرات * فلعل هذا الخبر الغريب بلغ ايضا مسامعهنّ * كيف لا واهوآء الرجال لا تخفى عن النسآ * والحسن فيهن قليل جدا * وانقيادهن الى القسيسين غريب * فان المراة منهن توثر قسيسها على زوجها واولادها واهلها جميعا * ولا يمكن ان تتخذ طعاما فاخرا من دون ان تهديه باكورته حتى اذا اكل منه اكلت هى *

١٤،٣،٢ وقد بلغنى ان امراة سوقية متزوجة اى من حزب شيخ السوق رات رجلا جميلا من الخرجيين فاستخسرته فيهم * وقالت لو دخل هذا الرجل كنائسنا لزادت بهجة ورونقا * فارسلت اليه عجوزا تدعوه اليها فلبّى الفتى دعوتها * لان عداوة السوقيّين والخرجيّين انما هى مقصورة على الضواطرة والنجشيّين والمحترفيّين لا مبلغ لها عند الرجال والنسآ * ففاضت معه فى الحديث الى ان قالت له ان كنت تتبع طريقنا فانى امكنّك من نفسى ولا امنع عنك شيا * فقال لها الشاب اما الذهاب الى الكنيسة فاهون ما يكون علىّ لكونها قريبة من منزلى * واما الاعتقاد فكلينى الى نيّتى * فانى آنف من هذا الاعتراف الذى يكلفكم به القسيسون من اهل كنيستكم * وليس من طبعى الكذب والتدليس حتى اعترف للقسيس بالصغائر واكتم عنه الكبائر * كما يفعله كثير من السوقيين * او اذكر له ما لم افعله واخفى عنه

breeches, for they reach only to the knee, while their shanks are clothed with black hose. It seems that the island is a mighty place, for all the priests on it are well-fed and fat. It is also the custom there for the priests and other great men and good to shave their mustaches and beards. The priests specifically however have to wear short, form-fitting drawers, and the beholder can make out what is beneath them.

As to their women, what surprised the Fāriyāq was the difference of their dress from that of the rest of the women of the Levantine and Frankish lands, 2.3.13
and the fact that many have mustaches and short beards, which they neither shave nor pluck, and I have heard that many Franks are attracted to mannish women, so perhaps this strange fact may have reached their ears too (and how could it not, when men's fancies are no secret to women?). Beauty is extremely rare among them, and their docility toward their priests is strange. A woman will sometimes favor her priest over her husband, her children, and the rest of her family. It is inconceivable for her to partake of some special dish until she has given him the first taste, and she will eat only after he has eaten.

I was told about a married Market-woman, meaning one belonging to the 2.3.14
party of the Market Boss, who saw a handsome Bag-man, and, deciding it was a pity he should be theirs, said, "If that man enters our church, it will grow in sparkle and allure." She therefore sent an old woman to him to invite him to visit her, and the young man obeyed her invitation, for the enmity between the Market-men and the Bag-men is limited to the market traders, the people who connive to drive up prices, and the professionals, and has no impact on ordinary men and women. She talked to him at length and eventually told him, "If you follow our path, I will give you the freedom of my body and forbid you nothing." The young man replied, "As to going to your church, nothing could be easier for me, for it is close to my house, and as to your creed, leave that to my conscience, for I reject that 'confession' that the priests of your church force on you. Lying and cheating are not in my nature that I should confess to the priest my peccadilloes and suppress my major transgressions, as do many Market-men, or tell him what I haven't done and hide from him what I have." At this the woman sighed and bowed her head, pondering and nodding. Then she said, "So be it. It will be enough for us if

ما فعلته * فتاوّهت المراة عند ذلك واطرقت وهى تفكّر وتحرك راسها * ثم قالت
لا باس انّا ليكفينا منك الظاهر كما افادنيه قسيسى * ثم تعانقا وتعاشقا وجعل يتردد
عليها وعلى الكنيسة معا * حتى ان الزوانى فى هذه الجزيرة متهوّسات فى الدين *
فانك تجد فى بيت كل واحدة منهن عدة تماثيل وصور لمن يعبدونه من القديسين
والقديسات * فاذا دخل الى احداهن فاسق ليفجر بها قلبت تلك التماثيل فادارت
وجوهها الى الحائط لكيلا تنظر ما تفعله فتشهد عليها بالفجور فى يوم النشور* قال ١٥،٣،٢
ومن خصائص اهل هذه الجزيرة انهم يبغضون الغريب ويحبون ماله وهوغريب *
فان مال الانسان عبارة عن حياته ودمه وذاته * حتى ان الانكليز اذا سالوا
عن كمية ما يملكه الانسان من المال قالوا كم قيمة هذا الرجل * فيقال قيمته مثلاً
الف ذهب * فكيف يتاتّى لاحد ان يبغض آخر ويحب حياته * وانهم يتجاذبون
كل غريب قدم اليهم * فياخذه واحد منهم بيده اليمنى ليريه النسآ * ويمسكه
الآخر بالاخرى ليريه الكنائس والدولة لمن غلب * ومن خصائصهم ايضا انهم ١٦،٣،٢
يتكلمون بلغة قذرة طفسة منتنة بحيث ان المتكلم يُشَم منه رائحة البخر اول ما يفوه *
والرجال والنسآ فى ذلك سوآ * واذا استنكهت امراة جميلة وهى ساكتة نشيت
منها عرفا ذكيا * فاذا استنطقتها استحالت الى بَخَر * ومنها انه اذا اصيبت احدى
النسآ بدآء فى احد اعضآئها ذهبت الى الصائغ وامرته بان يصوغ لها مثال ذلك
العضو من فضة او ذهب لتهديه للكنيسة * ومن كانت معسرة صاغته من الشمع
ونحوه * ومن ذلك ان حلق اللحى والشوارب مندوب وحلق ما سواهما محرّم * حتى
ان القسيسين يلحّون على النسآ فى السوال كثيرا حين يعترفن لهم عن قضيتى النتف
والحلق ويحرزونهن من ارتكاب ذلك * ومنها ان لاهل الكنائس عادة ان يخرجوا
فى ايام معلومة بما فى كنائسهم من الدُمى والتماثيل على ثقلها وضخمها * يحملونها على

you conform outwardly, or so my priest informs me." Then they embraced and made love, and he started paying visits to her and the church together. Even wantons on this island are obsessed with religion, and you'll see in their houses numerous statues and pictures of the saints, male and female, whom they worship, and when some lecher goes in to see one of them and perform debauchery with her, she turns the faces of the statuettes toward the wall so they can't see what she's doing and testify against her on the Day of Resurrection that she was a debauchee.

It is a curious fact about the people of this island that they hate strangers 2.3.15
but love their money, which is odd, for a person's money is an expression of his life, his blood, and his very self, to the extent that the British, when asking how much money a person possesses, say, "How much is the man worth?" to which the response may be, for example, "He's worth a thousand in gold." How can it occur to anyone to hate another and yet love his life? They contend with one another, too, over every stranger who comes their way. Thus, one will take his right hand to show him the women, another his other hand to show him the churches, and the winner takes all.

Another curious thing about them is that they speak a language so filthy, 2.3.16
dirty, and rotten that the speaker's mouth gives off a bad smell as soon as he opens it. The men and the women are alike in this. If you sniff at a beautiful woman who is silent, you'll find yourself intoxicated by a delicious scent, but if she utters a word, it's transformed into halitosis. Another is that if one of the women is afflicted with a disease in one of her limbs, she will go to a jeweler and tell him to make her a likeness of that limb out of silver or gold and give it to the church; a woman who is not well-off will make it of wax or the like. Another: the shaving of beards and mustaches is deplored and the shaving of everything else is forbidden, to the degree that the priests ask the women insistently during confession about the two issues of hair plucking and shaving and urge them to guard against committing any such acts. Also: the people of the church have a custom of taking, on certain specified days, the figures and statues, heavy and bulky as they are, from the churches and lifting them onto the shoulders of religious zealots who run through the streets with them making a lot of noise. Stranger still, they light candles

اكتاف المتحمّسين فى الدين فيجرون بها فى الشوارع وهم ضاجّون * واغرب من ذلك انهم يوقدون امامها الشموع حين يودّ كل انسان ان ياوى الى كهف فى بطن الارض من شدة توهج الشمس * وغير ذلك كثير مما حمل الفارياق على العجب * لان اهل ١٧،٣،٢
بلاده مع كونهم سوقيين ولهم حرص زائد على عداوة الخرجيين لا يفعلون ذلك * وح ثبت عنده ان الخرجيين هم على الهدى الّا فى اكل الخنزير * وان السوقيين على ضلال ما عدا استحسان نسائهم لغيسانىّ الخرجيّين * الا انه ليس من طريقة فى الدنيا الا وفيها ما يحمد وما يذم * وان الانسان تراه فى بعض الامور عاقلا رشيدا وفى غيرها جاهلا غويّا * فسبحان المتصف وحده بالكمال * وانما ينبغى للناقد المنصف ان ينظر الى الجانب الانفع ويقابله بغيره * فان راى نفعه اكثر من ضرره حكم له بالفضل * لا ان يمنّى نفسه بان يجد شيا من الاشيآء كاملا قال الشاعر

ومن ذا الذى تُرضى سجاياه كلها كفى المرء نُبلاً ان تعد معايبه

هذا وكما ان الجوع اسقط من فم صاحبنا الضَرِس المستجيع ضرسين * كذلك ١٨،٣،٢
اسقطت مشاهدة تلك الامور من راسه اعتبار السوقيين وبنى عمّهم من كلا جانبى الدين والرشاد * فظهر له ان افعالهم احرى ان تكون افعال المجانين * فلهذا ضاق صدره فى بلادهم وعيل صبره * مع احتياجه الى الطعام الطيّب الذى كان الفه فى الشام والى لباس يليق به * فان الخرجىّ افاده ان المفدّين على السلع الخرجية لا ينبغى لهم التحفّل بالملبوس * اذ المقصود من الخرج انما هو حمله فقط * مع ان السوقيين يحسبون ان الخرجيّين يستجلبون اليهم المفدّين بالمال والهدايا *
فلهذا كان الفارياق دائم الحزن والاسف * فلم يمكنه وقتئذ ان يتعلم لسان الخرجيين ١٩،٣،٢
وانما تعلم منهم بعض الفاظ تخصّ ترويج السلعة فقط * هذا وقد كان عند الخرجى المذكور خُرَيجىّ لئيم * شكس الاخلاق اصفر الوجه * ازرق العينين دقيق

before them, at a time when anyone else would want to take refuge in a cave under the ground from the excessive heat of the sun.

There are many other customs, too, that caused the Fāriyāq to wonder, 2.3.17
since the people of his country, even though they are Market-men and excessively hostile to the Bag-men, do not practice them. At this point he became convinced that the Bag-men were on the right path (except in eating pork) and that the Market-men were in error (except for their women's preference for young and good-looking Bag-men). However, there is no path in the world that does not have praiseworthy and blameworthy aspects, and one finds that individuals are rational and discerning at times and ignorant and misguided at others. Glory then to the One who alone may be described as perfect, and let the fair-minded critic look to the more beneficial aspects of each system and compare it with those of others. If he finds its positive qualities outweigh its negative qualities, he may judge it to be meritorious. He should not indulge in dreams of discovering perfection. As the poet says:[69]

And where is the man whose every feature pleases?
Sufficient nobility in a man it is that his vices be few enough to count.

Furthermore, just as hunger had caused two molars to fall from the mouth 2.3.18
of our ravenous and insatiable friend, so his witnessing such matters drove from his mind all respect for both the Market-men and their cousins,[70] where either religion and rationality were concerned, for it seemed to him that their acts were better considered those of madmen. Thus he felt oppressed in their country, and his patience was exhausted, not to mention that he felt in need of the delicious food that he had been accustomed to in the Levant, as well as of clothes that suited him, for the Bag-man had informed him that those who sold the Bag-men's wares should pay no attention to what they wore, the sole point of the bag being to carry it (even though the Market-men believe that Bag-men attract their salesmen by giving them money and gifts).

For these reasons, the Fāriyāq was always mournful and sad, and he 2.3.19
was unable, at that time, to master the language of the Bag-men, learning from them just a few words related to the promotion of the goods. In addition, there was in the house of the aforementioned Bag-man an evil junior Bag-man of spiteful ways with a yellow complexion, blue eyes, a thin tip to

ارنبة الانف كبير الاسنان * راى الفارياق يوما ينظر من طاقة له الى سطوح الجيران فنزغه الشيطان ان يسمّر الطاقة * فلما رآها الفارياق مسمرة تفآل انها خاتمة النحس * وهكذا كان* فانه مرض بعدها بايام قليلة * فاشار الطبيب على الخرجى بان يسفره الى مصر * فسافر من ثم ومعه كتاب توصية الى خرجى آخر*

his nose, and big teeth. One day he noticed the Fāriyāq looking though a window in his room at the neighbors' roof, and the Devil prompted him to nail the window closed. When the Fāriyāq saw that the window had been boarded up, he took it as a good omen that his bad luck could get no worse, and so it was, for within a few days he had fallen ill, the doctor had advised the Bag-man to send him to Egypt, and off he had set, carrying a letter of recommendation to yet another Bag-man.

الفصل الرابع

في منصّة دونها غصّة

ما زال البحر بحرا * ما برحت الريح ريحا * ما انفك طالع الفارياق هابطا * ما ١،٤،٢
فتئ لسانه فارطا * فلما بلغ الى الاسكندرية وجد فى محل الخرجى القديم خرجيا آخر قد دخل فى مضايق ذميمة لم يرض الشيخ خليل بن ايبك الصفدى ان يدخل فيها * فتخلّف عمن تقدمه وخبثت ريحه بين اقرانه * والحامل له على ذلك انه راى هوآ البلاد شديد الحرارة عليه * فارتاى ان يتخذ له هرمين يتسلقهما حين يحترّ * كما ان سلفه اتخذ هرما من الدنان * فافرغ عليهما من اللجين ما يسيل به واد
فشاع اسرافه هناك وملّه اصحابه * ثم سافر الفارياق من الاسكندرية الى مصر ٢،٤،٢
وادّى كتاب التوصية للخرجى * فانزله فى دار رفيق له وكانت محاذية لدار رجل من الشاميّين كان يجتمع عنده كل ليلة جماعة من المغنّين والعازفين بالات الطرب * فكان الفارياق يسمع الغنآ من حجرته * فهاج به الوجد والغرام * وتذكر اوقاته بالشام * وحنّ وصبا الى مجالس الأُنس * وخيّل له انه انتقل من عالم الجن الى عالم الإنس * واسفرت له الدنيا عن لذات مبتكره * وشهوات مدّخره * وافراح
صافيه * وامانى وافيه * فنسى ما كابده فى البحر من الدُوار والفُواق * وفى الجزيرة ٣،٤،٢
من الجوع وتسمير الطاق * وما اصابه من بَحّ التفديد * وترح التقليد * وراى لدولة مصر بهجة ورونقا * وفى عيشها رغدا مغدقا * فكانّ الناس كلهم مُعَرِسون *

Chapter 4

A Throne to Gain Which Man Must Make Moan

As long as sea's *sea* and wind's not ceased to *be*, the Fāriyāq's ascendant star will never cease to *slip*, his tongue to *trip*. When he reached Alexandria, he found a new Bag-man in the place of the old, one who had been through times so rough even Shaykh Khalīl ibn Aybak al-Ṣafadī[71] would have refused to put up with them. As a result, he had failed to advance, and his name was mud among his peers. He had been brought to this pass by his belief that the air in these lands was too warm for him, as a consequence of which he'd decided to make use of a pair of pyramids that he'd scale whenever the weather turned hot, just as his predecessor had made use of a pyramid of wine barrels. After he'd spent enough silver on the pair to fill a valley, the news of his extravagance got out and his friends became upset with him. 2.4.1

The Fāriyāq left Alexandria for Cairo and gave the letter of recommendation to the Bag-man, who put him up in the house of a colleague of his that was next door to the house of a Levantine, at whose home a group of singers and musicians used to gather each night. From his room the Fāriyāq would hear the *singing*, be moved by passion and *longing*, and, recalling his days in the Levant, yearn and ache to be ensconced amongst friends *again*, imagining he'd been transported from the world of jinn to that of *men*, that life had unveiled for him pleasures novel and lusts long in *abeyance*, joys untrammeled and hopes now in *abundance*. 2.4.2

Thus he forgot the miseries of dizziness and the deathly gasps he'd suffered at the *ocean's hand*, the hunger and boarding up of his window he'd suffered on *land*, the sore throat he'd contracted on his salesman's *mission*, the grief induced by blind *tradition*, and found in Egypt, as a state, sparkle and *self-confidence*, and, as a place to live, bounty and *opulence*, for all its 2.4.3

او مفاخرون ومنافسون * ولنسائها كياسة وظرفا وجمالا * ولطفا ولينا ودلالا * وتيها واختيالا * يخطرن فى الطرق بالحبر كالمنشئات * فيجعلن مجموع الهمّ على القلب فى شتات * وما انا باول واصف لهنّ انهن خلّابات للعقول * غلّابات للفحول * فقد وصفهن بذلك كل ناظم وناثر * وذكر مِحالهن كل من حاولهن من الاكابر والاصاغر * وفى المثل السائر * تراب مصر من ذهب * وغيدها نِعَمُ اللُعَب * وانها لمن غلب * واعجب ما يرى من احوالهن * حين يخرجن من مجالهن * ويتفلّتن من عكالهن * ما اذا ركبن الحمير الفارهة العالية * واستوين فوقها على منصّة مضمّخة بالغالية * فترى عَرفهن قد ملأ الخياشيم * وحَوَر اعينهن ٤،٤،٢
يذكّر الناس بحور جنات النعيم * فكل من ينظر حورية منهن يكبّر عند رؤيتها * ويستصغر الدنيا بجمال طلعتها * ومنهم من يهلّل لالتفاتتها * ويسبّح عند حركتها * ومنهم من يتمنى ان يكون ممسكا بركابها * او ماسا لجلبابها * او حاملا لنعالها * او رافعا لاذيالها * او بطانة لحبرتها * او بوابا لحجرتها * او رسولا بينها وبين عاشقها * او تبعا لتبعها ومرافقها * او مشّاطا يسوّى فرقها * او خياطا يرقع خرقها * او صائغا يصوغ لها سوارا * او حدّادا يصنع لها مسمارا * او بلّانيّاً يدلك بدنها * او هناً آخر يدانى هَنَها * وهى من فوق تلك المنصّة تتعزّز وتتمنع * وتشفن وتتطلّع * فترمى هذا بنظرة فتدميه * وذاك بغمزة فتُصبيه وتسبيه * فتعطل على التجار اشغالهم * وتبلبل من ذوى البطالة بالهم * حتى كانّ الحمار من تحتها يعرف قدر مَن حمل * ويدرى ما غرض من كبّر لرويتها وهلّل * فهو لا ينهق ولا يسمع له شخير * ولا يكرف كسائر الحمير * بل يسمُد على الخيل كبرا * ويمشى الخيلآ زهوا وفخرا * اما قائد الحمار فانه يرى ان قائد الجيش دونه فى المنزلة * وان الناس لفى افتقار اليه فهو الذى لا بدّ له من عائد وصلة * كيف لا وهو الموصوف بالسياسة *

people are like members of a never-ending wedding *celebration*, or jousters for ever engaged in competition and self-*acclamation*, while their women display their wit and *sophistication*, beauty, refinement, grace, and *coquetry*, pride and *vanity*, as they move through the streets like galleons in full sail in silk and velvet *wrapper*, causing the cares that cluster about the heart to *scatter*. I am not the first to describe them as seducers of the *mind*, conquerors of every virile male they *find*: thus has described them every master of prose and of the poetic *arts*, and any, old or young, who's sought to deceive them has mentioned their *smarts*. As the proverb that's going around would have it, "Cairo's dust is *gold*, its maidens are the best of playthings, and its spoils go to the *bold*."

The most amazing thing they do on slipping their hobbles and leaving their bridal *recesses* is straightway to mount tall, imposing *asses*, sitting upright atop them on a throne with galia moschata *daubed*, their scent thus being by every nostril *absorbed*, while the blacks of their irises and the whites of their *eyes* make men to think of the maidens of the gardens of *Paradise*. All who behold a houri of this type exclaim, "How great is *God*!" and see the world, beside the beauty of her visage, as but a paltry *sod*. One calls out to catch her *eye* and, having done so, "Praise the Lord!" goes up his *cry*. Another expresses his wish to hold her stirrup or her dress to *touch*, to carry her slippers or her train to *clutch*, to be a lining to her *shawl* or the porter at her *hall*, to be a go-between between her and her *lover* or her companions' follower's *follower*, to be a tire-woman dressing her *hair* or her tailor sewing up a *tear*, to be a jeweler fashioning for her wrist a *band* or a blacksmith forging her a nail by *hand*, to be a bathhouse attendant massaging her to release a *knot* or any other inconsequential thing that might bring him closer to her you-know-*what*, while she, from on top of that throne, *revels* and *repulses*, *glares* and *stares*, casting at this a glance that makes him *bleed*, at that a wink that steals his heart, never to be *freed*, bringing commerce to an *end* and sending the unemployed right round the *bend*. Even the jackass beneath her seems to know the worth of what he *bears* and understand what drives her halleluiah-shouting fans as they let fly their *cheers*, for he doesn't bray, is never heard to snort, and never sniffs (unlike the others) she-donkeys' *rears*. On the contrary, he lords it over every *horse* and struts in pride and glory as he pursues his *course*. As for the the donkey's driver, he thinks he's in a *class* outranking the army's topmost *brass*, and that the people are in need of his *ministrations*, 2.4.4

والقيادة والفراسة * وهنا قضية نسيت ان اذكرها * فلا بد من ان اقيدها فى هذا ٥,٤,٢
الموضع واحررها * وهى ان القلوب بروية المتبرقعات * اولع منها بروية المسفرات *
وذلك ان العين اذا رات وجها جميلا وان يكن رائعا شائقا غاية ما يمكن * فان
المخيّلة تستقر عليه وتسكن * فاما عند تبصّر الوجه المحجوب * مع اعتقاد القلب
بان صاحبه من الجنس المحبوب * ولا سيما اذا قام الدليل عليه بحلاوة العينين *
وبالهدَب وبزجِ الحاجبين * فان المخيّلة تطير بالافكار عليه * ولا تجد لها من
اَمَد تنتهى اليه * فيقول الخاطر (انتهى السجع لانه ملأ الصفحة) لعل هذا الوجه ٦,٤,٢

أُثْعُبانىّ	الاثعبان والاثعبانى الوجه الفَخْم فى حسن وبياض *
او ذو انسبات	يقال فى وجهه انسبات أى طول وامتداد *
او هو مُصفَّح	المصفح من الوجوه السهل الحسن *
او مُتْمعِدّ	المتمعد من الوجوه الظاهر البَشَرة الحسن السَحْنة *
او مدنَّر	يقال دنَّر وجهه تدنيرا تلالا *
او ملوَّز	الملوَّز من الوجوه الحسن المليح *
او مَخروط	المخروط من الوجوه ما فيه طول *
او ساجِع	الساجع الوجه المعتدل الحسن الخلقة *
او عَنْمىّ	الوجه الحسن الاحمر *
او فَدْغم	الفدغم الوجه الممتلى الحسن *
او ذو كلثمة	الكلثمة اجتماع لحم الوجه بلا جهومة *
او مَسْنون	يقال رجل مسنون الوجه مملّسه حسنه سهله *

ولعله جامع لجميع سمات الوسامة فاشتمل على خدين اسيلين * اسجحين او مكثّلين * ٧,٤,٢
وفى كل خدّ اذا ضحكت عمزة او هَزْمة او شَجْرة او عُكْوة او غُرْمة او فَحْصة او فيهما *

for which he requires presents and *oblations* (and how could it not be so, when he derives his very name from his "stable management (of affairs)," his "leadership qualities," and his "horse sense"?)[72]

And here's a matter to which I forgot to draw *attention* and so must enter here and *mention*: hearts are more easily set *alight* by women whose faces are fully veiled than those whose faces are in plain *sight*. This is because, if the eye beholds a beautiful *face* (even the most charming and intriguing that could be), the imagination rests and ceases to *race*. If, however, one gazes upon one that's got a veil on *top* (assuming that the heart believes its owner to belong to the beloved sex and especially if evidence of this is provided by the prettiness of eye, length of lash, and penciling of eyebrow), the imagination comes flying, freighted with thoughts, and finds no barrier at which to *stop*. 2.4.5

Then (and here the rhymed prose can end, because it's filled a page) the mind declares, "This face could be 2.4.6

uthʿubānī,	*uthʿubān* or *uthʿubānī* refers to "a face that is magnificent in its comeliness and whiteness"
or 'possessed of *insibāt*,'	"one says, 'There is in his face *insibāt*,' i.e., 'length and extension'"
or is *muṣfaḥ*,	"a *muṣfaḥ* face is smooth and handsome"
or *muthamʿidd*,	"a *muthamʿidd* face is full and comely"
or *mudannar*,	"one says, 'his face shone like a dinar' meaning 'it gleamed'"
or *mulawwaz*,	"a *mulawwaz* face is handsome and comely"
or *makhrūṭ*,	"a *makhrūṭ* face is one that has length"
or *sājiʿ*,	"a *sājiʿ* face is regular and comely of appearance"
or *ʿanmī*,[73]	"a handsome ruddy face"
or *fadgham*,	"a full handsome face"
or possessed of *kalthamah*,	"*kalthamah* is seamlessness of the flesh of the face without bloatedness"
or *masnūn*;	"one says, 'A man whose face is *masnūn*,' [meaning] his face is smooth, handsome, even"

or could bring together all the components of good looks to embrace smooth, lean, and wide, or compact and rounded, cheeks, with, in each cheek, when she laughs, a crinkle or a *dimple*, or a speckle or a *pimple*, a [?][74] or chin cleft, 2.4.7

or those cheeks might have on them

عُلْطة العلطة واللعطة سواد تخطه المراة فى وجهها زينة *
او في كل منهما خال عمّ حسنه * وعزّ فتنه *
او فيهما او فى احدهما خِداد (ميسم فى الخدّ) او تَرَخ (الشرط اللين) *
او وَحْص او عُد او ظَبْظاب * الوحص بثرة تخرج فى وجه الجارية المليحة
والظبظاب بثر فى وجوه الملاح ومثله العُدّ *
واشتمل ايضا على ثغرمنصّب * ذى شَنَب ورَتَل وحَبَب * ثغرمنصب مستوى
النِبتة والشنب مآ ورقّة وبرد وعذوبة فى الاسنان او نقط بياض فيها
او حدّة الانياب كالغَرْب تراها كالمنشار والرَتَل بياض الاسنان وكثرة
مائها والحَبَب تنضد الاسنان وما جرى عليها من المآء كقطع القوارير *
او على تفليج فى ثنايا من الدرّ * ذات أُشُر ووَشْر * أُشُر الاسنان وأُشَرها التحزيز
الذى يكون فيها خلقة او مستعملا يقال اشرت المراة اسنانها واشّرتها
والوشر تحديد المراة اسنانها وترقيقها *
او ان لها عِتّرة * تتهالك فى حبّها عِتّرة * العِترة أُشَر الاسنان ودقة فى غروبه
ونقآ ومآ يجرى عليه — والريقة العذبة وهى ايضا نسل الرجل ورهطه
وعشيرته الادنون ممن مضى وغبر *
او ان بذقنها نونة تعوذ بسورة ن * او ان شفتها ريًا او حوّآ او نَكِعة *
او ان فيها لَعَسا او ذبَا * او يتصبّب منها العسل تصبّبا *
او ان فيها تُرمله * تشفى من الوله * الترملة النقرة فى ظاهر الشفة العليا والنكعة
من الشفاه الشديدة الحمرة *
او ان فى طُرمتها طِرما * الطُرمة النبرة وسط الشفة العليا والطرم الشهد والزبد
والعسل *

a *ʿulṭah,* the *ʿulṭah,* or *luʿṭah,* is 'a black mark that a woman draws on her face for adornment'

or each might have a *mole* that adds beauty to the *whole,* and reinforces the charm of it *overall*;

or both, or one, might have a *khidād* (a brand upon the cheek) or a *tarkh* (a light incision);

or a *waḥṣ* or a *ʿudd* or a *ẓibẓāb* (the *waḥṣ* is 'the eruption that comes out on a pretty girl's face' and *ẓibẓāb* are 'eruptions on the faces of pretty girls; synonym *ʿudd*');

and this face might include also front teeth that are *munaṣṣab,* with *shanab, ratal,* and *ḥabab* (front teeth that are *munaṣṣab* are those that 'grow straight'; *shanab* is 'a fluid, or a softness, or a coolness, or a sweetness, on the teeth,' or 'spots of whiteness thereon,' or 'the canines being so sharp that they look like a saw' (synonym *gharb*); *ratal* is 'whiteness of the teeth and their extreme moistness' and *ḥabab* is 'even spacing of the teeth, and the fluid that passes over them making them look like pieces of glass),'

or a gap between the incisors caused by the milk, with *ushur* and *washr* (the *ushur* of teeth, or of a woman, are 'the file-marks on them that are either caused by nature or deliberately—one says, "the woman filed (*asharat* or *ashsharat*) her teeth"'; *washr* is 'a woman's sharpening and pointing her teeth'),

or the owner of this face might have a *ʿitrah* in love with which has fallen a *ʿitrah* (the first *ʿitrah* is 'the file-marks on the teeth and the precision with which they are sharpened,' and 'purity,' and 'a fluid that runs over [the teeth],' and 'sweet saliva'; the second is 'a man's offspring and his people and clan, consisting of his closer relations, both the living and the dead,'

or on her chin there might be a cleft that seeks protection in Sūrat Nūn,[75]

or her lip might be 'moist,' or 'red shading into black,' or *nakiʿah,* or have 'a blackness of gum and lip' or a 'dryness' or honey might ooze from it copiously, or she might have a *thurmulah* that heals love-sickness (a *thurmulah* is 'the depression that is on the outer part of the upper lip'; lips that are *nakiʿah* are 'bright red'),

or her *ṭurmah* might contain *ṭirm* (a *ṭurmah* is 'a swelling in the middle of the upper lip' and *ṭirm* is 'honeycomb, butter, or honey'),

او انّ لها تُرَفة * اشهى واعزّ من الترفة * الترفة هنة ناتئة وسط الشفة العليا ٨،٤،٢
خلقة وهى ايضا النعمة والطعام الطيب والشى الظريف[١] تخص به صاحبك *

او ان لها عُرَعُرة * على مثلها تهون الغرغرة * العرعرة بين المنخرين *

اوخَوْرَمة * تطيببها النفس عن الخُزَمة * الخورمة مقدم الانف او ما بين المنخرين
والخزّمة واحدة الخزّم وهو نبت كاللوبيا بنفسجي اللون شمه والنظر اليه مفرح جدا ومن امسكه معه احبّه كل ناظر اليه ويتخذ من زهره دهن ينفع لما ذكر *

او نَثْرة * عليها تنثر البدرة * النثرة الخيشوم وما والاه او الفرجة بين الشاربين حِيال وَتَرة الانف *

او ان لمراعفها غَفْرا * يكسر شوكة الاجرا * المراعف الانف وحواليه والغفر زئبر الثوب *

او ان لها خُنْعُبة * تشدّ العظام الوَرِبة * الخنعبة النونة او الهنة المتدلية وسط الشفة العليا او الشق ما بين الشاربين حيال الوترة ويقال فيه ايضا الخُنْبعة *

او عَرْتَبة * تصح بها القلوب الوصبة * العرتبة الانف او ما لان منه او الدائرة تحته وسط الشفة اوطرف وترة الانف *

اوعَرْتَمة * هى للحسن سمة * العرتمة مقدم الانف او ما بين وترته والشفة او الدائرة عند الانف وسط الشفة العليا ومثلها الهرثمة *

او ان على ملامظها وملاغمها لَغَما * ينفى سدما * ويشفى سقما * الملامظ ما حول الشفة والملاغم ما حول الفم كالملامج واللغم الطيب القليل *

---

١ كذا في القاموس وفي ١٨٥٥: الطريف.

or she might have a *turfah* more appetizing than any *turfah* (a *turfah* is 'a raised thing in the middle part of the upper lip (a congenital feature),' and it also means 'tasty food' and 'something nice that you give only to your friend'), 2.4.8

or she might have a *ʿurʿurah* besides which would pale the blaze on a horse's face (the *ʿurʿurah* is what is between the nostrils),

or a *khawramah* that would make the scent of the *khurramah* yet sweeter (the *khawramah* is 'the most forward part of the nose, or what is between the nostrils,' and *khurramah* is the unit noun from *khurram*, which is 'a plant like the black-eyed pea, violet in color, to smell and behold which brings such great joy that any who sees a person holding it falls in love with him; an ointment is made from its flowers that is good for the ailments mentioned'),

or a *nathrah* before which vast sums might be scattered (*tunthar*) (the *nathrah* is 'the nostril and the parts close to it, or the parting between the two wings of the mustache, in front of the septum'),

or her *marāʿif* have a *ghafr* that would repulse the most courageous (the *marāʿif* are 'the nose and its surroundings' and the *ghafr* is 'the nap on a garment'),

or she might have a *khunʿubah* that would stiffen rotten bones (the *khunʿubah* is the 'philtrum, or thing that is suspended in the middle of the upper lip, or the interstice between the two wings of the mustache, in front of the septum; also occurs as *khubnuʿah*'),

or a *ʿartabah* fit to cure the stricken heart (the *ʿartabah* is 'the nose, or the soft parts thereof, or the circle in the middle of the lip, or the end of the septum'),

or a *ʿartamah* that is an expression of beauty (the *ʿartamah* is 'the foremost part of the nose, or what is between the latter and the septum, or the circle in the middle of the upper lip' (synonym *harthamah*),

or she might have on her *malāmiẓ* and her *malāghim* a *lagham* fit to expel *grief* and bring to sorrow *relief* (the *malāmiẓ* are 'the parts around the two lips' and the *malāghim* are 'the parts around the mouth' (synonym *malāmij*) and *lagham* is 'a little perfume'),

او لعل لها نَبْرة * هى تمام النضرة * النبرة وسط النقرة فى ظاهر الشفة والنضرة الحسن *

او تُفْرة * يطيل الصب عليها زفرة * التفرة مثلثة الاول النقرة فى وسط الشفة العليا *

او حِثْرمة * تذر القلوب بها مغرمة * الحثرمة الدائرة تحت الانف وسط الشفة العليا او الارنبة او طرفها * ٩،٤،٢

او وَتِيرة * تفدى بالف وثيرة * الوتيرة حجاب ما بين المنخرين *

او ان لها خيشوما يبرئ كمها * ويطرى وَمَها * الخيشوم من الانف ما فوق نخرته من القصبة وما تحتها من خشارم الراس والومه شدة الحرّ*

او قَسامه * يمضى بها العاشق اقسامه * القسامة الحسن والوجه — او الانف وناحيتاه او وسط الانف الخ *

او ان لها ذَلَفا * يصحّ دنفا * الذلف صغر الانف واستوآ الارنبة او صغره فى دقة او غلظ واستوآ فى طرفه ليس بحدّ غليظ *

او خَنَسا تغيب له الخُنَّس * الخنس تاخر الانف عن الوجه مع ارتفاع قليل فى الارنبة وهى خنسآ والخُنَّس الكواكب كلها او السيّارة *

او كان انفها مُصفَحًا * المصفح من الانوف المعتدل القصبة *

او اشمّ * الشمم ارتفاع قصبة الانف وحسنها واستوآ اعلاها وانتصاب الارنبة *

او ان به قَنًى * قنى الانف ارتفاع اعلاه واحديداب وسطه وسبوغ طرفه او نتو وسط القصبة وضيق المنخرين هو اقنى وهى قنيآ *

او ان به غُرَضَين * يلهيان عن التغريض واللُجين * غرضا الانف ما انحدر من القصبة من جانبيه جميعا * والتغريض اكل اللحم الغريض والتفكه *

or it might be that she has a *nabrah* that is the acme of *naḍrah* (the *nabrah* is 'the central part of the depression in the visible part of the lip' and *naḍrah* is 'beauty'),

or a *tufrah* to bend his head over which is to prolong his moans (the *tufrah*, or *tafrah*, or *tifrah*, is 'the depression in the middle of the upper lip'),

or a *ḥithrimah* that leaves hearts infatuated (the *ḥithrimah* is 'the circle that is beneath the nose in the center of the upper lip' or 'the tip of the nose or its end'), 2.4.9

or a *watīrah* worthy to be ransomed for a thousand buxom and willing lasses (the *watīrah* is 'the partition between the two nostrils'),

or a *khayshūm* that would cure blindness or cool *wamah* (the *khayshūm* is 'the part of the nose above its front end starting from the bony part and the nasal gristle that lies beneath it' and *wamah* means 'extreme heat'),

or a *qasāmah* on which the lover swears his oaths (*qasāmah* is 'beauty, and the face . . . or the nose and its two sides, or the middle of the nose' etc.),

or a *dhalaf* that would cure illness (*dhalaf* is 'smallness of the nose and straightness of the tip of the nose, or its being small and fine, or a thickness of the nose and a straightness at its end without a thick edge'),

or a *khanas* before which the *khunnas* set (*khanas* is 'having a *retroussé* nose with a slight upward tilt to its tip, a woman with such a nose being called *khansā'*,' and the *khunnas* are 'all stars, or the planets'),

or her nose might be *muṣfaḥ* (a *muṣfaḥ* nose is one that has a straight bridge);

or *ashamm* (being *ashamm* means 'having the bridge of the nose elevated and handsome with a straight upper part and erectness of the tip'),

or it might be possessed of *qanā* (*qanā* of the nose is 'elevation of its upper part, crookedness of its middle, and length and fullness of its end, or prominence of the middle of the bridge and narrowness of the nostrils; a male with these characteristics is said to be *aqnā*, a female *qanyā*"),

or it might have two *ghurḍ*s fit to distract one from *taghrīḍ* and silver (the *ghurḍ* of the nose is the part that slopes down from the bridge on either side,' and *taghrīḍ* is 'eating fresh (*gharīḍ*) meat, and making merry');

او ان لها ناظرين * نفديهما بالناظرين الناظران عرقان * على حرفى الانف * ١٠،٤،٢

او ناحرتين * نذيل لهما النحور والمقلتين * الناحرتان عرقان فى اللَّحى وضلعان من اضلاع الصدر او هما الواهنتان والترقوتان *

او حافزا * يشرح قلبا حالزا * ويتلحّز له الشاعر تلحّزا * الحافز حيث يثنى من الشدق وقلب حالز ضيّق والتلحّز تحلّب فيك من اكل رمانة حامضة ونحوها شهوة لذلك كالتلزّج *

او ان خنّابتيها * تحوم القلوب عليها * الخناتبان طرفا الانف *

او ان لها صامغين * هما قرة العين * ورىّ الغين * الصامغان والصماغان والصمغان جانبا الفم وهما ملتقى الشفتين مما يلى الشدقين وهما ايضا السامغان لغة فى الصاد والغين العطش * ويا ليت شعرى هل يتكوّن فيهما صمغ شهد حتى سميا بهذا وهل هما منطبقان او منفتحان وهل يتلحّز لهما الشاعر المسكين كما تلحّز من الحافزين الله اعلم *

ثم يقول او ان لها حُترة * يديم الصبّ اليها[١] حَتْره * الحترة مجتمع الشدقين والحتر تحديد النظر * فهل من تلزّج معه * ١١،٤،٢

او ان لها ماضغين * يعوّذان من العين * الماضغان اصول اللحيين عند منبت الاضراس *

او غُنّبة * تهنّد الخلىّ سَنْبه * الغنبة على ما فى القاموس واحدة الغُنَب وهى دارات اوساط اشداق الغلمان الملاح * لكنّى رايت ربّة البرقع اولى بها فلا عِكاس ولا مِكاس * على هذا الاختلاس * والتنهيد التصبى والتشويق والسنبة الدهر *

ولعل عارضها * يتم معارضها * العارض صفحة الخد وجانب الوجه *

---

١ ١٨٥٥: اليهما.

or this girl might have *nāẓir*s for which we would give our eyes in ransom (the *nāẓir*s are 'two veins on either side of the nose'), 2.4.10

or *nāḥirah*s for which we would trample upon our upper chests and eyes (the *nāḥirah*s are 'two veins in the jawbone and two of the ribs of the chest, or they are the two short ribs, or the collar bones'),

or a *ḥāfizah* fit to relieve a heart that's oppressed and over which the poet's mouth would *yatalaḥḥaz* (the *ḥāfizah* is 'the fold in the corner of the mouth' and *yatalaḥḥaz* means 'to drool (of the mouth) from eating a sour pomegranate or the like because you find it so delicious (synonym *yatalazzaḥ*))';

or it might be that hearts would hover over her *khinnābah*s (the *khinnābah*s are 'the sides of the nose');

or that this girl would have *ṣāmigh*s to delight the heart and quench the *ghayn* (the *ṣāmigh*s, or *ṣamāgh*s, or *ṣamgh*s, are 'the sides of the mouth, meaning the place where the lips meet next to the corner of the mouth' (variant: the *sāmigh*s)); *ghayn* means 'thirst.'" (I would love to know whether they are so called because honeycomb forms at them, and whether they are pressed close together or parted, and whether the poor poet drools over the thought of them as he drooled over the *ḥāfizah*s, but God alone knows.)

Then the mind continues, saying, 2.4.11

"Or she might have a *ḥutrah* his love for which is prolonged by his *ḥatr* (the *ḥutrah* is 'the place where the corners of the mouth meet' and *ḥatr* is 'fixing of the gaze'" (and wouldn't he just be drooling?!),

or *māḍigh*s with which one might take refuge against 'the eye' (the *māḍigh*s are 'the points at which the jawbones start, at the place where the molars sprout'),

or a *ghunbah* that would *tuhannid* the fancy-free for a *sanbah* (*ghunbah*, according to the *Qāmūs*, is the singular of *ghunab*, which are 'circles in the center of the corners of the mouths of pretty boys,' though I have decided that our veiled lady has the better claim to them, so let there be no *protestation* or *negotiation* over this *appropriation*; *tuhannid* means 'entice' or 'cause to yearn' and a *sanbah* is 'an age');

and perhaps her *'āriḍ* will send her lover insane with desire (the *'āriḍ* is 'the flat of the cheek' or 'the side of the face'),

او ان لها عِلاطا * يشغف من ناظره نِياطا * العلاط صفحة العنق والنياط الفواد *

او بُلدة * تفتن اهل البلدة * البلدة نقاوة ما بين الحاجبين وثغرة النحر وما حولها او وسطها *

او ان لها مَحاجر* تباع لها المحاجر* المَجِر من العين ما دار بها والمحاجر الثانية ما حول القرية *

او اسارير* يعنو لها من جلس على السرير * الاسارير محاسن الوجه والخدّان والوجنتان *

او ان طُلَيْتها تبرى الطَليَآ * الطلية العنق او اصلها والطليآ قرحة كالقُوَبآ *

ولَدِيْدَيْها اللَدُود * اللديدان صفحتا العنق دون الاذنين واللدود وجع ياخذ فى الفم والحلق *

ولزيزيها اللَزّ* اللزيز مجتمع اللحم فوق الزور واللز الطعن * ١٢،٤،٢

ومفاهرها اعزالى ذى مسبغة من الفهيرة * المفاهر لحم الصدر والفهيرة محض يلقى فيه الرضف فاذا غلا ذرّ عليه الدقيق وسِيط *

وان سالفتيها تغنيان عن السلاف * السالفة ناحية مقدم العنق من لدن معلق القرط الى قَلْت الترقوة *

ونحرها عن نحر النهار* نحر النهار والشهر اوله *

وترائبها عن الأتراب * الترائب عظام الصدر او ما ولى الترقوتين منه والاتراب واحدها تِرب وهو اللِدَة * ويصح ان تكون ايضا بكسر الهمزة مصدر اترب الرجل اى كثر ماله فليسال القائل عن ايهما اراد *

or it may be that she has a *ʿilāṭ* to bewitch the *niyāṭ* of any who see her (the *ʿilāṭ* is 'the flat of the neck' and the *niyāṭ* is 'the heart'),
or a *buldah* that would enchant the people of a *baldah* (a *buldah* is a 'freedom from hair of the space between the eyebrows' or 'the pit between the two collar-bones, with the part around it, or the middle thereof' [and a *baldah* is 'a town']),
or *maḥājir* for which *maḥājir* might be sold (the *miḥjar* of the eye is 'that part of the face, below the eye, that may be seen through the type of veil called the *niqāb*' and the other *maḥājir* are 'the tracts surrounding a town or village'),
or *asārīr* to which one seated upon the bed (*sarīr*) is subservient (the *asārīr* are 'the beautiful features of the face' or 'the cheeks');
or it may be that her *ṭulyah* would cure a *ṭalyā'* (the *ṭulyah* is 'the neck, or the place from which it arises' and the *ṭalyā'* is 'an ulceration like a bubo'),
her *ladīd*s a *ladūd* (the *ladīd*s are 'the sides of the neck below the ears,' and the *ladūd* is 'a pain that affects the mouth and throat'),
and her *lazīz*s a *lazz* (the *lazīz* is 'the point where the flesh comes together above the throat' and *lazz* is 'a piercing'); 2.4.12
or that her *mafāhir* are dearer to the mail-clad knight than *fahīrah* (the *mafāhir* are 'the flesh of the breast' and *fahīrah* is 'pure milk into which heated stones are put; when it boils, flour is sprinkled over it and it is mixed' [and eaten]),
her *sālifah*s remove the need for even the best of *sulāf* (the *sālifah* is 'the side of the forepart of the neck, from the place of the suspension of the earring to the hollow of the collarbone' [and *sulāf* means 'wine']),
her *naḥr* ('throat') puts that of the day to shame (the *naḥr* of the day, or the month, is its beginning);
and her *tarā'ib*s are more to be valued than one's *atrāb* (the *tarā'ib* are 'the bones of the chest' or 'the part immediately following the two collarbones' and the *atrāb* (singular *tirb*) are one's 'coetaneans'; or the latter might also correctly be read as *itrāb*, a verbal noun, in the sense 'the man experienced *itrāb*,' meaning 'his wealth increased,' in which case the speaker would have to be asked which meaning he intended),"

الى غير ذلك من الاحتمالات التى لا بدّ منها لحصيف العقل المستحكم الراى * وانما اطلت الكلام هنا لكونى ناقلا له عمن تبصّر الوجه المحجوب * ودهش عن الاصابة فسال فمه سعابيب *

١٣،٤،٢ وغاية ما اقوله انا ان من شاعر امراة ليلا ولم يرها كما جرى لسيدنا يعقوب عَمّ وقع له ما وقع لصاحبنا هذا المكثر من اللعلّات والإنّات والآوّات * ولقائل ان يقول ان هذه القضية معكوسة فى شان المراة اللابسة * فان النظر اذا وقع عليها وهى متسترة وقفت معه المخيلة عند حدّ ما * بخلاف العريانة فان المخيلة والقلب عند النظر اليها يطيران عليها ولا يقفان على حدّ فالمخيلة تتصور اشياآ والقلب يشتهى اشياآ اخرى * وللمجيب ان يقول ان ذلك انما نشا عن الفرق الحاصل بين الوجه والجسم * فان الجسم من حيث كونه اكبر من الوجه اقضى طيران المخيّلة اليه * وحومان القلب عليه *

١٤،٤،٢ وردّ هذا القول جماعة منهم الصباباتى والمباعلىّ والالغزىّ وابو ارّ * بان كبر الجسم هنا ليس سببا للطيران والحومان * اذ لو لم يبدُ منه الا موضع واحد لكفى * فبقى الاشكال غير مدفوع * واجيب بان العلة فى ذلك انما هى لكون الجسم جسما والوجه وجها * وسُفّه هذا القول فانه تحصيل للحاصل * وقيل انما هو لكون الوجه محلاّ لاكثر الحواس * ففيه مخزن الشم والذوق والبصر وقريب منه مخزن السمع * وارتضاه جماعة منهم العَزهى والتيتآى والدَوذخى * وردّ بان هذه الحواس لا مدخل لها هنا * فان المراد من كونيّة المراة لا يتوقف عليها اصالة فهى مستغنًى عنها *

١٥،٤،٢ وقيل انما هو لكون الجسم يحوى اشكالا كثيرة * ففيه الشكل القمقمى والرمّانى والقرموطى والاطارى والخاتمى والقبّى والعمودى والهَدَفى والصادى والميمى والمدرّج والمخروط والهلالىّ ومنفرج الزاوية *

and so on, to include other possibilities that the man of insight and sound judgment will agree are necessary; I have prolonged my words here simply because I am copying them from one who looked deep into every veiled face(t)[76] and found himself, to his surprise, so stricken, that his mouth flowed with ropy saliva.

In the end, the point I'm trying to make is that a man who has slept with a woman wrapped up with her in a single undergarment but hasn't seen her as did Our Master Yaʿqūb,[77] peace be upon him, has suffered the same fate as our friend with all his maybes and ifs and buts.

Someone ought now to say, "The matter is the opposite of what's been *proposed* when we speak of a woman fully *clothed*, for if a man's glance falls upon her when she's decently covered, his imagination will take him no further than a certain point. It's different, however, if she is naked. Then the imagination and the heart, on beholding her, will fly toward her, stopping at nothing, for the imagination will picture certain things, while the heart will desire yet others." Then the defender of the original proposition should respond by saying, "This is simply a result of the face-body *differential*, for the body, being larger, brings the imagination flying to it and holds the heart hovering over it by a process *consequential*." 2.4.13

One party, among them Professors Amorato, Gropius, Randinski, and Copulatius,[78] have asserted that it is not the body's size per se that is responsible in such cases for any flying or hovering, for even if only one part of it were visible it would be enough and the issue therefore remains unresolved. To this the response should be that their argument consists simply of stating that a body is a body and a face a face, which shows that the assertion is ridiculous because it is a tautology. Others have claimed that the reason that the face is more arousing than the body is that the face is a locus for most of the senses, for it contains the repositories of smell, taste, and sight, with that of hearing close by. A second party, among them Professors Killjoy, Ejaculatio-Prematore, and Impotenza, has accepted this, but rejoinder has been made that these senses have no bearing here, for what is meant by "essence of woman" doesn't depend upon them anyway, so she is in no need of them. 2.4.14

It has also been claimed that the body is *more* arousing than the face because the body contains many different shapes. Thus, there is what is pear-shaped-with-a-long-neck, what is pomegranate-shaped, what is euphorbia-fruit-shaped, what is hoop-shaped, what is ring-shaped, what 2.4.15

وردّ بانه كقول من قال انه اكبر من الوجه وجوابه كجوابه * وقيل انما هو لكون العادة الاغلبية هى ان يكون الوجه حاسرا والجسم مستورا * فاذا راى الانسان ما خالف العادة هاجت خواطره وطارت افكاره * وقيل غير ذلك والله اعلم * ويحتمل ان هذه القاعدة التى استدركت ذكرها غير صحيحة فياليتنى نسيتها فان ذكرها اوجب المناقشة بين العلمآ * والحاصل ان الغرام البرقعى لما باض وفرخ ١٦،٤،٢
فى راس الفارياق غرّدت اطياره عليه لان يتخذ له آلة لَهْو * فما عتّم ان تابّط له طنبورا صغيرا من السوق * وجعل يعزف به فى شباك له مطلّ على دار رجل من القبط * وكان عند الخرجى خادم مسلم قد عشق ابنة القبطى فغار عليها من الطنبور * فسعى بالفارياق الى سيده قائلا اذا سمع المارّون فى الطريق صوت الطنبور من دارك ظنوا انها دسكرة او حانة او ثُكْنة (مركز الاجناد ومجتمعهم على لوآ صاحبهم الخ) لا دار للخرجيّين * لان هذه الآلة لا يستعملها غير الترك * فشكره الخرجى على ذلك واستصوب ما قاله واوعز الى الفارياق بالغآء الآلة * فالغاها وجعل يفكّر فى التملّص من ايدى هذه الزمرة التى لم يبرح اذاها واصلا اليه من كل شبّاك سوآ فى الجزيرة والارض * ثم بعد ايام قليلة هرب الخادم بالبنت وتزوّج بها بعد ان اسلمت والحمد الله رب العالمين *

is dome-shaped, what is pillar-shaped, what is in the shape of a prominent rock, what in is the shape of the letter *ṣād* and what is in the shape of the letter *mīm*,[79] what is in the shape of a set of steps, what is in the shape of a cone, what is in the shape of a crescent, and what is obtusely angled. To this, rejoinder has been made that it is the same argument as that made by those who claim that the body is more attractive because it is larger and may be refuted on the same grounds. It has also been claimed that the body is more exciting precisely because the face, under normal conditions, is revealed, while the body is concealed, and, should a person see anything that violates this norm, his thoughts will be plunged into commotion and his ideas fly in all directions. Other arguments have been made too and God alone knows the truth. It is also quite possible that this rule that I have advanced and retracted so often is incorrect, in which case, I wish I'd ignored it, for by mentioning it I have obliged us to engage in an academic discussion.

In sum, when this veil-passion was laid and hatched in the Fāriyāq's head, **2.4.16** the little birdies therein twittered to him that he should get himself a musical instrument, and, in no time at all, he had returned from the market with, under his arm, a small tambour, which he began playing at a window of his room that overlooked the house of a Copt. Now, the Bag-man had a Muslim servant, who had fallen in love with the Copt's daughter, and the tambour made him jealous, so he denounced the Fāriyāq to his master and said, "If the passers by in the street hear the sound of the tambour coming from your house, they will think it's a tavern or an inn or a *thuknah* ('headquarters and gathering place of soldiers under the banner of their commander,' etc.), not a Bag-men's abode, because this instrument is used only by the Turks." The Bag-man thanked him for this, accepted that what he said was true, and instructed the Fāriyāq to get rid of the instrument, which he did, while at the same time starting to think of how he could escape the hands of this band whose bane never ceased to get at him through every window, on island and on mainland. A few days later the servant fled with the girl and he married her, after she had converted to Islam, praise be to God, Lord of the Worlds.

الفصل الخامس

في وصف مصر

قد وصف مصر كثير من المورخين المتقدمين * ومدحها جمّ غفير من الشعرآ الغابرين * وها انا اليوم واصفها ومادحها بما لم يسبقنى اليه احد من العالمين * فاقول انها مصر من الامصار * او مدينة من المدن * او مَدَرة من المَدَر * او كورة من الكُوَر * او قصبة من القَصَب * او بَحْرَة من البُحَر * او ماهة من الماهات * او قرية من القرى * او قارية من القوارى * او عاصمة من العواصم * او صقع من الاصقاع * او دار من الديار * او بلدة من البلاد * او بلد من الابلاد * او قطر من الاقطار * او شى من الاشيآ * غير ان اهلها يقولون انها مصر الامصار * ومدينة المدن * وعاصمة العواصم * وشى الاشيآء الى آخره * وما ادرى فرق ذلك * وكيف كان فانها مدينة غاصة باللذات السائغة * متدفقة بالشهوات السابغة * توافق المحرورين من الرجال خلافا لما قاله عبد اللطيف البغدادى * يجد بها الغريب ملهى وسكنا * وينسى عندها اهلا ووطنا * ١،٥،٢

٢،٥،٢ ومن خواصها ان ما يذهب من اجسام رجالها يدخل فى اجسام نسائها * فترى فيها النسا سمانا كالاقط بالسمن على الجوع * والرجال كالحشف بالشيرج على الشبع * ومنها ان اسواقها لا تشبه رجالها البتة * فان لاهلها لطافة وظرافة وادبا وكياسة وشمائل مرضية واخلاقا زكية * واسواقها عارية عن ذلك راسا *

Chapter 5

A Description of Cairo[80]

Many an ancient historian toward Cairo has bent his *gaze* and on it hosts of poets past have lavished *praise*, and here now stand I, to describe it and to praise it as did no scholar in former *days*. Thus I declare: Cairo is one metropolis among metropoli, one city among cities, one settlement among settlements, one borough among boroughs, one seat among seats, one town among towns, one citadel among citadels, one village among villages, one urban center among urban centers, one capital among capitals, one locality among localities, one territory among territories, one land among lands, one township among townships, one region among regions, one thing among many things. Its people, though, would say, "It is *the* metropolis among metropoli, *the* city among cities, *the* capital among capitals, *the* thing among all other things" and so on, and I do not know how to account for the difference. However that may be, it is indeed a city replete with permissible pleasures, bursting with boundless appetites, answering to the needs of hot-humored men (contrary to what ʿAbd al-Laṭīf al-Baghdādī has said).[81] There the stranger finds amusement and *accommodation*, in it he forgets family and *nation*. 2.5.1

Among its curiosities[82] is that what leaves the bodies of its men enters the bodies of its women, and the women are therefore as fat as cottage cheese and clarified butter eaten on an empty stomach, while its men are like dry bread with sesame oil eaten on a full. Another is that its markets in no way resemble its men, for its inhabitants are full of refinement, sophistication, literary culture, and wit, qualities pleasing and morals pure, while its markets 2.5.2

ومنها ان مآها لا يشبه عيشها اى خبزها * فان الاول عذب والثاني تافه * ومنها ان العالِم فيها عالم والاديب اديب والفقيه فقيه والشاعر شاعر والفاسق فاسق والفاجر فاجر * ومنها ان نسآها يمشين تارة على الارض كسائر النسآ وتارة على السقف وعلى الحيطان * ومنها تذكّر المؤنث وتانث المذكر مع ان اهلها متقنون للعلم ٣،٥،٢
واى اتقان * ومنها ان حمّاماتها لا تزال تقرا فيها سورة او سورتان من القرآن فيها ذكر الاكواب والطائفين بها * فالخارج منها يخرج طاهرا وجنبا * واعجب من ذلك ان كثيرا من رجالها ليس لهم قلوب * وقد عوّض الواحد منهم عن قلبه بكتفين وظهرين وباربعة ايدى واربعة ارجل * ومن ذلك ان كثيرا من البنات اللاى يغسلن اقمصتهن فى بعض مجارى النيل يتعمّمن بقمصانهن بعد غسلهن ويمشين عريانات * ومنها ان قوما منهم بلغهم ان نسآ الصين يتخذن او بالحرى يُتَّخَذ لهن قوالب من حديد لتصغير ارجلهن عن المقدار المعهود * فجعلوا يشذّبون اصابعهم واعتقدوا ان اليد اذا كان بها اربع اصابع فقط كانت اخف للعمل وانفع لصاحبها * مع ان الاصابع والكفوف عندهم ليست مما يكسَى حتى تقضى عليهم بزيادة النفقة * كما هو شان الافرنج الذين لا يغادرون عضوا من اعضائهم الّا ويكسونه احتفالاً به وتفخيماً له او حذرا عليه من العدوى * ومن ذلك اى من الخواص لا من ٤،٥،٢
الاعضآء ان البنات اللاى يُستَخدَمن فى الميرى لحمل الآجر والجبس والتراب والطين والحجر والخشب وغير ذلك * يحملنه على روسهن وهن فرحات جامحات رامحات سابحات صادحات مادحات مازحات * غير آحّات ولا ترحات ولا دالحات ولا رازحات ولا كالحات ولا نائحات * ومن كان نصيبها من الآجرّ نظمت عليه موالا اجريّا * او من الجبس غنّت له اغنية جبسية * كانما هن سائرات فى زفاف عروس * ومن ذلك ان فيها ديوانين عظيمين يقال لكل منهما

are utterly without such things. Another is that its water in no way resembles its bread, which they call *ʿaysh*, for the first is sweet while the second is worthless. Another is that its scholars are scholars, its jurisprudents jurisprudents, its poets poets, its profligates profligates, its lechers lechers. Another is that its women walk sometimes on the ground like other women and sometimes on the ceiling or the walls.[83]

Another is the treatment of the feminine as masculine and of the mas- 2.5.3
culine as feminine,[84] even though its people are masters of scholarship (and what masters too!). Another is that, in their bathhouses, they constantly recite a sura or two of the Qur'an that mention "glasses" and "those who pass around with them," so that one emerges in a state of simultaneous ritual purity and impurity.[85] More amazing still, many of the city's men have no hearts, such men substituting for them two pairs of shoulders, two backs, four hands, and four legs.[86] And further, many of the girls who launder their shifts in the channels of the Nile, make them, once washed, into turbans, which they place on top of their heads; then they walk about stark naked. Another is that a tribe of them once heard that women in China use—or, more accurately, have used upon them—iron forms to reduce the size of their feet to below that of the norm, so they took to lopping off their fingers in the belief that if the hand has only four fingers, it will work more dexterously and be more useful to its owner.[87] This was despite the fact that they have no custom of covering their fingers and palms that would impose additional expense on them, unlike Franks, who leave no limb uncovered, either out of a desire to magnify the glory of those and show them off, or to guard against infection.

In addition to these (to these curiosities, that is, not these limbs), girls 2.5.4
employed in public works to carry bricks, plaster, dirt, mud, stones, lumber, and so on, do so on their heads, and do so joyfully, energetically, gallopingly, canteringly, cantabulatingly, celebratorily, and merrily, not sighingly, dejectedly, stumblingly, sinkingly, frowningly, or weepily. She to whose lot fall bricks will compose for them a brickish *mawwāl* or, if plaster, will sing to it a plastery song, as though walking in a bridal procession. And further, there are there two great offices, each called the Domestic Services Office. The first is presided over by a man and provides men with whatever they

الديوان المخدّمى * فالديوان الاول قيّمه رجل يجهز للرجال ما يلزمهم لتبريد فرشهم من هو * والديوان الثانى وهو دونه فى القدر والشان قيمته امراة تجهز لهم ما يلزمهم لتسخينهم من هى * واصل منشى الديوان الاول عجمىّ * وقد صار الان من الشهرة والنباهة عند العرب بحيث انك لا تزال تسمع بذكره والثنآء عليه فى كل
مقام ولا يكاد يخلو منه مجلس انس او غنآ او ادب * ومن ذلك ان البرنيطة فيها ٥،٥،٢
تنمى وتعظم * وتغلظ وتضخم * وتتسع وتطول وتعرض وتعمق * فاذا رايتها على راس لابسها حسبتها شونة * قال الفارياق وكثيرا ما كنت اتعجب من ذلك واقول * كيف صح فى الامكان وبدا للعيان ان مثل هذه الروس الدميمة * الضئيلة الذميمة * الخسيسة اللئيمة * المَهينة المُليمة * المستنكرة المشئومة * المستقذرة المهوّعة * المستقبحة المستفظعة * المستسمجة المستشنعة * المسترذلة المستبشعة * تقلّ هذه البرانيط المكرمة * وكيف انماها هوآ مصر وكبّرها الى هذا المقدار * وقد طالما كانت فى بلادها لا تساوى قارورة الفراش * ولا توازن نافورة[1] الفَراش * وكيف كانت هناك كالترب فاصبحت هنا كالتبر * يا هوآ مصر يا نارها يا مآها يا ترابها صيّرى طربوشى هذا برنيطة وان يكن احسن منها عند الله والناس وافضل * واجلّ وامثل * وللعين ابهى واكمل * وعلى الراس اطبق * وبالجسم اليق * وغير ذى قرون تملّق لتتلمّق * ويُرزَق عليها لترزق * قال فلم يغن عنى الندآء شيا وبقى راسى
مطربشا * وطرف دهرى مطرفشا * ومن ذلك ان قوما من الهُككآء المهاكيك فيها ٦،٥،٢
يمرأون ويبرقعون لحاهم ويزاحمون ذوات البراقع على مورد الإناثية * فتراهم يتخفّفون ويهجلون ويتبازون ويوكوكون ويوزوزون ويباغمون وهم اقبح خلق الله * ومن ذلك ان لضابط البلد شفقة زائدة على اهلها تقرب من حد الظلم * وذلك انه يامر جميع السالكين فى طرقها ليلاً ان يتخذوا لهم فوانيس وان كانت الليلة مقمرة *

١ ١٨٥٥: ناقورة.

need to cool their beds by way of hes, the second, of lower standing and status, is presided over by a woman and provides them with whatever they need to warm them up by way of shes. The founder of the first is of Persian origin and has now became so well-known and respected among the Arabs that you hear him mentioned with praise everywhere, and hardly a social, musical, or literary gathering is without his presence.

And further, the Frankish bonnet grows there and expands, gets thicker and huger, widens and lengthens and broadens and deepens to the point that, when you see one on its wearer's head, you think it must be a grain silo. Said the Fāriyāq, "I often used to wonder at this and say, 'How came it to be considered right and proper, or seem acceptable to the eye, that heads so misshapen, meager, and *miserable*, so vile and *contemptible*, so ignominious and meet to be *condemned*, so strange and so *ill-omened*, so evocative of filth and so *emetic*, so ugly to look at and so *pathetic*, so disgusting and *repulsive*, despicable and *convulsive*, should bear these most noble bonnets? And how could the air of Cairo have made them develop so and grow, when as long as they were in their own countries they weren't worth a bottle of bubbles or a fountain of frittilaries? And how can it be that there they were like dust, and here they've been metathesized into diamonds? O air, fire, water, dust of Cairo, turn this tarbush of mine into a Frankish bonnet (even if the former be better and of greater *élan* in the sight of God and *man*, more imposing and *correct*, to the eye more brilliant and *perfect*, to the head better *fitted*, to the body better *suited*, not equipped with horns that truckle for *tucker* and that the birds have to shit on if you're to find *succor*)!' But my cry helped not at all—the tarbush was on my head to *stay*, fate had turned to look the other *way*." 2.5.5

And further, a tribe of craving catamites there dress and talk like women and "veil their beards"[88] to keep them out of *sight*, jostling at the watering hole of femininity those who wear such veils by *right*, plucking out their facial hair, making eyes at men, dressing to the *nines*, mincing, tittupping, and speaking in sugary *whines*, though they are the ugliest of God's creatures. And further, the city's police chief is so solicitous of its people's welfare that it amounts almost to tyranny, for he commands everyone who walks its highways by night to have with him a lantern, even if the night is moonlit, out of 2.5.6

خفيةً ان يعثروا بشى فى اسواق المدينة فيسقطوا فى هوة اوجبّ فتنكسر ارجلهم او
تندقّ اعناقهم * ومن وُجد ليلاً يطوف من غير ذوى البرانيط وليس بيده فانوس
غُلّت رجله الى يده * ويده الى عنقه * وعنقه الى حبل * والحبل الى وتد *
والوتد الى حائط * والحائط الى ناكر ونكير * وتصلية سعير * ومن ذلك ان
لبنى حَنّا[1] فيها اسلوبا فى الكتابة لا يعرفه احد الا هم * ولهم حروف كحروفنا هذه
الا انها لا تقرا الّا اذا ادخلها الانسان فى عينه كذلك رايتهم يفعلون * ومنها انه
اذا مات منهم احد فلا يزال اهل الميت يندبونه وينوحون عليه حتى يؤوب اليهم
ووطبه ملآن من الطرّيخ * ومن خصائصها ايضا ان البغاث بها يستنسر *
والذباب يستصقر * والناقة تستبعر * والجحش يستمهر * والهرّ يستنمر * بشرط
ان تكون هذه الحيوانات مجلوبة اليها من بلاد بعيدة * ومن ذلك ان كثيرا من ٧,٥,٢
اهلها يرون ان كثرة الافكار فى الراس يكثر عنها الهموم والاكدار او بالعكس *
وان العقل الطويل يتناول البعيد من الامور * كما ان الرجل الطويل يتناول البعيد
من الثمر وغيره * وان تلك الكثرة سبب فى الاقلال * وهذا الطول موجب لقصر
الاجال * واوردوا على ذلك براهين سديدة * قالوا ان العقل فى الراس كالنور
فى الفتيلة * فما دام النور موقدا فلا بد وان تنفد الفتيلة ولا يمكن ابقاوها الا باطفآء
النور * او كالمآ فى الوادى * فاذا دام المآ جاريا فلا بد وان ينضب او ينصب
فى البحر فمتى حُقن بقى * او كالفلوس فى الكيس * فما دام المفلس اى صاحب
الفلوس يمدّ يده الى كيسه وينفق منه فنى ما عنده * الا ان تربط يده عن الكيس او
يربط الكيس عن يده * او كالتيس النازى * فانه اذا دام نزوه نزفت مادة حياته
فهلك فلا بد من نجفه * فمن ثم اصطلحوا على طريقة لتوقيف جريان العقل فى ميدان ٨,٥,٢
الدماغ حينا من الاحيان ليتوفر لهم فى غيره * وذلك بشرب شى من الحشيش

١ ١٨٥٥: حِنّا.

fear lest they trip over something in one of the city's marketplaces and fall into a hole or a pit and their legs be broken or their necks crushed. If anyone, other than someone wearing a Frankish hat, be found roaming around at night without a lantern in his hand, his foot is shackled to his hand, his hand to his neck, his neck to a rope, the rope to a peg, the peg to a wall, and the wall to Nākir and *Nakīr*, to the roasting of *hellfire*. And further, the Sons of Ḥannā[89] there have a way of writing that is known to none but themselves[90] and have letters like our own but which can be read only if one holds them within an inch of one's face, as I have seen them do. Another is that, when one of them dies, his family wails and keens over him in the hope that he will return to them, his milkskin filled with cured fish fry.[91] A further curiosity of the place is that ignoble birds there may pretend to be mighty eagles,[92] flies hawks, cow-camels bull-camels, donkey foals oryxes, and cats tigers—provided only that these animals have been imported from distant lands.

Further, many of its inhabitants believe that many thoughts in the head lead to many worries and vexations and vice versa, that the mind that ponders at length grasps the distant matter in the same manner that the tall man grasps the distant fruit, etc., that such abundance is a cause of destitution and such prolonged cogitation results in a shorter life. They adduce many pertinent proofs for this, saying that the mind is to the head as the light to the wick: if the light is left burning, the wick will be used up, and the latter can be preserved only if the former is extinguished; or that it's like the water in a water course: if the water keeps flowing, it must inevitably either soak into the ground or empty into the sea, but when it's contained it remains; or like money in a purse: so long as the exiguously monied one (meaning the owner of the money)[93] keeps putting his hand into the purse and spending, what he has will disappear (unless he tie down his hand so it can't reach the purse, or the purse so it can't reach his hand); or like a leaping billy goat: if he keeps on leaping, his vital juices will leak out and he will perish, so that a thong must be tied from his willy to his belly to prevent him from mounting the female. 2.5.7

Consequently, they have agreed among themselves on a method of halting the flow of the mind through the open arena of the brain at certain times so that it will be available to them at others, the method in question being to 2.5.8

او بمضغه او بالنظر اليه او بذكر اسمه *فحين يتعاطونه تغيب عنهم الهموم ويحضر السرور* وتولى الاحزان * ويرقص المكان * فمن يرهَم على هذه الحالة ودّ لو يُكتب فى زمرتهم ويدخل فى دائرتهم وان يكن قاضى القضاة * ومن ذلك ان طرقها لا تزال غاصة بالابل المحمّلة * فينبغى للسائر فيها اذا راها مقبلة ان يخلى لها الطريق * اَوْ لا فلا يامن ان يفقد احدى عينيه * وقد ينشا عن هذا الزحام فوائد كما فى حكاية المراة التى سارت مع امها لتحضر عرس اختها فطالعها من محلها *

smoke, chew, contemplate, or talk about, hashish, for when they consume it, care takes off and pleasure *advances*, grief turns its back and the whole place *dances*. Any who sees them in this state longs to be registered among their *company* and entered among their *constituency*, be he even the chief judge. And further, its roads are ever packed with loaded camels, and, if anyone walking them sees one coming, he has to make way; if he doesn't, there's no guarantee he won't lose an eye. This crowding may bring with it good things, as in the case of the woman who went with her mother to attend her sister's wedding: the rise in her fortunes came from her setting herself down.[94]

الفصل السادس

في لا شي

قد كنت اظن انى تركت الفارياق واخذت فى وصف مصر استريح فاذا هو هى او ١،٦،٢
اياها * فينبغى لى الان ان امكث فى ظل هذا الفصل الوجيز قليلا لانفض عنى غبار التعب ثم اقوم ان شا الله تعالى *

Chapter 6

Nothing

I had thought that, if I abandoned the Fāriyāq and set about describing Cairo, I'd find rest, but the second turned out to be just like the first, or, to put it differently, the *vice* was the same as the *versa*. I must now therefore sit myself down a while in the shade of this short chapter to brush off the dust of my labors. Then I shall arise once more, should the Almighty so allow. **2.6.1**

الفصل السابع

في وصف مصر

قد قمت حامدا لله شاكرا * فاين القلم والدواة حتى اصف هذه المدينة السعيدة ١،٧،٢
الجديرة بالمدح من كل من رآها * لانها بلد الخير ومعدن الفضل والكرم * اهلها ذوو لطف وادب واحسان الى الغريب * وفى كلامهم من الرقة ما يغنى الحزين عن التطريب * اذا حيّوك فقد احيوك * وان سلموا عليك فقد سلّموك * وان زاروك زادوك شوقا الى رويتهم * وان زرتهم فسحوا لك صدورهم فضلا عن مجالسهم * اما علماوها فان مدحهم قد انتشر فى الافاق * وفات فخرمن سواهم وفاق * بهم من لين الجانب ورقة الطبع وخفض الجناح وبشاشة الوجه ما لا يمكن المبالغة فى اطرائه * ولكل نوع من الناس عندهم اكرام يليق به سوآكان من النصارى او غيرهم * وربما خاطبوهم بقولهم ياسيدى ولا يستنكفون من زيارتهم ومخالطتهم ومعاشرتهم خلافا لعادة المسلمين فى الديار الشامية * وبذلك لهم الفضل على
غيرهم * وكانّ هذه المزية وهى حسن الخلق ورقة الطبع امر مركوز فى جميع اهل ٢،٧،٢
مصر * فان لعامتهم ايضا مخالقة ومجاملة * وكلهم فصيح اللهجة بيّن الكلام سريع الجواب * حلو المفاكهة والمطارحة * واكثرهم يميل الى هذا النوع الذى يسمونه الانقاط * وكانه المجازرة وهى مفاكهة تشبه السباب وهواشبه بالاحاجى * فان من لم يكن قد تدرّب فيه لا يمكنه ان يفهم منه شيا وان يكن شاعرا *

Chapter 7

A Description of Cairo

I am risen to my feet once more, praising and thanking God. Now, where are my pen and inkwell, that I may describe this happy city, which deserves the eulogies of all who behold it, for it is the home of good things, the motherlode of bounty and magnanimity? Its people are refined, cultured, and kind to the *stranger*, and there's such amiability in their speech that the grief-struck of getting any sadder need never be in *danger*. When they *hail* you, they *regale* you. When they *salute* you, they *save* you. After they've visited you, you can't wait to see them once *more*, and when you visit them, they open to you their hearts, to say nothing of their *door*. As for their scholars, praise of them has spread to every *quarter*, leaving the rest dead in the *water*. In fact, their geniality, natural delicacy, modesty, and welcoming mien cannot be over-extolled, while, for every condition of men among them, there is an appropriate respectful salute, be they Christians or others. The latter address the former as "My Master," and have no aversion to visiting them, mixing with them, or keeping company with them, in contrast with the custom of the Muslims of the Levant, and this a virtue to be credited to their account as against others. 2.7.1

It seems that these traits, of high moral character and natural delicacy, are things ingrained in all the people of Cairo, for their common folk too are good-natured and courteous. All of them are eloquent and articulate, quick-thinking and good at pleasant joking and joshing. Most have a liking for the kind of jokes they call *anqāṭ*, which are something like *mujārazah*, which is "a kind of joking back and forth that resembles mutual abuse,"[95] and are almost a kind of puzzle, for anyone not trained in them will find it impossible to understand the slightest thing about them, even if he's a poet. 2.7.2

٣،٧،٢ وكلهم يحب السماع واللهو والخلاعة وغناوهم اشجى ما يكون * فلا يمكن لِمَن اَلِفَه ان يطرب بغيره * وكذلك آلاتهم فانها تكاد تنطق عن العازف بها * واعظمها عندهم هو العود وقلّ اعتنآوهم بالناى * ولهم فى ضرب العود طرق وفنون تكاد تكون من المغيّبات * غير انى أُذمّ من غنائهم شيا واحدا * وهو تكرير لفظة واحدة من بيت او موّال مرارا متعددة حتى يفقد السامع لذة معنى الكلام * ولكن اكثر ما يكون ذلك من المتطفّلين على الفن * وبعكس ذلك طريقة اهل تونس فان غنآهم اشبه بالترتيل * وهم يزعمون انها كانت طريقة العرب فى الاندلس *

٤،٧،٢ ومما ينبغى ان يذكر هنا ان النصارى المولودين فى بلاد الاسلام الناهجين منهج المسلمين فى العادات والاخلاق هم ابدا دونهم فى الفصاحة والادب والجمال والكياسة والظرافة والنظافة * الا انهم انشط منهم على السفر والتجارة والصنائع واكثر اقداما وجَلَدا على تعاطى الاعمال الشاقة * وذلك ان المسلمين اهل قناعة وزهد وفى النصارى شره عظيم الى اتخاذ الديار الرحيبة * وقنية الخيل النجيبة * والجواهر النفسية والمتاع الفاخر لا حدّ لها * فاذا دخلت دار نصرانى من المتمولين بمصر رايت عنده عدة خوادم وخادمين ونحو عشرين قصبة للتبغ من اغلى ما يكون * وقدر نصفها من الاراكيل الثمينة * وثلث[١] غرفات مفروشات باحسن ما يكون من القماش * وآنية فضة للطعام والشراب والرائحة * واسرة عالية وطيئة وثيابا فاخرة وغير ذلك * ومع هذا فلا تجد عنده كتابا * ولو ان مشتريا شاء ان يشترى شيا من تاجر مسلم لوجد سعره ارخص من بضاعة النصرانى بربع الثمن * ولكن وجود هذه الشراهة انما هو فى الغالب عند النصارى الغربآ *

٥،٧،٢ فاما القبط فانهم اشبه بالمسلمين * وقلّ من تعاطى المتجر منهم * اما دولة مصر اذ ذاك فانها كانت فى الذروة العليا من الابهة والعزّ والفخر والكرم والمجد *

١ ١٨٥٥: ثلت.

All of them love music, amusements, and license, and their singing is the most tuneful possible; anyone who gets used to it finds that no other can move him. Similarly, their instruments seem almost to give tongue to the one who plays them, the most important being the lute, while they pay scant attention to the reed flute. They have methods and styles of playing the lute that seem almost to belong to the world of the divine mysteries. I would criticize their singing for one thing only, which is that they repeat a single word of a line of verse or a *mawwāl* so many times that the listener loses the pleasure of the meaning. However, this is mostly to be found among those who merely sponge off the art. At the opposite pole you have the method of the people of Tunis, whose singing is closer to chant; they claim that this was the way of the Arabs of al-Andalus. 2.7.3

It has to be stated here that the Christians native to the Islamic lands, who follow the Muslims in their customs and morality, are always inferior to them in the chasteness of their language, in literature, in aesthetics, in intelligence, in sophistication, and in cleanliness. They are, however, more active than them in travel, trading, and manufacturing, and bolder and more steadfast in taking on difficult tasks. This is because Muslims are a nation of self-denial and *abnegation* while Christians have an insatiable appetite for territorial *expansion*, not to mention the acquisition of pure-bred horses, precious gems, and luxury goods. If you enter the house of a wealthy Christian in Cairo, you'll find he has both serving women and serving men, around twenty tobacco pipes of the most expensive kind (half of them valuable waterpipes), three rooms upholstered in the best materials, silver vessels for eating and drinking, along with smooth, high beds, luxurious clothes, and so forth, and yet, for all that, not a single book. Also, if someone wants to buy something from a Muslim trader, he'll find it costs him twenty-five percent less than the Christian's goods. This avarice is, however, found, for the most part, only among foreign Christians. The Copts are more like the Muslims, and few of them practice trade. 2.7.4

As far as the Egyptian state is concerned, it had reached in those days a peak of splendor, strength, magnificence, munificence, and glory. Those inducted into its service enjoyed a huge salary in the form of money, clothing, and provisions, more than was customary in any other state. Its viceroy[96] awarded high rank and tokens of imperial favor to Muslim and Christian alike, 2.7.5

فكان للمتسمين بخدمتها مرتّب عظيم من المال والكسى والشِحَن مما لم يعهد فى دولة غيرها * وكان واليها يولى المراتب العلية وسمات الشرف السنية لكل من المسلمين والنصارى ما عدا اليهود * خلافا لدولة تونس فان شرفها عمّ الجميع * ومع عظم ما كان يكسبه التجار واصحاب الحرف وما يناله اهل الوظائف من الرزق العميم فكانت الاسعار بمصر رخيصة جدا فلهذا كنت ترى الناس قُصريّهم وعميّهم مقبلين على الشغل واللهو معا * فالبساتين غاصة باهل الخلاعة والقصوف * ومحال القهوة مجمع للاحباب * والاعراس مسموع فيها الغنآ والات الطرب من كل طرف * والرجال يخطرون بالخز والديباج * والنسآ ينوْن بما عليهن من الحلىّ * والخيل والبغال والحمير مسرجة ومكسوة بالحرير المزركش * الا ان صاحبنا الفارياق لم يكد يدخل ارضا سعيدة الا ويخرج منها وقد تغير حالها * فارجع معى الان لنخلصه من ايدى الخرجيين * فانى تركته يحاول ذلك مذ حين *

though not to Jews, in which Egypt differed from the Tunisian state, whose honors fell on all men equally.[97] Despite the large amounts earned by both merchants and craftsmen and the generous livings obtained by the servants of the state, prices in Cairo were exceedingly low, and, as a result, one might observe everyone, members of the elite and commoners, engaging together in work and play. The gardens overflowed with pleasure-seekers and revelers. The cafés were meeting places for friends. At the weddings, singing and musical instruments of every kind might be heard. The men swaggered in silk-wool and brocade, the women staggered under the weight of their jewelry. The horses, mules, and donkeys wore saddles and saddlecoths of embroidered silk. Any land blessed by fortune, however—if our friend the Fāriyāq ever entered it—inevitably changed for the worse before he exited it. Return, then, with me now so that we can release him from the hands of the Bag-men, for I left him a while ago engaged in trying to do just that.

الفصل الثامن

فى اشعار انه انتهى وصف مصر

قد غادرنا اى انا وجماعة المولفين الفارياق يحاول ان ينفض الخرج عن ظهره * ١،٨،٢
وانى الان من دونهم علمت انه بات ليلة وهو يفكّر فى ان كل شى اثبتته الصنعة فلا بد من ان تقلقله الاحوال * فمن ثم عزم على القلقلة * فخرج فى الصباح من معزفه واخذ يطوف فى الاسواق * ويحرك كتفيه عند كل خطوة ويقول * لا قلبنَّه لا طرحنَّه * لاركسنّه لابدحنّه * انه انقض ظهرى اى قرح اى عقر * هل انا
اليوم حمار لحمار يالنكر * فراه بعض الظرفآء وهو يحرك منكبيه فقال لا بد لهذا من ٢،٨،٢
شان فاقبل اليه ولطّف له المقال حتى استخرج سرّه من سرّته * وعلم حاله وسبب سفرته * فقال له لا عليك فان مصر حرسها الله معدن الخير والبركة * ولكن لا بدّ للفوز بذلك من حركة * قال واى حركة اعظم مما ترى * قال بل الامر دون ذلك * اَلَك اذن واعية * وفكرة مدركة وقدم ساعية * قال اجل * قال فاسمع
اذا ما اقول لك * ان بهذا المصر شاعرا مفلقا من النصارى له وجاهة ونباهة عند ٣،٨،٢
جميع الاعيان * قال ما هذه صفة شاعر وما ارى كلامك الّا متناقض الطرفين * فكيف فك هذا المعمى وتاويل هذه الاحجية * قال لا تناقض فانه شاعر بالطبع

Chapter 8

Notice that the Description of Cairo is Ended

We—that is, all my good friends and I—had left the Fāriyāq trying to shake the Bag-men's bag off his back. Now I, to the exclusion of the others, have come to know that he spent a night pondering the fact that everything that skill may set firmly in place external factors will shake to the core, and, this being the case, he decided to take the shaking business into his own hands. When morning came, he left the place where he'd been playing and started to wander through the markets, shaking his shoulders with every step and saying, "I shall turn him upside down! I shall give him the *push*! I shall send him back to where he came from! I shall beat him to *mush*! He has broken, meaning galled, meaning chafed, my back. Am I become today no better than one *ass* owned by another? A pretty *pass*!" 2.8.1

A man of some sophistication observed him shaking his shoulders and said to himself, "There is something afoot with this man" and approached him and spoke politely to him, finally extracting his secret from his *navel*, and learning his condition and the reason for his *travel*. "Never mind," he told him. "Cairo—God protect it!—is the mother-lode of good things and *benefaction*, though to win them you will have to take *action*." "What greater action can I undertake than what you observe?" he asked. "There's no call for such things," the other replied. "Have you a ready ear, a clever *mind*, a foot to effort *inclined*?" "I have," he said. "Then listen while I tell you," said the other. 2.8.2

"In this metropolis is a poet of great skill,[98] a Christian, who has influence and standing with the whole elite." Said the other, "These aren't the characteristics of a poet, and to me your words appear an oxymoron. How can this riddle be solved, this puzzle explained?" The other replied, 2.8.3

لا بالصنعة * والفرق بين ذلك ان الشاعر بالصنعة هو من يتكسّب بشعره فيمدح هذا ويكذب على هذا حتى ينال منهما شيا * فاما الشاعر بالطبع فانما هو الذى يقول الشعر لباعث من البواعث دون تكلّف وانتظار للجائزة * قال ليس هذا الفرق مما ذكره الآمدى * قال ابعث الامدى الى آمد واسمع منى * قال قد امَّدته فما الرشد * قال نصحى لك ان تكتب كتابا الى هذا العلامة وتلتمس منه فيما تطرى به مواجهته * فاذا تكرم بذلك فاذكر له ح ما انت تعانيه واستنجد به * فلا بد من ان يجيبك * فانه رجل متصف بمكارم الاخلاق ويحب دغدغة الافتخار * ولا سيما انه يرغب فى مجالسة ذوى الادب وتيسير اسباب معيشتهم * فتلطف اليه فى المقال * وانا ضامن لك ان تفوز منه بالامال * فشكره الفارياق على

٤،٨،٢ نصيحته ورجع الى محله راضيا مستبشرا * فلما جنَّ الليل اخذ القلم والقرطاس وكتب ما نصه * اهدى سلاما لو تحمله النسيم لعطر الافاق * ولو جعل للبدر هالة لما اعتراه المحاق * ولو مزجت به الصهبآ لما اعقب شربها صداعا * ولو استفّه مريض او لعقه لما لقى برحاً واوجاعا * ولو عُلّق على شجرة لزهت فى الحال اوراقها ولو فى الخريف * ولو سقيه الروض لانبت من كل زهر بهيج طريف * ولو جعل على اوتار عود لاطربت دون عازف * ولو تُغُنّى به فى مجلس لاغنى عن المشموم والمعازف * ولو علّق فى الآذان لكان شنوفا * ولو صقل به سيف كليل لجاء رهيفا * ولو مُثّل لكان حدائق ورياضا * وسلسبيلا ومحاضا * ولو نيط بالعمائم * لاغنى عن التمائم * ولو تختم به ولهان لاجزاه مُجزأ السُلوان * ولو كُتب على رجام لألَهى الثاكل عن النواح * او على خصر هيفا لقام لها مقام الوشاح *

"There is no contradiction: he's a poet by nature, not by trade, the difference being that the poet by trade is one who depends on his verse to make his living; thus he eulogizes this one and flatters that in order to get something from them. The poet by nature, on the other hand, speaks poetry because he cannot help himself—without having to force himself or in expectation of reward." "That's not the difference mentioned by al-Āmidī,"[99] said the Fāriyāq. "Then scoot al-Āmidī back to Āmid[100] and listen to me," said the other. "Voilà! I've *a-i-m-(e)-d* him and scooted him," he said, "so what's the scoop?" "I advise you to write a letter to this scholarly man and beg him, through the deployment of your praise, for an audience. If he is kind enough to grant this, use the occasion to tell him of your sufferings and seek his help. He is certain to say yes, for he is known for his noble morals and loves the titillation of high self-esteem. Your chances are especially good, because he loves to keep company with literary types and make their lives more comfortable. Speak to him courteously, and I guarantee you'll realize your hopes through him." The Fāriyāq thanked the man for his advice and returned to his lodging comforted and expecting the best.

When night came, he took his pen and paper and wrote the following: 2.8.4

> A greeting I send that, if 'twere carried on the breeze, the horizon with perfume would *freight* and if 'twere made a halo for the moon, would save the latter from its monthly *fate*; if 'twere added to the tawny wine, would cause no headache to follow its *potation* and if 'twere swallowed or licked by a sick man, would cause him no fever or *excruciation*; if 'twere hung upon a tree, though the season were autumn, would make its leaves straightway burst *out* and if 'twere used to water gardens, would make each charming and delightful flower *sprout*; if 'twere laid o'er the strings of a lute, would have them induce ecstasy without need of any agent *instrumental* and if at a gathering 'twere sung, would render all sweet-smelling plants and instruments purely *incidental*; if 'twere hung in the ear as a *pendant*, it would be one of those that, being from its upper rim *dependent*, are the more clearly *seen* and, if 'twere used to whet the dulled sword's edge, would make it *keen*; if 'twere portrayed, would be as blooming gardens and meadows of that *ilk* and soothing liquids and purest *milk* and if 'twere suspended from one's *headdress*, would render amulets *superfl'ous*; if 'twere worn as a ring by one by passion *misled*, would serve him in oblivion's *stead* and if 'twere written on a *tombstone*, would distract the grieving mother from making *moan*, or

او على انف مزكوم لما احوجه الى السعوط * او على ساق اعرج لكان له من قفزه
سبق وفروط * او على لسان ابكم لانحلت عقدته * او على كف بخيل لهان عليه
فى البذل ذهبه وفضته * او على اجاج لعاد فراتا * او على رمل لانبت الريحان
نباتا * وتحيات فاخرة * ذكية عاطرة * ارق من النسيم * واحلى من التسنيم *
واشهى من العافية على بدن السقيم * واجلى للعين من الاثمد * واغلى للناقد من
العسجد * واصفى من المآ الزلال * واعلق بالقلب من امل الوصال * واشغل
للبال * من هوى ذى دلال * وازهر من نور الصباح * وازهى من نَور الاقاح *
واعبق من شذا الراح * واثمن من الجوهر النفيس * واعز عند البستىّ من
التجنيس * وعند ابى العتاهية من الزهديات * وعند ابى نواس من الخمريات *
وعند الفرزدق من الفخريات * وعند جرير من الغزليات * وعند ابى تمام من
الحكم * وعند المتنبى من جزل الكلم * تهدى الى الجناب المكرم * المقام المحترم *
ملاذ الملهوفين * مستغاث المضيمين * ثمال المظلومين * ملجا المهضومين *
منهل القاصدين * مورد الطالبين * ادام الله سعده * وخلد مجده * وبعد ٥,٨,٢
ياسيدى فانى قدمت هذه الديار وانا حامل لخرج قد انقض ظهرى * وعيل به
صبرى * ولم اجد من يزحزحه عنى ولو قليلا * ولست اجد بنفسى الى التخلص
منه سبيلا * وقد هُديت الى نور معروفك فى جنح هذا العِماس * واُنبئت انك انت
وحدك معتق من هذا الارتباس * دون سائر الناس * فهل تسمح لى بان ازور
ناديك الكريم * وابث اليك مشافهة ما بى من البث المقيم * والضرّ الاليم *
فانك اهل لان تاخذ بيد من لا ناصر له * وان تصطنعه لك بالتفاتة تحقّق امله *

on the waist of a slender *lass*, would take the place of a *sash*, or on the nose of one with a *rheum*, for nose drops would leave no *room*, or on a cripple's *feet*, would make him hop ahead and all others in the race to the wellhead *beat*, or on a dumb man's *tongue*, would cause the knot therein to come *undone*, or on a miser's *hand*, would make it easier for him his gold and silver to *spend*, or on brackish water, would make it sweet at just one *go*, or on sand, would cause it to make even basil *grow*; plus salutations *ornamented*, sweet-smelling and *scented*, softer than the *breeze*, sweeter than heaven's *mead*, than good health for the sick a more sought-after *goal*, more brightening for the eye than *kohl*, dearer to the assayer than purest *gold*, clearer than sweetest water fresh and *cold*, dearer to the heart than hope of the beloved's *arms*, more distracting than a coquette's *charms*, brighter than the light of *morn*, more brilliant than the anemone's *bloom*, more fragrant than wine's *aromas*, more closely guarded than *tiaras*, dearer to al-Bustī than *paronomasias*,[101] to Abū l-ʿAtāhiyah[102] than ascetic *verse*, to Abū Nuwās[103] than poems about wine (and *worse*), to al-Farazdaq[104] than *panegyrics*, to Jarīr[105] than *lyrics*, to Abū Tammām[106] than *sagacity*, to al-Mutanabbī[107] than poems demonstrating rhetorical *capacity*—to be presented to that honored *person* of respected *station* who is the resort of the *depressed*, object of the entreaties of the *oppressed*, protector of those who've suffered *wrong*, refuge of the victims of the *strong*, watering hole of those who aspire to his *attention*, wellspring of those who seek his *intervention*, may God preserve his good fortune for ever and a *day*, and never let his glory fade *away*!

To proceed: Master, I am come to these territories bearing a bag that 2.8.5
has broken my *back* and in my patience made a *crack*, and I have found none to relieve me of even a little of the *encumbrance* and can see no way to rid myself of it without *assistance*. In the midst of this inky darkness I have been guided to your kindly *light*, informed that you alone, to the exclusion of any other *wight*, can free me from my *plight*. Will you then permit me to visit your noble circle and to you myself *unburden* of that from which I endlessly suffer, and of my dolorous hurt, in *person*? On you alone can I *rely* to take the hand of one without *ally*, knowing that, should you but look on him with favor, you'll make his wishes come *true* and help him obtain all he has in *view*, and should you take him to yourself, he will thenceforth owe you a debt of *gratitude* and of thankfulness for your pious *attitude*. Such a one thus asks this of you as a petitioner in the forecourt

وتنيله ما امله * وان تتخذه لك ما عاش رهين شكرك * ممنون برّك * فهو يرجو ذلك منك رجآ مَن لاذ بعقوة فخرك * فان رايت ان تفعل فذلك من احسانك * وطول امتنانك * والسلام* وكتب عنوانه يشرف بانامل سيدى الاكرم الاحسب الافخم الاوحد الافضل الاسعد الامثل الارشد الاكمل الامجد الاجل الخواجا
٦،٨،٢ فلان ادام الله بقاه بالعز والنعم * فلما بلغت هذه الرسالة الى الخواجا المذكور وطالع ما فى شرح السلام من التشابيه المتكلفة لم يتمالك ان ضحك منها وقهقه * وقال لبعض جلسائه ممن المّ بالادب * سبحان الله قد رايت اكثر الكتّاب يتهوسون فى اهدآ السلام والتحيات للمخاطب كانما هم مهدون له عرش بلقيس او خاتم سيدنا سليمن * فتراهم يشبهونه بما ليس يشبهه * ويغرقونه فى الاغراق ويغلونه فى الغلوّ حتى ياتى مبلولا محروقا * وربما جآوا بفقرتين متماثلتين فى المعنى كقول صاحب هذه الرسالة الان ثمال المظلومين ملجا المهضومين * ثم اذا انتقلوا من السلام الى الغرض اجادوا الكلام الى الغاية * وما ادرى ما الذى حسّن لارباب فن الانشآ ان يضيعوا وقتهم بهذه الاستعارات والتشبيهات المبتذلة * وبنظم الفقر المتماثلة فى المعنى * مع ان العالم يتاتّى له ان يبدى علمه بعبارة واحدة اذا كانت رشيقة اللفظ بليغة المعنى * وهذه الف ومائتا سنة قد مضت وما زلنا نرى زيدا يلوك ما لفظه
٧،٨،٢ عمرو * وعمرا يمضغ ما قاله زيد * فقد سرى هذا الدآء فى جميع الكتّاب * اما تفخيم المخاطب فى العنوان بالاجل والامجد والاسعد والاوحد وما اشبه ذلك فله وجه * وذلك انه لم تجرِ العادة فى بلادنا بان يكون تبليغ الكتب على يد البريد * وانما تبعث مع اشخاص ليست لهم خبرة بالطرق ولا بالديار فانها كما لا يخفى عاطلة عن التسمية خطّا * فاذا حملها رجل لا يعرف القراءة طفق يسال كل من لقيه فى الطريق عن

> of your *dignity*, and your willingness to oblige will be but further token of your kindness and far-reaching *benignity*. Farewell.

For the address he wrote:

> To be honored by the fingertips of my most generous, most nobly descended, most imposing, most unique, most bountiful, most fortunate, most exemplary, most well-guided, most complete, most glorious, most sublime master, Khawājā So-and-so, may God preserve him for ever in splendor and ease!

When this message reached the *khawājā* in question and the latter perused the affected similes employed in the elaboration of the greeting, he couldn't contain his laughter and guffaws and said to one of those seated with him in his salon, a man of culture, "Glory be! I find that most of our writers abandon themselves in their presentation of greetings and salutations to the addressee as unrestrainedly as if they were presenting him with the throne of Bilqīs or Our Master Sulaymān's ring,[108] comparing him to things he doesn't resemble, drowning him in immoderate praise, and boiling him over the fires of excess, with the result that he ends up soaked and singed. Sometimes they come up with two phrases that are identical in meaning, such as when the writer of this epistle here says 'object of the entreaties of the oppressed, protector of those who've suffered wrong.' Then, as soon as they move from salutation to content, they write excellently. I don't know why the writers of compositions have thought good to waste their time on such hackneyed metaphors and similes and on composing phrases of identical sense, when the scholar can, with ease, demonstrate his erudition in a single phrase if it's well worded and effective at conveying the meaning. Twelve hundred years have passed, and we still find Zayd chewing over what 'Amr[109] uttered and 'Amr masticating what Zayd said. This vice has entered the veins of every writer. 2.8.6

"When it comes to eulogizing the addressee in the address with 'the most sublime,' 'the most glorious,' 'the most fortunate,' 'the most exemplary,' and the like, there is a particular issue. The custom of delivering the mail via the postal service is not observed in our country; it is sent with persons who have no knowledge of the roads or the neighborhoods, which, as you will be aware, are innocent of any written signs. If the letter is borne by a man who doesn't know how to read, he will ask everyone he meets on the road about the addressee by name. If the address doesn't give a clue as to who he 2.8.7

اسم المخاطب * فان لم يكن العنوان دالاّ عليه التبس على القارى * فان كثيرا من الناس مشتركون فى الاسمآء وان كانوا مختلفين فى المكارم والاخلاق * وفضلا عن ذلك فقد يتفق ان مبلّغ الكتاب بعد ان يكون قد سال غير واحد عن اسم المخاطب ووجدهم كلهم امين * وبعد ان يكون قد اضاع نصف نهاره فى البحث عن الطريق * فلا يكاد يهتدى اليه الاّ ويجد عوّنا يترصده * حتى اذا لمحه تلقفه وبعثه الى احد الجهات التى اراد * فيبقى الكتاب عنده ثم ينتقل منه الى غيره * وربما لقى غيره ما لقيه هو فينتقل الكتاب الى آخر وهلم جراّ * فكان لا بدّ من الاستقصآء
٨،٨،٢ فى العنوان عن صفات المخاطب * فقال له جليسه اذن يجب ياسيدى ان يذكر فى العنوان جميع الصفات * فيقال للمخاطب مثلا اذا كان جميلا كيّسا غنيّا رشيق القد كبير العمامة عريض الحزام * الجميل الكيّس الغنى الى آخره * فقال اما وصف انسان بالجمال والغنى فهو من الموبقات له * واما بغير ذلك ككبر العمامة وعرض الحزام فليس من الصفات المخصصة اذ الناس فى ذلك سوآ * وما خالف ذلك فما اولاه بالاستعمال وستراه عن قريب مستعملا ان شآء الله * وهو وان يكن احيانا من المضحكات وذلك كانْ[1] تصف رجلا مثلا بالزَبَنيّة والكِنّية والحنطاوية والشَرَنْبثية والكِرْنيفية والزَلْهبية والزُخْرنيّة والسَنْطبيّة والعَرْزبيّة والعَشْجبيّة[2] والعِظْيَبيّة والحُوظيّة والأَرْطية والسناطية و الفُسْحمِيّة والجَهْضميّة والبرْطاميّة والحَتْرميّة الا انه احسن من ايقاع اللبس فى صفات المخاطب * فقد بلغنى ان كثيرا من الكتب التى تضمنت مقاصد مهمة لما لم يدل عنوانها بالنص والتوقيف على ذات المرسل اليه فُتحت ليعلم صاحبها * فكانت سببا فى ضرر المرسل والمرسل اليه * انتهت
٩،٨،٢ محاورتهما * واعلم هنا ان الخواجا المذكور لما بلغته الوكة الفارياق كان مريضا فلهذا

---

١ ١٨٥٥: كانّ. ٢ ١٨٥٥: العَنْجبيّة.

is, any who read it will be confused, for many share the same name, though they may differ in fine qualities and morals. In addition, it may happen that the one who is to deliver the letter, after asking more one than one person the name of the addressee and finding all of them to be illiterate and having wasted half his day searching for the way and and after failing in the end to be guided to it, finds a servant in the street watching him. As soon as he sees him, then, he seizes hold of him and sends him off in some direction he thinks correct. The letter stays with the new messenger for a while, and then he passes it on to someone else, and that someone else may face the same problems he did and so pass it on to another, etc., etc. One should therefore go into great detail when describing the addressee in the address."

His companion then said, "In that case, dear sir, all the addressee's characteristics should be mentioned in the address. If the addressee is, for instance, beautiful, intelligent, rich, shapely, of large turban, and broadly cummerbunded, he must be referred to as 'the beautiful, the intelligent, the rich,' etc." Responded the other, "As far as describing someone as beautiful, rich, and so on is concerned, to do so is a grave offense against him,[110] and as far as the rest, such as the size of his turban and the breadth of his cummerbund, is concerned, these are non-specific characteristics, for everyone's on the same footing in such matters. How much more appropriate it is to employ other forms of address, as you will soon see, God willing. Such other forms may on occasion make one laugh—as when one describes a man as being characterized, for example, by hypertrichotism, or hirsutism, or triticoidism, or hypermetacarpalism, or superrhysism, or partial hirsutism, or pyknism, or ectomorphism, or mesomorphism, or endomorphism, or somatomegalism, or exophthalmism, or planirostrism, or glabrotism, or acromegalism, or macrocephalism, or macrolabialism—but are better than others that create confusion over the addressee's distinguishing features. I'm told that many letters containing important messages that don't spell out the address explicitly and don't have directions have been opened so as to discover for whom they're intended, and this has been a cause of injury to both sender and recipient." Here ends their dialogue. 2.8.8

Be informed here that, when the the *khawājā* in question received the Fāriyāq's epistle, he was sick and so did not answer immediately. As a result, the Fāriyāq was left waiting days for his reply and finally came to 2.8.9

لم يجبه على الفور* فبقى الفارياق ينتظر جوابا اياما حتى اعتقد ان سجعه كله ذهب باطلا * اذ لم يكن يعلم السبب وكان فى خلال ذلك دائم الفكر والقلق * فانا الان ادعه فى هذه الحالة منتظر الجواب * وادع صاحبه يتداوى حتى يطيب *

واعرّج قليلا على منازل الالقاب والقاب المنزلة المتعارفة

وقتئذ بشرط ان تسمحوا لى

بان انتقل الى فصل

اخر

وهو

*

believe, being unaware, as he was, of the reason, that all his rhyming had gone for nought, and during this time he was prey to constant worry and anxiety. I shall leave him now in that state, waiting for an answer, and leave too the one who is to send it to take his medicine and get better, and turn aside for a little to the ranks of titles and titles of rank then recognized,

on condition that you allow me
to move on to a
new chapter,
namely
. . .

الفصل التاسع

فيما اشرت اليه

حد اللقب عند المشرقيين انه هنة ناتئة او زنمة او علاوة زائدة متدلدلة تناط بكونيّة ١،٩،٢
الانسان * وعليه قول صاحب القاموس العلاَقَى الالقاب لانها تعلّق على الناس *
وعند المغربيين اى الافرنج انه جُلَيدة تُكَوَّر فى الجسم * وشرح ذلك ان الهنة يمكن
قطعها واستئصالها مع السهولة وكذا الزنمة وكذا العلاوة يمكن ركسها وقلبها * فاما
الجليدة فلا يمكن فصلها عن الجسم الا بايصال الضرر الى صاحبه * وحاشية
ذلك اذ الشرح لا بد له من حاشية ولولاها لم يفهم له معنى * ان الزمنة عند
اهل الشرق غير موروثة الا ما ندر* فان لكل قاعدة شذوذا * والجليدة عند
الافرنج متوارثة كابرا عن صاغر* مثال ذلك لقب الباشا والبيك والافندى والاغا
بل الملك انما هو محصور فى ذات الملقب به فلا ينطلق منه الى ولده * فقد يمكن
ان يكون ابن الوزير او الملك كاتبا او نوتيا * فاما عند الافرنج فلا يصح ان يقال
لابن المركيز مريكيز او مركيزىّ * وقد يجتمع مطلق الزنمة والجليدة فى جهة بقطع
النظر عن كون الاولى متناهية والثانية غير متناهية * وذلك ان اصل كلّ منهما
فى الغالب أُكال يحدث فى ابدان ذوى الامر والنهى لهيجان الدم عليهم * فلا
يمكن تسكين هذا الهيجان وحكّ هذا الأُكال الا باحداث الهنة او الجليدة *

Chapter 9

That to Which I Have Alluded

The definition of a title in the minds of Orientals is that it is an insignificant fleshy protuberance or a flap of skin,[111] or an extra bag hung onto an already loaded camel, that dangles from a man's essential being. The author of the *Qāmūs* has said, "*ʿalāqā* means 'titles,' because they are hung onto people (*li-annahā tuʿallaqu ʿalā l-nās*)." To Occidentals, which is to say Franks, it is a second skin that wraps itself around the body. Our commentary on this is that an insignificant protuberance may be cut off and totally excised with ease, and the same goes for the skin tag and the extra bag, which may be overturned or inverted; the second skin, however, cannot be removed from the body without harm to its owner. Our super-commentary—for every commentary must have a super-commentary, however incomprehensible—is that the skin flap is not hereditary among the people of the East, or only rarely so (and every rule must have its exceptions). Among Franks, on the other hand, the second skin is passed from older to younger by inheritance. Examples of the former are the titles *Bāshā* ("Pasha"), *Bēh* ("Bey"), *Afandī* ("Effendi"), and *Aghā* ("Agha"). Even *Malik* ("King") is limited in its application to the person so titled and is not extrapolated from him to his son, for the son of a minister or a king may be a clerk or a sailor. Among Franks, however, it is incorrect to refer to the son of a marquis as a "marquisito" or as being "marquisate."[112] Regardless of the fact that the former is finite and the latter infinite, the essential meanings of "skin flap" and "second skin" may converge at a certain point, in that both generally have their origin in an itch that affects the bodies of those in positions of power because of the aggravation caused them by their blood. Such aggravation cannot be quieted, and such itches cannot be scratched, without creating either a flap or a second skin. 2.9.1

وبيانه ان الملك اذا غضب مثلا على زيد من الزيدين لذنب اقترفه * ثم بعث اليه ٢،٩،٢
ذلك الزيد بشفيع عريان ليترضاه سكّن هذا الاستشفاع ثورة ذلك الغضب *
واختلطت الكيفية الهيجانية بالماهيّة العريّة فانتجتا جليدة لمن كان يخاف سلخ
جلده * فتحلى بها بين اقرانه حلية موبدة ولم يخف من تداول القرون عليه *
والغالب فى الجليدة ان تحتاج الى جسمين * جسم مغضوب عليه وجسم شافع
فيه * والغالب فى الهنة ان تحتاج الى جسم واحد فقط * ومن الهنات هنات ٣،٩،٢
كنائسية وهى على نوعين * ترابيّة وهوائية * فالترابية ما كان لها مستقر او
اصل فى التراب فتنمى فيه وتثمر * وذلك كان يكون جاثليق من الجثالقة مستقرّا
فى دار او دير * وله إمرة على الناس يودون اليه عشورا ونحوه * فهو يامر فيهم
وينهى ويحكم ويقضى بحسب الاقتضآء او بحسب ما يعنّ له * ولا بدّ وان يكون
عنده كاتب يعى اسراره * وطباخ يشد فقاره * وخازن يخزن ديناره * وسجن
يحبس فيه من خالفه فى رايه او انكر عليه اطواره * وما اشبه ذلك * والهوائية
عكس ما تقدم وذلك كهنة المطران اتاسيوس التونجى صاحب كتاب الحكاكه فى
الركاكه * فان سيّده قلّده هذه الهنة ليحكم بها فى مدينة طرابلس الشام * غير
انه ليس فى هذه المدينة احد من اهل مذهبه حتى يودى اليه عشورا او يطبخ له
طعاما او يكتب له رسالة * فهو متقلد بها لمجرد الزينة فقط جريا على عادة بعض
المتقدمين الذين كانوا يطلقون هنة الامير * على راعى الحمير * وزنمة الملك * على
شيخ قرية عَفِك * والغرض من ذلك كله انفراد شخص عن غيره بصفة ما * واذ ٤،٩،٢
قد عرفت ذلك فاعلم ان الخواجا والمعلم والشيخ ليست القابا معدودة فى الهنات ولا
فى الجليدات اذ ليس فى تحصيلها ما يحتاج الى شفيع او اختلاط الكالّى بماهية

The archetype of this would be a king getting angry, for example, with some man or other for an offense he had committed, that man sending him a naked intercessor to placate him, this intercession soothing the eruption of the king's anger, the aggravational modality then combining with the gymnological quiddity, these two forming a second skin around the one who'd been in fear of losing his first skin through flaying, and he thenceforth flaunting this among his peers as a permanent adornment, never again to fear that fate might one day turn on him and gore him. In general, such second skins require two bodies—a body with which someone is angry and a body interceding on the former's behalf—while, in general, the insignificant protuberance requires just one. 2.9.2

One kind of insignificant protuberance is the ecclesiastical, which is of two sorts, the earth-bound and the air-borne. The earth-bound is that which has an abode or place of origin in the earth where it grows and bears fruit; such would be the case, for example, of some "catholicos" abiding in a house or a monastery who has authority over the people, who send him tithes and the like and whom he therefore commands, forbids, rules, and judges according to the requirements of the law, or whim. He is bound to have a secretary to keep his secrets off the *books*, to stiffen his backbone one or more *cooks*, a treasurer to hoard his golden *dinars*, a jail to hold anyone who differs from him in opinion or his ambitions *bars*, and so forth. The air-borne is the opposite of the preceding, an example being the protuberance borne by Metropolitan Atanāsiyūs al-Tutūnjī, author of *The Leavings Pile Concerning Lame Style*,[113] whose master has invested him with it so that he can use it to rule over Levantine Tripoli, even though there are none of his sect in that city to send him his tithes, make him his food, or write a letter for him; he has been invested with it, it follows, simply for decorative purposes, in keeping with the custom of certain ancients, who would give the protuberance of "emir" to one who raised donkeys and "king" to the shaykh of some benighted village. The object of all this is to set one individual apart from the rest by the use of some distinguishing mark. 2.9.3

Now that you have become aware of this, know too that the titles *Khawājā*, *Muʿallim*, and *Shaykh* are not to be considered either protuberances or second skins, because obtaining them calls neither for intercession nor for any pruritic combining with gymnological quiddities.[114] They are merely rags to cover the shame of the naked name that has been given its 2.9.4

عرية * وانما هى خرقة تستر عورة الاسم الذى اطلق على المسمَّى وهى غير مخيطة
فيه ولا مكفوفة ولا مشرّجة ولا ملفوفة * بل هى كالبطاقة شدت الى لابسها
ليعرف بها سعره * الا انه كثيرا ما يقع الغلط فى الصاقها بمن ليس بينه وبينها من
علاقة * فاهل مصر مثلا يطلقون لفظة معلم على نصارى القبط * وكلهم غير
معلِّمٍ ولا معلَّمٍ اذا قلنا انه مشتق من العلم * فاما اذا كان اشتقاقها من العلامة
فلا مشاحّة * ولفظة خواجا على غيرهم واصل معناها كالمعلِّم فبقى الاعتراض فى
محله * فاما لفظ الشيخ فانه فى الاصل صفة من اسنّ * ثم اطلق على من تقدم
فى العلم وغيره مجازا عمن تقدم فى السن * فان الطاعن فى السن يستحصف عقله
ويستحكم رايه وان انكره النسآ * فنُقلت مزيّنة الى من باشر العلم * والذى يظهر لى ٥،٩،٢
بعد التامل ان فى الهنات والجليدات لضررا عظيما على من تحلّى بها وخلا عنها *
الدليل الاول ان المتصف بها يعتقد بمجامع قلبه انه افضل من غيره خَلقا وخُلقا *
فينظر اليه نظر ذى القرن الى الاَجمّ * ويستكفى بهذه السمة الظاهرة عن ادراك
المناقب المحمودة والمزايا الباطنة ويخلد بها الى البلادة واللذات الموبقة * الثانى انه
لو نشبت فيه ربقة زحل يوما من الايام ودارت به دوائره فان لم يجد ذات جليدة
مثله لم يمكنه الجلد مع غيرها * وربما كان يهوى جارية عنده جميلة فى المطبخ او
فى الاسطبل فيحرمه منها ابوه او منصبه او اهله او اميره فيقع تعطيل على اهل
الجمال * وهو امر مكروه بل قد جزم بتحريمه جميع العلمآ * الثالث انه قد يتفق ان ٦،٩،٢
يتزوج بذات جليدة معسرة مثله غير موسرة * فاذا ولدت له اولادا لم يمكنه
ان يحضر لهم شيخا يعلمهم فى داره * ويستحيى ان يبعثهم الى المكتب ليتعلموا
مع جملة اولاد الناس * فتغدو اولاده من العجماوات ويتسلسل ذلك فى ذريتهم

bearer and are neither stitched, tacked, buttoned onto, or wrapped around it. In fact, they are more like a ticket tied onto the one wearing it to show his value. Frequently, however, the mistake is made of attaching them to persons to whom they have no connection. Thus in Egypt, for example, they apply the word *Muʿallim* to Coptic Christians, who are neither *muʿallim* nor *muʿallam*, if we are to derive the word from *ʿilm* ("knowledge"),[115] though if we are to derive it from *ʿalāmah* ("mark"), there can be no objection. They apply the term *Khawājā* to others too,[116] and as its original meaning is the same as that of *Muʿallim*, the same objection holds true. The word *shaykh* appertained originally to one who had reached old age; then it was applied to someone who had advanced in learning and other things, as a figurative extension of advancement in years, for the minds of the elderly are discriminating and their judgment is sound, even if women will have no more to do with them. This distinguishing characteristic was then transferred to those who engage in scholarly pursuits.

After pondering the matter, it seems to me that these protuberances and skin flaps do great injury both to those whom they adorn and those who are devoid of them. The first argument in support of this is that a person who bears one believes, in the depths of his heart, that he is better than others, physically and morally. Thus, he looks at the other as a ram with horns does at one without and contents himself with this external feature instead of seeking to attain praiseworthy qualities and meritorious inner traits, and this allows it to lead him in the direction of moral torpor and vicious pleasure. The second is that, should Saturn's noose get caught round his neck one day and drag him into the orbit of its adversities, if he fails to find a woman with a second skin like his, he'll be unable to withstand those adversities with any other; and it may happen that he fall in love with a beautiful serving girl who works in his house, in the kitchen or the stable, and his father, or his father-in-law, or his other relatives, or his emir, may tell him to have nothing to do with her, in which case beautiful girls will be left high and dry, which is regarded by Islamic law as reprehensible—nay, the scholars have all asserted authoritatively that it is absolutely forbidden. 2.9.5

The third is that it might happen that he marry a woman with a second skin who is as badly off as he and not well-heeled. Then, if she bears him children, he will lack the means to bring them a shaykh to teach them at home and he'll be too embarrassed to send them to the local school to learn 2.9.6

الى ما شا الله * الرابع ان الهنة والجليدة تقضيان على المتصف بهما بنفقات لا قّة * وتكاليف شاقة * تقضى به التفريط والا سراف * والتهالك والا شراف * وربما اوصلته اخيرا الى انشوطة حبل من مسد * الخامس ان الا نسان من اصل الفطرة ليس له هنة ولا جليدة فاحداثهما فيه بعد ذلك امر مغاير للطبيعة * او فى الاقل من الفضول او من البطر * وهناك ادلة اخرى اضربنا عن ايرادها

خوف الا طالة * فقد تبين لك ان الخواجا المشار اليه كان غير

ذى هنة ولا جليدة * ولعله كان يحصل على

احداهما لولا ميله بالطبع الى

الادب * ولكن

لكل شى

آفة *

along with everyone else's. Should this be the case, his children will grow up unlettered, and the process will repeat itself with their offspring for as long as God wills. The fourth is that both protuberance and second skin impose upon those who bear them devastating expenses and catastrophic costs, driving their owner to excessive outlay and *profligacy*, to collapse and imminent *bankruptcy*, which may even lead him, in the end, to the noose of a palm-fiber rope. The fifth is that humans in their native state have neither protuberance nor second skin and to add them at a later stage is contrary to nature, or at least a form of meddling or recklessness. Other arguments exist, but I have decided not to mention them here for fear of going on too long.

At least it must be clear to you by now that the Khawājā in question was
possessed of neither
protuberance nor second skin,
though perhaps,
had it not been for his natural inclination toward poetry,
he might have acquired one
or the other.
But everything has its drawbacks.

الفصل العاشر

في طبيب

مصح الله ما بك من السقم ياخواجا ينصر او مسح او مزح * على حدّ مَن قرا ١,١٠,٢
الصراط والسراط والزراط * ومن قال اجعلى فديتك بصاقا او بساقا او
بزاقا * انك غادرت الفارياق فى وسواس وبلبال * فهو ينتظر الجواب منك فى
الغدوّ والاصال * قال انى ليحزننى كثيرا ان قد بلغنى كتاب صاحبك وانا محموم
موجع الراس فلم يمكن لى ان اعجل اليه بالجواب * وكان بودى لو افعل ذلك معما
كنت اعانيه غير ان الطبيب رسول عزرائيل منعنى من الحركة * ولكن لا بدّ من
ان تسمع قصتى مع هذا القرنان * وهى انى اتخمت يوما من اكلة برغل اخذتها ٢,١٠,٢
بحذافيرها فاصبحت وبى غثيان * واتفق ان زارنى فى صباح ذلك اليوم بعض
الامرآء الذين ينبغى ان يقال لما اثبتوه نعم فى موضع لا ولما نفوه لا فى موضع نعم *
فرانى على تلك الحالة فقال ما بك * فاخبرته الخبر * فقال عليك بطبيبى الساعة
فهو امهر الاطبآء لانه قدم من باريس منذ ايام * ولولا ذلك لما اتخذته طبيبا
لى ولاهلى * قلت من عادتى ان اصبر على المرض الخفيف اياما واستعين على
معالجته بالاحتمآء والتوقى فقد يكون فى ذلك ما يغنى عن العلاج * فانى ارى
هولآء الاطبآء يعالجون الامراض بالخرص والتخمين * فما يهتدون الى العلة
والمعلول الا بعد ان تبلغ الروح الحلقوم * فيجربون مرة دوآء ومرة اخرى غيره *

Chapter 10

A Doctor

May God relieve you—or shrive you or deceive you,[117] following those who read *ṣirāṭ* or *sirāṭ* or *zirāṭ* or those who say "Demand the choicest of camels as your ransom!" and read the last word as either *buṣāq* or *busāq* or *buzāq*—of your sickness, Khawājā Yanṣur! You left the Fāriyāq in a state of unease and *apprehension,* waiting for an answer from you, morning and evening, in a state of *tension.* Replied the poet, "It grieves me greatly that your friend's letter should have reached me while I was feverish and had a headache, thus preventing me from responding quickly. I would have liked to do so, despite my sufferings, had not the doctor, envoy of 'Azrā'īl,[118] forbidden me to move. But you must hear the story of what happened to me with that cuckold. 2.10.1

"One day, I got indigestion from eating bulgur that I'd bolted down, lock, stock, and barrel, so that the next day I was ill and nauseous. It so happened that I was visited that morning by one of those emirs to whom, when they insist that something is thus and so, you have to say 'Yes' instead of 'No' and when they insist that it isn't, you have to say 'No' instead of 'Yes.' Seeing me in that state, he asked, 'What ails you?' so I told him what had happened. 'You must let my doctor see you right away,' said he. 'He is the most skillful of all doctors because he just arrived from Paris a few days ago. Were it not so, I wouldn't have taken him on as a physician for me and my family.' 'It is my custom,' I said, 'to endure minor illnesses for a few days, and seek to cure them through dieting and precaution, for this may render medicines unnecessary. I find that doctors treat illnesses by conjecture and guesswork, and, by the time they arrive at cause and effect, one's soul is almost coming out of one's gullet, for they try one medication this time and another the next.' 2.10.2

قال لولا ان المرض قد بلغ منك ما قلت هذا الكلام فلا بد من احضاره الان * ٣،١٠،٢
وما زال بى حتى بعثت اليه خادمى حيآ وخجلا * ثم خطر ببالى ان الآدِب عندنا
من فرط كرمه قد يجبر المادوب على الاكل * وربما القمه بيده ما تعافه نفسه *
ولكن لم اسمع ان احدًا تكرم بان يجبر غيره على علاج * فلم اتمالك ان ضحكت *
قال ما اضحكك * قلت لا شى * قال ما احد يضحك من لا شى فلا بد وان يكون
هناك شى * قلت فكّرت فى ذلك الطبيب الذى عاد مريضا فقال لاهله آجركم
الله فى مريضكم * فقالوا انه لم يمت بعد * قال يموت ان شاء الله * فضحكت *
قال لا عليك فان هذا الطبيب ليس مثل ذاك * وبعد فانك عزب ليس لك اهل
حتى يقول لهم ذلك * ثم ما عتّم الخادم ان جآ به وهو اشد منى مرضا ونحولا * ٤،١٠،٢
فالظاهر انه لم يكن له شغل حتى يخرجه من داره * فلما ان دخل جس نبضى ونظر
الى لسانى ثم زوى ما بين حاجبيه واطرق الى الارض وهو يهسّ اى يحدث
نفسه * ثم رفع راسه وقال لخادمى هات الطست * قلت ما تريد ان تفعل وانا
صاحب جثتى افلا تشاورنى * قال انه الفصد او الرمس * قلت هداك الله
ياشيخ انها اكلة برغل مع اللحم مما تسميه الناس كبيبة * قال انا اعرف ذلك انا اعرف *
انكم يااهل الشام كلكم تموتون بهذه الكبّة * فقد شيعت بها حين كنت فى بلادكم
اكثر من مئة جنازة * نعم هى الكبّة * قلت فى عجانك ان شا الله * قال لا تدخل
الكبة فى عجينى مطلقا * فالتفتّ الى الامير وضحكت فظهر لى انه هو ايضا لم
يفهم * وفى الاختصار فانه ما زال هو والامير يخطّئان رايى حتى استسلمت ٥،١٠،٢
للهلكة ومددت يدى * فاعمل فيها مبضعه اعمال السكين فى بطيخة * فخرج الدم
متبعقا حتى دخل فى عينيه فاطلق يدى وذهب ليغسل وجهه * ثم جا بعد هنيهة
وقد غشى علىّ * فتداركنى خادمى بمآ الزهر وغيره والامير ناظر الى دخان تبغه

"'If the disease hadn't already got to you,' he replied, 'you wouldn't be talking this way. We must bring him now,' and he kept on at me until, shamefaced and embarrassed, I sent my servant to him. Then it occurred to me that, among us, a host, from an excessive sense of hospitality, may force a guest to eat and even sometimes feed him with his own hand something the other cannot stomach but that I'd never heard of anyone doing the honors by forcing another to take medical treatment, so I couldn't stop myself from laughing. 'What's making you laugh?' he asked. 'Nothing,' I responded. 'No one laughs at nothing,' he said. 'There must be something going on.' I said, 'I thought of the doctor who visited a sick man and said to his family, "God recompense you for your loss!" "He isn't dead yet," they replied. "He will be soon, God willing," said the doctor, so I laughed.' 'Don't worry about it,' said the emir. 'This doctor isn't like that one, and anyway you're a bachelor and don't have any family he could say that to.' 2.10.3

"Presently, the servant came back with the doctor, who was sicker and thinner than me, for it seems he had no work that would take him out of the house. When he entered, he felt my pulse and looked at my tongue. Then he furrowed his brows and looked down at the ground, soliloquizing (which means 'talking to himself'). Next he raised his head and told my servant, 'Bring the basin.' 'What do you want to do?' I asked. 'It's my body. Shouldn't you consult me?' 'Either I bleed you or it's the tomb,' he said. 'God guide you aright, old man!' I said. 'All I did was eat bulgur with meat—what people call *kubaybah*.' 'I know that,' he said, 'I know. You Levantines—you all die of eating that *kubbah* stuff.[119] I must have buried a hundred cases when I was in your country. It's definitely the *kubbah*.' 'A *kubbah* up your patootie, God willing!' I said. 'There's no *kubbah* whatsoever in my patties!' he replied.[120] I turned to the emir and laughed, but, as far as I could tell, he didn't get it either. 2.10.4

"To keep it brief, he and the emir kept on finding fault with my opinion until I surrendered myself to destruction and put out my hand, and he worked away at it with his scalpel like someone cutting a watermelon with a knife and out came the blood, spurting everywhere, some of it even getting into his eyes, which made him let go of my hand and go off to wash his face. When he returned after a short while, I had fainted, so my servant ministered to me with orange-blossom water and other things, while the emir gazed at the smoke made by his tobacco and the doctor whispered in his ear. When I 2.10.5

والطبيب يسارّه * فلما افقت ربط يدى وخرج مع الامير وقالا احترز لنفسك
فانا نعودك عن قريب * فقلت فى نفسى لا اعادكما الله * فلما كان الغد جآ الطبيب ٦،١٠،٢
متابّطا اعشابا * فقلت ما هذه الاعشاب * قال حقنة قلت تكفينى واحدة *
قال ان الامير يقول لك ينبغى ان تحتقن ان لم يكن لنفعك فلاكرامه * فقلت فى
نفسى لا باس باكرامه فى الحقنة * الا انه قد خالف العادة مرة اخرى فان عادة
المزور ان يحلّف الزائر باسم الله واسمآ ملئكته و رسله وكتبه واليوم الآخر وبالبعث
ان ياكل او يشرب شيا على اسمه * وهذا زائر يلحّ علىّ بالاحتقان * ثم استعملت
الحقنة * ثم وافانى اليوم القابل ومعه حقة * فقلت وما بيدك * فقال مسهل
مما اصنعه للامير * فاستففته * ثم جانى فى الغد وليس بيده شى * فاستبشرت ٧،١٠،٢
وقلت له قد وَهَنت منّى القُوَى بقوة المسهل * قال ينبغى ان تتخذ اليوم حمّاما
فى غاية السخونة لكى تعرق وقد جرّبته فى ذوى الامير فوجدته بعد المسهل انفع ما
يكون * ثم تولّى هو بنفسه تسخين المآ وانزلنى فى مغطس كنت اتخذته لنفسى * فلما
دخلته لفحنى حرّه حتى غشى علىّ بعد ان سمط جلدى * فأُخرِجت منه على رَمَق
من الحياة * فتداركنى خادمى بالمشمومات حتى افقت * ثم جانى فى الغد وليس ٨،١٠،٢
بيده شى ففرحت ايضا وقلت لعله قد نفد ما فى وطاب علاجه وكان الحمّام آخر ما
عنده * فسالنى عن حالى * فقلت هو كما ترى * قال عليل * قلت واىّ عليل *
قال ينبغى ان تفصد * فسقط علىّ كلامه كجلمود صخر حطّه السيل من عل *
وقلت كانك تهمّ باعادة ما صنعته اوّلاً فمتى ينتهى هذا الدور * قال لا بدّ ان احد
هذه العُلُوج (جمع علاج) يزيل ما بك * قلت اجل اما الاول فهوانت واما الثانى
فهودمى او روحى * ثم تجلّدت وتمنعت وقلت له قل للامير انى والحمد لله عزب
فلاى سبب يحاول تسفيرى سريعا فلم يفهم * وقال انى اريد ان افصدك لا ان انقل

revived, he bandaged my hand and left with the emir, the two of them telling me to look after myself and that they'd come and visit me soon, while I said, under my breath, 'May God never bring you back!'

"Next day, the doctor returned with an armful of medicinal plants. 'What are those plants for?' I asked. 'An enema,' he replied. 'One will be enough for me,' I said. He replied, 'The emir says you have to take enemas, if not for your sake, then to do him honor.' 'There's no harm in honoring him with an enema,' I thought to myself, 'but once again he's going against custom, which is that the person visited should adjure the visitor by the name of God and the names of His angels, His apostles, His books, and the Last Day and the Resurrection, to take something to eat or drink for his sake, but here it's the visitor, and he's insisting on flushing me out!' Then I took the enema. The next day, he showed up again, carrying a small pot. 'What's that in your hand?' I asked. 'A laxative,' he replied, 'of the kind I make specially for the emir.' So I swallowed it down. 2.10.6

"Then the following day he came to me carrying nothing, so I rejoiced and told him, 'The laxative was so powerful it's drained me of all my strength.' 'Today,' he replied, 'you have to take the hottest bath possible, so that you sweat. I have tried it before on the emir's family and found it to be most beneficial.' He undertook to heat the water himself and made me get into a bathing tub that I'd bought. When I got in, the heat struck me with such force that I fainted, though it had time to scald my skin first. I was pulled out at my last gasp, and my servant ministered to me with pungent herbs until I recovered. 2.10.7

"The day after that he came to me carrying nothing, and I was again delighted and thought, 'Maybe he's exhausted his box of tricks and the bath was the last thing he had up his sleeve.' He asked me how I was. 'As you see,' I responded. 'Sick?' he said. 'Sick indeed,' I answered. 'You have to be bled,' he said, his words falling on my ears like 'a rugged boulder hurled from on high by the torrent'[121] and I said, 'It seems you're going back to what you began with. When will this cycle end?' He replied, 'One of these *giaours* (plural of *cure*)[122] is bound to get rid of what you have.' 'That's true,' I said. 'As for the first named, that's you, and as for the second, that's my blood or living spirit,' and I stood firm and refused, saying, 'Tell the emir that I am, thank God, a bachelor, so why is he trying to send me away from here so quickly?' but he didn't get it.[123] 'I want to bleed you,' he said to me, 'not be 2.10.8

٩،١٠،٢ عنك * قلت فانا لا اريد فارحنى اراحك الله * فاولانى كتفه وولّى * ثم لم يلبث ان بعث الىّ برقعة الحساب وتقاضانى فيه خمسمائة قرش * فانه زعم ان عنده ناسا فى الريف من الفلاحين يجمعون له تلك الاعشاب مع انها مما ينبت على حيطان ديار القاهرة * وماكفاه ذلك حتى توعّدنى بانى اذا تاخّرت عن قضائه كما تاخرت عن الفصد الثانى يرفع القضية الى ديوان قنصله * فنقدته المبلغ المذكور بتمامه

١٠،١٠،٢ وقلت لا بارك الله فى الساعة التى ارتنا وجوه العجم وادبارهم * وها انا اليوم والحمد لله احسن حالا * ومرادى ان اجتمع بصاحبك * ولكن لا بد من اكرامه قبل الزيارة * ثم انه امر غلامه بان ينتقى تختا من الثياب الفاخرة وان يتوجه بها الى الفارياق * فانه كان وقتئذ مبرنطا * ثم كتب له رسالة وجيزة مع ابيات قليلة تتضمن استدعاءه الى مجلسه فى اليوم القابل * وتفصيل ذلك ياتى فى الفصل التالى *

your messenger.' 'But I don't want you to,' I said, 'so grant me rest, may God grant you the same.'

"At this he showed me his back and departed, sending me soon after his 2.10.9
bill, in which he demanded of me five hundred piasters, for he claimed to have people in the countryside among the peasants who collected those medicinal plants for him, even though they were the same that sprout from the walls of Cairo's houses. Not content with this, he threatened that, if I was as reluctant to pay as I had been to get bled the second time, he'd bring a case against me in his consul's office.[124] I paid him, therefore, the aforementioned sum in full, saying to myself, 'God damn the hour that showed us foreigners' faces, and their backsides!'

"Now here I am today, feeling much better, and I'd like to meet with your 2.10.10
friend. Before the visit, though, I must do him some honor"—and he ordered his servant to select a trunkful of fine clothes and take it to the Fāriyāq, who at the time was dressing as a Frank. Then he wrote him a short message with a few lines of verse inviting him to his salon the following day, details to come in the following chapter.

الفصل الحادى عشر

في انجاز ما وعدنا به

كان للفارياق صاحب من الديار الشامية يتردد عليه * فلما وفد الخادم بالرسالة ١،١١،٢
وتخت الثياب كان هو حاضرا * فقال للفارياق انا اذهب معك الى الخواجا ينصر
فقد سمعت بذكره غير مرة واحبّ ان اراه * فقال له الفارياق ولكن لعلّ فى الإِزْوآ
اسآة ادب فى حق المَزُور(١) * فان المدعوّ لا يليق به ان يستصحب احدا
معه * قال لا باس فان هذه عادة الافرنج فاما فى مصر فيمكن للمدعوان
يستصحب ايّا شآء * وللمستصحَب ايضا اذا لقى واحدا فى الطريق من معارفه ان
يستصحبه * ولهذا ايضا ان يستصحب آخر وللاخر آخر حتى يصيروا سلسلة
اصحاب * بحيث لا يكون فى السلسلة حلقة انثوية * وكلهم يكلمون المَزور من دون
محاشاة وينالون منه الاكرام ويترحَّب بهم * ولا يمكن ان يسال احدا منهم فيقول
له وانت ما حاجتك واىّ كتاب وصاة عندك الىّ * وما اسم زوجتك او اختك
وما سنّهن * وفى اى حارة يسكنّ كما تفعل اصحابك الافرنج * فلا تخش من الرجل
جَبْها * وبعدُ فان لنا عليه دالّة الادب * فهى تغنينا عن دالّة النسب * فاجابه ٢،١١،٢
الى ذلك وسارا اليه معا * والفارياق يرفل بثيابه وقد اتخذ له عمامة كبيرة * فتذكر
يومئذ عمامته بالشام وسقطته تلك المشئومة * فلما استقرا بمجلس المشار اليه بعد

(١) ازوى الرجل جآ ومعه آخر *

Chapter 11

The Fulfillment of What He Promised Us

The Fāriyāq had a friend from the Damascene lands who used to visit him, and he was with him when the servant arrived with the letter and the set of clothes. He told the Fāriyāq, "I shall go with you to see Khawājā Yanṣur, for I have often heard him mentioned and would love to meet him." "But," the Fāryaq said, "turning up with another (*al-izwāʾ*)(1) may be considered a discourtesy to the person visited, for it is inappropriate for an invitee to bring a companion with him." "Forget about that," said his friend, "for it's the Frankish way. In Egypt, on the other hand, a guest may bring anyone he wishes, and his companion too, should he come across any acquaintance on the way, has the right to bring him along with him, and the latter too has the right to bring along another, and that other another, till they turn into a chain of friends, the only condition being that none of the links be female; all of them, without exception, talk to the person being visited, are treated to his hospitality, and are welcomed by him. He can't question one of them and say, 'You! What do you want, what letter of introduction do you have, and what are the names of your wife and your sister, and how old are they, and on what street do they live?' like your Frankish friends. Have no fear that the man will receive us harshly. And anyway, we have literature to commend us to him, and that will relieve us of the need to invoke pedigree." 2.11.1

(1) *al-izwāʾ* is "a man's coming accompanied by another."

So the Fāriyāq agreed to his request, and they set off to see the man together, the Fāriyāq strutting along in his new clothes; he had also got himself a large turban that made him think of his turban in Lebanon and his ill-fated fall.[125] When they'd settled down in the aforementioned salon and been greeted and received with warmth and welcoming faces, and once 2.11.2

الترحيب والتلقى بالبشر والبشاشة * وبعد معاقبة اوحشتنا لآنستنا * ومداركة آنستنا لاوحشتنا * ومواترة سلامات طيّبين * وموالاة طيبين سلامات * كما جرت العادة عند الخاصة والعامة * قال الخواجا للفارياق قد سرّنى قدومك الى هذه الديار والله سبحانه وتعالى قد اسبغ علىّ نعمته لا شركك فيها * فقد قال الشاعر

قالوا البعال الذّ شى يشتهَى   فاجبتهم هذا ضلال بيّن
اسدآ معروف الى ذى حاجة   اشهى وابقى وهو امر هيّن

على انى لا اقول ان بك حاجة الىّ لكنى لحنت من شكواك انك محتاج الى ذى مروة يواسيك او يسليك او يتوجع * وقد وجب علىّ القيام بما يسليك ما انت معانيه * سوآء كان ذلك بالمواساة او بالنصيحة * ولا سيما انه قد ظهر لى انك منشّم فى طلب العلم * وقد عانيت القريض * ولكن فى كلامك ما انتقدته عليك * وليس هذا وقت نقد وتقييد * وانما اسالك اىّ كتاب من الادب قرات * فابتدر ٣،١١،٢
صاحبه وقال قرا كتاب بحث المطالب * فقال له لقد عجلت فى الجواب * فان هذا الكتاب فى النحو لا فى الادب * الا انكم ياتلاميذ الجبل تحسبون ان من قرا هذا الكتاب فكانما قد استوعب العربية كلها دون افتقار معه الى شى من كتب اللغة والادب والشروح * وان الطالب منكم اذا اراد ان ينمق كتابا او خطبة فانما يستعمل بعض اسجاع مبتذلة ساكنة الروىّ * خيفة ان يلتبس عليه المرفوع بالمنصوب * ويتطالل الى بعض استعارات باردة * وتشبيهات جامدة * حشوها الالفاظ الركيكة والمعانى المتقلقلة من دون معرفة ما يستعمل من الفعل ثلاثيا او رباعيا * وما يتعدى به من حروف الجرّ * فعند قوله هذا تذكّر الفارياق قول المطران

"We've been looking forward to meeting you" had been followed up with "You bring us good cheer," and "You bring us good cheer" had fallen fast on the heels of "We've been looking forward to meeting you," and after the salutations of kindly men had followed hard on the kindliest of salutations, as is the custom among both elite and commoners, the Khawājā said to the Fāriyāq, "I am delighted with your arrival in these lands and that God, Glorious and Almighty, has granted me His blessing in allowing me to make you my partner here, for as the poet has said,

Sexual congress, they claimed, is the most desirable thing
But that, I replied, is clearly misguided.
A favor done to one in need
Is more gratifying, of more lasting effect, and easily provided

"—which doesn't mean I'm saying that you're in need of me, though I did infer from your complaint that you require a doughty friend to keep you in good cheer, or shore up your spirits, or share your sorrows; and the duty of keeping your spirits up so long as you are preoccupied, whether by providing consolation or offering advice, has fallen to me, especially as it's clear to me that you are new to the pursuit of knowledge and interested in rhyming. Notwithstanding this, there are things in your writing that I might criticize you for, though this is not the time for criticism or the listing of faults. I would like to ask you, however, what books of literature you have read."

Here his friend took the lead in anwering in his stead and said, "He's read 2.11.3
the *Baḥth al-maṭālib* (*The Discussion of Issues*)."[126] "You were too quick with your answer!" the Khawājā replied. "That's a book on grammar, not literature, though you students from the Mountain reckon that any who's read it has effectively imbibed all that the Arabic language has to offer and feel no need to complement it with any of the books on the lexicon or literature, or the commentaries. When one of you students wants to pen a book or a speech in high-flown style, he uses a few hackneyed rhyme words with no vowel on the rhyme consonant, for fear of getting confused between *-u* and *-a*.[127] They strain to produce a few mediocre metaphors and rigid similes that they've stuffed with feeble phrases and faltering figures without any knowledge of which verbs, triliteral or qadriliteral, should be used, or which should be used with a preposition to make them transitive." When the man said this, the Fāriyāq remembered how the metropolitan had written to Qayʿar Qayʿār

لقيعر قيعار واولجت فيها * فذكرها للخواجا المذكور فغلب عليه الضحك حتى فحص
الارض برجله * ثم قال نعم وان لفى كتب الكنيسة كلها اغلاطا فاضحة من هذا ٤،١١،٢
النوع * فقد قرات فى كتاب منها عن بعض الرهبان انه كان من التواضع على جانب
عظيم حتى انه كان كلما مرّ عليه رئيسه يقوم وينتصب عليه * اى له * وعن آخر
انه بلغه عن راهبة ما انها كانت ذات كرامات ومشاهدات * فكان يستمنى دائما
ان يراها * اى يتمنّى * وعن آخر انه كان خرج من ديره وغاب عنه مدة طويلة ثم
رجع فوجد رئيسه الاول قد مات وولى رئاسته احد اصحابه * وانه بعد ان تفاوضا
وتباشرا قلده الرئيس خدمة تهبيب الرهبان ليلاً * اى ايقاظهم من هبّ اذا
قام * وعن بعض المطارنة انه كان اذا وعظ فى الكنيسة ينتعظ له كل من يسمعه *
اى يتّعظ * وغير ذلك مما لا يحصى بل قد ورد فى الانجيل وكلام الرسل كلام
فاسد المعنى ومنشاه فيما اظن جهل المعرّبين * فمن ذلك ما ورد فى انجيل متى خطابا
عن المسيح عمّ * احذروا لا يضلكم احد فانه سياتى باسمى كثيرون قائلين انا هو المسيح
فلا تصدقوهم * والمراد ان يقال ان كثيرا ينتحلون اسمى فيدّعى كل منهم بانه هو
المسيح * وشتان ما بين الكلامين * وفى رسالة مار بولس الى طيموتاوس * ولتكن
الشمامسة ازواج زوجة واحدة * ومقتضاة اشتراك الشمامسة فى بضع واحد *
معاذ الله ان يكون كلامى هذا ازدرآء بالدين وانما اوردت ذلك شاهدا على جهل
من عرّب والّف من اهل ملتنا * نعم ان بعض المطارنة قد الفوا تاليف مفيدة جوّدوا
عبارتها وحرروا معانيها * الا ان الجمهور من اهل الكنيسة جهال اغبيآء لا يعجبهم
الا الكلام الفاسد الركيك * ولقد افضى بنا هذا الاستطراد الى غير الغرض * ٥،١١،٢
فلنعد الى ما كنا بصدده وهو اسعافك ايها الخدين بما يريحك من حمل الخرج *

"*wa-awlajtu fī-hā*"[128] and he mentioned this to the aforementioned Khawājā, who laughed so hard he scuffed the ground with his foot.

"Indeed," he said, "all church books are full of horrible mistakes of that sort. I once read in one, of a certain monk, that he was 'endowed with great humility, to the extent that, whenever the head of his monastery passed him, he stood up *to him* (*'alayh*)' (meaning *for him* (*lahu*)), and of another that 'he was told, of a nun, that she was a wonder-worker and a seer of visions, and he constantly *wanked* to see her' (for he *wanted* to see her), and, of another, that he left his monastery and was absent for a long period; then he returned and found that its former abbot had died and one of his friends had taken over his position, and, after they'd consulted and congratulated one another, the abbot appointed him 'to smut up the monks at night,' meaning 'to wake them up' (from *habba* meaning 'to rise'),[129] and, of a certain metropolitan, that 'when he preached a homily in the church, everyone who heard him stood erected,' meaning 'stood corrected,' and so on and so forth, with too many examples to count. Indeed, even in the New Testament and the words of the apostles there is language whose meaning has been corrupted, the source of such corruption lying, I believe, in the ignorance of those who translated them into Arabic. For example, in the gospel according to St. Matthew, there is an oration handed down from Christ, peace be upon him, in which he says, 'Take heed that no man deceive you. For many shall come in my name, saying, I am Christ; so do not believe them,' but what is meant is that 'many shall adopt my name, and each shall claim that he is the Messiah'—and what a difference there is between the two versions![130] And in St. Paul's epistle to Timothy it is written, 'Let the deacons be the husbands of one wife,'[131] when what is meant is that the deacons should jointly pay one dowry. God forbid that these words of mine should be taken as showing contempt for religion; I cite them only as testimony to the ignorance of those of our community who worked as translators into Arabic and composers of prose. True, some metropolitans have composed useful works excellently expressed and with well turned figures, but the mass of the clergy are stupid ignoramuses who like only poor, lame language. 2.11.4

"This aside has diverted us from our goal. Let us return to what we were about, which was how to help you, my dear friend, relieve yourself of the burden of the bag. Would you be interested in being a scribe in the establishment of a certain rich prince who wishes to set up a Panegyricon[132] in which 2.11.5

هل لك فى ان تكون كاتبا عند رجل من السَّراة الاغنيآ يريد ان ينشى ممدحا يكتب فيه بلغات مختلفة مساعيه ومعاليه * فيكون شغلك فيه فى كل يوم نظم بيتين او اكثر بحسب الاقتضاء * قال فقلت انى ياسيدى ما بلغت من العلم ما يوهّلنى ٦,١١,٢
الى هذه الرتبة * ونحن هنا فى بلد العلم والادب فاخشى ان يتصدّى لى قوم يزيفون كلامى ويخطّئوننى * فاخجل والله بعدها من ان انظر الى وجه مخلوق من البشر * فانى رجل احب الخمول وان بضاعتى فى ذلك لمزجاة * قال لا تخش من ذلك فان اهل مصر وان كانوا قد تقصّوا حدّ العلم وبرعوا فى الفضل والادب على غيرهم * الّا انهم لا يتعنّتون على الناظم او الناثر بلفظة يخلّ فيها عفوا * او بمعنى يخطى فيه سهوا * فانهم اهل سماح ومياسرة * على ان من نبغ فى الشعر ان لم يلق من ينتقد قوله مرة ومن يخطّئه اخرى فلا يمكنه ان يصل الى مرتبة الشعرآء المجيدين * ولو بقى ينظم ابياتا ويودعها سمعه فقط لما عرف الخطا من الصواب قط * فلا يكاد احد يصيب الاّ عن خطا * وقد جرت العادة بين الشعرآء بان ما يستهجنه بعضهم ٧,١١,٢
من المعانى والالفاظ يستحسنه البعض الآخر * فلا يزال الشاعر والمولف بين اثنين عاذل وعاذر * ومخطّئ ومصوّب * ومفسّق ومبرّى * ومعترض ومناضل * وراتق وفاتق * وممزق ورافئ * وخارق وراقع * وحاظر ومسوغ * ومضيّق وموسّع وقائل لمَ وقائل لانّ * حتى ترجح حسناته سيئّاته * وتتداول الناس ابياته * وقد طالما حاول الشهرة اناس بالقول المردود * والكلام المقصود * فمنهم من نظم ابياتا مهملة اى عارية عن النقط فاهملت * ومنهم من التزم فيها الحبك بان يجعل فى اول كل بيت منها حرفا من حروف اسم الممدوح فتركت والغيت * ومنهم من جعل دابه التجنيس والتوريات البعيدة فردّت وزيفت * واكتفوا من ذلك

to record in writing, in different languages, his mighty deeds and noble virtues? Your work there would be to compose each day two or more lines of verse, as needed."

The Fāriyāq went on, "I told him, 'I am not, Sir, a scholar senior enough to qualify for such a rank. Here we are in the land of scholarship and literature, and I fear some group may obstruct my path, claiming that what I say is spurious and erroneous, after which I'll be too ashamed to look any man in the face, for I'm a man who prefers obscurity, and what I have to offer in this respect is but meager.' 'Don't worry about that,' he told me. 'The people of Egypt, though they may have reached the limits of learning and surpass all others in merit and culture, would not pick a quarrel with a writer, be it of poetry or prose, who made a hash of a word *unintentionally* or trashed a trope *inadvertently*. They are a tolerant and easy-going people. At the same time, though, if one who wants to make a name for himself in poetry finds no one on one occasion to critique his work and on another to find fault with it, he will never reach the rank of the truly celebrated poets, and, if he keeps composing verses and trusting to his ear alone, he will never learn to distinguish the incorrect from the correct. Almost no one succeeds without first making mistakes. 2.11.6

"'Also, it has become the custom for some poets to condemn the rhetorical figures and words that others commend, so that the poet or prose writer is always caught between two—between a critic and a commender, a fault-finder and an excuser, an accuser and a defender, an opponent and an ally, a render and a mender, a ripper and a darner, a perforator and a patcher, a forbidder and a permitter, a narrower and a widener, one who asks, "Why?" and one who answers, "Because!"—until, in the end, his good qualities come to outweigh his bad, and everyone circulates his verses. How often people have tried to attain fame through compositions that deserve to be *rejected* and *not accepted*. Some wrote verses using only unpointed letters, meaning those that are devoid of dots, and these were *neglected*;[133] some in their verses cleaved to "binding," by which they make the first letter of each line of the poem one of the letters of the name of the person being eulogized, and these were disregarded and *disrespected*; and some took paronomasia and far-fetched punning as their path, and these were refused and condemned as too *affected*. All that such poets sought from such things was celebrity among their fellows, and they cared nothing for blame or rebuttal, and I pray God 2.11.7

بمجرد الشهرة بين قومهم ولم يبالوا بالتعرض للّوم والتفنيد * وانى اعيذك من ان تعدّ فى جملة هولآء * فانى رايت فى انشائك نزوات افكار لطيفة تدل على قريحة جيدة * وسليقة متوقدة * وبعد فمن ذا الذى ما سآء قط * قال فقلت والله ٨،١١،٢
انلك علىّ لمنتين عظيمتين * الاولى عنايتك بمعاشى * والثانية تنشيطك اياى الى النظم * فقد كنت جزمت بان لا اقول الشعر الا مكتوما عن الناس وها انا لك

ياسيدى من الشاكرين * وبكرمك من الزائرين * ثم

انصرف من عنده داعيا له وقد اضمر

مفارقة الخرجى

فى اليوم

القابل

*

that you are not to be counted among their number, for I saw in your composition hints of refined ideas that point to an excellent *intuition*, and a lively inborn *disposition*. But, to get back to our original discussion, who has never done wrong?'"

Said the Fāriyāq, "I told him, 'By God, now you have two great claims on my gratitude! The first is your concern for my welfare, the second your galvanizing me to write verse, for I had resolved to do so only far from people's eyes. 2.11.8

Behold now, My Master, my *gratitude*
and hear me broadcast, like a lion roaring, your generous *attitude*!'"

Then he left his house, calling down blessings on the other's name,
having decided that he would part company with the Bag-man
the following day.

الفصل الثانى عشر

فى ابيات سَرِيَّه

لم يكن لصاحبنا الفارياق عند الخرجى من الاثقال الّا جثته فقط * فلذا تابّط ١،١٢،٢
طنبوره ووضع دواته فى حزامه وقال له * قد اغاثنى الله وارانى طريقا غير التى
طرقتها لى انت وحزبك الخرجيون * فانا اليوم مفارقك لا محالة * قال كيف تفارقنى
وما اسات اليك فى شى * قال هذا الطنبور يشهد عليك بانك سوئتنى * قال ان
العازف به لا تقبل له شهادة فكيف تصح شهادته هو مع كونه سببا فى جرح شهادة
صاحبه * قال بل تصح كما صحت شهادة حجر ابائك * وانه لينطق بمساويك كما
نطقت اتان جدّك * ويدكّ حصون عِنقاشيّتك كما دكّ المدن بوق ربيبك * قال
ما هذا الكلام * قال وحى والهام * قال لا باس فى ان تعزف به فقد علمت ان
الخادم عن حسد شكاك * قال بل انى عازف به عند من يقولون لى زِد ويُعاد
واحسنت والله * لا عند عجم لا يذكرون اسم الله الا فى الابتهال * قال قد خلّطت
واشططت * قال قد فرّطت وقسطت * قال انك كنود * قال انك من اليهود *
ثم ولّى عنه وهو سامد الراس جاحظ العينين من الغيظ * وسار واكترى محلّا
آوى فيه الطنبور وتوجه الى الممدح * فما استقر به المجلس الّا وورد بشير اليه ٢،١٢،٢
وبيده رقعة فيها بيتان يراد ترجمتهما * فلما عرُضا على مترجمى اللغات العجمية واديت

Chapter 12

Poems for Princes

Our friend the Fāriyāq had no heavy baggage at the Bag-man's house other than his own body, so he took his tambour under his arm, put his pen-box in his belt, and told the man, "God has come to my aid and shown me a path different from that laid down for me by you and your company of Bag-men. Today I shall leave you and nothing shall dissuade me." "How can you leave me, when I've done you no injury?" asked the other. "This tambour," replied the Fāriyāq, "bears witness against you that you did." "If the tambour-player isn't acceptable as a witness, how can the witness of the instrument itself—the reason for the discounting of its owner's witness—be valid?"[134] "On the contrary," said the Fāriyāq "it's as valid as your father's mare's, can announce your sins as loudly as your grandfather's she-ass, and can demolish the castles where you store your peddlers' goods as well as any kingly trumpet!"[135] Said he, "What am I to make of such a *peroration*?" "That it's revelation and *inspiration*!" he replied. "It doesn't matter if you play your tambour," the Bagman said, "for I've discovered that the servant only brought the complaint against you out of envy." "Never!" said the Fāriyāq. "I'm going to play it to people who tell me, 'More!' and 'Encore!' and 'Well done!' and '*Allāh*!'[136] not to foreigners who only say God's name when praying." "You're a trouble-maker and have gone too *far*!" said the man. "And you've let me down and haven't treated me *fair*!" the Fāriyāq retorted. "You're *untrue*!" he said. "And you're a *Jew*!" he responded. Then he turned his back on him, head held high, eyes bulging with fury, and set off, and he rented a room, where he stowed his tambour and made his way to the Panegyricon. 2.12.1

He had barely had time to take his seat before a messenger appeared before him with a piece of paper in his hand, on which were two lines of 2.12.2

ترجمتهما الى جهبذ الممدح انتهت النوبة اخيرا الى الفارياق * فاخذ القلم وكتب

ركب السرىّ اليوم خير جواده   ياليته منا امتطى اكتافا
اذ ليس فينا رامح او رافس   بل كلنا يغدو به رفّافا

فلما قابل الجهبذ هذين البيتين بالاصل وجدهما يشتملان على المعنى اشتمال البطن على الجنين او الامعآ على العَفَج * مع عدم الحشو بالالفاظ التى يستعملها الشعرآ غالبا لسد ما فى ابياتهم من الخلل * فاعجب بهما جدا وقال * هما حريّان بان يفضلا على الترجمة العجمية * فانى لا ارى فيها الا معاظلة الفاظ ولكن لعل هذه عادة القوم فدعهم وعادتهم * غير انه لما اشتهر البيتان عند ٣,١٢,٢
اهل النقد اعترض بعض ان قوله رامح او رافس من الالفاظ المترادفة فتكون الاولى او الثانية لغوا * فالاولى ان يقال جامح او رامح وفيه مع ذلك سجع * واجيب بان للفظة رامح معانى كثيرة منها الثور له قرنان واسم فاعل من رمح اذا طعن بالرمح او صار ذا رمح * ورمح البرق لمع * ورُدّ بان الثور ليس له مدخل هنا بقرنيه * فان الناس لا تركب الثيران وان اشار اليه المتنبى فى الغبب * واسم الفاعل بمعنى طاعن لا يناسب المقام * لان المركوب لا يكون طاعنا *
ثم ورد فى اليوم القابل بشير ثان معه رقعة فيها بيتان اخران فقال الفارياق ٤,١٢,٢

قام السرى مبكّرا لصبوحه   فارتجت الارضون من تبكيره
اَوَما ترى ذى الشمس من شباكه   مدّت اليه شعاعها لسروره

verse that were to be translated, for after they had been presented to those translating into languages other than Arabic and delivered by them to the Grand Panjandrum of the Panegyricon, it was finally the Fāriyāq's turn. He took up his pen and wrote,

The prince this day rode the best of his steeds
  But would that he'd taken his seat on our backs!
Among us there's none that bucks or kicks (*rāmiḥ aw rāfis*)—
  Nay, through him, all of us are turned into hacks.

When the Grand Panjandrum compared these verses to the original, he found that they encapsulated the meaning as the belly does the fetus or the intestines the duodenum, without at the same time stuffing it with the words that poets usually use to fill in the weak spots in their poems. Delighted, he said, "These verses are preferable to the translations made by the foreigners, in which I find only repetition. But maybe such is their way, so let us leave them to their own devices."

However, when the verses became known to the critics, some objected that *rāmih* and *rāfis* were synonymous, so either the first or the second had to be considered an error, and it would have been better if he'd written *jāmiḥ* ("bolts") *aw rāmiḥ*, which, in addition, form a doublet. To this response was made that the word *rāmiḥ* has many meanings, among them "a bull with two horns," and it may be used as the verbal adjective of *ramaḥa* meaning "to thrust with the lance (*rumḥ*)" or in the sense "he became armed with a lance"; there's also *ramaḥa l-barq* meaning "the lightning flashed." To this the riposte would be that there's no way for a bull to get in there with his horns because people don't ride bulls, even if al-Mutanabbī raises such a possibility in the ode of his known as *Al-Ghabab* (*The Wattle*),[137] and that the verbal adjective from "to thrust" is inappropriate since a "mount" cannot "thrust." 2.12.3

The following day a second messenger appeared bringing a piece of paper on which were two more verses, and the Fāriyāq wrote, 2.12.4

The prince arose betimes—all earth shaking
  At that early rising—to partake of his matitudinal potation.
Or could it be that the sun reached out to him with its rays,
  Through his window, on beholding his elation?

فاعترض على البيت الثانى انه غير لفق للاول * واجيب انه متفرّع عليه ومرتبط به * لان الارضين لما ارتجت وخشى العالمون سطوته ترضّته الشمس بشعاعها * وردّ بان ترضى الشمس كان متراخيا عن ارتجاج الارضين فلا يفيد * واجيب بان الترضّى حاصل على اى حال كان * فان الشمس لا يمكنها ان تطلع قبل وقت الطلوع *
٥،١٢،٢ وضحك قوم من هذا التعليل * ثم ورد فى اليوم الثالث بشير آخر فقال الفارياق

نام السرىّ مهنأً بالامس لم يخطر بخاطره الشريف هموم
ان نام نامت امّة الثقلين او ان قام قامت والكرىّ جريم

فاعترض على لفظة الثقلين انها ثقيلة * وان امّة حقها ان تكون امّتا * وردبان اللفظة
٦،١٢،٢ خفيفة ولا عبرة فى كونها مشتقة من الثقل * ثم ورد فى اليوم الرابع بشير آخر فقال

شرب السرىّ فحلّ شرب المُسْكر فاستغن عن فتوى الفقيه المنكِر
اذا اصرّ على الخلاف محرِّم فاعمد الى حدّ الحسام الابتر

فاعترض عليه انه مبالغة قبيحة تفضى الى الكفر وتعطيل الشرع * واجيب عنه بانه
٧،١٢،٢ طبق الاصل * ثم ورد فى اليوم الخامس بشير آخر فقال

خرج السرىّ مع السريّة ماشيا غلسا الى الحمّام كى يتنعما
من كان يدعك جسميهما خُلقت يداه على المدى ان تلثما

فاعترض عليه ان الاولى ان يقال ماشيين * ورد بانه لا محظور منه فان السرى هو الاصل بدليل تغليب ماشيين * ثم اعترض ان الافصح ان يقال جسمهما

Objection was made that the second verse is poorly tacked on to the first, to which the response is that it follows naturally from it and is linked to it because when the earth shook, it scared mankind with its brutal power, and then along came the sun and reassured it with its rays. The riposte to this was that the sun's reassurance would have been feeble compared to the shaking of the earth and so would have done no good, to which the response is that such reassurance is an inescapable fact, as the sun cannot rise before sunrise. Certain persons made fun of this explanation.

The third day, another messenger appeared, and the Fāriyāq wrote, 2.12.5

The prince slept soundly last night
With nary a care in his noble head.
When he sleeps, the nation of men-and-jinn sleeps too.
When he rises, it rises, and then it's a crime to be a-bed.

Objection was made to the word "men-and-jinn" (*al-thaqalayn*) on the grounds that it was "heavy" (*thaqīlah*), and that "nation" ought to have been put in the dual.[138] The response is that the word is light and its derivation from *thiqal* ("heaviness") has no bearing.[139]

The fourth day, another messenger appeared, and he wrote, 2.12.6

The prince drank, thus rend'ring the consumption of wine permitted—
He dispensed with the lawyer's rule that says it's not admitted.
Should any who say it's a sin insist,
The aid of your sharpest sword enlist!

Objection was made to the ugly exaggeration amounting to blasphemy and disregard for the Revelation, to which the response is that it just follows the original.

The fifth day, another messenger appeared, and he wrote, 2.12.7

The prince repaired with his squadron on foot (*māshiyan*)
To the bathhouse in the pre-dawn dark, there to luxuriate.
The pair of hands that has scrubbed their two bodies but once
Are thenceforth something one cannot but osculate.

Objection was made on the grounds that it would have been more proper to say "on their two sets of feet" (*māshiyayn*), to which the riposte would be that there's nothing wrong with "on foot" because appeal to the rule of

او اجسامهما * واجيب بان الافصح لا ينفى الفصيح * ثم قيل انه ارتكب ضرورة بحذف حرف الجر فى المصراع الاخير اذ حق الكلام ان يكون خلقت يداه بان * على ان تثنية اليد هنا لا معنى لها فان الداعك لا يدعك بكلتا يديه * واجيب بانه لا مانع من حذف الجر مع اَنْ * وان التثنية للايذان بان كل الجوارح مخلوقة لخدمة الممدوح * ثم ورد فى اليوم السادس بشير اخر فقال ٨،١٢،٢

خلع السرىّ اليوم نعليه على   مُثنٍ عليه مبالغ فى مدحه
فاستبشروا ياعصبة الشعرآ من   هذا السخآء بيمنه وبسخه

فاعترض عليه بان اليمن والسخ بمعنى واحد * واجيب بانه كقول الشاعر والفى قولها كذبا ومينا * ثم ورد فى اليوم السابع بشير آخر فقال ٩،١٢،٢

حكّ السرىّ اليوم اسفل جسمه   باظافر ظفرت بكل مؤمّل
فالناس بين مصفّر ومرتّل   ومدفّف ومزمّر ومطبّل

فاعترض عليه صرف اظافر * واجيب بان ذلك غير محظور لا سيما وقد وليها قوله ظفرت * ثم ورد فى اليوم الثامن بشير آخر فقال ١٠،١٢،٢

طوبى لمن فى الناس اصبح حالقا   راس السرىّ الاحلس الملحوسا
لا زال محفوفا بلطف الله ما   حلقت[١] له شعرًا شريفا موسى

١ ١٨٥٥: حلتت.

taghlīb as applied to *māshiyayn* implicitly admits that the prince may stand for both.[140] Further objection was made that it would have been chaster to say "the body (singular) of each of the two" or "the bodies (plural) of each of the two,"[141] to which the response would be that chaster does not invalidate chaste. Then it was claimed that he had committed the fault of bending the rules of grammar under pressure from the exigencies of verse by omitting the preposition in the last hemistich, since correct diction would require *bi-an* in place of *an*, not to mention that the use of the dual here in reference to "hands" is meaningless, for the scrubber doesn't use both hands. To this the response would be that one is allowed to omit the preposition with *an*, while the dual is there to announce that the scrubber's every limb was created to serve the object of the panegyric.

On the sixth day, another messenger appeared, and he wrote, **2.12.8**

To a eulogist extreme in his praise this day
  The prince, they say, gave his shoes away.
Rejoice, ye band of poets, at one so free with both wealth (*yumn*)
  And pelf (*sunḥ*)!

Objection was made that *yumn* and *sunḥ* mean the same, to which the response would be that it's the same as when the poet[142] says, "And I find her words to be both falsehood and ballyhooing."

On the seventh day, another messenger appeared and he wrote, **2.12.9**

The prince this day scratched his nether parts
  With nails (*aẓāfir*) that had nailed down (*ẓafirat*) his every aspiration,
So everyone either whistled or chanted
  Or beat the tambourine or blew the pipes or drummed, in jubilation.

Objection was made that that *aẓāfir* should not be treated as though it were inflected, to which the response would be that it is not forbidden to treat it as such, especially given that it is followed by the word *ẓafirat*.[143]

On the eighth day, another messenger appeared, and he wrote, **2.12.10**

Blessed is he who shaves of a morn
  The piebald (*aḥlas*) clean-licked (*malḥūs*) princely pate!
May it remain bordered with God's grace as long as razor
  Can find upon it one noble hair to abbreviate!

فاعترض عليه بان الملحوس غير وارد فى صفة الراس* واجيب بانه لا باس به هنا للجناس * ثم قيل ان محفوفا مع ذكر الراس ثقيلة * واجيب بانها خفيفة بالنسبة الى راس السرىّ * قلت وكان الاولى ان يعاب عليه قوله طوبى لمن * فانه مطلق لا يفيد ان السرى حلق راسه فى يوم معيّن * غير ان الجناس فى المصراع الثانى شفع فى البيت كله * ثم ورد فى اليوم التاسع بشير آخر فقال ١١،١٢،٢

بَسَم الزمـان عن المنى وتنوّرا   لمـا اسـتحمّ سـريّنا وتنورا
ان المعالى من اسافله زهت   والشعر بالشِعر اكسِب مفخرا

فاستحسن هذان البيتان جدا لما فيهما من المطابقة والجناس التامّ وغيره الا قوله مفخرا * ثم ورد فى اليوم العاشر بشير آخر فقال ١٢،١٢،٢

تحب السرىّ واى شهم ماجد   بين البـرية مثله لا يحب
ذى سنّة فُرضت على كل الورى   ان المخالف منهم ليُصلّب

فعيب عليه لفظة تحب واجيب بانها فصيحة بمعنى سعل * ثم ورد فى اليوم الحادى عشر بشير آخر فقال ١٣،١٢،٢

عطس السرىّ فكلنا يبكى دما   وارتاعت الارضون والافلاك
حرس الاله دماغه عن عطسة   اخرى تموت برعبها الاملاك

ثم ورد فى اليوم الثانى عشر بشير آخر فقال ١٤،١٢،٢

Objection was made that "clean-licked" isn't a quality associated with heads, to which the response would be that it was allowable there for the sake of the paronomasia.[144] Then it was claimed that "bordered" in association with "head" was "heavy," to which the response would be that in the prince's case the border was quite light. In my opinion, they would have done better to criticize him for writing "Blessed is he who . . . ," because the phrase is absolute and doesn't indicate that the prince was shaved on a particular day, though the paronomasia in the second hemistich puts in a good word for the line as a whole.

On the ninth day, another messenger appeared, and he wrote, 2.12.11

Time's lips parted to reveal a radiant fate,
The day our prince took a bath and was rendered depilate.
His noble nether parts thus appeared less hoary
And poetry, through his pubes, gained in glory.

These two verses were very well received because of the antithesis and the perfect paronomasia and so on that they contain. Except for the words "in glory."[145]

On the tenth day, another messenger appeared, and he wrote, 2.12.12

The prince coughed (*qaḥaba*), and what glorious and gallant gentleman
Of his ilk, among the human race, has never had a cough?
It's a habit imposed upon all mankind,
And any who hasn't should be hung on a cross!

Fault was found with the word *qaḥaba*, to which the response was made that it is a chaste word meaning "he coughed."[146]

On the eleventh day, another messenger appeared, and he wrote, 2.12.13

The prince sneezed, so tears of blood we wept, one and all,
While both globe and celestial sphere recoiled in horror.
God protect his brains from another such sneeze
Lest it so scare the angels that they die of terror!

On the twelfth day, another messenger appeared, and he wrote, 2.12.14

فسّى الامير فاىّ عرف عاطر   فى الكون فاح واىّ مسك ديفا
ياليت اعضاآ العباد جميعهم   تغدو لنشوة ذا العبير انوفا

فعيب عليه قوله فسّى * اذ التكثير هنا لا معنى له * واجيب بان القليل المنسوب الى السرىّ كثير * وعليه بظلّام للعبيد * فان ادنى ما يكون من الظلم فى حق البارى تعالى كثير * ثم ورد فى اليوم الثالث عشر مبشّران فقال ١٥،١٢،٢

حبق السرىّ اليوم فى وقت الضحى   والجوّ ادكن ليس يسفر عن شَرَق
فتعطّرت ارجاؤنا باريجه   فكان من حبَق له عَرْف الحَبَق

فاستحسنا لما فيهما من التجنيس * ثم ورد فى اليوم الرابع عشر مبشران اخران فقال ١٦،١٢،٢

قد أُسهل اليوم السرىّ فكلنا   فرح ففى اسهاله التسهيل
فاستبضعوا خزاً اليه مطرّزا   وتسابقوا ان البطىَ قتيل

فاستحسن البيت الاول للجناس * وعيب عليه قوله مطرزا * اذ التطريز هنا لا موجب له بل فيه ايلام * واجيب بانه طبق الاصل * وان حق الترجمة ان لا تزيد على الاصل المترجم منه فى المعنى ولا تنقص عنه ولا سيما فى الامور المهمة الخطيرة * وقد كان يجب ان يعاب عليه قوله فكلنا فرح وان علله بقوله ففى اسهاله التسهيل * اذ المتبادر ان التسهيل مسبّب عن حتف الممدوح وكانّ الجناس شفع فيه *

The prince let off a string of silent farts, and what heady odor
Within the universe was spread, what musk unpent!
Would that the limbs of all mankind
Into noses might turn, to inhale that scent!

Fault was found with the word *fassā* ("let off a string of silent farts"), since the repetitive form[147] has no meaning here, to which the response would be that even what is little becomes much when attributed to a prince; a similar logic applies to the words *ẓallām li-l-ʿabīd* ("a (repeated) oppressor of mankind"), [148] since the least degree of outrage (*ẓulm*) against what is due to the Almighty Creator in terms of the ruler's dealing justly with His creation is too much.

On the thirteenth day, two messengers appeared, and he wrote, **2.12.15**

The prince at mid-morn this day let off an audible fart,
The sky being dark, no hint of sun revealed,
And all parts of our land with its perfume were scented
For t'was a fart (*ḥabq*) that the scent of basil (*ḥabaq*) concealed.

These lines were well received because of the paronomasia that they contained.

On the fourteenth day, two other messengers appeared, and he wrote, **2.12.16**

The prince's bowels this day were loosened (*ushila*) and as one
Did all rejoice, for his looseness (*ishālihi*) brought him ease (*tashīl*).
They purchased some silk-wool for him, embroidered,
And rushed to claim that constipation's a fatal disease.

The first verse was well received because of the paronomasia but fault was found with "embroidered" because there's no call for embroidery in this context, indeed, it would cause pain; to which the response was that it follows the original and a good translation neither adds to nor subtracts from the original from which it is taken, especially where important and significant matters are involved. Fault should have been found with the words "as one did all rejoice" (albeit he does go on to explain what he means, by saying "for his looseness brought him ease"), for the hearer's natural first reaction is that the looseness of the bowels will lead to the death of the object of the panegyric; the paronomasia, however, may be considered to draw a veil over this solecism.

ثم ان الفارياق بعد انقضآ هذه المدة الذكية راى من الواجب ان يزور صاحبه ويخبره بما جرى له * فلما تشرف بمجلسه ساله الخواجا عن حاله * فقال له قد كنت اود ياسيدى ان ازورك قبل الان لكن خشيت ان يعلق بناديك اثر من الرائحة التى شملتنى * فقال له لا ضير فى ذلك ولا سيما اذا تعودت عليها * وان ناديّ[1] لا يبرح كل يوم يعبق به امثالها من زيارة امثال السرىّ وهذا شان امّ دَفار * ولكن كيف حالك من جهة المعيشة * قال قد اكتريت لى دارا صغيرة واشتريت حمارا * واتخذت خادمة لتصلح لى الدار * وخادما ليصلح الحمار * وانا الان بجاهك وفضلك فى احسن حال * ثم انصرف من عنده داعيا له * ١٧،١٢،٢

(سرّ بينى وبين القارى) ١٨،١٢،٢

قد كان طبيب الجزيرة نصح للفارياق ان يجانب النسآ اى يبتعد عنهن لا انه يلصق بجنبهن فان فى قربهن حَيْنا له فالنفى قوله كذبا ومينا *

١ ١٨٥٥: نادِيَ.

With this redolent episode behind him, the Fāriyāq decided it was his duty to visit his friend and let him know how things had gone. After he had been honorably received and seated in the man's salon, the Khawājā asked how he was, to which the Fāriyāq replied, "I would have wished, sir, to visit you sooner but was afraid that some trace of the smell that was all over me would fill this gathering of yours." "It would have done no harm," the other returned, "for I am used to it, and not a day goes by in this salon without similar smells filling it from the visits of the Prince and his like, which is an insalubrious calamity. But how are you doing in your everyday life?" "I've rented a small place," said the Fāriyāq, "bought a donkey, acquired a maid to take care of the first, hired a manservant to take care of the second, and am now, thanks to your patronage and bounty, doing very well." Then he left him, calling down blessings upon his head. 2.12.17

(A Secret between Me and the Reader) 2.12.18

The doctor on the island advised the Fāriyāq to set women to one side—meaning to keep his distance from them, not stick to their sides—for proximity to them would be his *undoing*. He dismissed his words as "both falsehood and *ballyhooing*."[149]

الفصل الثالث عشر

في مقامة مقعدة

١،١٣،٢ لا يمكن لى ان ابيت الليلة مستريحا حتى انظم اليوم مقامة * فقد عودت قلمى فى هذا الموضع موالاة السجع * وترصيع الفقر الرائعة للعقل الرائقة للسمع * الشائقة للطبع * فاقول * حدّس الهارس بن هثام قال * بينا انا امشى فى اسواق مصر ٢،١٣،٢ واسرح ناظرى فى محاسنها * واتهافت على النظر الى جَمال شوافنها * فتدركنى جِمال مدائنها * فالطأ بقرار حائط واضبأ بآخر * واجعل يدى تارة على عينى وتارة على ما هو اصغر منها او اكبر * اذ اومأ الىّ فتى من حانوت له * عليه لوائح هيبة ومنزلة * وحَوبة فى الترائب متخلّله * غير متحلله * فقال ان شئت ان تصعد الى هنا ٣،١٣،٢ الى ان ينفض زحام الابل * وتنساغ غصّة هذا الاَزْل الاَزِل * فانك لدينا لمن المقرّبين * وانى باكرامك لقمين * فوجدت دعوته كدعوة الداعى بحىّ على الفلاح * وقلت ما يابى السماح * الّا من فاته الصلاح * وعَمِه عن النجاح * كيف لا وقد اوشكت جوارحى ان تعود مجروحه * وضاقت باحمال ابلكم الارض وهى فسيحه * فابتسم ابتسامة اسفرت عن لحَن للقول سريع * وطبع الى ايلاء المعروف ذريع ثم ٤،١٣،٢ صعدت اليه فوجدت عنده نفرا عليهم عمائم مختلفة * ولهم وجوه مؤتلفة *

Chapter 13

A *Maqāmah* to Make You Sit

I shall not sleep well tonight unless I compose a *maqāmah* first. I have made it the custom of my pen at this point[150] to do nothing but *rhyme*, producing elegant periods that charm the *mind* and are appetizing and pleasing to the ear. I thus declare: 2.13.1

Faid al-Hāwif ibn Hifām in lifping tones, "Once, as I walked through Cairo's markets, my eyes o'er their attractions wandering *aglaze*, the beauty of their sideways-glancing girls absorbing my *gaze*, overtaken by camels from its every *zone*, so that now I was against this wall crushed, now at the foot of that one *thrown*, at one moment placing my hand over my eye, at another over something that might smaller or larger be, a young man signaled to me from a store he seemed to *own*—a youth bearing every sign of prestige and high-standing—with an agitation that pierced one's *chest* and settled there to *rest*. 2.13.2

"'If you like,' said *he*, 'climb up here with *me*, till this crush of camels has *dispersed* and the hideous climax of these distressing straits has passed its *worst*, for you are to us as a close *friend* and to do you honor I *intend*.' I found his invitation as compelling as 'Hie ye to security!'[151] so said, 'None refuses the offers of the *kind* but he who's devoid of righteousness and to the path of prosperity is *blind*. How can I say no, when my limbs are once more about to be injured and the loads on your camels' *backs* leave no place in this land, broad as it is, on which to make *tracks*?' He smiled, indicating a wit quick to *answer*, a nature ever alert to render a *favor*. 2.13.3

"Having climbed up to where he was, I found with him a party of men each wearing a turban of a different *fashion*,[152] their faces full of good-natured *compassion*. After I'd uttered a friendly salutation them to greet and 2.13.4

فلما سلّمت متودّدا * وتبوّأت ما بينهم مقعدا * قال رب الحانوت هل لك فى ان تنتظم معنا فى سلك جدال قد شغلنا من الضحى * وجعلنا له الآذان كِثفال الرحى * فهو دائر على كل منّا بالمناوبه * ومستدرك ختامه باوّله بالمعاقبه * دون دَرَك ومعاقبه * اذ ليس فيه افضآ الى البحث في الاديان * وانما هو امر مباح
٥،١٣،٢ لكل انسان * فقلت ان كان مرجعه الى العقل فقد كلّفتمونى إِدًا * وشططتم فى انتظامى معكم جدًا * اذ لست بصاحب اسفار* بل حليف تطواف واسفار * وان كان الى الطبع فان بى لطبعا سليما * وخُلقا قويما * قال هذا الثانى هو مركز دائرته * وفيصل محاورته * قلت فاملأ اذنى اذا من جدالك * والْقِ علىّ اعدال عِدالك * قال اعلم * فرج الله عنك كل غم * انى انا والحمد لله من المسلمين المومنين بالله وبرسوله * وبوحيه وتنزيله * وان صاحبى هذا الودود * واشار الى احد القعود * هو من النصارى والآخر من اليهود * والآخر امَّعة ما له اعتقاد ولا جحود * وانّا قد تنازعنا كاس البحث فى الزواج * وافضنا فيه كما تفيض من عَرَفات
٦،١٣،٢ الحجّاج * اما النصرانى فانه يزعم ان طلاق المراة مفسدة من اعظم المفاسد * ومندمة تمنى المطلّق بالنَغَص والمكايد * ووجه فسادها على مقتضى زعمه * وقدر فهمه * ان الزوجة اذا علمت انها تكون عند زوجها كالمتاع المنتقل * وكالثوب[١] المبتذل * موقوفة على بادرة تفرط منها * او هفوة تنقل عنها * لم تخلص له سريرتها * ولن تمحض له مودتها * بل تعيش معه ما عاشت فى انقباض وإبجاس * ووحشة وابتئاس * ونكد وياس * وتدليس والباس * واذا انزلته منزل مبتاعها * واعتقدت ان متاعه غير متاعها * وانه لا يلبث ان يلاعنها او يبارئها *

١ ١٨٥٥: كثوب.

found among them a seat, I was asked by the owner of the store, 'In a debate that since the middle of the morning has kept us busy, would you care to take your *turn* (a debate for which we've made our ears like the cloth that's spread to catch the crumbs beneath the *quern*)? From each to each the turn's *relayed*, each one's opening words amplifying, in sequence, what the last one *said*, there being no punishment or consequences to be *paid*, for it's not a matter here of calling religion into *question*; it's an issue into which any may make *investigation*.'

"'You ask of me a terrible thing,' said I, 'and go too far by including me among your ranks, if your appeal be to the *mind*, for I'm no book-worm, but rather one to roaming and travel *inclined*. If, though, your appeal is to natural *intuition*, then mine, naturally, is sound, just as upright is my *disposition*.' 'The second,' said he, 'is the point round which it all revolves, the factor in our discussion that will lead to a *decision*.' 'Fill, then,' said I, 'my ears with your *debate* and throw upon my back the matched loads of argument between which you *hesitate*.' 'Know,' said he, God save you all *grief*, 'that I, to God be thanks, am a Muslim who to God and His messenger, His inspiration and His revelation, owes *belief*. My dear friend here (and he pointed to one of the seated) is a Christian, the other a *Jew*, the next a man with no ideas of his own, who to neither belief nor unbelief will *hew*. Know too that the debate whose cup we've wrested from each other in *turn*, and in which we've taken as many separate ways as pilgrims leaving 'Arafāt,[153] has matrimony as its *concern*. 2.13.5

"'Now, the Christian claims that to divorce a woman is a very grave *sin*, an occasion for regret bringing its initiator naught but trouble and *chagrin*. The proof of its evil, according to his claim and in keeping with his degree of comprehension, is that, once a wife finds she's no more to her husband than a disposable chattel or worn-out bit of *kit*, her presence hostage to any chance mistake or trivial *slip*, she'll never again honestly share with him her *introspection* or grant to him her sincere *affection*. On the contrary, as long as she's with him she'll be depressed and full of *misapprehension*, lonely, sad, bad-tempered, and prone to *desperation*, practicing deceit and *falsification*. If she thinks of him as someone by whom she's been *bought*, believes his belongings aren't hers and that soon enough sworn allegations of adultery will be *brought*, or that he'll leave her, or strip her of her clothes, dress her in those of a *divorcée*, and tell her, "Back to your *family*!" or 2.13.6

او يخالعها او يكسوها ثياب التِّهَّمة * ويقول لها الحقى باهلك * او استفلحى بامرك * او انت علىّ كظهر امّى * او حبلك على غاربك * وعودى الى كناسك * عند اهلك وناسك * فما انت لى باهل * وما انا لك ببعل * لم تحرص على حاجة ولا على سرّ * ولم يهمّها ما ينزل به من الشرّ * وربما خانته فى عرضه وماله * وكادت له مكيدة فضحته بها بين اقرانه وامثاله * وهناك محذور آخر * ادهى وانكر * وانكى واضر * وامضّ وامرّ * وهو ان المراة اذا فركت زوجها بان رأت منه ما تخاف غائلته * لم يهمها ان تربّى عَيّله اوتستكفى عائلته * فان المراة لا تحبّ ولدها الا اذا احبت بعلها * ولا تحب بعلها الا اذا ادام وصلها * وآتاها سؤلها * ومن كان له زوجة يُولها فواده * ولم يخل لها وداده * فاتخذته عدوا خصيما * لا اليفا حميما * فهو جدير بان يرثى له شامته * ويرجع عنه سامته * فان صدره والحالة هذه مورد الشجون * وراسه منبت القرون * ومنزله منزل الاكدار * وحالته فى الجملة حالة اهل النار * الا انى اعترض على مذهب من حظر الطلاق * وتقيد بزوجته دون اطلاق * بان الزوجة اذا علمت ان جسم زوجها قد اُدغم فيها * واصبح سره فى فيها * فصارا فردا لا زوجا * سوآ هبطا وهدة او صعدا اوجا * وانه لا يُفكّ هذا الالتحام الّا بمقراض الِحمام * ولا تحلّ عقدة هذه الكينة * الا بانحلال جميع اجزآء الطينة * انها اذا مرضت مرض هو معها * واذا رات رايا فلا بدّ له من ان يواطئها عليه ويجامعها * نشزت عليه وتنمرت * وطغت وتجبرت * فتارة تسومه شرآ لباس وحُلىّ * وتارة تتعنّت عليه بامر تذيقه فيه الصُلىّ * فويل له اذا حبا * ثم ويلان اذا ابَى * وان غاب عنها ليلة قامت قيامة كيدها عليه * وان تشاغل

"Good luck on your own!" or "You are to me as my mother's back!"[154] or "Your nose-rope's on top of your hump!"[155] or "Return to your covert, [156] among your kith and kin, for you're no family to *me* and I'm no husband to *thee*!" she'll never be solicitous of his secrets or what he may *need* and to whatever evils may befall him she'll pay no *heed*.

"'She may betray him with regard to his honor or his *monies* and lay traps 2.13.7 to make him an object of scandal before his peers and *cronies*. And there's another danger too, more calamitous still and leading to greater *sorrow*, more injurious and harmful, yet more painful and harder to *swallow*, which is that, if a wife hates her husband because of what she's suffered at his hands and fears what havoc he may *wreak*, she'll not bother to care for his children or the welfare of his household *seek*, for if a woman doesn't love her husband, she'll not love his offspring and his *seed*; she'll love her husband only if he maintains their union and fulfills her *need*. Any man who has a wife to whom he does not give his heart and devote his entire *affection* will be taken by her as a deadly foe, not a friendly *companion*, in which case he's to be pitied even by those who observe his misfortunes with *glee* and those who inveigh against him should leave him *be*, for when things reach this point his breast becomes a wellspring of sorrow, his head a place for horns to grow, his home a camping-ground for *ire*, and, in short, his condition that of Those Who Dwell in *Fire*.

"'I, on the other hand, object to those who'd forbid *divorce* and the obli- 2.13.8 gations of their wives *enforce*, on the grounds that, if a wife knows her husband's body with hers is *one*, that his secrets are on her *tongue*, making them like a single person, not a *pair*, whether they plumb the depths or rise to great heights in the *air*, that naught but the file of death this solder can *fray*, naught untie the knots of this condition but the dissolution of their earthly *clay*—so that, should she sicken, he too falls *ill* and, if she takes a stand, he must (un)buckle to her *will*, her every demand *fulfil*[157]—then she'll rebel and *disobey*, play tyrant and insist she have her *way*. One time she'll force him to buy jewelry and *clothes*, another insist on his swallowing some other bitter *dose*; then woe unto him if he *concurs*, and double woe if he *demurs*! If he spends one night away from home, all her guile on him she'll *vent*, and if some profitable business of his distracts him from her, she'll do anything she can to his *detriment*. Thus he makes it his habit to placate and *flatter her*, to play up to and *humor her*, to pay her compliments when she gives him the

عنها بامر له فيه نفع جرّت جميع المضارّ اليه * فدابه التودّد اليها والتملّق * والمداراة والترفق * ومجاملته لها اذا جفت * ومخالقته اياها اذا انفت * وتانّثه معها اذا تذكّرت * وتصعصعه منها اذا تشزّرت * وهل يطيب عيش لمن علم انه طوع لهوى غيره * وان لا مناص له من ضيره * فاما شان الاولاد * وهو الداعى الى تحمّل ٩،١٣،٢
هذا الكُباد * فان الزوجين اذا كانا على حالة النفور والعناد * والخلاف واللِحاد * لم تكن تربيتهما لولدهما الا اغرآء بالاقتدآ بهما * وتدربا على الفساد بسببهما * فيكون اهمالهم من غير تربية عند طلاق امّهم اَوْلى * وان الوفاق هو المصلحة الاولى * على انّا نعلم من التجربة * منذ سنّ الله تعالى الزواج وحبّبه * ان المراة اذا علمت ان لزوجها استطاعة على طلاقها * وتملصاً من وثاقها * حرصت على ان تحبب اليه وتلاينه * وتياسره وتخادنه * وتخالقه وتداريه * وتتلافاه وتراضيه * وتجامله وتسانيه * خيفة ان يتنغص عيشها بفراقه * او تحرَم من خَلاقه * فان لم يحصل بينهما الوفاق * فالطلاق الطلاق * ورای صاحبنا هذا اليهودى قريب مما رايت * فلا يخالف الا فى اسباب الطلاق وهى كيت وكيت * فاما صاحبنا الامّعة * فانه متردد فى هذه القضية المنكعة * فتارة يقول ١٠،١٣،٢
ان الطلاق ادعى الى الراحة * وتارة انه موجب لنكد العيش وصفق الراحة * وطورا يزعم ان المُتْعة او الزواج الى اجل مسمّى اوفق * حتى اذا انقضى يجدد العهد بينهما ويوثق * الى ان يتفارقا عن تراض * ويقضيا لهما وعليهما ولا قاض * فهو اخف على الشَجَ * وانفى للحَرَج * وان يكن يفعله بعض الهمج * وحينا يقول بل التسرّى اسرّ * واهنأ واقر * ان لم يكن من القرينة مفرّ * واونة يختار الاقتصار على خويدمة رُعبوبة * وآونة على وحدة العزوبة * والتناول مما تفيزه به الفرص المرقوبة * واخرى على جب الآلة * ان كان الجبّ ينجى من الحبالة *

cold shoulder and be nice to her if she leads him a *dance*, to play the woman with her when she plays the man, and cower when she looks at him *askance*. Can life be sweet when one knows he's a pawn to the whims of *another* and at his hands condemned to *suffer*?

"'As for the children (the reason for putting up with this pain in the liver), if a couple are in a state of aversion and *contumely*, conflict and *contumacy*, the way they bring them up will be simply an invitation to *imitation*, a training, through their agency, in *abomination*, and how much better it would be to divorce the *mother* and leave them sans upbringing, concord being a factor more important than any *other*. In addition we know—from experience gained since the day the Almighty decreed that marriage be the law and saw that it was *good*—if a woman knows her husband can divorce her and slip from her clutches, she'll treat him lovingly and as she *should*, indulge him and be a good *friend*, go along with his whims and help him *unbend*, put right anything that's wrong and agree with his *views*, compliment him and use language that *soothes*, fearing lest her life become unbearable should he leave her or she be deprived of what he owes her of this world's *joy*, for if there's no concord between them, "Divorce! Divorce!" will be his *cry*. This Jewish friend of ours doesn't differ in his opinion *much*, for he disagrees with me only over the conditions for divorce (which, for him, are such and *such*). 2.13.9

"'As for our wishy-washy *friend*, he's at sea as to where this thorny issue will *end*. Sometimes he says divorce leads to ease, at others that it must disturb life's *calm* and be nasty as a slap with the *palm*. On occasion he claims that a set period for legal dalliance[158] or marriage is more likely to lead to a successful *conclusion*, for even when that ends the contract may be renewed, with official *collusion*, until the two part without any *grudge* and settle it all mutually without recourse to a *judge*, this being less likely to create inconvenience and expose the purse to *ravages* (albeit it's also the practice of certain *savages*). On others he says that, on the contrary, keeping a concubine is more comfortable, pleasant, and restorative for the *listless*, and there is no substitute for keeping a *mistress*. At moments, he decides to make do with a plump little serving girl as wife, at others with the bachelor's solitary *life* (taking any, much-anticipated, opportunities as may be on offer), at yet others to cut off his tackle *completely* (supposing, if we may, that one can slice through such snares so *neatly*).' 2.13.10

قال وذلك انى صعّدت فى درجات هذه الخطّة ونزلت فى دركاتها * وعانيت ١١،١٣،٢ ضروبا من اخطارها وهلكاتها * فوجدت عند كل درجة منها مهواة تغيب فيها الاحلام * وتضيع الافهام * وتَهِن القُوى * ويستطاب التوَى * ويصغر كل عظيم من البلا * حتى كأنّ هذه الحاجة ليست من الحَوج فى شى * وما لها به من صلة لحَىّ * فهى دآء لا آسى له * وثوب قشيب مسموم يسر ناظره وحامله * لكن يقرّح اوصاله ومفاصله * وكل امر فى الدنيا فانما يصح قياسه على عقول الكَيّسى من الناس * ويعالج بالصبر او الياس * الا هذه الحَوبة فان المرجع فيها الى الطباع *

ولا يفيد معه رشد ولا زَماع * ثم اَنَّ انين الثَكلى * وقال وانى ازيد على ما قاله ١٢،١٣،٢ الامعة قولا * ولا اخشى من احدكم عذلا * فاقول ولكم تصدعت قلوب من ذلك الصدع * واشتقت من ذلك الوَمّاح مشاقّ لا يطيقها طبع * وكم من رؤس لاجله دُعكت ورضّت * وعقول اَفِنت وحَرِضت * واعناق دقّت * وعيون لقّت * واسنان هُتِمت * وانوف شُرِمت * وشعور ندفت * ولحًى نتفت * وايدٍ قطّعت * وانساب ضيّعت * وكتائب كتّبت * وكتب كُتبت * (حاشية من جملتها هذا الكتاب) وخيل رُكضت * وسيوف ومضت * ورماح شُرّعت * واحزاب تترّعت * وجبال دكّت ونسفت * وبيوت اقوت وعفت * واملاك حُربت * وملوك استخربت * وبلدان خربت * بل امم تهالكت وفنيت * وقرون اندرجت ونسيت * ثم تاوّه وقال وسلعة نَفدت * ودنانير نُقدت * قال الهارس فعلمت ١٣،١٣،٢ انه قد صدعه الصدع بماله * وعظّه بلهاته عند تغلغله فيه وايغاله * ولذاك كان يفيض فى حديثه ويخوض فيه * ليعلم هل من مصاب مثله وعنده علم ما يشفيه *

"The speaker now declared, 'We're discussing all this because I've descended the staircase of this business from top to *bottom* and suffered each of the kinds of danger and perdition with which it's *rotten*, for at every step I found a chasm into which discernment *vanished* and where reason was *banished*, where strength waned and bankruptcy was to be *relished*, a chasm beside which all other disasters seemed *diminished*, to the point that I became convinced that it plays no useful *role* and benefits not one living *soul*. It's a sickness none can cure, a smart but poisoned garment that pleasure to those both who see and those who wear it *brings* but ulcerates their joints and *limbs*. With the exception of this *curse*, any matter in the world may be sized up by the astute and dealt with for better or for *worse*, for it all goes back to the individual's *disposition* and neither good sense helps, nor resolute *decision*.' 2.13.11

"Then said he, moaning like a mourning mother, 'To the words of the wishy-washy man I would add what *follows* (and I fear not the censure of my *fellows*): How many a heart has been tied to the *rack*[159] by reason of that *crack*, by reason of that *cleft* how many of all tranquility *bereft*! How many a head for its sake has been softened and *contused*, how many a mind weakened and *abused*, how many a neck *chopped* and eye *popped*, how many a tooth *split* and nose *slit*, how many a head of hair shaved smooth and beard plucked out, how many a hand cut off and lineage *lost*, how many a brigade raised and tome *off tossed*' (a category to which this tome belongs) 'or horse galloped or sword *flashed* or lance flourished or band into battle *dashed* or mountain crumbled and *shattered* or house abandoned, its stones *scattered*, or possession plundered, or king by adversity *crushed*, or land reduced to *dust*—nay, how many a nation has disappeared and been *dismembered*, how many a generation receded and ceased to be *remembered*!' And then he sighed and added, 'Or goods *depleted* and gold coins *deleted*.'" 2.13.12

Said al-Hāwif, "Then I realized that 'the crack' had cracked him in his *pocket*, and its 'uvula' bitten him, once well inserted in its *socket*. That was why he'd gone on at such length in his discourse and waded so *far out*: to discover if any other had suffered as had he and knew of aught that might bring a cure *about*. Now he turned to me, his eyes full to the *brink*, and said, 'And you, what do you *think*?' 'Verily,' I replied, 'it is a very great *woe*,[160] a dilemma fit to make tears *flow*. For long the greatest scholars have been confounded as to the *affair*, and of ever understanding it the wisest of sages 2.13.13

ثمّ التفت اليّ مستعبرا * وقال وانت فما ترى * قلت والله انها لاحدى الكُبَر* ومعضلة تفيض لها العبَر * قد طالما ارتبك فيها العالم النحرير* وضل عن علمها اللبيب الخبير* لا جرم ان معرفة الافلاك وكواكبها * وايشآء معادن الارض وعجائبها * واسرارها وغرائبها * لَاَهْون عليّ من ان اقول فى هذه المسألة نعم اَوْ لا * فما ارى الّا سكوتى عنها اَوْلى * ثم بينا هم يوجبون ويسلبون * ويوجزون ويسهبون * اذا بالفارياق مرّ علينا راكبا على حمار فاره * سامد سامه * فلما بصرت به قلت له نزال نزال * وحىّ على هذا العِدال * فما نرى غيرك جديرا بايضاحه * وبشفائنا من صُماحه * قال فى اى امر مريج كنتم تخوضون * وعن اى نكر مشيج انتم تجيضون * قلنا له فى الزواج * فهلمّ العلاج * فابتدر وقال * على ارتجال *

مسالة الزواج كانت ثم لا تزال طول الدهر امرا معضلا
ان يكون الطلاق يوما حُلّلا للزوج ايّان ابتغاه فعلا
فليس عندى رشدا ان تُحظلا زوجته عنه ولا ان تُعضَلا
ان لم يصيبا للوفاق سبلا فدعهما فليفعلا ما اعتدلا
ايان شاآا طلّقا وانفصلا

قال فضحكنا من افتحاره مالم يذكر فى الكتب *وقلنا له الى حمارك عن كثب * فما نرى رايك الّا بِدّعا *ولقداسات جابة بعدان اصبت سمعا *ثم تفرقنا كما اجتمعنا *وعجبنا مما سمعنا *

are in *despair*. Let there be no misapprehension, knowing each celestial sphere and every *star*, diving where lie Earth's metals and wonders *bizarre*, or comprehending its secrets and things *exotic*, would be easier by far for me than giving a yes or no on such *a topic*. So it seems to me I'd better say nothing.' Then, while they all argued to and fro, at length and in brief, who but the Fāriyāq should come riding briskly *by* on a trotting donkey that bowled along, its head held *high*. Catching sight of him, I called, 'Get down, get down, and hie thee to this locus of *indecision*, for none but you, we think, is capable of ridding us of its reek and presenting the facts with some *precision*!' He asked, 'Into what muddled matter have you *waded* and regarding what muddy miasma do you seek to be *persuaded*?' We told him, 'Matrimony. Now give us your remedy *instantaneously*!' at which he launched into the following, quite *spontaneously*:

The question of marriage has e'er a thorny matter been
    And so for ay it will remain.
If divorce should e'er to the husband
    Be permitted, at the drop of a hat his rights he'll claim.
I don't think it right then that his wife be stopped
    From divorcing him too or from wedding again.
If they can't agree on a friendly way out,
    Let them do what's moderate:
Whenever they want, get a divorce and separate.

"We laughed at his adoption of a position not found in the books in any shape, form, or *way* and told him, 'Back to your donkey without *delay*! We think your opinion's quite *absurd*, and ill you answered though well you *heard*!'[161] Then we split up just as we'd *congregated*, each marveling at what he'd heard *debated*."

الفصل الرابع عشر

في تفسير ما غمض من الفاظ هذه المقامة ومعانيها

ليس فى لغتنا هذه الشريفة ولا فى لغة امة اخرى من الامم لفظة تدل على فاعل ومفعول او فاعلين اشتركا فى فعل واحد للذتهما ونفعهما * واحتاجا الى من يدخل عليهما ليتعرف منهما اى رفع ونصب يجرى بينهما * وبيانه ان لفظة الزواج عندنا معناها ضمّ واحد الى آخر حتى يصير كل واحد منهما زوجا لصاحبه * ولكن من دون قيد مكان ولا زمان * فلو تزوج زيد بهند في سهل او على قنة جبل او كهف فى يوم الاحد او الاثنين او السبت بشرط التراضى بان يكتب الرجل للمراة صكا موذنا بزواجه بها او يشهد على ذلك رجلين لصحّ * هكذا كانت سنّة السلف المتقدمين من الانبيآ وغيرهم كما هو مسطور فى تواريخهم * بل لم يكونوا يقيدون انفسهم لا بالصك ولا بالشهود * اما لفظ النكاح فمعناه احراز امراة على اى وجه كان * وذلك لان عرب الجاهلية لم يكن عندهم آداب للنكاح والطعام وغيرهما حتى جآ الشرع فعرّفه وميز الحلال من الحرام منه * قال ابو البقآ في الكليات — ولكن لم اجده فى فصل النون فان رايته فى غيره انجزت ما وعدت به * وكنت اريد استشهد بكلامه على ان اسم النكاح لم يزل الى الان مستعملا

(margin: ١،١٤،٢ at line 1; ٢،١٤،٢ at line 9; ٣،١٤،٢ at line 13)

Chapter 14

An Explanation of the Obscure Words in the Preceding *Maqāmah* and Their Meanings[162]

There is no word in this noble tongue of ours, or in that of any other nation, for an active subject or a passive object, or two actives, who, having participated in one and the same act for their own pleasure and advantage, are in need of someone to burst in upon them to inform himself as to what kind of "raising" and "erecting" they are engaged in.[163] This may be demonstrated by the fact that our word *zawāj* ("marriage") means the joining of one thing to another in such a way that each forms a conjunct (*zawj*) with its companion without, however, specification of time or place. Thus, if Zayd enters into conjunction (*tazawwaja*) with Hind on a plain or on a mountain top or in a cave, or on a Sunday or a Monday or a Saturday, and provided there is mutual consent to the man's writing the woman a document publicly proclaiming that he has formed a conjunction with her, or he brings two men to bear witness to the same, then all is as it should be. This was the way of the earliest prophets and others, as recorded in their histories; in fact, they didn't even tie themselves down with documents or witnesses. 2.14.1

As to the word *nikāḥ* ("copulation"), it means having a woman, however that may come about. This is because the Arabs of the Days of Barbarism had no conventions governing intercourse, or eating, or anything else. Then the Revelation came and classified the categories of intercourse and distinguished the permitted from the forbidden. Abū l-Baqā' states in *al-Kulliyyāt* (*The Universals*)[164]—well, I can't find it in the chapter on the letter *nūn* but if I come across it in someone else's work, I promise to get you the reference. 2.14.2

I'd hoped to cite what he has to say, namely that the noun *nikāḥ*[165] remains in use until now and occurs in books of jurisprudence innumerable times, 2.14.3

وانه فى كتب الفقه اكثر من ان يحصى * وهو حجة على من انكره من النصارى وعلى من استعاذ من ذكره * وانما استعملته العلمآء من دون محاشاة لاسباب * الاول انه استعمل قديما من الجاهلية فاثبتته العاقلية * الثانى لوروده في القرآن * الثالث لاشتماله على اربعة احرف وفاقا للطبائع والعناصر والجهات * الرابع لورودها في اسرار سور القران * فالنون في ن والقلم وما يسطرون والكاف فى كهيعص والالف في الم والحآ فى حم * الخامس انك اذا قلبت هذه اللفظة بدا لك منها معنيان شريفان * الاول اسم فاعل من حيي والثانى فعل امر من كان * وبه برزت الموجودات الى العيان * وتجلّت الحقائق لذوى العرفان * السادس لخفة اللفظ وحلاوته * السابع لكون اوله يدل على آخره وآخره على اوله * وقد سمى بعضهم هذا النوع دلالة الاول على الاخر وبالعكس * قال وفائدته انه لو استشهد القاضى احدا على فاعله فنطق بالنون والكاف ثم غشى عليه او على القاضى تلجّزا لذلك * عَرَف من بقي غير مغشى عليه بالمجلس القاضوى ما اراده القائل * وكذلك لو طرا عليه عند ادآ الشهادة ما قطعه عن الكلام شوقا وهيبة فلم يسمع منه الا الالف والحآء لدل هذا الجزء الاخير مع قلة حروفه على جميع ما يراد من المدلول * قلت وهو تعليل بديع غير ان هذه التسمية ٤،١٤،٢
لا توجد فى كتب البيانيين والبديعيين * ولست احب الالفاظ الطويلة فالاولى ان ينحت له لفظ من تلك الجملة بحيث يسلم الطرف * فان قلت بل قد استعملت الفاظا طويلة جدا فى وصف البرنيطة بقولك المستقبحة المستفظعة مع انه كان يمكنك ان تصفها بالفاظ قصيرة * قلت كان ذلك من باب مراعاة النظير* فان طول البرنيطة يقتضيه * فاما مدلول اللفظ الذى نحن بصدده فانه قصير*

which is an argument against those Christians who deny this and anyone who throws up his hands in horror when it's employed. Scholars of religion used it without embarrassment for several reasons. The first is that it was used anciently in the Days of Barbarism and that same usage was then confirmed in the Era of Rationality. The second is that it occurs in the Qur'an. The third is that it is composed of four letters and thus accords with the humors, the elements, and the directions. The fourth is that the letters of which it is composed occur among the "mysterious letters"[166] of the chapters of the Qur'an; thus the *nūn* occurs in "*Nūn*. By the Pen and what they inscribe,"[167] the *kāf* in *kāf-hā'-yā'-ṣād*,[168] the *alif* in *alif-lām-fā'*,[169] and the *ḥ* in *ḥā'-mīm*.[170] The fifth is that if you write the word backward, you will find two noble meanings, the first being an active participle of the verb *ḥ-y-y*, the second an imperative verb formed from *kāna*;[171] thus God's creation is *revealed*, the essential truths made manifest to those whose eyes can pierce the veil to arrive at what's *concealed*. The sixth is the lightness of the word on the tongue and its sweetness to the taste. The seventh is that its beginning signifies its end and its end its beginning, this kind of word play being called by some "the signifying of the end by the beginning and vice versa." The advantage this bestows lies in the fact that, if a judge calls on someone to bear witness against the commissioner of such an act and the witness utters the letter *nūn* followed by the letter *kāf*[172] and then swoons, or the judge swoons, from lasciviousness, those left standing in the judge's chambers will understand what the speaker was trying to say. Similarly, should he be overcome in the course of his testimony by such longing and dread that he can no longer speak and all that can be heard from him is the *alif* and the *ḥā'*,[173] this last part of the word, though consisting of only a small number of letters, will provide all the signification that could be asked for.

I declare, "This analysis is indeed elegant. It is not, however, to be found 2.14.4
in the books of the rhetoricians and the stylists. Personally, I'm not fond of long words, so the best thing would be to create a new, shorter, one from that assemblage of letters by keeping only the end.[174] If it be said, 'But you used very long words when you described a bonnet as being *mustaqbiḥah* and *mustafẓi'ah*[175] even though you could just as well have described it with short words,' I reply, 'That falls under the rubric of "maintenance of consistency," for it is required by the height of the bonnet, whereas what is signified by the word in question doesn't take long.'"

ثم انى كنت ابتدات كلاما في اول هذا الفصل ولم انهه فان القلم زلق بى الى معنى ٢،١٤،٥
آخر على عادته * واظن ان الجناب الرفيع او الحضرة السنية لم يفهماه فمن ثم اقول الان * انه اذا كان المراد من الزواج ان كلّا من الزوجين يزاوج صاحبه لنفسه لا لاهل البلد وللمعارف والاصحاب كما كان عليّان ياكل فخذ الدجاجة لامّ عليّ * لم يكن من المعقول ان يدمق عليهما ذو قُبَّعة فيقول للمراة لا تتزوجى هذا لكونه لم يسمّ بطرس * ثم يقول للرجل لا تتزوج هذه لانها لم تسمّ مريم * او ان يقول هذا يوم الاحد لا يصح فيه الزواج * وهذه حجرة لا يحلّ فيها البعال * والّا لصح ان يقول لهما أريانى الميل فى المكحلة * ومثل هذا الكلام لعمرى لا يليق لاحد ان يقوله او يكتبه * ثم ان المراة هى من الاشيآء التى لكثرة تكرر النظر اليها كالشمس ٢،١٤،٦
والقمر لم يودّ العقل حق اعتبارها * وبيانه ان الله عز وجل خلق المراة من الرجل لتكون بمنزلة معين له على مصالحه المعاشية ومونس له فى وحشته وهمومه * الا انّا نرى ان هذه العلة الاصلية كثيرا ما تستحيل عن صيغتها الاولوية حتى ان بلآء الرجل وهمه ووحشته ونحسه وشقاوته وحرمانه بل هلاكه يكون من هذه المراة * فتنقلب تلك الاعانة احانة * وتلخيصه ان الانسان وُلد في هذه الدنيا محتاجا الى اشيآء كثيرة لازمة لحفظ حياته * وذلك كالاكل والشرب والنوم والدفء * والى اشيآء اخرى غير لازمة للحيوة وانما هى لتقويم طبعه حتى لا يختلّ * وذلك كالضحك والكلام واللهو وسماع الغنآ واتخاذ المراة * الا ان هذا الاخير مع كونه جعل فى الاصل لتقويم الطبيعة * اذ يمكن للرجل ان يعيش حينا ما من دونه * فقد غلب على سائر اللوازم المعاشية التى لابد منها * الا ترى ان من يحلم بامراة يجد منها فى الحلم ما يجده منها فى اليقظة * وليس كذلك من يحلم بانه اكل عسلا او شرب سلافا * بل وقوع هذا نادر جدا حتى للجائع والعطشان * وقد طالما رضيت

I started to say something at the beginning of this chapter and didn't finish it, the pen, as usual, having drawn me unawares into another topic, and I doubt that Your Elevated Honor or Sublime Presence understood it. I now therefore declare: "If the ideal of marriage be that each of the two spouses take his companion for his own sake and not for that of his countrymen, acquaintances, or friends, the way that 'Ulayyān ate Umm 'Alī's chicken's thigh,[176] it would be unreasonable for someone wearing a bonnet to intrude upon them and tell the woman, 'Don't marry so-and-so because he wasn't given the name Buṭrus' and then to the man, 'Don't marry so-and-so because she wasn't given the name Maryam' or 'Today's Sunday, and marriage is not allowed' or 'This room isn't licensed for the contraction of marriages.' Nor would it be proper for him to say to them, 'I want to see the kohl-stick stuck in the pot.' Such things, I swear, are not fit to be spoken or written of by any. 2.14.5

"Then again, the woman is one of those things that, like the sun or the moon, are so much looked at that the mind doesn't pay them the attention they deserve. This may be demonstrated by the fact that God, Mighty and Powerful, created woman from man to be a helpmeet to him in his daily *affairs* and a comfort to him in the midst of his anguish and *cares*. It seems to us, though, that this underlying intention is so frequently distorted that man's calamities, care, loneliness, ill fortune, wretchedness, and deprivation, nay even his perdition, come from woman, thus turning that *collaboration* into a cause of *aggravation*. In brief, one is born into this world in need of many things required for one's survival (such as food, drink, sleep, and warmth) and others that are not but that exist rather to rectify one's nature so that it does not become imbalanced (such as laughter, speech, recreation, listening to songs, and having women). This last, however, while originally created for the rectification of nature (as evidenced by the fact that a man can live for a while without it), has gained the upper hand over all other mundane requirements of life which cannot be foregone. Observe that a man who dreams of a woman gets from her in his dream what he would have had were he awake, while this is not true of one who dreams of eating honey or drinking the best wine, which is anyway something that very rarely happens, even to one who is hungry or thirsty. How often have our friends the poets been content to see the image of the beloved in their 2.14.6

اصحابنا الشعرآ بطيف الخيال من المحبوب * وما احد منهم رضى على جوعه بان يبعث اليه ممدوحه بكاس مدام فى الحلم او ثريدة * واذا تناول الانسان طعاما طيبا لونا كان او لونين بقى عدة ساعات مكتفيا بما ناله غير مفكر فى القِدْر ولا فيما يقتدر فيها * حتى يعاوده الجوع فيطفق ح يفكّر فى تناول طعام آخر * ولكن لم يسمع عن احد من الناس فى حالتى الجوع والشبع انه كان كلما راى طائرا فى الجو اشتهى ان يقع على سفوده فى البيت حتى يسترطه * او انه كان لا يزال يبصّص فى دكاكين الطباخين والبدّالين والزياتين ويلاوص من ثقوب اقفالهم ومن خصاص
ابوابهم وشقوق حيطانهم على ما عندهم من اصناف الماكول * نعم ان الجائع فى ٧،١٤،٢
بلادنا يحسب كل مستدير رغيفا كما يقال * وفى بعض بلاد الافرنج ربما حسب ايضا المستدير والمطاول وذا شقّ كظِلف الشاة وذلك لتفننهم فى اشكاله * غير ان الجائع الى النسآء ليس له شكل ينتهى اليه * وكذلك قضية الشرب فان الظمان بعد ان يروى غليله بالمآ فاذا جئ اليه بكاس من التسنيم عافه * وكذلك البردان المحتاج الى الدفء فانه متى لبس ما يدفئه من الثياب وتحمّله بين الناس لم يتطالل بعد ذلك الى كل ثوب ينظره فى دكاكين التجار معرضا للبيع * ولو راى مثلا قوس قزح او روضة مدبجة بالازهار البهيجة لم يتمنّ ان تكون الوانها فى سراويله او قميصه * وانما يراها ويستحسنها مجرد استحسان من دون ان يشغل بها خاطره ولبّه * ولا يحلم ليلته تلك انه راى روضة انيقة او يتصور وهو متوسّد على فراشه انها لوكانت حِيال مخدّته لزاد ذلك فى تنعيمه او عمره * وقس على ذلك النائم اذا نام كفايته على فراش غير وطئ فان منظر الفراش الوثير بعده لا يهمّه * والحاصل ان للانسان عقلا فى يافوخه يدله على ما ينفعه ويضره ويسوءه ويسره * وان فى كل من معدته وحلقومه ميزانا قويما يزن به ما هو محتاج اليه من الطعام والشراب *

dreams! None, however, was ever content to have the object of his eulogies send him a glass of wine or a pot of porridge in a dream. Likewise, if a person partakes of some tasty food, be it of one kind or two, he will remain satisfied with what he's eaten for a number of hours and give no thought to the cooking pot and its potential contents. Then, when revisited by hunger, he will start thinking again of having another meal. Never, however, has it been heard that one in a state of hunger or thirst, on seeing a bird, would wish for it to fall onto the spit in his house so that he could gulp it down or keep ogling the cooks', grocers', and oil chandlers' shops or peering through their keyholes, the chinks in their doors, or the cracks in their walls at the different kinds of food inside.

"True, in our country 'the hungry man thinks that everything round is a loaf,' as the saying goes, and it may be that in some Frankish countries, where they have so many different kinds of food, they harbor similar thoughts about everything round, oblong, or cloven like a sheep's hoof, but one who is hungry for women has no one shape to fix on. The same goes for drink, for a thirsty man, having once quenched his longing with water, will feel aversion to drinking more, even if a glass filled with the nectar of paradise is brought him. Similarly, one who is cold and needs warmth, once he has put on some clothes to warm himself and cut himself a fine figure in public, will not thereafter stand on tiptoes to peer at every garment he sees displayed for sale in the merchants' stores. Were he to see, for example, a rainbow or a meadow brocaded with gay flowers, he wouldn't want the same colors to be on his drawers or his shirt; he would see it and simply find it beautiful without exercising his mind and heart over it or dreaming that same night of an elegant garden or imagining as he lay on his bed that, if it were next to his pillow, he'd feel more comfortable or live longer. The same goes for the sleeper: if he gets enough sleep on his hard bed, the subsequent sight of a luxuriously comfortable bed will be of no interest to him. In sum, everyone has a brain in his cranium that guides him to what will benefit him and what will hurt him and to what will do him harm and what will bring him pleasure, and, in both his stomach and his gullet, there is an accurate set of scales that measures what food and drink he needs and that enables him to grasp the meaning of the saying, 'One meal precludes many another.' 2.14.7

٨،١٤،٢ وبه يدرى مضمون قولهم ربّ اكلة حرمت اكلات * فامّا فى امر المراة فالقانع العزوف يغدو شرها رغيبا * والرشيد غويا * والحليم سفيها * والمهتدى ضالا * والحكيم عَمِها * والعالم جاهلا * والفصيح عييّا وبالعكس * والصَبُور جزوعا ولا عكس * والفتى شيخا ولا عكس * والغنى فقيرا وبالعكس * والفظّ لطيفا ولا عكس * والسمين نحيفا وبالعكس * والمعافى مبتلى ولا عكس * والمتثبّت متغشمرا وبالعكس * والبخيل كريما ولا عكس * والساكن متحركا وبالعكس * والطرد عكسا وبالعكس * وهلم جرا * واذا راى امراة تبغضه فربما احبها * او تجفوه كلف بها * او تعرض عنه تعرّض لها * او تملّق اليه وتملثه فُتِن بها * او ترميه بحقيبتها على ثقلها جُنّ بها * الا ولو حضر مجلسا كان فيه

امراة وضيئة	حسنة نظيفة *
وهيّئة	حسنة الهيئة *
ومُخْبَأة	الجارية المخدرة لم تتزوج بعد *
وذَبَأة	الجارية المهزولة المليحة الخفيفة الروح *
وجَرْبآ	الجارية المليحة *
وخِدَبّة	ضخمة *
وخُرْعُوب	الشابة الحسنة الخلق الرخصة او البيضآ اللينة الجسيمة اللحيمة الرقيقة العظم *
وخَنِبة	الجارية الغنجة الرخيمة *
ورَطْبة	معروف *
وسَرْهَبة	المراة الجسيمة الطويلة *
وشَطْبة	الطويلة الحسنة الخلق * ٩،١٤،٢

"Where women are concerned, though, the self-denying ascetic becomes a lustful lecher, the reasonable man a slave to his passions, the clement ruler a tyrant, the well-guided person a lost soul, the wise man an idiot, the scholar an ignoramus, the eloquent a stutterer (and vice versa), the patient man a prey to his impulses (but not vice versa), the young man old (but not vice versa), the rich man a pauper (and vice versa), the lout a sophisticate (but not vice versa), the fat thin (and vice versa), the healthy an invalid (but not vice versa), the steady-going reckless (and vice versa), the miser generous (but not vice versa), the immobile mobile (and vice versa), and all things their opposites (and vice versa, and so on, and so forth). If a man finds a woman who hates him, how often will he fall in love with her, if one who ignores him devote himself to her, if one who avoids him throw himself in her path, if one who flatters him and offers him false hopes become infatuated by her, if one who throws him her bag,[177] however heavy, go mad for her—unless he attend a gathering where there's 2.14.8

a *waḍīʾah,*	"a woman who is comely and clean"
or a *hayyiʾah,*	"a female who is comely of form"
or a *mukhbaʾah,*	"a secluded girl who has not yet married"
or a *dhabʾah,*	"a thin, cute, jolly girl"
or a *jarbāʾ,*	"a cute girl"
or a *khidabbah,*	a female who is "huge"
or a *khurʿūb,*	"a supple, shapely young woman or a fine-boned, fleshy, stout, soft, white young woman"
or a *khanibah,*	"a coquettish girl of thrilling voice"
or a *raṭbah,*	too well known to require definition[178]
or a *sarhabah,*	"a tall, stout woman"
or a *shaṭbah,*	"a shapely girl" 2.14.9

وشِطْبة	الجارية الحسنة الغضة الطويلة *
وشَنْبا	ذات شنب وقد ذكر تحت البرقع *
وصَقْبة	الطويلة التارّة *
وصَهْباً	الصَهَب حمرة او شقرة فى الشعر كالصُهبة والصهوبة *
وعَجْباً	المراة يتعجب من حسنها *
وقَبّاً	الدقيقة الخصر الضامرة البطن *
وكَبْكابة	المراة السمينة *
ومكدوبة	النقية البياض *
وكاعِب	التي نهد ثديها *
ولَعُوب	الحسنة الدَلّ * ١٠،١٤،٢
ووَطْباً	العظيمة الثدى والوَطب الثدى العظيم *
وهَدْباً	الكثيرة شعر الهدب *
وذات صُلُوته	الصَلْت الجبين الواضح وقد صلت ككرم *
وصَمُوت الخلخالين	غليظة الساقين لا يسمع لهما حسّ *
وخَوْثاً	الحَدَثة الناعمة *
وبَلْجاً	البُلْجة نقاوة ما بين الحاجبين هو ابلج وهى بَلْجاً *
ومِبْهاج	حسنة *
وجائعة الوشاح	ضامرة البطن ومثله غَرْثى الوشاح *
وخَدَلَّجة	المراة الممتلئة الذراعين والساقين *
ودَعْجاً	الدَعَج سواد العين مع سعتها * ١١،١٤،٢
ورَجْراجة	يترجرج عليها لحمها *

or a *shiṭbah,*	"a tall, blooming, shapely girl"	
or a *shanbā',*	"having lustrous teeth" (of a female); mentioned under *burqu'*[179]	
or a *ṣaqbah,*	a female who is "tall and full-bodied"	
or a *ṣahbā',*	["a red-headed woman"] "*ṣahab* is redness or blondness of the hair; synonyms *ṣuhbah* and *ṣuhūbah*"	
or a *'ajbā',*	"a woman whose beauty is to be wondered at"	
or a *qabbā',*	a female who is "slim-waisted and slender-bellied"	
or a *kabkābah,*	"a fat woman"	
or a *makdūbah,*	"a pure white woman"	
or a *kā'ib,*	a woman whose breasts stand up	
or a *la'ūb,*	a female "with a nice way of flirting"	**2.14.10**
or a *waṭbā',*	a female who is "large breasted"; a *waṭb* is "a large breast"	
or a *hadbā',*	a female "having thick eyelashes"	
or a *dhāt ṣulūtah,*	["having a clear, or prominent and straight, brow"] "*ṣalt* means 'a clear brow'; *ṣaluta* means 'to develop such a brow'"	
or a *ṣamūt al-khulkhālayn,*	"having legs so thick that her anklets make no sound"	
or a *khawthā',*	a female who is "young and smooth"	
or a *baljā',*	*buljah* is having "a space between the eyebrows"; masculine adjective *ablaj*, feminine *baljā'*	
or a *mibhāj,*	a female who is "shapely"	
or a *jā'i'at al-wishāḥ,*	a female who is "slender-bellied"; synonym *gharthā' al-wishāḥ*	
or a *khadallajah,*	"a woman with plump arms and legs"	
or a *da'jā',*	["a dark- and wide-eyed woman"] "*da'aj* is . . . blackness of the eye combined with wideness"	**2.14.11**
or a *rajrājah,*	a woman whose flesh quivers upon her	

وزجّآ — الزَجَج محركة دقة الحاجبين فى طول والنعت ازج وزجآ *

ومُعَذْلجة — الممتلئة الناعمة الحسنة الخلق *

ومفلّجة الاسنان — الفلج تباعد ما بين الاسنان *

وبَيْدَح — بادِن ونحوه بَلْدح *

ودَحُوح — عظيمة *

وذات سَجاحة — سَجِح الخدّ سهل ولان وطال فى اعتدال *

ودُمْلُجة — الضخمة التارّة *

وصَلْدَحة — عريضة وكذا سلطحة وصلطحة *

وفُقّاح — المراة الحسنة الخَلْق * ١٢،١٤،٢

ووَضّاحة — البيضآ اللون الحسنته *

وبَيْدَخة — تارّة *

وبُلاخيّة — عظيمة او شريفة *

وصَمِخة — المراة الغضّة *

وطُباخيّة — الشابّة المكتنزة *

وفتخآ الاَخلاف — ناقة فتخا الاخلاف ارتفعت اخلافها قِبَل بطنها ذمّ وفى المراة والضّرع مدح *

وفِرْضاخة — ضخمة عريضة او طويلة عظيمة الثديين *

وقُفاخ — المراة الحادرة الحسنة الخلق *

ولُباخيّة — لحيمة *

وهَبَيَّخة — الناعمة التارّة *

وبَخَنْداة — المراة التامة القصب كالبَخَنْدَى * ١٣،١٤،٢

or a *zajjāʾ*,	"*zajaj* is the delicate lengthening of the eyebrows, and the delineating [thereof]"; masculine adjective *azajj*, feminine *zajjāʾ*
or a *muʿadhlajah*,	"a plump, smooth, shapely woman"
or a *mufallajat al-asnān*,	["a gap-toothed woman"] "*falaj* is having a distance between the teeth"
or a *baydaḥ*,	a female who is "corpulent"; similarly, *baldaḥ*
or a *daḥūḥ*,	a female who is "large"
or a *dhāt sajāḥah*,	["a smooth-cheeked woman"] "*sajiḥa*, of the cheek, means that it became smooth, soft, and moderately long"
or a *dumluḥah*,	a female who is "huge and full-bodied"
or a *ṣaldaḥah*,	a female who is "broad"; similarly, *salṭaḥah* and *ṣalṭaḥah*
or a *fuqqāḥ*,	"a shapely woman" 2.14.12
or a *waḍḍāḥah*,	a female who is "of a pleasing white color"
or a *baydakhah*,	a female who is "full-bodied"
or a *bulākhiyyah*,	a female who is "large or noble"
or a *ṣamikhah*,	" a blooming woman"
or a *ṭubākhiyyah*,	"a sturdily-built young woman"
or a *fatkhāʾ al-akhlāf*,	["a high-breasted woman"] "a she-camel whose *akhlāf* ('teats') are *fatkhāʾ* has them raised (toward the belly) (a blameworthy quality in she-camels, but praiseworthy in women and women's udders)"
or a *firḍākhah*,	a female who is "huge and broad" or "tall and with large breasts"
or a *qufākh*,	"a fat woman of comely physique"
or a *lubākhiyyah*,	"a female who is fleshy"
or a *habayyakhah*,	a female who is "smooth and full-bodied"
or a *bakhandāh*,	"a woman with a perfectly developed figure"; also *bakhandā* 2.14.13

وبُرَخداة	الجارية الناعمة التارّة *
ومُبَرَنْدة[1]	الكثيرة اللحم *
وثأدة	المكتنزة الكثيرة اللحم *
وثَوْهَدة	السمينة التامة الخلق وكذا الثَهْودة والفَوْهدة *
وثَهْمَد	السمينة العظيمة *
وجَدّآ	الصغيرة الثديين *
وجَيْدآ	الطويلة الجيد الدقيقته *
وبَضّة المُجرّد	بضّة عند التجرّد *
وخَبَنْداة	جارية خَبَنْداة تامة القصب أو تارّة ممتلئة اوثقيلة الوركين وساق خَبَنْداة مستديرة ممتلئة *
وخَرِيد	الخريد البكر لم تمسس اوالخفرة الطويلة السكوت الخافضة الصوت المتسترة كالخريدة والخرود *

(تنبيه المراة الجَشُوب الدِرْدِحة الضَمْزِر اللَهْبَرة العُكْبُرة القُعَسُوس الجُبّاعة الثَدْمة اكثر دلّا وغنجا من جميع هولآ)

ورِخْوَدّة	اللينّة العظام السمينة *	١٤،١٤،٢
ورِعْديد	رخصة *	
ورَهيْدة	الشابة الرخصة الناعمة *	
وعُبُرد	الجارية البيضآ الناعمة ترتجّ من نَعمتها *	
وعَضاد	المراة الغليظة العضد *	
وعُمُدّة	الشابة الممتلئة شبابا كالعُمُدانيّة *	

---

١ ١٨٥٥: مُبَرْنَدة.

or a *burakhdāh,*	"a smooth, full-bodied girl"
or a *mubarnadah,*	a female who is "well-fleshed"
or a *tha'dah,*	a sturdily-built "well-fleshed woman"
or a *thawhadah,*	"a fat, shapely woman"; also *thahwadah* and *fawhadah*
or a *thahmad,*	a female who is "fat and large"
or a *jaddā',*	a female who is "small-breasted"
or a *jaydā',*	a female "having a long, finely formed neck"
or a *baḍḍat al-mujarrad,*	"revealing tender skin on undressing"
or a *khabandāh,*	"a girl described as *khabandāh* has a perfectly formed figure, or is stoutly built, or has heavy haunches; a leg so described is rounded and full"
or a *kharīd,*	"a *kharīd* is an untouched virgin, or a bashful woman who maintains long silences, speaks in a low voice and conceals herself from public view"; also, *kharīdah* and *kharūd*

(Note: women who are nanoid, endomorphic, adipose, fubsy, hebetudinous, impulchritudinous, chamaephytic, and troglodytic are more coquettish and sensual than any of the above.)

or a *rikhwaddah,*	a female who is "soft-boned and fat" 2.14.14
or a *ri'dīd,*	a female who is "soft to the touch"
or a *rahīdah,*	"a smooth, soft, young woman"
or a *'ubrud,*	"a girl who is white and smooth and quivers with good living"
or a *'aḍād,*	"a woman thick of upper arm (*'aḍud*)"
or a *'umuddah,*	"a young woman bursting with youthfulness; synonym *'umudāniyyah*"

وغادة المراة الناعمة الليّنة البيّنة الغَيد *

وغَيْدآ المتثنّية ليناً *

ومَقْصَدة المراة التامة العظيمة تعجب كل احد والتى الى القِصَر *

ومأدة الجارية الناعمة *

ومَمْسودة مجدولة الخلق * ١٥،١٤،٢

وأُمْلُود المراة الناعمة اللينة *

وناهِد كاعب *

وبَهِيْرة السيدة الشريفة والصغيرة الخلق الضعيفة وكذا البَهِيلة

وبَشِيرة جميلة *

ومبشورة الحسنة الخلق واللون *

وتارّة ممتلئة الجسم *

وتُرّة الحسنآ الرعنآ *

وجُحاشرة الضخمة الحادرة الجسم[١] العبلة المفاصل العظيمة الخلق *

وجَهْرآ مونث الاجهر وهو الحسن المنظر والجسم التامّة والاحول المليح الحولة *

وحادرة السمينة او الحسنة الجميلة * ١٦،١٤،٢

وأَحْوَرِيّة البيضآ الناعمة *

وحَوارِيّة الحَوارِيّات نسآ الامصار *

وحَوْرآ الحَوَر ان يشتد بياض العين وسواد سوادها وتستدير حدقتها وترق جفونها ويبيض ما حواليها او الخ *

---

١ كذا في القاموس وفي ١٨٥٥: الجسيمة.

or a *ghādah*, "a smooth, pliant woman of patent pliability"

or a *ghaydā'*, "a woman who walks with an affected swaying, out of pliability"

or a *maqṣadah*, "the large, perfect woman who pleases all men and tends to shortness"

or a *ma'dah*, "a smooth girl"

or a *mamsūdah*, a female who is trimly built 2.14.15

or a *umlūd*, "a soft, pliable woman"

or a *nāhid*, a female who is "full-breasted"

or a *bahīrah*, "a noble lady, of small stature and weak"; synonym *bahīlah*

or a *bashīrah*, a female who is "beautiful"

or a *mabshūrah*, a female who is "comely of face and body"

or a *tārrah*, a female who is "full-bodied"

or a *turrah*, a female "comely and frivolous"

or a *juḥāshirah*, "a huge woman, of beautiful physique and large joints, and well built"

or a *jahrā'*, feminine of *ajhar*, which means "a male of comely, perfectly formed appearance and body, or a male with an attractive squint"

or a *ḥādirah*, "a fat, or comely and beautiful, woman" 2.14.16

or an *aḥwariyyah*, a female who is "white and smooth"

or a *ḥawāriyyah*, "the *ḥawāriyyāt* [plural] are the women of the great cities"

or a *ḥawrā'*, ["having *ḥawar*"] "*ḥawar* is when the white of the eye is extremely white and the black extremely black and the pupil is rounded, the eyelids delicate and surrounded by white," etc.

وذات تدهكر ترجرج *

ومُدَهْمَرة المراة المكّلة المجتمعة *

ومزنَّرة طويلة جسيمة *

وزَهْرآ المراة المشرقة الوجه *

ومَسْبورة الحسنة الهيئة *

ومسمورة الجارية المعصوبة الجسد غير رخوة اللحم *

وشَغْفر المراة الحسنآ *

وصَيِّرة الحسنة الصورة * ١٧،١٤،٢

وعَبْقَرة تارة جميلة *

وعَبْهَرة الرقيقة البشرة الناصعة البياض والسمينة الممتلئة الجسم كالعبهر والجامعة للحسن فى الجسم والخلق *

وعَنْجَرة المكّلة الخفيفة الروح *

ومُعْصر التى بلغت شبابها وادركت او دخلت فى الحيض او راهقت العشرين *

وغَرّآء بيضآ وكذا فَرّآ *

وذات افترار افترضحك ضحكا حسنا *

وفَرْآ الممتلئة لحما وشحما او التى قاربت الادراك *

وقُفاخِريّة النبيلة العظيمة من النسآ *

ومُرْمورة المرمورة والمرمارة الجارية الناعمة الرجراجة *

ومَشْرة الاعضآ ريّا *

ومَطِرة لازمة للسواك أو للتنظف والاغتسال * ١٨،١٤،٢

or a *dhāt tadahkur*,	a female "whose body shakes"
or a *mudahmarah*,	a compact, well-knit woman
or a *muzannarah*,	a female who is "tall, large-bodied"
or a *zahrā'*,	"a woman of radiant face"
or a *masbūrah*,	a female "of comely form"
or a *masmūrah*,	"a girl with a sinewy body and no loose flesh"
or a *shaghfar*,	"a comely woman"
or a *ṣayyirah*,	a female "of comely appearance" 2.14.17
or a *ʿabqarah*,	a female who is "full-bodied and beautiful"
or a *ʿabharah*,	a female "with delicate, shining white skin or who is fat and full-bodied, synonym *ʿabhar*; also a female who brings together all beautiful qualities of body and physique"
or a *ʿajanjarah*,	a female "of compact physique and a light spirit"
or a *muʿṣir*,	"a girl who has completed her girlhood and attained or entered into the menses, or who is approaching twenty"
or *gharrā'*,	"white"; synonym *farrā'*
or a *dhāt iftirār*,	[a woman "with a pleasant laugh"] "*iftarra* means 'he laughed a pleasant laugh'"
or a *fazrā'*,	a female who is "fleshy and fat-laden, or approaching the onset of the menses"
or a *qufākhiriyyah*,	"a large, noble woman"
or a *murmūrah*,	"a *murmūrah*, synonym *mirmārah*, is a girl whose skin is smooth and whose flesh quivers"
or a *mashrat al-aʿḍā'*,	"a fragrant woman"
or a *maṭirah*,	a female who "constantly uses the teeth-cleaning stick, or cleans herself, or washes" 2.14.18

وذات مكْرة المكرة الساق الغليظة الحسنآ *

ومَمكورة المطوية الخلق من النسآ والمستديرة الساقين او المدمجة الخلق الشديدة البَضْعة *

ومارِيّة بيضآ برّاقة (من مار) *

وذات نَضْرة حسن وبهجة *

ووَثيرة الوثيرة الكثيرة اللحم او الموافقة للمضاجعة *

(تنبيه المراة الرّبسة الدِعْفصة الدِنْقصة القُنْبُصة الصَعْلة الطَهْمل الضَلْفع الضَوْكعة الرَصعآ القُشْوانة[1] الكروآ اكثر دلّاً وغنجا من جميع هولآ) *

وهُدَكِر المراة التي اذا مشت حرّكت لحمها وعظامها * ١٩,١٤,٢

وهَيْدَكُور الكثيرة اللحم والشابة الضخمة الحسنة الدلّ كالهُدكورة *

وبِلِز المراة الضخمة او الخفيفة *

وعُكْموزة الحادرة التارّة *

وغَمّازة الجارية الحسنة الغمز للاعضآ *

وكِناز كثيرة اللحم صُلْبة *

وآنِسة الجارية الطيبة النَفْس *

وبَيْهس الحسنة المشى *

وخَرُوس البكر فى اول حملها *

وخَنْسآ تقدم ذكرها تحت البرقع *

ومُرْكِس الجارية طلع نهدها فاذا اجتمع وضخم فقد نهد * ٢٠,١٤,٢

وعَيْطَموس المراة الجميلة او الحسنة الطويلة التارة كالعُطْموس *

---

١ كذا في القاموس وفي ١٨٥٥: القَشْوانة.

or a *dhāt makrah,*	[a woman "possessed of a *makrah*"] "a *makrah* is a comely, thick calf"
or a *mamkūrah,*	"a woman with a curvaceous physique and rounded calves, or one who is of slender waist and corpulent"
or a *māriyyah,*	a female who is "of a brilliant white"; from [the verb] *māra*
or a *dhāt naḍrah,*	[a woman "possessed of *naḍrah*"] "i.e., of comeliness and good looks"
or a *wathīrah,*	"the woman who is *wathīrah* has much flesh, or is ready to be bedded"

(Note: women who are dirty crockadillapigs, shorties, runts, trolls, long-necked pinheads, midgets, wide-wooed woofers, waddlers, bitty-butted beasts, scrawnies, and spindle-legs are more coquettish and sensual than any of the above.)

or a *hudakir,*	"a woman who brings her flesh and her bones into play when she walks"	2.14.19
or a *haydakūr,*	a female "with a lot of flesh on her" and "a huge young woman who is attractively coquettish"; synonym *hadkūr*	
or a *biliz,*	"a huge, or a light, woman"	
or a *ʿukmūzah,*	a female who is "thick and full-fleshed"	
or a *ghammāzah,*	"a girl skilled at massage"	
or a *kināz,*	a female "with much flesh, and solid"	
or a *ānisah,*	"a cheerful girl"	
or a *bayhas,*	a female who "walks well"	
or a *kharūs,*	"a girl who has not yet brought forth, in the first period of her pregnancy"	
or a *khansāʾ,*	["snub-nosed"] already mentioned under *burquʿ*	
or a *murkis,*	"a girl whose breasts are emerging; when they become compact and large, they are said to have 'become full' (*nahada*)"	2.14.20
or a *ʿayṭamūs,*	"a beautiful woman, or a comely, tall, full-bodied woman"; synonym *ʿuṭmūs*	

وعَلَطميس الجارية التارة الحسنة القوام *
وعانِس التى طال مكثها فى اهلها بعد ادراكها حتى خرجت من عداد الابكار *
وقُدْمُوسة ضخمة عظيمة *
وقِرْطاس الجارية البيضاَ المديدة القامة *
وكَنيسة المراة الحسناَ *
ولَعْساَ من فى لونها ادنى سواد *
ولَمِيْس اللينة الملْمس *
وعَشَّة المراة الطويلة القليلة اللحم او الدقيقة عظام اليد والرجل *
وخربَصة المراة الشابة التارّة *
ودَخُوض الجارية الممتلئة شحما *
ورخْصَة معروف *
وبَضْباضة بَضّة الرخصة الجسد الرقيقة الجلد الممتلئة *
وخَرِيْضة الجارية الحديثة السن الحسنة البيضآء التارة * ٢١،١٤،٢
ورَضْراضة في معنى رجراجة *
وغَضّة غضيضة الطرف الغضّة الناضرة والغضيض من الطرف الفاتر الطرف *
وفارض ضخمة *
وفَضْفاضة الجارية اللحيمة الجسيمة الطويلة *
ومُفاضة الضخمة البطن *
وخُوْطانة جارية خوطانة وخوطانية كالغصن طولا ونَعمة * ٢٢،١٤،٢

or a *ʿalṭamīs,*	"a full-bodied girl of attractive physique"	
or a *ʿānis,*	"a female who has remained so long with her family after having reached puberty that she is no longer counted among the virgins"	
or a *qudmūsah,*	a female who is "huge and big"	
or a *qirṭās* ,	"a white girl of lanky physique"	
or a *kanīsah,*	"a comely woman"	
or a *laʿsāʾ,*	"one who has the slightest hint of blackness to her complexion"	
or a *lamīs,*	a female "soft to the touch"	
or a *ʿashshah,*	"a tall woman with little flesh, or one with fine-boned hands and feet"	
or a *kharbaṣah,*	"a young, full-bodied woman"	**2.14.21**
or a *dakhūṣ,*	"a girl full of fat"	
or a *rakhṣah,*	["soft"] "too well known to require definition"	
or a *baḍbāḍah baḍḍah,*	a female who is "soft-bodied, delicate-skinned, full-fleshed"	
or a *kharīḍah,*	"a full-fleshed, white, comely, youthful girl"	
or a *raḍrāḍah,*	synonym of *rajrājah*	
or a *ghaḍḍah ghaḍīḍat al-ṭaraf,*	["a blooming girl with a drowsy eye"] "*ghaḍḍah* is 'blooming' (*nāḍirah*); an eye that is *ghaḍīḍ* is 'drowsy'(*fātir*)"	
or a *fāriḍ,*	a female who is "huge"	
or a *fadfāḍah,*	"a tall, well-built, fleshy girl"	
or a *mufāḍah,*	a female who is "huge-bellied"	
or a *khūṭānah,*	"a girl who is *khūṭānah*, or *khūṭāniyyah,* is smooth and tall as a tree branch"	**2.14.22**

وسَبِطة الجسم حسنة القدّ *
وشَطّة حسنة القوام طويلة *
وشِناط المراة الحسنة اللون والقوام *
وذات عَنَط وعَيَط طويلة العنق حسنته *
وذات شِناظ مكتنزة اللحم كثيرته *
ومُلَعَّظة الجارية السمينة الطويلة الجسيمة *
وبَتْعاَ الشديدة المفاصل والمواصل من الجسد *
وبَرِيْعة فائقة الجمال والعقل *
وبزيعة طريفة مليحة كيّسة *
ومُتِلع الحسنا لانها تتلع راسها تتعرض للناظرين اليها * ٢٣،١٤،٢
وسنيعة الجميلة اللينة المفاصل اللطيفة العظام *
وشَبْعى الخلخال والسوار ضخمة تملاهما سمنا *
وشَمُوع مَزّاحة لَعُوب *
وصَمْعاَ الصغيرة الاذن والاذن الصغيرة اللطيفة المنضمّة الى الراس *
وضَرْعاَ عظيمة الضرع *
وفَرْعاَ تامّة الشعر*
ولَعّة عفيفة مليحة *
ولاعة التى تغازلك ولا تمكنّك (قلت لانها تلوع مغازلها بذلك) *
وأنُوف طيبة رائحة الانف *
وخَنْضَرِف المراة الضخمة اللحيمة الكبيرة الثديين * ٢٤،١٤،٢

or a *sabṭat al-jism*,	a female "of pleasing figure"	
or a *shaṭṭah*,	a female "of pleasing physique and tall"	
or a *shināṭ*,	"a woman of pleasing color and physique"	
or a *dhāt ʿanaṭ wa-ʿayaṭ*,[180]	a female "having a long and attractive neck"	
or a *dhāt shināṭ*,	a female "fully and copiously fleshed"	
or a *mulaʿʿaẓah*,	"a well-built, tall, fat girl"	
or a *batʿāʾ*,	a female "having strong joints and sinews to her body"	
or a *barīʿah*,	a female "outstanding in beauty and brains"	
or a *bazīʿah*,	a female who is "quick-witted, witty, and charming"	
or a *mutliʿ*,	a female who is "attractive because she stretches out her neck (*tutliʿu ʿunuqahā*) when addressing those who look upon her"	2.14.23
or a *sanīʿah*,	a female who "has beautiful, soft joints and fine bones"	
or a *shabʿā l-khulkhāl wa-l-siwār*,	a female who is "huge and fills her anklets and bracelets with fat"	
or a *shamūʿ*,	a female who is "merry and playful"	
or a *ṣamʿāʾ*,	"a female with small ears, or a small, fine ear that is flattened against the head"	
or a *ḍarʿāʾ*,	a female who is "large-uddered"	
or a *farʿāʾ*,	a female "with perfect hair"	
or a *laʿʿah*,	a female who is "chaste and cute"	
or a *lāʿah*,	a female who "flirts with you but doesn't let you" (because, I believe, she torments (*talūʿu*) her suitor by so doing)	
or a *anūf*,	"a female with a sweet-smelling nose"	
or a *khanḍarif*,	"a huge, fleshy woman with large breasts"	2.14.24

وذَلْفاَ	نقدم ذكر الذَلَف تحت البرقع *
وذات سَجَف	السجف دقة الخصر وخماصة البطن *
وسُرْعُوف	المراة الطويلة الناعمة *
وسَيْفانة	الطويلة الممشوقة الضامرة *
وظريفة	الظَرف انما هو فى اللسان او حسن الوجه والهيئة او يكون فى الوجه واللسان او البَزاعة وذكا القلب او الحِذق او لا يوصف به الا الفتيان الازوال والفتيات الزولات لا الشيوخ ولا السادة *
وقِرْصافة	القِرْصافة من النسآ التى تتدحرج كانها كرة *
وقِصاف	المراة الضخمة *
ولَفّاء	واحدة اللُفّ للجوارى السمان الطوال *
وحسنة المَعارف والموقفين	المعارف الوجه وما يظهر من المراة والموقفان الوجه والقدم او العينان واليدان وما لا بدّ لها من اظهاره *
ومهفهفة	ضامرة البطن دقيقة الخصر*
وهَيْفآ	الهَيَف ضمر البطن ورقة الخاصرة * ٢٥،١٤،٢
وبَرّاقة	الحسنآ لها بهجة وبريق كالابريق *
وبُهْلُق	المراة الحمرآ جدا *
وحارُوق	نعت محمود للمراة عند الجماع *
وخِرْباق	الطويلة العظيمة او السريعة المشى *
ورشيقة	حسنة القدّ لطيفته *
ورَقْراقة	التى كانّ الماء يجرى فى وجهها *

or a *dhalfā'*,	["smallness and straightness of the nose"] *dhalaf* has been mentioned above under *burquʿ*
or a *dhāt sajaf*,	[possessed of] "*sajaf*, which is narrowness of the waist and lankness of the belly"
or a *surʿūf*,	"a smooth, tall woman"
or a *sayfānah*,	a female who is "thin, svelte, and tall"
or a *ẓarīfah*,	"*ẓarf* [the quality of being *ẓarīfah* ('charming, witty, sophisticated')] may be used only of the tongue, or of comeliness of face and appearance, or of both tongue and face, or of graciousness and quickness of both sensibility and wits, or it may be that only lively young men and women may be described as having it, not old men or lords"
or a *qirṣāfah*,	"a *qirṣāfah* is a woman who rolls like a ball"
or a *qiṣāf*,	"a huge woman"
or a *laffā'*,	singular of *luff* meaning "tall, fat girls"
or a *ḥasanat al-maʿārif wa-l-mawqifayn*,	["a female comely of those parts that may be seen"] the *maʿārif* are "the face and those parts of a woman that show" and the *mawqifān* are "the face and the feet, or the eyes and the hands and whatever has to be shown"
or a *muhafhafah*,	a female "lank-bellied and small-waisted"
or a *hayfā'*,	["slender-waisted"] *hayaf* [the quality of being *hayfā'*] is "lankness of the belly and delicacy of the haunches" 2.14.25
or a *barrāqah*,	"a beautiful female possessed of brio and brilliance"; synonym *abārīq*[181]
or a *buhluq*,	"a very ruddy woman"
or a *ḥārūq*,	"having a certain quality welcomed in a woman during copulation"[182]
or a *khirbāq*,	a female who is "tall and large, or a fast walker"
or a *rashīqah*,	a female who is "comely and refined of figure"
or a *raqrāqah*,	a female who "looks as though water were running over her face"

ورُوقة حسناً تعجب *

وسَوقاً الطويلة الساقين او الحسنتهما *

وعَبِقة المراة التى اذا تطيّبت بادنى طيب لم يذهب عنها اياما *

وعاتق الجارية اول ما ادركت *

وعَشَنَّقة طويلة ليست بضخمة ولا مُثقلة *

وغُبَرُقة العينين واسعتهما شديدة سواد سوادهما *

وغُرانق امراة غرانق وغرانقة شابة ممتلئة * ٢٦،١٤،٢

وذات غَرنقة غزل بالعينين *

وذات لمّة غُرانقة ناعمة تفيّئها الريح *

وفُنُق جارية فنق ومفناق منعمة *

ولَبقة الحسنة الدلّ واللبسة *

ومُلصقة الضيقة المتلاحمة *

ولِهقة شديدة البياض *

(تنبيه المراة الطُرطبة المتخجبة الزّغادبة العَكَا ذات الحردبة والسُنطبة البلَعثة الخرثا الحنظوب[1] العُكبرة المُثَدَّنة الخَطلا اكثر دلاً وغنجا من جميع هولاً) *

وممشوقة خفيفة اللحم * ٢٧،١٤،٢

ورَوْدكة حسناً فى عنفوان شبابها *

وضِبِرك المراة العظيمة الفخذين *

وضَكضاكة قصيرة مكتنزة *

وضُنّاكة الصلبة المغصوبة اللحم *

---

١ ١٨٥٥: الحُنظوب.

or a *rūqah,*	a female who is "comely and admired"
or a *sawqāʾ,*	a female "with long, or comely, legs"
or a *ʿabiqah,*	"a woman who continues to give off a pleasant smell for days though she applies to herself the smallest amount of perfume"
or a *ʿātiq,*	"a girl who has just reached the start of puberty" **2.14.26**
or a *ʿashannaqah,*	a female who is "tall without being huge or ponderous"
or a *ghubruqat al-ʿaynayn,*	a female "having wide eyes with intensely black pupils"
or a *ghurāniq,*	"a woman who is *ghurāniq,* or *ghurāniqah,* is young and full-bodied"
or a *dhāt gharnaqah,*	[a female "possessed of *gharnaqah,*" which means] "flirtatiousness of the eyes"
or a *dhāt limmah ghurāniqah,*	[a female "possessed of a lock of hair that is"] "smooth and played with by the wind"
or a *funuq,*	"a girl who is *funuq* or *mifnāq* is pampered"
or a *labiqah,*	a female "pleasing in her coquetry and way of dressing"
or a *mulṣaqah,*	a female who is "small and well-knit"
or a *lahiqah,*	a female who is "extremely white"

(Note: women who have dilated dugs or deflated bellies, who are blubber-lipped, gross, flighty and gangly, fleshy, hippo-haunched, ill-starred and vile, gross-bodied, and flabby-fleshed, with pendulous pendentives, are more coquettish and sensual than any of the above.)

or a *mamshūqah,*	a female who is "lightly fleshed" **2.14.27**
or a *rawdakah,*	a female who is "comely, in the bloom of youth"
or a *ḍibrik,*	"a woman with huge thighs"
or a *ḍakḍākah,*	a female who is "short and plump"
or a *ḍunʾakah,*	a female who is "solid and sparely fleshed"

ومُعْرَوْرِكة متداخلة *

وعَكوّكة القصيرة الملزّزة او السمينة *

وعَضَنَّك اللفّا التى ضاق ملتقى فخذيها مع ترارتها *

وعاتِكة المراة المحمرّة من الطيب *

ومُفلّك التى استدار ثديها *

ومَكماكة المكماكة والكمكامة القصيرة المجتمعة الخلق * ٢٨،١٤،٢

وهَبْرَكة الجارية الناعمة *

واسيلة الخدّين الاسيل من الخدود الطويل المسترسل *

ومُبتَّلة الجميلة كانها بُتّل حسنها على اعضائها اى قطّع والتى لم يركب بعض لحمها بعضا وفى اعضائها استرسال *

وبَهْلَكة المراة الغضة الناعمة *

وجُمول جَملآ الجمول السمينة والجملآ الجميلة والحسنة الخلق من كل حيوان *

وخَدْلة المراة الغليظة الساق المستديرتها او الممتلئة الاعضا لحما فى دقة عظام كالخَدْلآ *

وخَلّة المراة الخفيفة *

ودَحْمَلة الضخمة التارة *

ودُمَحِلة السمينة او الحسنة الخلق *

ومِكسال نعت للجارية المنعمة لا تكاد تبرح من مجلسها مدح * ٢٩،١٤،٢

ورَخيمة رَخُمت الجارية صارت سهلة المنطق فهى رخيمة ورخيم *

or a *muʿrawrikah,*	a female who is "well-knit"
or a *ʿakawwakah,*	a female who is "short and compact, or fat"
or a *ʿaḍannak,*	"a tall, fat (*laffāʾ*) female, the point of convergence of whose thighs has been narrowed by plumpness"
or a *ʿātikah,*	a female who is "stained red with perfume"
or a *mufallik,*	"a girl whose breasts have rounded out"
or a *makmākah,*	a *makmākah* and a *kamkāmah* are females who are "short and compactly built" **2.14.28**
or a *habrakah,*	"a smooth girl"
or a *asīlat al-khaddayn,*	["smooth and even, or long, of cheek"] "a cheek that is *asīl* is long and even"
or a *mubattalah,*	"a female so beautiful it is as though her comeliness had been cut up (*buttila,* i.e., *quṭṭiʿa*) and distributed to all of her limbs and who does not have parts of her flesh riding on top of other parts, and in whose limbs there is looseness"
or a *bahlakah,*	"a smooth, blooming woman"
or a *jamūlun jamlāʾ,*	"a *jamūl* is a female who is fat and a *jamlāʾ* is a female who is beautiful and comely of form, whether human or non-human"
or a *khadlah,*	"a woman with thick, rounded legs, or whose limbs are full-fleshed with fine bones"; synonym *khadlāʾ,*
or a *khallah,*	"a light woman"
or a *daḥmalah,*	a female who is "huge and full-bodied"
or a *dumaḥilah,*	a female who is "fat and comely of physique"
or a *miksāl,*	[literally, "sluggish"] "epithet for a coddled girl who can scarcely get up from her seat (a compliment)" **2.14.29**
or a *rakhīmah,*	["a woman with a thrilling voice"] "one says *rakhumat al-jāriyah,* meaning 'the girl acquired a thrilling voice'; adjective *rakhīmah* and *rakhīm*"

ورَقيمة	المراة العاقلة البَرْزة وفى ب ر ز امراة بَرْزة بارزة المحاسن او متجاهرة كهلة جليلة الخ *
وميْسانة الضُحَى	مدح ونحوه نؤوم الضحى *
وحسنة الخفّين	اى صوتها واثر وطئها يقال اذا حسن من المراة خفيّاها حسن سائرها *
وغانية	المراة التى تُطلَب ولا تطلب او التى غنيت بحسنها عن الزينة *

(تنبيه المراة القُرزُح القَيلع الخِنجل الحِزمل الحمكّة الخنْثل الجبَلة[1] الجهبلة الحنكلة القيعلة اكثر غنجا وتدعبا من جميع هولآ) *

٣٠،١٤،٢ وسياتى تتمة وصف الحسان فى الفصل السادس عشر من الكتاب الرابع اذ لم يبق لى من حراك وقوة لذلك واحسب القارى نظيرى * وانما اقول * نعم لو كان فى ذلك المجلس السعيد جميع هولآ الحسان على اختلاف الوانهن لودّ ان ينظمهن كلهن فى سلك واحد ويجعله فى عنقه كسبحة اوليآ الله المفردين * ومن ماراني فى ذلك رجعته الى قصة سيدنا سليمن عم * فانه معما اوتى من الحكمة * وما ادراك ما الحكمة * فقد كان سلكه يشتمل على الف امراة * منهن ثلثمائة

٣١،١٤،٢ سُرّيات والباقى سَرِيّات * فكان له فى كل يوم امراتان ونصف وكسور* اَلا ولو انه اى الرجل راى الشمس طالعة والبدر بازغا والكواكب مضيئة لكان اول ما يخطر بباله ان يقول * لقد تزينت هذه السمآ بهذه النيّرات البهية * فمتى تزيّن حجرتى بواحدة من اخواتهن او باثنتين او بثلاث او بعشر او بالسبحة كلها * ولو راى غوطة او ربوة او جبلين متناوحين او نوّفا او حُشّة او هدفا او شَقّبا

[1] كذا في القاموس وفي ١٨٥٥: الجَبَلَة.

or a *raqīmah,*	"a noted, intelligent woman"; and under *b-r-z* "a 'noted woman' (*imra'ah barzah*) is one whose good qualities are conspicuous (*bārizah*), or 'a bold, mature, magnificent' female, etc."
or a *mīsānat al-ḍuḥā,*	"a compliment: a female who slumbers deeply in the forenoon"; similar is "*[imra'atun] na'ūmu l-ḍuḥā* ('a woman who sleeps in the forenoon')"
or a *ḥasanat al-khafiyyayn,*	[literally "comely of the two that appear"] meaning her voice and her footprint; one says, "if the two things that appear of a woman are comely, the rest of her will be comely"
or a *ghāniyah.*"	"a woman who is pursued and does not herself need to pursue, or whose beauty is such that she may dispense with adornment"

(Note: women who are brevo-turpicular, magno-pinguicular, vasto-oricular, ignobilar, exiguo-deformicular, flaccido-ventricular, obesar, rancidular, nigero-malo-incultular, and hyper-rustico-rapacular are more sensual and bolder than any of the above.)

The continuation of this description of feminine charms will come in Chapter 16 of Book Four, as I have no strength or energy left and imagine my reader doesn't either. I merely declare: Indeed, were all these charms in all their variety present at such a happy gathering, he would want to string them all on a single thread and put them round his neck, like prayer beads round the necks of God's Chosen Friends, and I refer any who challenge me on this to the story of Our Master Sulaymān, peace be upon him, whose thread, for all that he was given wisdom—and what wisdom!—had on it a thousand women, three hundred of whom were concubines, the rest great ladies, which means that each day he had two-and-half-plus-a-bit women. 2.14.30

Why, were any man to see the sun rising, the full moon coming out, and the stars shining, the first thing it would occur to him to say would be, "Now that the sky has been adorned with these glorious heavenly bodies, when will my chamber be adorned with one of their sisters, or two, or three, or ten, or an entire string of prayer beads?" Likewise, if he beheld a dip or a mound, two hills standing next to one another or a perky little bump, a large dome or a high mountain, a hollow or a rounded dune, a little sand hill or the stern of a ship, a branch bending or a sea surging, a trough between waves, 2.14.31

او قَوْزا او دِعْصا او كَوْثلا او خُوْطا[1] يتاوّد او بحرا يتموّج او عَوْطبا او طاووسا او تفاحا او رمّانا او عقد درّ منظوم او شيا آخر يروق العين لسبق وهمه الى امراة * بل ربما تصوّر واحدة لم يكن قد راها قط ولا وجود لها فى الاعيان * ولو راى سفينة ماخرة فى اليمّ وعليها شراعها لشبّهها بامراة ترفل بثيابها فى الطرق كما كان داب احد الخرجيين المتورّعين * ولو راى حمامتين تتزاقّان وتتلاسنان قال ليت لى الان من ازقّها وتزقّنى والاسنها وتلاسننى وانقرها وتنقرنى * ولو راى ابا بُرائل بين ضغادره يلقمهن مما لديه * ويصفق لهن بجناحيه ويجثئلّ اليهن ويتجفّل ثم يحلج بينهن لود ان يكون نظيره * وحسبك بذلك من دناة ٣٢،١٤،٢
واهانة لهذه الصورة البشرية التى يقال فيها انها خلقت على مثال الخالق تعالى عن الشبيه والنظير * الا ولو انك القيته فى جب سيدنا يوسف * وفى فلك سيدنا نوح * وفى بطن حوت سيدنا يونس * وعلى ناقة سيدنا صالح * ومع اصحاب الكهف * لصرخ قائلا المراة المراة * ومن لى بالمراة * ولو انزلته فى

بُنانة	الروضة المعشبة *
ورَقْمة	الروضة وجانب الوادى او مجتمع مائه *
ودَقِيرة	الروضة الحسنآ العميمة النبات *
ووَدِيفة	الروضة الخضرآ *
وغَلْبآ	الحديقة المتكاثفة *
وعُلْجوم	البستان الكثير النخل *
ومَخْرفة	البستان *
وحديقة	الروضة ذات الشجر *

[1] كذا في القاموس وفي ١٨٥٥: خَوْطا.

a peacock, apples, pomegranates, a necklace of strung pearls, or anything else that pleases the eye, he would immediately fantasize about a woman; indeed, he might imagine one whom he'd never even seen and on whom he'd never clapped eye. And if he beheld a ship plowing the high seas, its sail set, he would liken it to a woman strutting the highways in her fine clothes, as a certain venerable Bag-man used to do. If he beheld two doves feeding each other with their mouths and cooing to each other, he'd say, "Would there were with me now one whom I might feed and who might feed me too, to whom I might coo and who might coo to me, whom I might peck and who might give me a peck!" If he beheld a rooster among his hens, feeding them morsels of his own food, flapping his wings at them, bristling and puffing up his feathers, and then stalking among them, he would want to be like him.

Enough, though, of such low-mindedness and abuse of that human form 2.14.32
which is said to have been shaped in the image of the Creator (too sublime though He be to have like or peer)—despite which, should you come across him down Our Master Yūsuf's well even, or on board Our Master Nūḥ's ark, or in the belly of Our Master Yūnus's whale, or on the back of Our Master Ṣāliḥ's[183] camel, or with the People of the Cave, he'd be shrieking, "A woman! A woman! Who will get me a woman!", and if you set him down in a

bunānah,	"a verdant meadow"
or a *raqmah*,	"a meadow, or the side of a watercourse, or the confluence of its waters"
or a *daqīrah*,	"a beautiful meadow covered in vegetation"
or a *radīfah*,	"a green meadow"
or a *ghalbā'*,	"a dense garden"
or a *'uljūm*,	"a grove of many palms"
or a *makhrafah*,	"a grove"
or a *ḥadīqah*,	"a meadow with trees"

وفي حُجْرة وعِلّية وغرفة ومقصورة وخِدر وحَجَلة ومِنَصّة *

وسِدار شبه الخِدر والموصَّد الخدر * ٣٣،١٤،٢

وحُشّة القبة العظيمة *

وجُنْبُذة كالقبة *

وعَرْش الخيمة والبيت الذى يستظل به كالعريش *

وكِرْح بيت الراهب ومثله الركح *

وكُوخ البيت المسنّم من قصب *

وصومعة بيت للنصارى *

ورِيْع الصومعة *

وفَنْزَر بيت يتخذ على خشبة طولها نحو ستين ذراعا للربيئة *

وبَهْو البيت المقدم امام البيوت *

وحِلّة جماعة بيوت الناس او مئة بيت والمجلس والمجتمع * ٣٤،١٤،٢

وفُسْطاط السرادق من الابنية ومثله المضرب *

وكِبْس بيت من طين *

وحِفْش البيت الصغير جدا *

وجَنْز البيت الصغير من الطين *

وخُصّ البيت من القصب او — *

ورَدْهة البيت الذى لا اعظم منه *

ومَجْلُوه البيت الذى لا باب فيه ولا ستر *

ووَأْم البيت الدفئ *

واُقْنة بيت من حجر *

or in a chamber or an upper room or a compartment or a ladies' bower or an alcove or on a dais,

or a *sidār*,	"something like a ladies' chamber (*khidr*)"; the *khidr* is also called a *muwaṣṣad*	2.14.33
or a *ḥushshah*,	"a large dome"	
or a *junbudhah*,	"[a thing] like a dome"	
or a *ʿarsh*,	"a tent, or a housing used for shade like a trellis"	
or a *kirḥ*,	"a monk's abode"; synonym *rukḥ*	
or a *kūkh*,	"a hump-shaped house of reeds"	
or a *ṣawmaʿah*,	[a monk's cell] "an abode of the Christians"	
or a *rīʿ*,	"a *ṣawmaʿah*"	
or a *fanzar*,	"a chamber placed on top of a piece of wood of some sixty spans as a watch-tower"	
or a *bahw*,	[a hallway or antechamber] "a chamber advanced in front of other chambers"	
or a *ḥillah*,	"a group of residential dwellings, or a hundred dwellings, or a place for sitting, or a gathering place"	2.14.34
or a *fusṭāṭ*,	"the structure called a *surādiq* ('an enclosure around a tent'), similar to a *miḍrab*"	
or a *kibs*,	"a dwelling of mud"	
or a *ḥifsh*,	"a very small dwelling"	
or a *janz*,	"a small dwelling of mud"	
or a *khuṣṣ*,	"a dwelling of reeds, or . . . ."[184]	
or a *radhah*,	"the largest kind of chamber"	
or a *majlūh*,	"a dwelling that has no door or anything to preserve its privacy"	
or a *wa'm*,	"a warm dwelling"	
or a *uqnah*,	"a dwelling of stone"	

وطِراف	البيت من اَدَم *	
ووَسُوط	بيت من بيوت الشعر او هو اصغرها *	٣٥،١٤،٢
وطَنَف	السقيفة تشرع فوق باب الدار*	
ونُزُل	ما هيّئ للضيف ان ينزل عليه *	
ومَغْنى	المنزل الذى غنى به اهله ثم ظعنوا او عامّ *	
ومَعْهَد	المنزل المعهود به الشى *	
ومَعان	المباَة والمنزل *	
ونَدِىّ	مجلس القوام نهارا او — *	
ومُرتَبَع	الموضع يرتبعون فيه فى الربيع *	
ومَصِيف ومَشْتى	معروف *	
ودَسْكرة	بناء كالقصر حوله بيوت او — *	
ومَشْرَقة	موضع القعود في الشمس بالشتآ *	٣٦،١٤،٢
ومَضْحاة	ارض مضحاة لا تكاد تغيب عنها الشمس *	
وظُلّة	شى كالصفّة يستتر به من الحرّ والبرد *	
ومَشْرَبة	الغرفة والعلية والصفة *	
وسُعْنة	الرَّفن او مطلق المِظَلة *	
ومظلّة	الكبير من الاخبية *	
وساباط	سقيفة بين دارين تحتها طريق *	
وعِرْزال	بيت صغير يتخذ للملك اذا قاتل الخ *	
وكِنّ	البيت *	
وقَيطون	المخدع *	

or a *ṭirāf*,	“a dwelling of hide”	
or a *wasūṭ*,	“a dwelling like the hair tent, or smaller”	2.14.35
or a *ṭanaf*,	“the projecting roof over the door of a house”	
or a *nuzul*,	“a place prepared for guests to stay in”	
or a *maghnā*,	“an abode whose people had no need of it and so departed, or [a house] generally”	
or a *maʿhad*,	“an abode dedicated to a specific purpose”	
or a *maʿān*,	“a home or an abode”	
or a *nadī*,	“a place where people gather and sit by day, or . . .”[185]	
or a *murtabaʿ*,	“a location where they[186] reside at the time of the autumn rains”	
or a *maṣīf* or *mashtā*,	[“a summering or a wintering spot”] “too well known to require definition”	
or a *daskarah*,	“a building like a palace with houses around it, or . . .”[187]	
or a *mashraqah*,	“a place to sit in the sun in winter”	2.14.36
or a *maḍḥāh*,	[“a land of sunshine”] “a land that is *maḍḥāh* is one that is sunny almost all the time”	
or a *ẓullah*,	“something like a portico in which one finds shelter from the heat and the cold”	
or a *mashrabah*,	“a chamber, or upper chamber, or portico”	
or a *suʿnah*,	“a rooftop shelter from the heat and humidity, or any shelter whatsoever”	
or a *miẓallah*,	“the larger kind of tent”	
or a *sābāṭ*,	“a roofing between two houses with a street beneath it”	
or a *ʿirzāl*,	“a small house used for the king when he is at war, or . . .”[188]	
or a *kinn*,	“a house”	
or a *qayṭūn*,	“a closet”	

وسَرَب الحفير تحت الارض * ٣٧،١٤،٢
ودِيْماس الكنّ والسَرَب والحمّام *
وبُرج معروف *
وصَهْوة البرج في اعلى الرابية *
وصَرح القصر وكل بنا عال *
وعَقْر البنآ المرتفع *
وطِرْبال كل بنآ عال *
وأَزَج ضرب من الابنية *
وإِيوان الصفة العظيمة كالازج *
ورِواق بيت كالفسطاط او سقف فى مقدّم البيت *
واُجُم كل بيت مربع مسطح وبضمتين الحصن * ٣٨،١٤،٢
وكَعْبة الغرفة وكل بيت مربّع *
واُطُم القصر وكل حصن مبنى بحجارة وكل بيت مربع مسطح *
ووَشِيع عريش يبنى للرئيس فى المعسكر*
وسُنَّيق بيت مجصّص *
وجَوْسق القصر*
ودَوْشَق البيت ليس بكبير ولا صغير او البيت الضخم *
وقُهْقور بنآ من حجارة طويل *
وبُغْبور الحجر الذى يذبح عليه القربان للصنم *
وزُور مجلس الغنآ *
وبُدّ بيت الصنم * ٣٩،١٤،٢

or a *sarab*,	"a subterranean excavation"	2.14.37
or a *dīmās*,	"a *kinn*, or a *sarab*, or a bathing chamber"	
or a *burj*,	[tower] "too well known to require definition"	
or a *ṣahwah*,	"a tower on top of a hill"	
or a *ṣarḥ*,	"a palace, or any tall building"	
or a *ʿaqr*,	"a high building"	
or a *ṭirbāl*,	"any tall building"	
or a *azaj*,	"a kind of building"[189]	
or a *īwān*,	"a large portico, like the *azaj*"	
or a *riwāq*,	"a house like a *fusṭāṭ*, or a roof at the front of a house [i.e., an arcade]"	
or a *ajam*,	"any square, roofed house; spelled *ujum* it means 'a fortress'"	2.14.38
or a *kaʿbah*,	"a room, or any square house"	
or a *uṭum*,	"a palace, or any fortress built of stone, or any square, roofed house"	
or a *washīʿ*,	"a trelliswork structure constructed for the chief in a camp"	
or a *sunnayq*,	"a house plastered with gypsum"	
or a *jawsaq*,	"a palace"	
or a *dawshaq*,	"a house that is neither large nor small, or a huge house"	
or a *quhqūr*,	"a tall stone structure"	
or a *bughbūr*,	"a stone on which an offering is sacrificed to an idol"	
or a *zūr*,	"a gathering place for singing"	
or a *budd*,	"the house of an idol"	2.14.39

وزُون	الموضع تجمع فيه الاصنام وتنصب وتزيّن *
ومسجد	معروف *
وكنيسة	معروف *
وفُهْر	مدارس اليهود تجتمع اليه في عيدهم او — *
ومِدْراس	الموضع يقرا فيه القرآن ومنه مدراس اليهود *
وبي كوكبان	حصن باليمن رصّع داخلة بالياقوت فكان يلمع كالكوكب *
والجَوْسق	دار بنيت للمقتدر فى دار الخلافة فى وسطها بركة من الرصاص ثلثون ذراعا فى عشرين *
وقصر النعمان الذى بناه السِنِمّار	هو رجل اسكاف بنى قصرا لنعمان بن امرء القيس فلما فرغ القاه من اعلاه لئلاّ يبنى لغيره مثله او هو غلام لأُحَيحة بنى أُطمة فلما فرغ قال له لقد احكمته قال انى لاعرف فيه حجرا لو نزع لتقوض من عند آخره فساله عن الحجر فاراه موضعه فدفعه احيحة من الاطم فخرّ ميتا *
والجعفرىّ	قصر للمتوكل قرب سرّ من راى *
والمارد	حصن بدومة الجندل * ٤٠،١٤،٢
والاَبلق	حصن بتيمآ قصدتهما الزبا فعجزت فقالت تمرّد مارد وعزّ الابلق *
وصِرْواح	حصن بناه الجن لبلقيس *
ودار الخيزران	بمكة بنتها خيزران جارية الخليفة *
وقصر بَهْرام جُور	من حجر واحد قرب همذان *
وقصر غَفْرآ	بالشام *

or a *zūn*,	"a place where idols are gathered, erected, and adorned"
or a *masjid*,	["mosque"] "too well known to require definition"
or a *kanīsah*,	["church" or "synagogue"] "too well known to require definition"
or a *fuhr*,	"the *midrās* ('midrash') of the Jews in which they gather on their festival, or . . ."[190]
or a *midrās*,	"a place in which the Qur'an is recited; origin of the *midrās* of the Jews"
or Kawkabān,	"a castle in Yemen whose inside was studded with rubies so that it shone like a star"
or al-Jawsaq,	"a house built for al-Muqtadir[191] inside the caliph's house in which was a pool of lead[192] thirty cubits by twenty"
or Qaṣr al-Nuʿmān,	[the Palace of al-Nuʿmān][193] that was built for him by al-Sinimmār; the latter was an artisan who built a palace for al-Nuʿmān, son of Imru' al-Qays; when he finished it, the latter threw him from its highest point so that he could never build another like it; or he was a slave of Uḥayḥah[194] who built a castle; when he finished, Uḥayḥah asked him, "Have you made it strong?" and he responded, "I know a stone in it which, if pulled out, will lead to its utter collapse" and Uḥayḥah asked him which stone it was, so he showed it to him, and then Uḥayḥah pushed him off the castle and he was killed
or al-Jaʿfarī,	"a palace of al-Mutawakkil's[195] close to Surra Man Ra'ā"
or al-Mārid,	["the Defiant"] "a castle at Dawmat al-Jandal"[196] **2.14.40**
or al-Ablaq,	["the Piebald"] "a castle at Taymā', one of two that al-Zabbā' tried and failed to take, leading her to say, 'al-Mārid defied me, and al-Ablaq was too strong'"
or Ṣirwāḥ,	"a castle built by the jinn for Bilqīs"
or Dār al-Khayzurān,	"at Mecca, built by Khayzurān,[197] the caliph's slave girl"
or Qaṣr Bahrām Jūr,	"made from a single rock, near Hamadhān"
or Qaṣr Ghafrā',	"in Syria"

والبديع بنآ عظيم للمتوكل بسرّ من راى *

و زُعَيرة حصن قرب الكرك *

وقصر عِسَل بالبصرة *

والنَدّ حصن باليمن *

والغُفر حصن بها * ٤١,١٤,٢

وسَمدان حصن بها عظيم *

والشَخَب حصن بها *

وثَربان حصن بها *

وهِرّان حصن بها *

وشُواحِط حصن بها *

والمَوْهَبة حصن بها *

والظَفِير[1] حصن يمانى صنعا *

ولَسِيس حصن باليمن *

والنُجير حصن قرب حضرموت *

وغُمدان قصر باليمن بناه يشرخ باربعة وجوه احمر وابيض واصفر واخضر وبنى داخله قصرا بسبعة سقوف بين كل سقف اربعون ذراعا *

لما انفك ان يصرخ ويقول المراة المراة * ومن لى بالمراة * ولا عيش الا مع المراة *

ولو انزلته فى

شِعْب بوّان احدى الجنان الاربع * ٤٢,١٤,٢

وصنعآ د باليمن كثيرة الاشجار والمياه تشبه دمشق *

---

١ كذا في القاموس وفي ١٨٥٥: الظُفَيْر.

or al-Badīʿ,	"a large building of al-Mutawakkil's, at Surra Man Raʾā"
or Zuʿayrah,	"a castle close to al-Karak"
or Qaṣr ʿIsl,	"at Baṣrah"
or al-Nadd,	"a castle in Yemen"
or al-Ghufr,	another castle there 2.14.41
or Samadān,	another castle there, large
or al-Shakhab,	another castle there
or Tharabān,	another castle there
or Hirrān,	another castle there
or Shuwāḥiṭ,	another castle there
or al-Mawhabah,	another castle there
or al-Ẓafīr,	a castle east of Ṣanʿāʾ
or Lasīs,	"a castle in Yemen"
or al-Nujayr,	"a castle close to Haḍramawt"
or Ghumdān,	"a palace in Yemen built by Yashrukh, with four faces, one red, one white, one yellow, and one green, inside of which he built another palace with seven roofs, each roof forty cubits distant from the next"

he still wouldn't stop yelling, "A woman! A woman! Who will get me a woman?" and "No life without a woman!" and if you set him down in

Shiʿb Bawwān,	"one of the four paradises" 2.14.42
or Ṣanʿāʾ,	"a town in Yemen with many trees and much water resembling Damascus"

والسُغْد بساتين نزهة واماكن مثمرة بسمرقند *

والشَعْران جبل قرب الموصل من اعمر الجبال بالفواكه والطيور *

والوَهْط بستان ومال كان لعمرو بن العاص على ثلثة اميال من وَجّ كان يُعرَّش على الف الف خشبة شرا كل خشبة درهم *

وبَلَنسية د شرقى الاندلس محفوف بالجنان لا ترى الا مياها تدفع ولا تسمع الا اطيارا تسجع *

ومُرْسية د اسلامى بالمغرب كثيرة المنازه والبساتين *

وثَمانين بلد بناه نوح عم لما خرج من السفينة ومعه ثمانون نفسا *

وجابَلَص د بالمغرب ليس ورآه انسى *

والراهُون جبل بالهند هبط عليه آدم عم *

والجُودىّ جبل بالجزيرة استوت عليه سفينة نوح عم *

وقاف جبل محيط بالارض او من زمرذ وما من بلد الا وفيه عرق منه وعليه مَلَك اذا اراد الله ان يهلك قوما امره فحرّك فخُسِف بهم *

والقِيق جبل محيط بالدنيا ومثله الفِيق *

والساهِرة ارض يجردها الله يوم القيامة *

لما انفك يصرخ ويقول المراة المراة * ومن لى بالمراة * ولا عيش الا مع المراة * بلَ لو صعد الى

المِشْريق باب للتوبة في السمآ * ٤٣،١٤،٢

وطوبى شجرة في الجنة *

وعلّيين في السمآ السابعة تصعد اليه ارواح المومنين جمع عِلّى *

or al-Sughd,	"pleasure gardens and places filled with fruiting trees, in Samarqand"
or al-Shaʿrān,	"a mountain close to Mosul, one of the mountains most overflowing with fruits and birds"
or al-Wahṭ,	"an orchard, or a property belonging to ʿAmr ibn al-ʿĀṣ[198], three miles from Wajj[199], that took a million pieces of wood to trellis, each piece costing one dirham"
or Balansiyyah,	[Valencia] "A town in eastern al-Andalus, surrounded by gardens where all one can hear is water gushing and birds caroling"
or Mursiyyah,	[Murcia] "An Islamic town in the Maghreb, with many parks and orchards"
or Thamānīn,	[literally, "Eighty"] "A town built by Nūḥ, peace be upon him, when he left the ark with eighty souls"
or Jābalaṣ,	"a town in the Maghreb, beyond which nothing human lives"
or al-Rāhūn,	"a mountain in India, on which Adam, peace be upon him, fell"[200]
or al-Jūdī,	"a mountain in al-Jazīrah[201], on which the ark of Nūḥ came to rest"
or Qāf,	"a mountain that surrounds the earth, or one made of emeralds, a vein of which is present in every town and on which is an angel to whom God, should He wish to destroy a people, gives an order, which the angel carries out, causing them to be swallowed up by the earth"
or Qīq,	"a mountain that surrounds the world, also called Fīq"
or al-Sāhirah,	"a land that God will strip bare on the Day of Resurrection"

he wouldn't stop yelling, "A woman! A woman! Who will get me a woman?" and "No life without a woman!" In fact, even if he ascended to

al-Mishrīq,	"a gate for repentance, in Heaven"	2.14.43
or Ṭūbā,	"a tree in Heaven"	
or ʿIlliyyīn,	"in the Seventh Heaven, to which the souls of the Believers ascend; plural of *ʿIllī*"	

والضُراح البيت المعمور فى السمآ الرابعة *

وبُرقَع اسم للسمآ السابعة او الرابعة او الاولى *

والحاقورة اسم للسمآ الرابعة *

والصاقورة اسم للسمآ الثالثة *

والغُرفة السمآ السابعة وكذا عَرُوبا وفيها سدرة المنتهى *

وعِقيَوْن بحر من الريح تحت العرش فيه ملئكة من الريح معهم رماح من الريح ناظرين الى العرش تسبيحهم سبحان ربنا الاعلى *

والاَعْراف سور بين الجنة والنار*

لاخذ يزعق بمجامع حلقومه ويقول المراة المراة * فانى ما دمت بشرا لا بدّ لى من المراة * ولو اريته من الغرائب

السَكِينة شى كان له راس كراس الهر من زبرجد وياقوت وجناحان * ٤٤،١٤،٢

والكِلْواذ تابوت التوراة *

وقُرطى ماريّة هى مارية بنت ارقم او ظالم كان فى قرطها مائتا دينار او جوهر قوّم باربعين الف دينار او درّتان كبيضتى حمامة لم يرَ مثلهما قط فاهدتهما الى الكعبة *

وقنطرة خُرَّذاذَ امّ اردشير[١] بسمرقند بين ايدج والرباط من عجائب الدنيا طولها الف ذراع وعلوها مائة وخمسون اكثرها مبنى بالرصاص والحديد *

---

١ كذا في القاموس وفي ١٨٥٥: خُرَّزاذا امّ ازدشير.

or al-Ḍurāḥ,	"the Prosperous House in the Seventh Heaven"
or Burquʿ,	"a name for the Seventh, Fourth, or First Heaven"
or al-Ḥāqūrah,	"a name for the Fourth Heaven"
or al-Ṣāqūrah,	"a name for the Third Heaven"
or al-Ghurfah,	"the Seventh Heaven, also called ʿArūbā; it contains the lote tree beyond which none may pass"[202]
or ʿIqyawn,	"a sea of wind beneath the Throne in which there are angels of wind with spears of wind gazing at the Throne whose Magnificat is 'Glory to Our Lord Most High!'"
or the Aʿrāf,	"a wall between Paradise and the Fire"

he would set about yelling with all the force his throat could muster, "A woman! A woman! So long as I am human, I must have a woman!" and if you were to show him such wonders as

the Sakīnah,	"a thing that had a head like a cat's, made of chrysolite and ruby and with two wings"	2.14.44
or the Kilwādh,	"the Ark of the Torah"	
or Māriyyah's Earrings,	"she was Māriyyah, daughter of Arqam, or Ẓālim, who had two hundred dinars in her earrings, or jewels valued at forty thousand dinars, or two pearls like pigeon's eggs the like of which had never been seen before, so she gave them to the Kaaba"	
or the Bridge of Khurradhādh, the mother of Ardashīr,	"in Samarqand, between Aydaj and the fort, one of the wonders of the world, one thousand cubits in length and one hundred and fifty in height, mostly constructed of lead and iron"	

وتابوت تاحة — هى تاحة بنت ذى الشُفَر قال ابن هشام حفر السيل عن قبر باليمن فيه امراة فى عنقها سبع مخانق من در وفى يديها ورجليها من الاسورة والخلاخيل والدماليج سبعة سبعة وفى كل اصبع خاتم فيه جوهرة مثمنة وعند راسها تابوت مملو مالاً ولوح فيه مكتوب باسمك اللهم اله حمير انا تاحة بنت ذى شفر بعثت مائرنا الى يوسف فابطا علينا فبعثت لاذتى بمُدّ من وَرِق لتاتينى بمُد من طحن فلم تجده فبعثت بمدّ من ذهب فلم تجده فبعثت بمد من بحرىّ فلم تجد فامرت به فطُحن فلم انتفع به فاقتفلت فمن سمع بى فليرحمنى وايّة امراة لبست حليا من حليى فلا ماتت الّا ميتتى[1] *

وذا الفَقار — سيف العاص بن منبّه قتل يوم بدر وكان كافرا فصار الى البنى صلّعم ثم صار الى علىّ *

والكَشُوح — من السيوف السبعة التى اهدتها بلقيس الى سليمن عمّ *

والِجنّ — حىّ من الجن منهم الكلاب السود البهم او سفلة الجن وضعفاوهم وكلابهم اوخلق بين الانس والجن *

واَوْرم الجَوْز — قرية بحلب فيها اعجوبة وهى ان المجاورين لها من القرى يرون فيها بالليل ضونار فى هيكل فيها فاذا جاوه لا يرون شيا *

والرِئّ — جنّى يُرَى فيُحبّ *

---

[1] ١٨٥٥: ميتى.

the Sepulcher of Ṭāḥah, — "Ṭāḥah was the daughter of Dhī l-Shufr; Ibn Hishām[203] says that a flash flood washed away the earth from a grave in Yemen in which was a woman around whose neck were seven ropes of pearls and on whose hands and feet were seven times seven bracelets, anklets, and armlets and on each of whose fingers was a precious stone and at whose head was a chest full of money and a tablet on which was written 'In Your Name, O God, God of Ḥimyar![204] I am Ṭāḥah, daughter of Dhī Shufr [sic]. I sent our purveyor to Yūsuf, but he made no haste to help us, so I sent my trusted lady-in-waiting with a bushel of silver that she might bring us a bushel of flour, but she could find none, so I sent a bushel of gold, and still she could find none, so I sent a bushel of fine pearls, and still she could find none, so I ordered the pearls brought and had them ground up, but I benefited nothing and had no food to give out, so let any who hears my plight be merciful to me, and let no woman who dons one piece of my finery die any death other than mine.'"

or Dhū l-Faqār, — "the sword of Sayf ibn Munabbih who was killed at the battle of Badr;[205] he was an unbeliever, so his sword became the property of the Prophet (peace and blessings upon him) and of ʿAlī[206]"

or the Kashūḥ, — "one of the seven swords that Bilqīs presented to Sulaymān, peace be upon him"

or the Ḥinn, — "a tribe of the jinn to which jet-black dogs belong, or the meanest and weakest of the jinn and their dogs, or creatures between men and jinn"

or Awram al-Jawz, — "a village near Aleppo in which is a wonder, to wit, that at night the neighboring villages see firelight there in a tabernacle, but when they go to it they find nothing"

or the Raʾiyy, — "a jinni who, once seen, is loved"

وفرس قاين الذى قال له هِجّدَم	يقال اول من ركبه ابن ادم القاتل حل على اخيه فزجر الفرس فقال هِجْ[1] الدم فخفف *
والعصافير	شجر يسمّى من راى مثلى له صورة كالعصافير كثيرة بفارس * ٤٥،١٤،٢
والنَسناس	جنس من الخلق يثب احدهم على رِجْل واحدة فى الحديث ان حيّا من عاد عصوا رسولهم فمسخهم الله نسناسا لكل انسان منهم يد ورجل من شق واحد ينقزون كما ينقز الطائر ويرعون كما ترعى البهائم وقيل اولئك انقرضوا والموجود على تلك الخلقة خلق على حدة اوهم ثلثة اجناس ناس ونسناس ونسانس او النسانس الاناث منهم اوهم ارفع قدرا من النسناس اوهم ياجوج وماجوج اوهم قوم من بنى آدم او خلق على صورة الناس وخالفوهم فى اشيا وليسوا منهم *
ودُعْموصا	رجل زنّا مسخه الله دعموصا لدويبة او دودة سودآ تكون في الغدران اذا نشت *
وعَبّودا	عبد اسود اول الناس دخولا الجنة *
وعامِر بن جَدَرة	اول من كتب بخطنا *
ومُرامرا	اول من وضع الخط العربى *
وابا عُرْوة	رجل كان يصيح بالاسد فيموت فيشقّ بطنه فيوجد قلبه قد زال عن موضعه *

١ ١٨٥٥: هج.

or Qāyin's horse, called Hijdam,	"it is said that, when Adam's son, the murderer, first mounted him, he charged his brother, but the horse held back, so he said, 'Bestir thy blood! (*hij al-dam*),' so it surged forward"
or the ʿAṣāfīr,	"a kind of tree called 'Who Has Seen My Like?' which has the shape of birds (*ʿaṣāfīr*), plentiful in Persia" 2.14.45
or the Nasnās,	"a species of creature that jumps on one foot; in the hadith it says that a tribe of ʿĀd[207] rebelled against their prophet, so God turned them into Nasnās, each one of whom had a hand and a foot on one side of the body and who hopped like birds and grazed like beasts; it is also said that those have become extinct and that what currently exists of that form are a separate species, or that they are of three kinds—*nās*, *nasnās*, and *nasānis*;[208] or that the *nasānis* are the females, or that they are a higher form than the *nasnās*, or that they are Yākhūkh and Mākhūkh,[209] or that they are a group of humans, or creatures that are in the shape of people but differ from them in certain things and are not of them"
or Daʿmūṣā,	"an adulterer whom God turned into a *daʿmūṣā*, meaning a certain creeping thing, or a black worm such as is found in rain pools when they dry up"
or ʿAbbūdā,	"a black slave, the first person to enter Paradise"
or ʿĀmir ibn Jadarah,	"the first person to write using our script"
or Murāmirā,	"the inventor of the Arabic script"
or Abū ʿUrwah,	"a man who shouted, 'Lions!' and then died, and when his belly was cut open, his heart was found to have moved from one place in his body to another"

وطَهْمُورث ملك من عظما الفرس ملك سبعمائة سنة *

والوَضّاح رجل ملك الارض وكانت امه جنّية فلحق بالجنّ *

والرابضة ملئكة أُهْبِطُوا[١] مع ادم وبقية حملة الحجة لا تخلو الارض منهم *

واليَبْرُوح اصل اللفّاح شبيه بصورة انسان *

وسُكَيْنة اسم البقّة الداخلة انف نمروذ * ٢،١٤،٤٦

وطاخِية نملة كلمت سليمن عم *

وعَيجَلوف اسم النملة المذكورة فى القرآن *

والتُخَس دابة بحرية تنجى الغريق تمكّنه من ظهرها ليستعين على السباحة وتسمى الدلفين *

والجَسّاسة دابة تكون في الجزائر تجسّ الاخبار فتاتى بها الدجال *

والرُخّ طائر كبير يحمل الكَرْكَدّن *

والكركدن دابة تحمل الفيل على قرنها *

والزَبَعْرى دابة تحمل الفيل بقرنها *

والعَقام سمك وحيّة تسكن البحر وياتى الاسود من البر فيصفر على الشط فتخرج اليه العقام فيتلاويان ثم يفترقان فيذهب كل منهما الى منزله *

وبنت طَبَق سلحفاة تبيض تسعا وتسعين بيضة كلها سلاحف وتبيض بيضة تنقف عن حية *

والفَلَتان طائر يصيد القردة * ٢،١٤،٤٧

---

١ كذا في القاموس وفي ١٨٥٥: هبطوا.

or Ṭakhmūrath,	"one of the great kings of the Persians, who reigned for seven hundred years"
or al-Waḍḍāḥ,	"a man who ruled the earth; his mother was of the jinn, so he returned to them"
or the Rābiḍah,	"angels" who descended "with Adam, or the remainder of the bearers of the Proof, which no part of the earth is without"[210]
or the *yabrūḥ*,	"the mandrake root, which resembles a human"
or Sukaynah,	"the name of the bedbug that got up Numrūdh's nose" **2.14.46**
or Ṭākhiyah,	"an ant who spoke to Sulaymān,[211] peace be upon him"
or ʿAyjalūf,	"the name of the ant mentioned in the Qur'an"[212]
or the *tukhas*,	"a sea beast that rescues drowning men by offering them its back to save them from having to swim; also called the *dulfīn* ('dolphin')"
or the *jassāsah*,	"a beast to be found on islands that seeks out news and passes it on to the Antichrist"
or the *rukhkh*,	"a large bird that can lift a rhinoceros"
or the *karkadan*,	["rhinoceros"] "a beast that can lift an elephant on its horn"
or the *zabaʿrā*,	"a beast that can carry an elephant on its horn"
or the *ʿaqām*,	"a fish, or a snake that lives in the sea—the lion comes from the land and whistles on the shore, the *ʿaqām* comes out to it, and they intertwine; then they part and each returns to its dwelling"
or *bint ṭabaq*,	[literally, "daughter of a plate"] "the tortoise, which lays ninety-nine eggs, all of which are tortoises, and one more, which hatches to reveal a snake"
or the *falatān*,	"a bird that hunts apes" **2.14.47**

والبُلَت طائر محترق الريش ان وقعت ريشة منه فى الطير احرقته *

والسَمَنْدل طائر بالهند لا يحترق بالنار *

والتِهِبِّط طائر اغبر يتعلق برجليه ويصوت بصوت كانه يقول انا اموت انا اموت *

والأُنَن طائر كالحمام صوته انين أُوِّهِ اوه *

والزماح طائر ياخذ الصبى من مهده *

والهَدِيل فرخ على عهد نوح عم مات عطشا او صاده جارح من الطير فما من حمامة الا وهى تبكى عليه *

والقَرَقْفَنَّة طائر يمسح جناحيه على عينى القنذع الديّوث فيزداد لينا *

والقَقَنَّس طائر عظيم بمنقاره اربعون ثقبا يصوت بكل الانغام والالحان العجيبة المطربة ياتى الى راس جبل فيجمع من الحطب ما شآ ويقعد ينوح على نفسه اربعين يوما ويجتمع اليه العالم يستمعون اليه ويتلذذون ثم يصعد الى الحطب ويصفق بجناحيه فينقدح منه نار ويحترق الحطب والطائر ويبقى رمادا فيتكوّن منه طائر مثله ذكره ابن سينا فى الشفآ *

لمدّ عنقه وجعل اصابعه فى اذنيه واذّن صارخا * هاى هاى المراة المراة * اروني المراة * ما يجزئني شي عن المراة * ولو انك لاعبته

٤٨,١٤,٢ بالجُنابَى لعبة للصبيان *

وحَدَبْدَبَى لعبة للنبيط *

والطَبْطابة خشبة عريضة يلعب بها بالكرة *

والقِرِطِبَّى ضرب من اللعب ونوع من الصراع *

or the *bulat*,	"a bird with burning feathers which, should they fall on other birds, burn them"
or the *samandal*,	"a bird in India that cannot be burned by fire"
or the *tihibbiṭ*,	"a grayish bird that clings on with its feet and makes a sound as though it were saying '*anā amūt anā amūt*, I am dying, I am dying'"
or the *unan*,	"a bird like a dove whose sound is a moan—'ouhi-ouhi'"
or the *zummāḥ*,	"a bird that takes children from their cradles"
or the *hadīl*,	"a chick in the days of Nūḥ, peace be upon him, that died of thirst or was caught by some bird of prey, so that every dove now weeps for it"
or the *qarqafannah*,	"a bird that wipes the eyes of the complacent wittol with its wings, making him yet more pliant"
or the *faqannas*,	"a large bird with forty holes in its beak that sings every exhilarating, wonderful tune and air; it comes to the top of a mountain and collects as much firewood as it wants and sits and mourns for itself for forty days, during which everyone gathers to listen to it and take pleasure; then it climbs atop the firewood and claps its wings, and fire is struck from them, and the firewood and the bird catch fire, and it turns to ashes; then a new bird just like it is formed from them; Ibn Sīnā mentions it in the *Shifā'* (*The Cure*)[213]"

he would crane his neck and cup his ears with his hands[214] and cry to all the world, "Hey! Hey! A woman! A woman! Show me a woman! Nothing can take the place of a woman for me," and if you were to seek to divert him with

a *junābā*,	"a child's game"	**2.14.48**
or a *ḥadabdabā*,	"a game of the Nabataeans"	
or a *ṭabṭābah*,	"a broad stick used when playing ball"	
or *qarṭibbā*,	"a way of playing, or a kind of wrestling"	

والكِبْكِب لعبة *

والكُوبة النرد او الشطرنج *

والهَبْهاب لعبة للصبيان *

وكُتُكُتَى لعبة *

والبُحَيْثَى لعبة بالبُحاثة اى التراب *

والكُتُكُثَى لعبة بالتراب *

والطَثّ لعبة للصبيان يرمون بخشبة مستديرة تسمى المِطَثّة * ٤٩،١٤،٢

واللُوثة خرقة تجمع ويلعب بها *

والاُنْبُوثة لعبة يدفنون شيا فى حفير فمن استخرجه غلب *

والشِطْرنج معروف *

والخَرِيج لعبة يقال لها خَرَاجِ خَرَاجِ *

والفَنْزَج رقص للعجم *

والقَجْقَجة لعبة يقال لها عَظْمِ وضّاح *

والكُجّة لعبة ياخذ الصبى خرقة فيدوّرها كانها كرة *

والكَجْكَجة لعبة تسمى است الكلبة *

والجُمّاح تمرة تجعل على راس خشبة يلعب بها الصبيان *

والجَمْح رمى الصبى الكعب بالكعب حتى يزيله عن مكانه * ٥٠،١٤،٢

ودِحِنْدِح لعبة للصبية يجتمعون لها فيقولونها فمن اخطاها قام على رجل وحجل سبع مرات *

والدّاح نقش يلوّح للصبيان يعلّلون به ومنه الدنيا داحة *

والرُجّاحة حبل يعلّق ويركبه الصبيان *

or *kibkib*,	"a game"	
or *kūbah*,	"backgammon, or chess"	
or *habhāb*,	"a children's game"	
or *kutkutā*,	"a game"	
or *buḥḥaythā*,	"a game using *buḥāthah* (i.e., 'soil')"	
or *kuthkuthā*,	"a game using soil"	
or *taṭhth*,	"a children's game, in which they throw a round piece of wood called a *miṭaththah*"	2.14.49
or a *lūthah*,	"a piece of cloth, picked up and played with"	
or *unbūthah*,	"a game in which they bury something in a hole they make and the one who gets it out wins"	
or *shiṭranj*,	["chess"] "too well known to require definition"	
or *kharīj*,	"a game also called *kharāji kharāji*"	
or *fanzaj*,	"a non-Arab dance"	
or *qajqajah*,	"a game, also called 'Waḍḍāḥ's Bone'[215]"	
or *kujjah*,	"a game in which the child takes a piece of cloth and twists it until it takes the shape of a ball"	
or *kajkajah*,	"a game also called *ist al-kalbah* ('bitch's butt')"	
or a *jummāḥ*,	"a date placed on the end of a stick that children play with"	
or *jamḥ*,	"a child's kicking the heel of another child with his own in order to dislodge it from its place"	2.14.50
or *diḥindiḥ*,	"a children's game, in which they gather and then say this word, and any who mispronounces it has to stand on one leg and hop seven times"	
or *dāḥ*,	"gewgaws that one waves at children and by which they are pacified; from it derives the saying *al-dunyā dāḥah* ('the world is a gaudy toy')"	
or a *rujjāḥah*,	"a rope that is suspended and that children climb"	

والدُبّاخ لعبة *
والدُماخ لعبة للاعراب *
والمِطخة خشبة يلعب بها الصبيان *
والطَرِيدة لعبة تسميها العامة المَسّة والضَبْطة فاذا وقعت يد اللاعب من آخر على بدنه[1] او راسه او كتفه فهى المسّة واذا وقعت على الرجل فهى الاَسْن *
والنَرد معروف *
والمواغدة لعبة وان تفعل كفعل صاحبك *
والبقّار لعبة * ٢،١٤،٥١
والبُقَّيرَى لعبة *
والجِعِرَّى لعبة للصبيان وهو ان يحمل الصبى بين اثنين على ايديهما *
والحاجُورة لعبة تخط الصبيان خطّا مدورا ويقف فيه صبى ويحيطون به لياخذوه *
والدِكر لعبة للزنج والحبش *
والسَحّارة شى يلعب به الصبيان *
والسُدَّر لعبة للصبيان *
والعَرعرة لعبة للصبيان *
والشَعارير لعبة *
والمِنجار لعبة للصبيان او الصواب الميجار *
والتُوَز خشبة يلعب بها بالكِجّة * ٢،١٤،٥٢

---

[1] ١٨٥٥: بدنه رأسه.

or *dubbākh,*	"a game"	
or *dumākh,*	"a game played by the Arabs of the desert"	
or a *miṭakhkhah,*	"a piece of wood that children play with"	
or a *ṭarīdah,*	"a game, called by the common people *al-massah wa-l-ḍabṭah* ('touch and grab'); if a player's hand falls onto another's trunk, head, or shoulder, it is called *massah,* and if it falls onto his leg it is called *asn*"	
or *nard,*	["backgammon"] "too well known to require definition"	
or *muwāghadah,*	"a game, in which you do the same as your companion does"	
or *baqqār,*	"a game"	2.14.51
or *buqqayrā,*	"a game"	
or *jiʿirrā,*	"a children's game in which the child is carried between two others on their hands"	
or *ḥājūrah,*	"a game in which children draw a circle and a child stands inside it and they surround him to try to grab him"	
or *dikr,*	"a game of the negroes and Ethiopians"	
or *saḥḥārah,*	"something children play with"	
or *suddar,*	"a children's game"	
or *ʿarʿarah,*	"a children's game"	
or *shaʿārīr,*	"a game"	
or *minjār,*	"a children's game; the correct form may be *mījār*"	
or a *tūz,*	"a piece of wood with which they play at *kujjah*"	2.14.52

والعَرْز عرز لفلان قبض على شى فى كفه ضامّا عليه اصابعه يريه منه شيا لينظر اليه ولا يريه كله *

والقُفَّيْزَى لعبة للصبيان ينصبون خشبة ويتقافزون عليها *

والنُفّاز لعبة لهم يتنافزون فيها اى يتواثبون *

والبُكْسة الكجة *

والحَوالِس لعبة للصبيان *

والدُسَّة لعبة *

والدَعْكَسة لعب للمجوس كالرقص *

والفِسْفِسَى لعبة لهم *

والفاعوس لعبة لهم *

والبَوْصاً لعبة لهم ياخذون عودا فى راسه نار فيديرونه على رؤسهم * ٥٣,١٤,٢

والرَقّاصة لعبة *

والحُوطة لعبة تسمى الدارة *

والخُطّة لعبة للاعراب *

والضَبْطة لعبة لهم *

والتَضَرْفُط وهو ان تركب احدا وتخرج رجليك من تحت ابطيه وتجعلهما على عنقه *

والضُرَيْفِطيّة لعبة لهم *

والمَقْط مقط الكرة ضرب بها الارض ثم اخذها *

والمِرْصاع دُوّامة الصبيان وكل خشبة يُدحَى بها *

or *ʿarz,*	"when someone plays at *ʿarz,* he takes something in his hand and closes his fingers over it and shows a part of it for another to see but doesn't show him all of it"
or *quffayzā,*	"a children's game in which they erect a piece of wood and compete at jumping over it"
or *nuffāz,*	"a game of theirs in which they compete at bounding, or leaping"
or a *buksah,*	"[the *buksah* is] the *kujjah*"
or *ḥawālis,*	"a children's game"
or *dussah,*	"a game"
or *daʿkasah,*	"a pastime of the Magians, similar to dancing"
or *fisfisā,*	"a game they play"
or *fāʿūs,*	"a game they play"
or *bawṣāʾ,*	"a game they play, in which they take a stick with fire at its end and pass it around on their heads" 2.14.53
or *raqqāṣah,*	"a game"
or *ḥūṭah,*	"a game that they also call *dārah*"
or *khuṭṭah,*	"a game played by the Arabs of the desert"
or *ḍabṭah,*	"a game they play"
or *taḍarfuṭ,*	"this is when you climb onto someone's back and stick your legs out from under his armpits and put them around his neck"
or *ḍurayfiṭiyyah,*	"a game they play"
or *maqṭ,*	"to play *maqṭ* with the ball is to cast it onto the ground and then catch it"
or a *mirṣāʿ,*	"a child's spinning top or any piece of wood that is thrown down to hit a mark in a game"

واليَرْمَع الخُذْروف *

وقَلَوْبَع لعبة لهم *

والحَفَة اللعب بالكرة * ٥٤،١٤،٢

والخُذْرُوف شى يدوره الصبى بخيط فى يديه فيسمع له دوىّ ويسمّى ايضا الخُذْرة والقرصافة والخذروف ايضا طين يجن يعمل شبيها بالسكّر يلعب به الصبيان *

والزُحْلوفة تزلّج الصبيان من فوق التل الى اسفله *

والعَياف العياف والطريدة لعبتان لهم *

وقاصّة قرصافة لعبة لهم *

والحُزُقّة ضرب من اللعب *

والدَبّوق لعبة *

والزُحْلوقة الارجوحة *

والشَفَلَّقة لعبة وهوان يكسع انسانا من خلفه فيصرعه *

والعَفّقة لعبة *

والعُقّة التى يلعب بها الصبيان * ٥٥،١٤،٢

والقِرَق لعب السُدَّر *

والكُرَّك لعبة لهم *

ودِبَّى حَجَل لعبة *

والدُخَيْلياّ لعبة لهم *

والدِرَقّلة لعبة للصبيان *

والدِرَكّلة لعبة للعجم او ضرب من الرقص اوهى حبشية *

or a *yarmaʿ*,	"the same as a *khudhrūf*"
or *qalawbaʿ*,	"a game they play"
or *jaḥfah*,	"playing ball" 2.14.54
or a *khudhrūf*,	"a thing that a child turns with a string in his hands and that produces a humming sound; also called a *khudhrah* or a *qirfāṣah*; *khudhrūf* is also clay that is kneaded until it is made into something like sugar that children play with"
or *zuḥlūfah*,	"the sliding of children from the top of a mound to its bottom"
or *ʿayāf*,	"*ʿayāf* and *ṭarīdah* are two games they play"
or *qāṣṣah qirfāṣah*,	"a game they play"
or *ḥuzuqqah*,	"a kind of pastime"
or *dabbūq*,	"a game"
or a *zuḥlūqah*,	"a swing"
or *shafalaqqah*,	"a game consisting of striking a person from behind and then throwing him to the ground"
or *ʿafqah*,	"a game"
or a *ʿuqqah*,	"such as children play with"[216] 2.14.55
or *qirq*,	"a pastime of the frivolous"
or *kurrak*,	"a game they play"
or *dibbā ḥajal*,	"a game"
or *dukhayliyāʾ*,	"a game they play"
or *diraqlah*,	"a children's game"
or *diraklah*,	"a game played by non-Arabs, or a kind of dance; or it may be Ethiopian"

والفِئال لعبة للصبيان يخبّون الشى فى التراب ثم يقسمونه ويقولون فى ايّها هو *

والفِيال لعبة لفتيان العرب *

والدُمَّة لعبة *

والدُوّامة التى يلعب بها الصبيان فتدار وتسمى ايضا المِرْصاع *

والمَرْغمة لعبة لهم * ٥٦,١٤,٢

والشَّحمة لعبة لهم *

وعَظْم وضّاح لعبة لهم *

والمِهْزام عود يجعل فى راسه نار يلعبون به *

والبَرْطَنة ضرب من اللهو كالبرطمة *

والتُوْن خرقة يلعب عليها بالكجة *

والطُبَن لعبة لهم *

والقِنّين لعبة للروم يتقامر بها *

والكُبْنة لعبة *

والدَمَه لعبة للصبيان *

والمِجْذا خشبة مدورة تلعب بها الاعراب *

والمخاساة خاساه لاعبه بالجوز فردا او زوجا *

والقُرَة لعبة *

والقُلَة عودان يلعب بهما الصبيان *

لشحر فاه وشحاه وعجاه وزاد صراخا وضجيجا وهو يقول المراة المراة * الا فلاعبونى بالمراة * ولو انك طرّبته

or *fi'āl*,	"a children's game consisting of hiding something in the dirt and then dividing the dirt into parts and saying, 'Which part is it in?'"
or *fiyāl*,	"a game played by Arab youths"
or *dummah*,	"a game"
or a *duwwāmah*,	[the "spinning top"] "that children play with, making it revolve; also called *mirṣā'*"
or *marghamah*,	"a game they play" 2.14.56
or *shaḥmah*,	"a game they play"
or *'aẓm Waḍḍāḥ*,	"a game they play"
or *mihzām*,	"a stick on top of which fire is placed and which they play with"
or *barṭanah*,	"a kind of diversion, also pronounced *barṭamah*"
or a *tūn*,	"a piece of cloth that they play with, like the *kujjah*"
or *ṭuban*,	"a game they play"
or *qinnīn*,	"a game played by the Greeks on which they gamble"
or *kubnah*,	"a game"
or *damah*,	"a children's game"
or a *mijdhā'*,	"a round piece of wood with which the Arabs of the desert play"
or *mikhāsāh*,	"to play *mikhāsāh* with someone is to play with him at walnuts, saying 'Odd or even?'"
or *quzzah*,	"a game"
or *qullah*,	"two sticks that children play with"

he would open wide his mouth in a rictus and yell yet louder and more noisily, saying "A woman! A woman! Give me a woman to play with!" and if you charmed his ear with

بالرَّباب	معروف *	٢,١٤,٥٧
والعَرطبة	العود او الطنبور او الطبل او طبل الحبشة *	
والكُوبة	البَربط والطبل الصغير المخصّر *	
والدِرِّيج	شى كالطنبور يضرب به *	
والصَنج	شى يتخذ من صُفر يضرب احدهما على الاخر وآلة باوتار يضرب بها معرّب والصيار صوت الصنج *	
والوَنج	ضرب من الاوتار والعود او المعزف *	
والعود	معروف *	
والمِزمار	ما يزمّر به ويقال له ايضا الزَمّخر والزَنبق والصُلبوب والنقيب والقَصّابة والهُبنوقة *	
والمِزهر	العود يضرب به *	
والشَبّور	البوق ويقال له ايضا القُبع والقُثع والقُنع والصُور *	
والطنبور	معروف *	٢,١٤,٥٨
والكَنّارات	العيدان او الدفوف او الطبول او الطنبور *	
والكُوس	الطبل *	
والبَربَط	العود *	
والشِياع	مزمار الراعى *	
والهَيرَعة	اليراعة يزمر بها الراعى *	
والدف	معروف *	
والمُستُقة	آلة يضرب بها الصنج ونحوه *	
والعَركَل	الدف والطبل *	

a *rabāb*,	["rebec, spike-fiddle"] "too well known to require definition"	2.14.57
or a *ʿarṭabah*,	"a lute, or a tambour, or drums, or the drums of the Ethiopians"	
or a *kūbah*,	"a lute, or a small goblet drum"	
or a *dirrīj*,	"a thing like a tambour that is played"	
or *ṣanj*,	"a thing made out of brass, one piece of which is struck against the other, or a stringed instrument that is played (an Arabized non-Arab word); the sound made by the *ṣanj* is referred to as *ṣiyār*"	
or *wanaj*,	"playing on strings or a lute or any musical instrument"	
or *ʿūd*,	["lute"] "too well known to require definition"	
or *mizmār*,	"what is blown on as though it were a reed; also called *zamkhar* or *zanbaq* or *ṣulbūb* or *naqīb* or *qaṣṣābah* or *hubnūqah*"	
or a *mizhar*,	"the *ʿūd* ('lute') on which one plays[217]"	
or a *shabbūr*,	"a trumpet, also called *qabʿ* or *quthʿ* or *qunʿ* or *ṣūr*"	
or a *ṭunbūr*,	["tambour"] "too well known to require definition"	2.14.58
or *kannārāt*,	"lutes, or large tambourines, or drums, or the tambour"	
or a *kūs*,	"a drum"	
or a *barbaṭ*,	"a lute"	
or a *shiyāʿ*,	"a shepherd's pipe"	
or a *hayraʿah*,	"a reed on which a shepherd blows"	
or a *duff*,	["large tambourine"] "too well known to require definition"	
or a *mustuqah*,	"an instrument with which cymbals and the like are struck"	
or a *ʿarkal*,	"a drum or a tambourine"	

والصَغانة	من الملاهى معرّبة *
والطُبَن	الطنبور او العود *
والقِنّين	الطنبور*
والكِران	العود او الصنج *
والوَنّ	الصنج *

لظل فاغرا فاه وهو يزعق ويقول المراة المراة * الا فطرّبونى بالمراة * ولو اطعمته *

الجُوذاب	طعام يتخذ من سكر ورز ولحم *	٢,١٤,٥٩
والقَبيب	الاقط خلط رطبه بيابسه *	
والكَباب	معروف *	
والسَنّوت	الزبد والجبن والعسل وضرب من التمر*	
واللَفيتة	العصيدة المغلّظة او مرقة تشبه الحيس*	
والنَفيتة	طعام اغلظ من السخينة *	
والعُلاثة	سمن واقط يخلط *	
والغَبيثة	لت الاقط بالسمن كالعبيثة *	
والسِكباج	معروف *	
والطَباهجة	اللحم المشرّح *	
والنابجة	طعام جاهلىّ *	٢,١٤,٦٠
والاَخِيخة	دقيق يعالج بالسمن او الزيت *	
والقَفيخة	طعام يعالج بالتمر والاهالة *	
والكامَخ	ادام *	
والثريد	معروف *	

or a *ṣaghānah*,	“a musical instrument (Arabized)”
or a *ṭubn*,	“a tambour or a lute”
or a *qinnīn*,	“a tambour”
or a *kirān*,	“a lute or the *ṣanj*”
or *wann*,	“the *ṣanj*”

he would remain open-mouthed, crying out and saying, “A woman! A woman! Will you not charm me with a woman?” and if you were to feed him with

jūdhāb,	“a dish made of sugar, rice, and meat”	2.14.59
or *qabīb*,	“moist and dry curds mixed together”	
or *kabāb*,	[“kebabs”] “too well known to require definition”	
or *sannūt*,	“butter, or cheese, or honey,[218] or a kind of date”	
or *lafītah*,	“thickened wheat gruel, or a broth resembling *ḥays*[219]”	
or *nafītah*,	“a dish thicker than *sakhīnah*”	
or *ʿulāthah*,	“clarified butter and curds mixed together”	
or *ghabīthah*,	“curds kneaded with clarified butter; synonym *ʿabīthah*”	
or *sikbāj*,	[“meat cooked in vinegar”] “too well known to require definition”	
or *ṭubāhajah*,	“sliced meat”	
or *nābijah*,	“a dish of the Days of Barbarism”	2.14.60
or *akhīkhah*,	“flour made with clarified butter or oil”	
or *qafīkhah*,	“a dish made with dates and drippings”	
or *kāmikh*,	“pickles”	
or *tharīd*,	[“crumbled bread moistened with broth”] “too well known to require definition”	

والرشيدية طعام معروف فارسيته رشته *

والرَّهيدة البُرّ يدق ويصب عليه لبن *

والشَهِيدة البَرَق المشوى *

والقَدِيد اللحم المشرّر المقدّد *

والحَنِيذ حنذ الشاه شواها وجعل فوقها حجارة محماة لينضجها فهى حينذ *

والزُماوَرْد طعام من البيض واللحم ويسمى ايضا الميسَّر * ٦١،١٤،٢

والبَرابِير طعام يتخذ من فريك السنبل والحليب *

والبُورانية طعام ينسب الى بوران بنت الحسن بن سهل زوج المامون *

والجاشِريّة طعام *

والجَعاجِر ما يتخذ من العجين كالتماثيل فيجعلونها فى الربّ اذا طبخوه *

والحَرِيرة دقيق يطبخ بلبن او دسم *

والحَكَر السمن بالعسل يلعقهما الصبى *

والمَخْبور الطعام المدسّم والخُبْرَة الثريدة[١] الضخمة — والطعام واللحم وما قُدّم من شى وطعام يحمله المسافر فى سفرته وقصعة فيها خبز ولحم بين اربعة اوخمسة *

والخَزِيرة شبه عصيدة بلحم *

والصَحِيرة اللبن الحليب يغلى ثم يصب عليه السمن *

والغَذِيرة دقيق يحلب عليه لبن ثم يحمى بالرضف * ٦٢،١٤،٢

---

١ والخُبْرة الثريدة: كذا في القاموس وفي ١٨٥٥: الخُبْرة والثريدة.

or *rashīdiyyah,*	"a well-known dish; in Persian *rishtah* ('noodles')"
or *rahīdah,*	"pounded wheat over which milk is poured"
or *shahīdah,*	"grilled lamb"
or *qadīd,*	"jerked, sun-dried meat"
or *ḥanīdh,*	"*ḥanadha l-shāh* means 'he grilled the ewe by placing on top of it heated stones to cook it'; the result is called *ḥanīdh*"
or *zumāward,*	"a dish of eggs and meat, also called *muyassar*" 2.14.61
or *barābīr,*	"a dish made of parched ears of wheat and fresh milk"
or *būrāniyyah,*	"a dish attributed to Būrān, daughter of al-Ḥasan ibn Sahl, the wife of al-Ma'mūn"[220]
or *jāshiriyyah,*	"a dish"
or *ja'ājir,*	"whatever is made of dough, such as figurines, that they then place in inspissated fruit juice and cook"
or *ḥarīrah,*	"flour cooked with milk or fat"
or *ḥakr,*	"clarified butter with honey that children lick"
or *makhbūr,*	fatty dishes or[221] "*khubrah,* or *tharīdah ḍakhmah* ('great *tharīdah*') . . . or food generally, or meat, or the part of a thing that is offered, or food that a traveler takes with him on his journey, or a large wooden bowl containing bread and meat for between four and five persons"
or *khazīrah,*	"something resembling *'aṣīdah* ('a paste of flour and clarified butter') with meat"
or *ṣaḥīrah,*	"fresh milk that is boiled and onto which clarified butter is poured"
or *ghadhīrah,*	"flour to which fresh milk is added and which is then heated with hot stones" 2.14.62

والفُرفور	سويق من ثمر اليَنبوت *
والمُرّىّ	ادام الكامخ *
والمَضِيرة	مريقة تطبخ باللبن المضير*
والنَّجِيرة	لبن يخلط بطحين او سمن *
والوَغِير	لبن يغلى ويطبخ *
والخَاميز	مرق السكباج *
والخَنِيز	الثريد من الخبز الفطير*
والمُرَزَّز	الطعام المعالج بالرز*
والبَسِيسة	لت الاقط المطحون بالسمن *
والحَمِيسة	القليّة * ٦٣،١٤،٢
والحَيْس	تمر يخلط بسمن واقط فتعجن شديدا *
والكَسِيس	لحم يجفف على الحجارة فاذا يبس دق فيصير كالسويق *
والهَرِيسة	معروف *
والبوش	طعام بمصر من حنطة وعدس يجمع ويغسل فى زنبيل ويجعل فى جرة ويطين ويجعل فى تنّور *
والجَشِيش	السويق وحنطة تطحن جليلا فتجعل فى قدر ويلقى فيه لحم او تمر فيطبخ *
والرَشْرش	السمين من الشوآ *
والقَمِيشة	طعام من اللبن وحب الحنظل ونحوه *
والمكَرَّشة	طعام يعمل من اللحم والشحم فى قطعة مكورة من كرش البعير*
والكَوْشان	طعام من الرز والسمك *

or *furfūr*,	"mush made of thorny carob fruit"
or *murrī*,	"pickles as condiments"
or *maḍīrah*,	"broth cooked with sour milk"
or *najīrah*,	"milk mixed with meal or clarified butter"
or *waghīr*,	"boiled or cooked milk"
or *khāmīz*,	"broth made of *sikbāj* ('meat cooked in vinegar')"
or *khanīz*,	"*tharīdah* ('crumbled bread with broth') made from flaky pastry"
or *murazzaz*,	"food made with rice"
or *basīsah*,	"milled curds pounded with clarified butter"
or *ḥamīsah*,	"synonym of *qaliyyah* ('broth made of camel meat')" **2.14.63**
or *ḥays*,	"dates mixed with clarified butter or curds and then well kneaded"
or *kasīs*,	"meat dried on stones and beaten when dry until it becomes like *sawīq* ('parched barley meal')"
or *harīsah*,	["a condiment made with chili peppers" or "a sweet confection made with flour, butter, and sugar"] "too well known to require definition"
or *bawsh*,	"in Egypt, a dish of wheat and lentils washed together in a sieve, placed in a jar, sealed with mud, and put in a clay oven"
or *jashīsh*,	"mush and finely milled wheat placed in a pot into which meat or dates are tossed and which is then cooked"
or *rashrash*,	"the drippings from the grill"
or *qamīshah*,	"a dish of milk and colocynth or similar seeds"
or *mukarrashah*,	"a dish made of meat and fat wrapped in camel tripes"
or *kawshān*,	"a dish of rice and fish"

والآمِص — الآمص والاميص طعام يتخذ من لحم عجل بجلده او مرق السكباج المبرّد المصفّى من الدهن * ٢,١٤,٦٤

والخَبِيص — طعام من التمر والسمن ويسمى ايضا البَرُوك *

والعَمّص — ضرب من الطعام *

والكَرِيص — طبخ الحُمّاض باللبن فيجفف فيوكل فى القيظ *

والمَصُوص — طعام من لحم يطبخ وينقع فى الخل او يكون من لحم الطير خاصة *

والاَقِط — شى يتخذ من المخيض الغنمى *

والمُبَرْقَط — طعام يفرّق فيه الزيت كثيرا *

والبَهَط — الارز يطبخ باللبن معرب *

والخَلِيط — الجدى اذا سلخ فشوى *

والسَمِيط — الجدى اذا نزع شعره فشوى *

والسُرَيطآ — حساً كالحريرة * ٢,١٤,٦٥

والسُوَيطآ — مرقة كثر ماوها وثمره اى بصلها وحمصها وسائر الحبوب *

والتَشْيِيط — لحم يشوى للقوم *

والخَدِيعة — طعام لهم *

والخَذِيعة — طعام بالشام من اللحم مشتق من خذع اى حزّز وقطع والمخذّع الشِوآء *

والخَلْع — لحم يطبخ بالتوابل فى وعآ من جلد او القديد المشوى فى وعآ باهالته *

والرَضِيعة — البُرّ يدق بالفهر ويبلّ ويطبخ بالسمن *

or *āmiṣ*, “*āmiṣ*, or *amīṣ*, is a dish made of calf meat with the skin, or *sikbāj* broth cooled and with the fat strained off” 2.14.64

or *khabīṣ*, “a dish of dates and clarified butter, also called *barūk*”

or *ʿamṣ*, “a kind of food”

or *karīṣ*, “sorrel cooked in milk and then dried; eaten in hot weather”

or *maṣūṣ*, “a dish of meat cooked and marinated in vinegar, or especially of fowl meat”

or *aqiṭ*, “something made from buttermilk of sheep and goats”

or *mubarqaṭ*, “a dish into which a large amount of oil is worked”

or *bahaṭṭ*, “rice cooked with milk (an Arabized word)”

or *khalīṭ*, “kid, skinned and grilled”

or *samīṭ*, “kid, stripped of the hair and grilled”

or *suraytā’*, “a soup, synonym *ḥarīrah*” 2.14.65

or *suwaytā’*, “a broth with a lot of water and trimmings, meaning onions, chickpeas, and grains of any kind”

or *tashyīṭ*, “meat grilled for the whole group”

or *khadīʿah*, “a dish of theirs”

or *khadhīʿah*, “a dish, in the Levant, of meat, the word deriving from *khadhaʿa* meaning ‘to shear’ or ‘cut’; *mukhadhdhaʿ* means ‘grilled meat’”

or *khalʿ*, “meat cooked with spices, or in a container made of hide, or jerked meat grilled in a container with its drippings”

or *raṣīʿah*, “wheat pounded with a stone pestle, moistened, and cooked with clarified butter”

والوَضيعة حنطة تدق فيصب عليها السمن فيوكل *

والثميغة ما رقّ من الطعام واختلط بالوَدَك *

والخَطِيفة دقيق يذر عليه اللبن ثم يطبخ *

والصفصفة السكباجة * ٦٦،١٤،٢

والطِحرف حسا رقيق دون العصيدة *

والمُوخِف طعام من اقط مطحون يذر على مآ ثم يصب عليه السمن *

والاَلُوقة طعام طيب او زُبد برُطَب *

والحَرُوقة طعام اغلظ من الحسا *

والمدقَّقة من الطعام مولدة *

والرَوْذَق الحمل السميط وما طبخ من لحم وخلط باخلاطه*

والزُرَيقآ الثريدة بلبن وزيت *

والسَلِيقة الذرة تدق وتصلح او الاقط خلط به طراثيث وما سُلق من البقول ونحوها *

والسويق معروف *

والشُبارق ما اقتطع من اللحم صغارا وطبخ * ٦٧،١٤،٢

والوَشيق لحم يقدد حتى ييبس او يُغلَى اغلاة ثم يقدد ويحمل فى الاسفار*

والولِيقة طعام يتخذ من دقيق ولبن وسمن *

والدَلِيك طعام من الزبد واللبن او زبد وتمر ونبات وثمر الورد الاحمر يخلفه ويحلو كانه رُطَب الخ *

والرِبيكة اقط بتمر وسمن *

or *waḍīʿah,*	"pounded wheat onto which clarified butter is poured before eating"	
or *thamīghah,*	"soft food mixed with fat"	
or *khaṭīfah,*	"flour sprinkled with milk and cooked"	
or *ṣafṣafah,*	synonym of *sikbājah*[222]	**2.14.66**
or *ṭiḥrif,*	"a thin soup thinner than *ʿaṣīdah* ('thick gruel of flour and clarified butter')"	
or *mūkhif,*	"a dish of ground curds sprinkled onto water onto which clarified butter is then poured"	
or *alūqah,*	"delicious food, or butter with *ruṭab* dates[223]"	
or *ḥarūqah,*	"a dish thicker than *ḥasāʾ* ('soup')"	
or *mudaqqaqah,*	"a kind of food (a post-classical word)"	
or *rawdhaq,*	"lamb roasted with the wool removed, or any meat cooked and mixed together"	
or *zurayqāʾ,*	"crumbled bread with broth to which milk or oil is added"	
or *salīqah,*	"millet bruised and dressed, or curds mixed with legumes, or boiled pulses and the like"	
or *sawīq,*	["parched barley meal"] "too well known to require definition"	
or *shubāriq,*	"meat cut into small pieces and grilled"	**2.14.67**
or *washīq,*	"meat cut into strips and dried or well boiled and then cut into strips and taken on journeys"	
or *walīqah,*	"a dish made of flour, milk, and clarified butter"	
or *dalīk,*	"a dish made of butter and milk, or of butter and dates, or a plant to which red rose hips may be admixed, in which case it becomes as sweet as moist fresh dates," etc.	
or *rabīkah,*	"curds with dates and clarified butter"	

والسَّهيكة طعام *

والفَرِيك طعام يفرك ويلت بسمن وغيره *

واللَّبيكة اقط ودقيق او تمروسمن يخلط *

والوَدِيكة دقيق يشاط بشحم *

والبَكِيلة دقيق بالرب او بالسمن والتمر *

والحَذَل حب شجر ويختبز * ٦٨،١٤،٢

والطَفَيْشَل نوع من المرق *

والعَوَكَل ضرب من الادام *

والزَوْم طعام لاهل اليمن من اللبن لذيذ *

وابا عاصم السويق والسكباج *

والهُلام طعام من لحم عجل بجلده او مرق السكباج المبرد المصفى من الدهن *

والسَخِينة طعام رقيق يتخذ من دقيق *

والكُبان طعام من الذرة لليمنيين *

والتَلْبينة حسآ يتخذ من نخالة ولبن وعسل *

والجَليهة تمر يعالج باللبن *

والإرَة القديد ولحم يغلى بالخل اغلآة فيحمل فى السفر *

والآصِية طعام كالحسى بالتمر *

والإطْرِيَّة طعام كالخيوط من الدقيق *

والكَدَى لبن ينقع فيه التمر تسمَّن به البنات *

ولو اطعمته من انواع الكمأة الذُبَح والفَرحانة والقُرحان والغَرد وبنات اَوبر والجماميس ٦٩،١٤،٢

or *sahīkah,*	"a dish"
or *farīk,*	"a food that is rubbed and pounded with clarified butter and other things"
or *labīkah,*	"curds mixed with flour or dates and clarified butter"
or *wadīkah,*	"meal parched with clarified butter"
or *bakīlah,*	"flour with inspissated fruit juice or clarified butter and dates"
or *ḥadhal,*	"the seeds of a tree that are baked" 2.14.68
or *ṭafayshal,*	"a kind of broth"
or *ʿawkal,*	"a kind of condiment"
or *zawm,*	"a dish of the people of Yemen, made of milk and delicious"
or *abū ʿāṣim,*	"either *sawīq* or *sikbāj*"
or *hulām,*	"a dish of calf's flesh with the skin, or *sikbāj* broth cooled and with the fat strained off"
or *sakhīnah,*	"a soft dish made of flour"
or *kubān,*	"a millet dish of the Yemenis"
or *talbīnah,*	"a soup made with bran, milk, and honey"
or *jalīhah,*	"dates worked with milk"
or *irah,*	"jerked meat, or meat well boiled with vinegar, and taken on journeys"
or *āṣiyah,*	"a soup-like dish with dates"
or *iṭriyyah,*	"a dish like threads, made of flour"
or *kadā,*	"milk in which dates are steeped and which is used to fatten girls"

and if you were to feed him with all the different kinds of fungi, such as 2.14.69
dhubaḥ truffles or *farḥānah* truffles or *qurḥān* truffles or *ghard* truffles or the little earth-colored truffles they call "Daughters of Awbar" or *jamāmīs*

والفَقْع والبِرْنِيق والدُعْلوق والقَعْبل والعُرْجون والعُرهون ومن انواع السمك القُباب والهازِبَى والكَنْعَت والكَنْعد والخُبّاط وهى اولاده والبَيْنِيث والمُدَّج والاَبْدح والقُدّ والغُوبَر والزِمّير[1] والزُنْجور والاُشْبور والطَنْز والانقليس والجُوفَى واللُخْم وابا مَرِينا *

والصِلِنْباح سمك طويل دقيق * ٧٠،١٤،٢

والحافِيرة سمكة سودآ *

والجِرّىّ سمك طويل املس لا ياكله اليهود وليس عليه فصوص *

والصَرْصَران سمك املس *

والغارّة سمكة طويلة *

والقَيْصانة سمكة صفرآ مستديرة *

والشَبُّوط سمك دقيق الذنب عريض الوسط لين المسّ صغير الراس كانه بَرْبط *

والجِنّيس سمكة بين البياض والصفرة *

والضِلَعة سمكة صغيرة خضرآ قصيرة العظم*

والحَفّة سمكة بيضآ شاكة

والعُفّة سمكة جردآ بيضآ طعم مطبوخها كالارز* ٧١،١٤،٢

والخُذّاق سمكة لها ذوائب كالخيوط *

والحاقُول سمك اخضر طويل *

والقَتَن سمكة عريضة قدر راحة *

والغلآ سمك قصير*

والهِفّ السمك الصغار الهاربة *

---

[1] كذا في القاموس وفي ١٨٥٥: الزِمير.

truffles or soft white *faqʿ* truffles or long red (or short black) *birnīq* truffles or *dhuʿlūq* truffles or *qaʿbal* truffles or the *ʿurjūn* mushrooms that look like *faqʿ* truffles or *ʿurhūn* mushrooms (which are a kind of truffle), or with all the different kinds of fish, such as the *qubāb* (which resembles the *kanʿad*) or the *hāzibā* (one of which is called a *huffah*) or the *kanʿat* (which is the same as the *kanʿad*) or the *kanʿad* (which is a sea fish) or the *khubbāṭ* (the young of the *kanʿad*) or the *baynīth* (a sea fish) or the *muddaj* or the *abdaḥ* or the *qudd* (a sea fish) or the *ghawbar* or the *zimmīr* or the *zunjūr* or the *ushbūr* or the *ṭanz* or the *anqalīs* (which looks like a snake) or the *jūfā* or the *lukhm* (a sea fish) or the *abū marīnā* or

the *ṣilinbāḥ*,	"a species of long, slim fish"	2.14.70
or the *ḥāffīrah*,	"a black fish"	
or the *jirrī*,	"a species of long, smooth fish not eaten by the Jews and having no scales"	
or the *ṣarṣarān*,	"a smooth species of fish"	
or the *ghārrah*,	"a long fish"	
or the *qayṣānah*,	"a round, yellow fish"	
or the *shabbūṭ*,	"a species of fish with a slim tail and broad middle, soft to the touch and with a small head, as though it were a lute"	
or the *jinnīs*,	"a fish halfway in color between white and yellow"	
or the *ḍilaʿah*,	"a small, green fish with short bones"	
or the *ḥaffah*,	"a bony white fish"	
or the *ʿuffah*,	"a white scale-less fish that tastes like rice when cooked"	2.14.71
or the *khudhdhāq*,	"a fish with thread-like feces"	
or the *ḥāqūl*,	"a long, green fish"	
or the *qatan*,	"a fish as broad as the palm of the hand"	
or the *ghalāʾ*,	"a short fish"	
or *hiff*,	"small fry that flee"	

والنَّلَم صغار السمك *

والصَّحْناة ادام يتخذ من السمك الصغار*

والصِّيرَ الصحناة او شبهها والسميكات المملوحة يعمل منها الصحناة *

والحَرِيْد السمك المقدد *

والقَرِيب السمك المملوح ما دام فى طرآته * ٧٢،١٤،٢

والطِّرِّيخ سمك صغار تعالج بالملح *

والحُساس سمك صغار تجفف *

والنَّشُوط سمك يمقر فى مآ وملح *

والاِرْبيان سمك كالدود *

والصُّعْقر بيض السمك *

والسِّكَّل سمكة سودآ صخمة *

والزَّجْر سمك عظام *

والبال الحوت العظيم *

والاَطُوم سمكة بحرية غليظة *

والجَيْذرة سمكة كالزنجى الاسود الضخم * ٧٣،١٤،٢

والبُنْبُك دابة كالدلفين *

والجَلَ سمكة طولها ثلثون ذراعا *

واللِّيآ سمكة تتخذ منها الترَسة الجيدة وهو ايضا شى كالحمص شديد البياض توصف به المراة *

والتُّخَس تقدم ذكرها فى الغرائب *

or *balam*,	"small fry"
or *ṣaḥnāh*,	"a condiment made from small fry"
or *ṣīr*,	"*ṣaḥnāh* or something resembling it, or the salted fish from which *ṣaḥnāh* is made"
or *ḥarīd*,	"sun-dried fish"
or *qarīb*,	"salted fish when still moist" **2.14.72**
or *ṭirrīkh*,	"small fish treated with salt"
or *ḥusās*,	"small fish that are dried"
or *nashūṭ*,	"fish that are macerated in water and salt"
or the *irbiyān*,	"a species of fish like worms"
or *ṣuʿqur*,	"fish eggs"
or the *sikl*,	"a huge, black fish"
or *zajr*,	"large fish"
or the *bāl*,	"the mighty whale"
or the *aṭūm*,	"a thick sea fish"
or the *jaydharah*,	"a fish like a huge black negro" **2.14.73**
or the *bunbuk*,	"a beast like a dolphin"
or the *jamal*,	"a fish thirty cubits long"
or the *liyyāʾ*,	"a fish from which high-quality shields are made; also something like chickpeas, extremely white, to which women are compared"
or *tukhas*,	previously mentioned under "the wonders"

ومن المحار

السُلَج	اصداف بحرية فيها شى يوكل *
والدُلّاع	ضرب من محار البحر*
والقَرْثع	دويبة بحرية لها صدفة *
والجُمَّل	لحم يكون فى جوف الصدف*

ومن انواع الخبز

الطُرْمُوث	خبز المَلّة ومثله المُفْتأد والمُضْباة والطُرْموس والإِصْطَكْمة والأُصْطُكْمة * ومن الغرائب هنا ان صاحب القاموس اورد التى بالكسر بعدا ش م والتى بالضم بعد ص ط م * ٧٤،١٤،٢
والرَّحْلة	الرقيقة من الخبز وكذا الصَرِيقة *
واللُحُوح	خبز شبه القطائف *
والانْبخانى	خبزة انبخانية ضخمة *
والخُبْرة	الثريدة الضخمة *
والمَشْطور	الخبز المطلىّ الكامخ *
والسِلَّجْن	الكعك *
والخَنيز	الثريد من الخبز الفطير*
والرَشْرش	اليابس الرخو من الخبز كالرَشْراش *
والهَشاش	الخبز الرخو اللين *
والمُرَبَّقة	الخبزة المشحمة ونحوها المروّلة *
والرُقاق	الخبز الرقيق *
والضَغِيغة	خبز الا رز المرقق *

or of shellfish, such as

sulaj,	"seashells containing something edible"
or the *dullāʿ,*	"a kind of shell found in the sea"
or the *qarthaʿ,*	"a small sea creature with a shell"
or *jummaḥl,*	"flesh found in the interior of the shell"

or of the various kinds of bread, such as

ṭurmūth,	"bread made in the ashes, similar to *mufta'ad, muḍbāh, ṭurmūs, iṣṭakmah,* and *uṣṭukmah*" (an oddity here is that the author of the *Qāmūs* puts the form with *i* after the entry for the root *ʾ-sh-m* and that with *u* after *ṣ-ṭ-m*) 2.14.74
or *zalaḥlaḥah,*	"a thin bread, synonym *ṣarīqah*"
or *luḥūḥ,*	"bread resembling *qaṭā'if* ('small triangular doughnuts fried in butter and served with honey')"
or *anbakhānī,*	"a huge puffed-up loaf of fermented dough"
or *khubrah,*	"a huge mess of crumbled bread moistened with broth"
or *mashṭūr,*	"bread wiped with sour condiments"
or *sillajn,*	"cake"
or *khanīz,*	"crumbled unleavened bread moistened with broth"
or *rashrash,*	"floppy dry bread; synonym *rashrāsh*"
or *hashāsh,*	"soft floppy bread"
or *murabbaqah,*	"a bread made with fat; *murawwalah* is similar"
or *ruqāq,*	"flaky bread"
or *ḍaghīghah,*	"layered rice bread"

والمُلَّى الخبزة المنضجة *

ومن اجناس اللبن

السَمَعج اللبن الدسم الحلو ومثله السَمْلج والسَمْهج والسمهجيج * ٧٥،١٤،٢

والقُطَبِيّة لبن المعز والضان يخلطان او لبن الناقة والشاة *

والشَمِيط ما لا يُدرَى احامض هو ام حقين من طيبه *

والجُلَعطِيط اللبن الرائب الثخين ومثله لبن عُجَلِط وعثلط وعذلط وعكلط وعلبط * تقدم نحوى بغيض كان يتكلم بالاعراب الى لبّان فقال يالبان اعندك لبن عُثَلِط علبط عجلط فقال له اللبان تنصرف او تُصفَع *

والكَفْنة الزبدة المجتمعة البيضآ *

واللّياخة الزبد الذائب مع اللبن *

والقِشْدة الزبدة الرقيقة *

والقِلْدة القشدة والتمر والسويق يخلّص به السمن *

والنَهِيد الزبد الرقيق *

والعَكِيس اللبن الحليب تصب عليه الاهالة *

والثميرة اللبن الذى ظهر زبده *

والنَخِيسة لبن العنز والنعجة يخلط بينهما *

والإِمخاض الحليب ما دام فى المِمخضة *

والحالُوم ضرب من الاقط او لبن يغلظ فيصير شبيها بالجبن الطرى *

ومن الحلواء

or *mullā*, "a well-cooked bread"

or of the different kinds of milk, such as

samʿaj, "sweet, fatty milk; similar are *samlaj*, *samhaj*, and *samhajīj*" 2.14.75

or *quṭabiyyah*, "goat and sheep milk mixed, or camel and sheep milk mixed"

or *shamīṭ*, "milk that is so tasty that it is impossible to tell if it is curdled or fresh milk mixed with curdled"

or *julaʿṭīṭ*, "thick buttermilk; other terms with the same meaning are *ʿujaliṭ*, *ʿuthaliṭ*, *ʿudhaliṭ*, *ʿukaliṭ*, and *ʿulabiṭ*"; once an insufferable grammarian, who insisted on speaking literary Arabic, went up to a milkman and said, "Milkman, hast thou any milk that is *ʿuthaliṭ*, *ʿulabiṭ*, or *ʿujaliṭ*?" to which the milkman replied, "Be off before I give you a slap on the back of your neck!"

or *kafkhah*, "a white blended butter"

or *liyākhah*, "butter melted with milk"

or *qishdah*, "a runny butter"

or *qildah*, "*qishdah*, dates, and parched barley meal made with pure clarified butter"

or *nahīd*, "runny butter"

or *ʿakīs*, "fresh milk onto which drippings have been poured"

or *thamīrah*, "milk whose butter has appeared"

or *nakhīsah*, "goat or ewe milk mixed together"

or *imkhāḍ*, "fresh milk while still in the churn"

or *ḥālūm*, "a kind of curds or milk thickened until it turns into something like moist cheese"

or of sweet things, such as

الوَطيئة تمر يخرج نواه ويعجن بلبن والاقط بالسكر والكعك * ٧٦،١٤،٢

والعَبِيبة طعام وشراب من العُرفط حلو *

والبُرْت السكّر *

والضَيح العسل والمقل *

والمَلَخ عسل في جلّنار المَظّ *

واليَعْقيد طعام يعقد بالعسل *

والفارِد ابيض السكر واجوده *

والقَنْد عسل قصب السكر *

والفانيذ ضرب من الحلوآ *

والصَقْر عسل الرُطَب والدبس *

والاِكْبِر شى كانه خبيص يابس ليس بشديد الحلاوة يجى به النحل *

والفالوذ م ويسمى ايضا الرِعْديد والمُزَعزع والزَلِيل والكَمْص والمُزَعفَر *

والماذِىّ العسل الابيض او الجديد او خالصه وجيده *

والمُسيَّر حلوآ *

واللوزِيْنَج معروف معرب *

والوَخِيز ثريد العسل * ٧٧،١٤،٢

واللَّوَاص الفالوذ والعسل *

والسِرطِراط الفالوذ او الخبيص *

والمَجِيع تمر يعجن بلبن *

والقَطائف معروف *

والكُرسُفىّ نوع من العسل *

waṭī'ah,	"pitted dates kneaded with milk, or curds with sugar and cake"	2.14.76
or *'abībah,*	"a food and a drink made from mimosa (sweet)"	
or *burt,*	"sugar"	
or *ḍayḥ,*	"honey, or ripe doum fruit"	
or *malakh,*	"honey from wild pomegranate blossoms"	
or *ya'qīd,*	"a dish thickened with honey"	
or *fārid,*	"the whitest, best sugar"	
or *qand,*	"sugar-cane molasses"	
or *fānīd,*	"a kind of sweetmeat"	
or *ṣaqr,*	"molasses of fresh moist dates, or inspissated fruit juice"	
or *ikbir,*	"something like dry *khabīṣ* ('dates mixed with clarified butter') that is not extremely sweet and is brought by bees"	
or *fālūdh,*	["blancmange"] "too well known to require definition; also called *ri'dīd*, *muza'za'*, *zalīl*, *kamṣ*, and *muza'far*"	
or *mādhī,*	"white, or new, honey, or the purest and best honey"	
or *muyassar,*	"a sweet dish"	
or *lawzinj,*	[dish made with almonds (*lawz*)] "too well known to require definition; an Arabized word"	
or *wakhīz,*	"moistened crumbled bread made with honey"	2.14.77
or *lawāṣ,*	"blancmange with honey"	
or *siriṭrāṭ,*	"blancmange, or *khabīṣ* ('dates mixed with clarified butter')"	
or *majī',*	"dates kneaded with milk"	
or *qaṭā'if,*	[small triangular doughnuts fried in butter and served with honey] "too well known to require definition"	
or *kursufī,*	"a kind of honey"	

والطِرْم الشهد والزبد والعسل *

والمَنّ كل طلّ ينزل من السمآ على شجر او حجر يحلو وينعقد عسلا ويجف جفاف الصمغ الخ *

والزَلابِية حلوآ معروف *

ومن الثمر

الصَرَبَة شى كراس السنور فيه شى كالدبس يمص ويوكل * ٧٨،١٤،٢

والعُتْرُب شجر كالرمان يوكل *

والبُوت شجر نباته كالزعرور *

والرَغْثآ عنب له حبّ طوال *

والجَوْح البطّيخ الشامى *

والصَدَح ثمرة اشدّ حمرة من العُنّاب *

والمُلاحىّ عنب ابيض طويل ونوع من التين *

والعَنْجَد الزبيب او ضرب منه *

والفِرْصاد التوت او حمله او احمره *

والقَثَد نبت يشبه القثآ او الخيار *

والكَشَد حب يوكل *

والمَرِيد التمر ينقع فى اللبن * ٧٩،١٤،٢

والمَغْد ثمر يشبه الخيار *

والحَناذ المشمش *

والصُفْرِيّة تمر يمانى يجفف بُسرًا فيقع موقع السكر فى السويق *

والضَمِير العنب الذابل *

or *ṭirm,*	"honeycomb, or butter, or honey"
or *mann,*	"any dew that falls from the sky onto trees or rocks and is sweet and coagulates to form honey and dries like gum"
or *zalābiya,*	["fritters"] "a sweet dish, too well known to require definition"
or of fruit, such as	
ṣarabah,	"something like a cat's head with something like inspissated juice on it that is sucked or eaten" 2.14.78
or *ʿutrub,*	"a tree, like the pomegranate, whose fruit is eaten"
or *būt,*	"a tree whose foliage is like that of the azarole"
or *raʿthāʾ,*	"grapes with a long fruit"
or *jawḥ,*	"Levantine watermelons"
or *ṣadaḥ,*	"a fruit redder than the jujube"
or *mulāḥī,*	"long white grapes, or a kind of fig"
or *ʿanjad,*	"raisins, or a particular kind thereof"
or *firṣād,*	"the mulberry, or its fruit, or such of its fruit as is red"
or *qathad,*	"a plant resembling squirting cucumber, or cucumbers"
or *kashd,*	"an edible berry"
or *marīd,*	"dates steeped in milk" 2.14.79
or *maghd,*	"fruits resembling cucumbers"
or *ḥanādh,*	"apricots"
or *ṣufriyyah,*	"Yemeni dates dried before ripening and used in place of sugar when making parched barley meal"
or *ḍamīr,*	"withered grapes"

والزِنْبار التين الحلوانى *

والسُكّر من احسن العنب *

والزَغْرآ ضرب من الخوخ *

والشَعْرآ ضرب منه ايضا *

والمِغْثَر شى ينضحه[1] الثمام والعُشر والرِمْث كالعسل وكذا المِغْفَر *

والغَوْفر البطيخ الخريفى او نوع منه * ٨٠،١٤،٢

والقُبّز عنب ابيض طويل *

والمَرْمار الرمّان الكثير المآء لا شحم له *

والنَهِر العنب الابيض والكُلافِىّ عنب ابيض فيه خضرة *

والجَوْزة ضرب من العنب *

والمِشْلَوز المشمش الحلو *

والبَلَس ثمر كالتين *

والضَّغابيس صغار القثآ او نبات كالهليون *

والمَيْس نوع من الزبيب *

والكِشْمِش عنب صغار لا عجم له الين من العنب *

والضُرُوع عنب ابيض كبار الحب * ٨١،١٤،٢

والاَقْاعىّ عنب ابيض يصفرّ اخيرا حبه كالورس *

والمَيْعة شجرة كالتفاح لها ثمرة بيضآ اكبر من الجوز توكل ولبّ نواها دسم يعصر منه الميعة السائلة (فى قول)

والغاف شجر له ثمر حلو جدا *

---

[1] ١٨٥٥: ينضجه.

or *zinbār*,	"figs from Ḥulwān"
or *sukkar*,	"the best grapes" [literally, "sugar"]
or *zaʿrāʾ*,	"a kind of peach"
or *shaʿrāʾ*,	"another kind [of peach]"
or *mighthar*,	"something honey-like exuded by panic grass, milkweed, and the dwarf tamarisk; synonym *mighfar*"
or *ghawfar*,	"rainy-season watermelons, or a kind thereof" **2.14.80**
or *qubbaz*,	"long, white grapes"
or *marmār*,	"pomegranates with much juice and little pulp"
or *nahir*,	"white grapes; *kulāfī* are white grapes with a touch of green"
or *jawzah*,	"a kind of grape"
or *mishlawz*,	"sweet apricots"
or *balas*,	"fruits resembling figs"
or *ḍaghābīṣ*,	"small squirting cucumbers, or a plant resembling asparagus"
or *mays*,	"a kind of raisin"
or *kishmish*,	"small, seedless grapes softer than [regular] grapes"
or *ḍurūʿ*,	"white grapes with a large berry" **2.14.81**
or *aqmāʿī*,	"white grapes whose berries eventually turn as yellow as *wars*[224]"
or *mayʿah*,	"a tree like the apple with edible fruit larger than walnuts, whose kernels are fatty, liquid storax (*mayʿah*) being squeezed from them" (according to one definition)
or *ghāf*,	"a tree with very sweet fruit"

والباسِق ثمرطيبة صفرآ *

والرازِقيّ العنب الملّاحى *

لزاد شحرفٍ وزعيقا وزياطا وضجيجا وهو يقول المراة المراة * الا فلحسونى المراة *

ولوانك سقيته من الشراب

الرحيق ممزوجا بالبند الرحيق الخمر او اطيبها او الخالص او الصافى والبند الذى يسكِر من المآ * ٨٢،١٤،٢

والسَلْسل ممزوجة بالسلسل السلسل المآ العذب ومن الخمر اللينة *

والمِسْطار مزاجها العَضْرس المِسْطار الخمر الصارعة لشاربها والعضرس المآ البارد العذب والثلج *

والإسْفِنط مزاجها النَقِز الاسفنط المطيب من عصير العنب او ضرب من الاشربة او اعلى الخمر * والنقز المآ الصافى العذب *

والخرطوم ممزوجة بالمآ الزلال الخرطوم الخمر السريعة وما زلال كغراب سريع المرّ فى الحلق بارد عذب صاف سهل سلس *

والمعتَّقة مزاجها الفُرات المعتقة الخمر القديمة والفرات المآ العذب جدا *

والمثلَّث شراب طبخ حتى ذهب ثلثاه *

والفضيخ عصير العنب وشراب يتخذ من بُسر مفضوخ *

والفَقّد شراب من زبيب او عسل كالفُقّدد *

والمَقَدىّ شراب من عسل * ٨٣،١٤،٢

والداذِىّ شراب الفسّاق *

or *bāsiq*,	"a tasty yellow fruit"	
or *rāziqī*,	"long white grapes"	

he would open his mouth even wider and shriek, shout, yell, and clamor yet more, saying, "A woman! A woman! Get me a woman to lick!" and even if you provided him by way of drink

raḥīq mixed with *band*,	*raḥīq* is "wine, or the best-tasting thereof, or the purest, or what is clear" and *band* is "water that intoxicates"	2.14.82
or *salsal* mixed with *salsal*,	*salsal* is "sweet water, or smooth wine"	
or *misṭār* with which *ʿaḍras* has been mixed,	*misṭār* is "wine that fells the one who drinks it" and *ʿaḍras* is "sweet, cold water, or ice"	
or *isfinṭ* with which *naqiz* has been mixed,	*isfinṭ* is "perfumed grape juice, or a sort of drink, or the finest wine" and *naqiz* is "sweet, clear water"	
or *khurṭūm* mixed with *zulāl water*,	*khurṭūm* is "fast-acting wine" and *zulāl* (on the pattern of *ghurāb*) water is "water that is flowing, easy, clear, sweet, cold, and quick to pass down the throat"	
or *muʿattaqah* mixed with *furāt*,	*muʿattaqah* is "old wine" and *furāt* is "very sweet water"	
or *muthallath*,	"a drink that is cooked until two-thirds of it is gone"	
or *faḍīkh*,	"grape juice, or a drink made from split unripe dates"	
or *faqd*,	"a drink from raisins or honey; synonym *fuqdud*"	
or *maqadī*,	"a drink from honey"	2.14.83
or *dādhī*,	"the drink of the depraved"	

والجُمْهورىّ شراب مسكر او نبيذ العنب اتت عليه ثلث سنين *

والخُسْروانى شراب *

والسَكَر الخمر ونبيذ يتخذ من التمر *

والغُبَيْرآ السُكركة وهى شراب من الذرة *

والمِزْر نبيذ الذرة والشعير *

والكَسِيس نبيذ التمر *

والبِتْع نبيذ العسل المشتدّ او سلالة العنب *

والسُقُرْقَع شراب يتخذ من الذرة او من الشعير والحبوب *

والجِعَة نبيذ الشعير * ٨٤،١٤،٢

والفُقّاع هذا الذى يشرب لما يرتفع فى راسه من الزَبَد *

والباذِق ما طبخ من عصير العنب ادنى طبخة فصار شديدا *

والخَليطَين ما ينبَّذ من البُسر والتمر معًا او من العنب والزبيب او منه ومن التمر ونحو ذلك *

والصَرِىّ المآ من البسر الاحمر والاصفر يصبونه على النبق فيتخذون منه نبيذا *

والعَكِىّ سويق المقل *

والاَطْواق لبن النارجيل وهو مسكر جدا سكرا معتدلا ما لم يبرز شاربه للريح فان برز افرط سكره الخ *

والصَعْف شراب من العسل او يشدَخ العنب فيطرح ثم يغلى *

والنبق دقيق يخرج من لبّ جذع النخلة حلو يقوى بالدبس ثم يجعل نبيذا *

or *jumhūrī*,	"an intoxicating drink, or three-year-old grape wine"
or *khusruwānī*,	"a drink"
or *sakar*,	"wine, or a fermented drink made from dates"
or *ghubayrā'*,	"*sukarkah*, which is a drink made from millet"
or *mizr*,	"a fermented drink from millet and barley"
or *kasīs*,	"date wine"
or *bit'*,	"a fermented drink made from fortified honey or the best grapes"
or *suqurqa'*,	"a drink made from millet or barley and other grains"
or *ji'ah*,	"a fermented drink from barley" 2.14.84
or *fuqqā'*,	"what is drunk when foam rises to its surface"
or *bādhiq*,	"wine that is cooked as lightly as possible and thus fortified"
or *khalīṭān*,	"a fermented drink made of unripe and ripe dates together, or of grapes and raisins, or of the latter plus dates or the like"
or *ṣarī*,	"juice of red and yellow unripe dates that they pour onto lote fruit and make into a fermented drink"
or *'akī*,	"ripe doum-fruit mash"
or *aṭwāq*,	"coconut milk, which is highly intoxicating—moderately so, as long as the drinker does not go out into the wind, but if he does go out, he becomes extremely drunk," etc.
or *ṣaf'*,	"a drink made from honey or grapes that are crushed, whose skins are discarded, and whose juice is then boiled"
or *nabq*,	"a flour that is extracted from the heart of the palm-tree trunk, that is sweet and is fortified with inspissated juice and then made into a fermented drink"

والسَلِيل الشراب الخالص *

والمَعْمول المعمول من الشراب ما فيه اللبن والعسل *

والطِلآ الخمر وخاثر المنصَّف وهو الشراب طبخ حتى ذهب نصفه *

لعرِبد وزاد صراخا وصياحا وهو يقول المراة المراة * الا فاسقونى المراة *

بل لو سقيته من الخفاح والكوثر * ومن رحيق مختوم * مزاجه من تسنيم * ٢،١٤،٨٥

وجعلته فى جملة من يطوف عليهم ولدان مخلدون * باكواب واباريق وكاس من معين * وفاكهة مما يتخيرون * ولحم طير مما يشتهون * فى سِدر مخضود * وطلح منضود * وظل ممدود * ومآ مسكوب * وفاكهة كثيرة * لا مقطوعة ولا ممنوعة * وفرش مرفوعة * وعنده جنّتان* ذواتا افنان * فيهما عينان تجريان * فيهما من كل فاكهة زوجان * من دونهما جنتان * مدهامّتان * فيهما عينان نضّاحتان * فيهما فاكهة ونخل ورمان * فيهن خيرات حسان * فيها فاكهة والنخل ذات الأكمام * والحب ذو العَصْف والريحان * بين متكئين على رفرف خضر وعبقرى حسان * بين متكئين على فرش بطائنها من استَبْرق * وعلى فرش موضونة * يسقون فيها كاسا كان مزاجها زنجبيلا * عينا فيها تسمى سلسبيلا * ويطوف عليهم ولدان مخلدون اذا رايتهم حسبتهم لولوا منثورا * عاليَهم ثياب سندس خضر واستبرق وحُلوا اساور من فضة * لما رايته والحالة هذه راضيا من دون المراة * فاعوذ بالله من هذا الانسان * ومع ذلك اى مع كون وجود الطعام والشراب للرجل الزم من وجود المراة اذ الاول مخلوق لحفظ الحياة والثانى

لتقويم الطبيعة على ما سبق ذكره * فان وجود المراة اصعب منهما واكثر تعذّرا ٢،١٤،٨٦

واغلى سعرا * اذ الطعام والشراب يوجدان فى كل مكان وزمان * حتى ان اهل

or *salīl,*	"a pure drink"
or *maʿmūl,*	"any drink containing milk and honey"
or *ṭilāʾ,*	"wine, or *khāthir al-munaṣṣaf,* which is a drink that is cooked until reduced by half"

he would frown, and scream and shout yet more, saying, "A woman! A woman! Give me a woman to drink!"

Nay, even if you watered him with the waters of al-Faḥfāḥ and al-Kawthar[225] or with fine honey wine with which *tasnīm*[226] has been mixed, and added him to the company "among whom pass immortal youths bearing goblets and ewers and a cup from a spring"[227] and "such fruits that they shall choose and such flesh of fowl as they desire" "mid thornless lote trees and serried acacias and spreading shade and outpoured waters and fruits abounding—unfailing, unforbidden—and up-raised couches," and who have "two gardens abounding in branches, therein two fountains of running water . . . therein of every fruit two kinds and besides these two gardens . . . and green, green pastures . . . and two fountains of gushing water . . . and fruits, and palm trees, and pomegranates . . . and maidens good and comely . . . and fruits and palm trees with sheaths and grain in the blade and fragrant herbs" with among them those who "recline upon green cushions and lovely druggets" and those who "recline upon couches lined with brocade . . . upon close-wrought couches" who "shall be given to drink a cup whose mixture is ginger, and therein a fountain whose name is Salsabīl; immortal youths shall go about them, when thou seest them one supposest them scattered pearls . . . with upon them green garments of silk and brocade, adorned with bracelets of silver," never, even in such a state, will you see him consenting to go without a woman, and I seek refuge with God from such a person: despite all of the foregoing (meaning the availability to the man of food and drink), he will insist upon a woman being present, since the first is created for the sustenance of life and the second to rectify his nature, as mentioned. 2.14.85

The presence of a woman is harder to ensure than that of either food or drink, demands more effort, and is costlier, for food and drink are to be found in every place and at every time; even the people of hell have food in the form of *zaqqūm*,[228] molten copper, and cactus thorn, and drink in the form of foul pus, and shade from a smoking blaze,[229] but they do not have women in the form of "fire from a smokeless blaze"[230] or from among the demons, and there are no women present on board ship or in a monastery (except 2.14.86

سقر لهم طعام من الزقّوم والمُهل والضَريع * وشراب من غسلين * وظل من يحموم * ولكن ليس لهم نسآ من مارج من النار او من الشياطين * ولا وجود للمراة ايضا فى السفينة ولا فى دير الرهبان الا نادرا * ولا لراكب فرس او حمار او جمل او بغل * ولا لساعٍ على القدم * ولا لمباشر الحرب ولا لمسجون * ولا لقبيح الخلقة الا اذا كان جميل الدينار والجِلآ * ولا لشاعر مملق وان تملّقهن وسهر الليالى فى وصف محاسنهن والتشبب بها * ولا لمن به تشويلية وترويلية وزَلِقيّة وزُمالِقيّة وزِهلِقيّة وتيتائية واذليلائية ونَغنعيّة وهلُوكية وشكّازية وثَيتليّة وعِنّينية وحَرِيكيّة وطَمَسلية ومَنجوفية وحصورية وسَرِسية وعجيرية وذَوذَخية وحَوقلية وهَوذلية ووَخواخية وعِذيَوطيّة وعِضيوطية وعِظيوطية وثنّية وثُموتية وضَفيطيّة ومُجيّائية وعِتولية * فان قيل ان الادرم لا خبز له ايضا * قلت يمكن ان يدق له الخبز ناعما فيمضغه ويجتزئ به * ولكن كيف السبيل الى مضغ المراة مع التيتائيّة واخواتها *

ثم انه كما وقعت البلبلة عن ذات المرأة وحارت العقول فى السرّ الذى ٨٧،١٤،٢
اودعه الله فيها * من جهة انه اول الاسباب فى عمران الكون وخرابه * اذ لا يكاد يحدث فى العالم خطب جليل الا وتراها من خلله واقفة وراءه او بالحرى مضطجعة * كذلك حصل التشويش والتخليط فى اسمها * فالمراة فى لغتنا الشريفة مشتقة من مرؤ الطعام اذ صار مرّيئا هنيئا حميد المغبّة * الا انها كثيرا ما تكون طعاما ذا غصّة وشجا وتخمة وتختير وتخثير * ثم ان همزها للوصل ووصلها للهمز * وجمعها من غير لفظ المفرد وهو متعدد * وفى بعض اللغات هى ويل الرجل * وفى بعضها سَوأة *

occasionally) or available to a man riding a horse or a camel or a mule, or to one running on foot, or to one fighting a war, or to a prisoner, or to a man with an ugly face (unless his money or his pedigree are attractive), or to an unctuous poet even though he flatter them and spend his nights describing their charms and rhapsodizing over them, or to one who has erectile dysfunction, or a tendency to premature ejaculation, premature climax, rapid climax, or early ejaculation, or to come immediately on penetration or to go soft before it, or one who suffers from weak erections, or from going soft after being stiff, or is too quick to come, or comes just from talking to a woman, or suffers from impotence, or lack of libido, or frigidity, or lack of virility, or thwarted sexual capacity, or lack of sexual interest in women, or lack of sexual drive, or lack of studliness, or lack of manly vigor, or floppiness of the member, or poor performance, or sexual inertia, or sheer inability, or coming too fast, or behaving like a female jerboa, or lack of virility or machismo, or sexual ignorance, or shooting his wad the moment he enters, or indifference to women. If it be said that the toothless man can eat no bread either, I would reply that he can have bread pounded for him until it's soft and then chew on and work it over with his gums, but when you're one of those who come immediately on penetration, or suffer from any consanguine conditions, how are you ever going to find a way to chew over a woman?

In addition, just as confusion reigns over the very nature of womankind **2.14.87**
and men's minds are at a loss to understand the mystery with which God has endowed her, from the perspective that she is first cause of both the flourishing and the ruination of the universe, for almost nothing of great import takes place in the world but you'll discover when you peep through its chinks that there's a woman standing (or more likely lying) behind it, so likewise muddling and mixing are present in her name. Thus the word *imra'ah* ("woman") in our noble language is derived from the verb *mara'a*, used of food to mean "it was wholesome, healthy, and of beneficial effect,"[231] though in fact a woman is often a food to choke or gag on, one that causes indigestion, spoils one's appetite, and makes one's stomach heave. Furthermore, the glottal stop (*hamz*) in *imra'ah* is for purposes of elison (*waṣl*), and the elision (*waṣl*) in it is for purposes of compression (*hamz*),[232] while its plural is constructed from a different root than that of the singular and has numerous forms,[233] and in one language the word denotes "man's woe" and in another "pudendum."[234]

فاما الزوجة وهى المفهوم منها انها امراة وزيادة ونصف امراة ونصف رجل فقد ٢،١٤،٨٨
خصّت ترضيا لها باسماكثيرة * من ذلك القرينة واشتقاقها معلوم * والعازبة
واشتقاقها من عزب اى بعد لانها تعزب عن ابويها الى زوجها او بالعكس او
عنه الى غيره * والحُرْمة * واللحاف لانها تدفى الرجل بحر جسدها كما سياتى *
والحَدادة[١] والنِضر العِرس والحَليلة واللباس والجَثَل والحال والخُضُلّة والشاعة والحَنّة
والرُبُض والنَعْل ولست ارضى بهذه فالاَوْلى محوها * ومن الغريب انها سميت
لباسا ولحافا ولم تسمّ سروالا * قال بعض العلمآء اذا اراد الله ان يقضى خيرا على ٢،١٤،٨٩
الارض قيّض له امراة فكانت الوسيلة الى اجرآئه * واذا اراد الشيطان ان يقضى
شرّا توسل اليه ايضا بامراة * وقد اختلفوا فى تاويل هذا القول * فالخرجيون
على ان دخول المراة فى قضية ملك الانكليز كان للخير المحض * والسوقيون على انه
كان للشر الجهنمى * وكذلك قضية ملكتى الانكليز وقضية ايرين زوجة ليو الرابع
وثيودورة زوجة ثاوفيليوس * وغير ذلك مما لا يحصى * واعلم هنا انه لم تجر العادة
بان يتخذ من النسآ بابا او مطران او رئيس جيش او رئيس سفينة او قاض * ذلك
لاتقاء باسهن وسطوتهن * فان الرجال مستعبدون للنسآ بالطبع خلوا من هذه
المراتب العلية فكيف بهن اذا ولينها * فان قيل ان الافرنج يتخذون منهن ملكات
ويفلحون * قلت قد تقرر عندهم انه اذا كان رئيس الدولة انثى كانت ادارة الاحكام
والعمل كله لذكر * ولعل ذلك من مشاكل الامور الانثوية فان هذا التعليل يصدق
ايضا على كون البابا وغيره يتخذ من النسآ * ولعلى قد اطلت الكلام هنا على
النسآ مع انه ربما يوجد فيهن قصار غير جديرات بالطويل منه * فينبغى لى الان
تطليقهن والعود الى ما كنت بصدده * وساعود اليهن فى موضع آخر ان شا الله *

١ ١٨٥٥: الحدادة.

In contrast, a wife, by which is understood "a woman plus" or "half a woman plus half a man," has been allocated numerous names out of respect, among them *qarīnah* ("consort"), whose etymology is well known,[235] and *ʿāzibah*, which derives from *ʿazaba*, meaning "to distance oneself," because she distances herself from her parents when she goes to her husband or vice versa,[236] or when she goes away from him altogether, etc., and *ḥurmah* ("the protected one"), and also *al-liḥāf* ("the quilt") because she warms the man with the heat of her body, as will be explained,[237] and *ḥadādah*[238] and *niḍr* and *ʿirs*[239] and *ḥalīlah* ("co-dweller") and *al-libās* ("the bloomers") and *jathal* and *ḥāl* ("burden") and *khuḍullah* ("comfort, ease" or "a soft woman") and *shāʿah*[240] and *ḥannah* and *rubuḍ* and *al-naʿl* ("the sole") (though I don't approve of the last and it would be better if it were deleted). It's strange that she is called "the bloomers" and "the quilt" but not "the underdrawers." 2.14.88

A certain scholar has said that if God wishes to do something good on earth, he chooses a woman as the means to its accomplishment, and if the Devil wishes to do something evil, he also uses a woman for his ends. People differ over the interpretation of this statement. The Bag-men believe that the accession of women to the throne of England was an unalloyed blessing,[241] while the Market-men believe it was an infernal evil; similar are the cases of the two queens of England[242] and of Irene, wife of Leo IV, and Theodora, wife of Theophilus,[243] and so on without number. Note here that it has not been the custom to make women popes, metropolitans, heads of armies, ships' captains, or judges, out of fear of their intrepid and powerful natures. What would happen if men, who by nature worship women, were to vacate these high posts and they to assume them? If it be said that the Franks take them as queens and do well, I would respond that it has been decided among them that, if the head of state is a female, the management of the laws and all official work go to a male. This may be one of the most difficult issues relating to women, for the same analysis applies equally to women being popes or anything else. I may have gone on at too great a length here about women, overlooking the fact that there are to be found among them some who are too short to justify a long discussion. Now, then, it is time for me to divorce myself from them and return to the matter in hand, though I shall come back to them at some other point, God willing. 2.14.89

الفصل الخامس عشر

. . . . في ذلك الموضع ☜

Chapter 15[244]

. . . . Right There! ☞

الفصل السادس عشر

في ذلك الموضع بعينه

لم يطاوعنى القلم على الانتقال من هذا الموضع الشهى الى الكلام فى الفارياق ١،١٦،٢
وامثاله * بل لعله هو نفسه يروم ذلك ايثارا له على ذاته * فلا بد اذا من الرجوع
الى وصف النسآ من دون اعتذار اليه فاقول * قال بعض الفحول من العلمآء ان ٢،١٦،٢
المراة اشرف من الرجل وافخم وانبل واحلم وافضل واكرم * امّا وجه كونها اشرف
فلان شاهدى تانيثها واقفان فى محل مرفوع * بحيث يمكن لها ان تراهما او
تريهما ايان شات من دون تطاطى راس وانحنآ * وفى ذلك من العز والشرف
ما لا يخفى * الا ترى ان بعض الادبآ قال ان من عزّ لا ان يقولها الانسان وهو
رافع راسه * ومن ذُلّ نعم ان يقولها وهو خافضه * اما شاهدا الرجل فهما
منكوسان فى محل منخفض بحيث لا يقدر ان يراهما الا اذا تطاطا وانحنى *
وامّا وجه كونها افخم فلان ساقيها اللتين هما عمودان لهيكل الجسم * وبطنها ٣،١٦،٢
الذى هو منبت لتكوّن النسمة * وعجزها الذى هو مورد للاعجاز * تكون افخم
من ساقى الرجل وبطنه وعجزه وامّا وجه كونها انبل فلانها تنبل بما يلقى اليها مدة
تسعة اشهر * وامّا وجه كونها احلم فلانّ سِمَةَ الحلم ترى فى شاهدى تانيثها *

Chapter 16

Right Here!

The pen has refused to obey my command to leave this stimulating spot and talk of the Fāriyāq and his like, and he too indeed, in all likelihood, would rather stay put than talk about himself. Thus there is no help for it but to resume my description of women, without tendering him any apology. 2.16.1

I thus declare: certain of our most eminent scholars have said that the woman is more honorable than the man, more imposing, nobler, more clement, more virtuous, and more generous. The argument for her being more honorable rests on the fact that the two witnesses to her feminity stand in an elevated position, enabling her to see them and to make them seen whenever she wishes, without bowing her head or bending over, and in this lie a pride and a nobility that cannot be concealed. Are you not aware that a certain litterateur has claimed that "the pride of 'No' lies in one's saying it with one's head raised, while the humiliation of 'Yes' lies in saying it with it bowed?" The two witnesses to a man's masculinity, on the other hand, are withdrawn, in a position that allows him to see them only if he bends over and bows down. 2.16.2

The argument for her being more imposing lies in the fact that her legs, which are the columns upon which the mass of the body stands, her belly, which is the nest in which the soul is formed, and her backside, which is a source of paralyzing inaction, are more imposing than the legs, belly, and backside of the man. The argument for her being nobler lies in the fact that she is treated with the respect due to nobility for a period of nine months because of what is cast into her. The argument for her being more clement lies in the fact that the mark of clemency[245] is visible on the two witnesses to her femininity. 2.16.3

٤،١٦،٢ واما وجه كونها افضل فلانها خلقت من الرجل وعقبه * وهو خلق من تراب * لكنها اذا ماتت (معاذ الله من ذلك) تستحيل الى تراب كالرجل لا الى اصلها الذى اخذت منه اى لا تصير رجلا ولا ضلعا * واما وجه كونها اكرم فلانها ارق فوادا وارحم قلبا والين طبعا * فاذا رات احدا محتاجا الى شى من عندها لم تضن به عليه * وناهيك ما جآ عن مادح السيدة زبيدة اذ قال

ازبيـدة ابنـة جعفـر   طوبى لزائـرك المـثاب
تعطـين من رجـليك ما   تعطى الاكف من الرغاب

فلما انكر الوصفآ عليه ذلك وهمّوا بضربه انتهرتهم واحسنت اليه لعلمها انه لم يخطئ الوصف * وقال فحل اخران المراة تعمّر فى الغالب اكثر من الرجل * وسبب ذلك ٥،١٦،٢ انها لما كانت مفطورة على اللين والطفولة والنعومة كان لها ان تتلقى ما يستقبلها من الحوادث بالصبر والتانّى * فتكون به مَيْلَعا اى تارة تميل الى هذا الشق وتارة الى ذلك * فَمَثَلُها كمثل الغصن الرطيب يميل مع الريح فلا ينقصف * فاما الرجل فانه لما كان مفطورا على القسوحة واليبوسة فمتى دهمه امر تصلّب له واقتسح فلا يلبث ان يعطب به * فمثله كمثل الشجرة اليابسة اذا قويت عليها الريح * قال ومن خواصها ايضا ان الخمرة لا تبلغ منها قدر ما تبلغ من الرجل * واختلفوا فى تعليل ذلك * فذهب قوم الى ان فى دم المراة قوة جاذبية تغلب على الخمر فتجذبه سفلا فلا يصعد الى دماغها * وزعم بعض ان فى المراة نوعا من الخمر يسمى رضابا وهو فيها قوى جدا * بحيث اذا خالطه الشراب اىّ شراب كان ذهب بقوته * والقطرة من هذا النوع تباع احيانا ببدرة واحيانا براس انسان او بعنقه * ومن خواصها ان ٦،١٦،٢ شعرها يكون اطول من شعر الرجل * وشِعرها ابلغ من شعره * وشعورها ادق *

The argument for her being more virtuous lies in the fact that she was created from and subsequent to the man and that he was created from dust. She, on the other hand, were she to die (which God forbid), would turn to dust like the man, not to the origin from which she was taken, i.e., would not become either a man or a rib. The argument for her being more generous lies in the fact that she is more tender-hearted, more kindly-minded, and more gentle-natured. If she sees someone to be in need of something she has, she will not begrudge it to him, on which topic it is enough to cite what the eulogist had to say about Mistress Zubaydah when he wrote, 2.16.4

O Zubaydah, Jaʿfar's daughter,
Happy the visitor you reward!
You grant as many wishes with your feet
As your hands accord.

When her attendants reproached him for these words and rose to beat him, she scolded them and thanked him, for she knew that his description was not wrong.[246]

Another eminent scholar has stated that a woman generally lives longer than a man, because her inborn suppleness, childlikeness, and smoothness allow her to face events with patience and deliberateness so that she is flexible with them, meaning that she bends now to this side, now to the other, being in this like the supple branch that bends with the wind and does not snap. Man, on the other hand, given his innate hardness and dryness, holds himself rigid and unyielding in the face of whatever may befall him and is, as a consequence, quickly destroyed by it, being in this like the dry tree in the face of the tempest. Another of her singular charactestics is that alcohol does not affect her as much as it does the man, and people differ over why this is so. Some believe that there is an attractive force in the woman's blood that overcomes the alcohol and draws it downward so that it doesn't ascend to her brain. Others claim that the woman herself contains a kind of alcohol called *ruḍāb*[247] that is so strong within her that if you mix it with any other drink whatsoever the latter loses its strength; a single drop of this type of alcohol is sold sometimes for an enormous sum of money and sometimes for a man's head or his neck. 2.16.5

Further peculiarities of hers are that her locks are longer than a man's, her lyrics more eloquent, and her likes more precise, and that sleeping with 2.16.6

ومشاعرتها انفع * اما الاول فلم يختلف فيه اثنان * واما الثانى فلانها اذا قالت شعرا فانما تقوله فى رجل فهو يعجب الرجال ويبلغ منهم بالطبع * ويعجب النسآ بالطبع والصنعة ايضا * ولعل ذلك مشكل آخر من المشاكل الانثوية * فانى ارى هذا التعليل يصدق على الرجل فانه انما يقول الشعر فى امراة * ويمكن ان يجاب بان الشاعر المجيد اكثر شعره يكون فى غير الغزل * وذلك كاختلاق مدح يفتريه
٧،١٦،٢ على امير* او وصف مجلس انس او حرب ونحوه * واما الثالث فلانها اذا مرّت مثلا بحانوت بزّاز ورات بزّا شفافا اترنجى اللون * فاول ما تلمحه تقول لك هذا يصلح لليل * وربما كان فكرك وقتئذ فى كتاب تطالعه او فى شرآ حمار تركبه * واذا رات ديباجا اخضر قالت بديها هذا يصلح للشتآ * او كتانا ابيض فاخرا خصّصته بالصيف * ثم اذا مرّت بدكان جوهرى او اذا تهوّستَ انت واخذتها اليه قالت لك على الفور هذا الحجر الماس يصلح لان يجعل فصا فى خاتم للبنصر* وهذه الياقوتة فى خاتم للخنصر* وهذه الزمرذة فى خاتم للمتوسطة * وهذا الفيروزج فى خاتم للسبابة * وهذه الفريدة فى خاتم للابهام * وهذه اللآلى الكبيرة لقلادة فى العنق * وهذه الصغيرة لسوار * وهذه السلاسل الذهب المرصعة توضع فى العنق مع القلادة وتدلّى الى الخصر ويعلق بها ساعة من ذهب * وهذه الشنوف الثقيلة للشتآ * وتلك الخفيفة للصيف * وهذه المتوسطة للربيع والخريف* وفكرك لم يزل مشغولا بالحمار * فان قيل ان الكاف فى فكرك خطاب مطلق لكل قارى وربما تشرف كتابك هذا بمطالعة امير او غيره من السادة العظمآ فلا يصح توجيه الخطاب اليه * لان الامير لا يفكر فى الحمير* قلت قد ورد فى سفر التكوين فى الفصل السادس والثلثين ان عانة من ولد سعير الحورى كان يرعى حمير ابيه زبعون وكان اميرا * بل قد علّق عليه فى بعض النسخ جِلآ دوك وهو اعظم من الامير*

her inside her slip is more fortifying. As to the first, no two will disagree. As to the second, the reason is that, when she makes up verses, she always composes them about a man and as a result it both pleases and affects men through nature, while simultaneously pleasing women through both nature and art. (This may be another of the knotty issues relating to women, for it seems to me that this analysis applies to the man only, for the only thing he composes verse about is women. This may be answered by saying that most of the output of the brilliant poet is directed to activities other than the love lyric, such as dreaming up praises with which to tell lies about some emir or describing a party or a war or something of the sort.)

The third argument may be illustrated by the fact that, if she passes a cloth merchant's store, for example, and catches sight of some translucent, citron-colored fabric, the moment she notices it she'll tell you that it would be perfect for the evening, while your thoughts at the time may be elsewhere—on a book to read or on buying a donkey to ride. If she sees some green silk brocade she'll tell you in the most matter-of-fact way that it would be perfect for winter or, if some extra-fine white linen, she'll assign it to summer. Similarly, if she passes a jeweler's store, or you're besotted enough to take her to one, she'll tell you immediately that that diamond would make a perfect bezel for a signet ring on her little finger, that ruby for one on her fourth finger, that emerald for one on her middle finger, that turquoise for one on her index finger, and that perfect pearl for one on her thumb; that those large pearls would make a collar for her neck, these little ones a bracelet, and those gem-studded gold chains could be placed around her neck next to the necklace so as to hang down to her waist, with a gold watch suspended from them, while those heavy earrings are for the winter, those light ones for the summer, and those medium ones for the spring and fall—during which time your thoughts are still preoccupied with the donkey. If it be objected that the second-person pronoun attached to the word "thoughts" is addressed indiscriminately to all readers and that your book may experience the honor of being read by an emir or other mighty lord, in which case it would be inappropriate to address him in this way, for an emir doesn't think about donkeys, I declare, in Chapter 36 of the Book of Genesis, it says that Anah, descendant of the son of Seir the Horite, used to graze the asses of his father Zibeon, and he was an emir; in fact, in some copies the title "duke" is appended to his name, and a duke is higher than an emir.[248] 2.16.7

ثم انها اى المراة لم تلبث حالة كونها ناظرة الى تلك الجواهر ان تقسم اهل المصر ٨،١٦،٢
جميعا الى خمسة اقسام

القسم الاول فى تهيئة الجواهر *

من التِجاب	ما اذيب مرة من حجر الفضة *
والمَشْخَلَبة	خرز بيض تشاكل اللولو او الحلىّ يتخذ من الليف والخرز وقد تسمىّ الجارية مَشْخَلبة بما عليها من الخرز وليس على بنائها شى * قلت وفى محفوظى ان ابن الاثير حكاها بتقديم الخآ على الشين دون هآ *
والضِئْب	حبّ اللولو *
والقَصَب	ما كان مستطيلا من الجوهر..... والدرّ والرطب والزبرجد الرطب المرصّع بالياقوت *
واليَشَب	حجر معروف *
والبَهْت	حجر معروف *
والكِبْريت	الياقوت الاحمر والذهب او جوهر معدنه خلف التُبَّت بوادى النمل وفى ت ب ت تبّت كسكر بلاد بالمشرق ينسب اليها المسك الاذفر *
والياقوت	معروف *
والدَهْنَج	جوهر كالزمرذ *
والزِبْرج	جوهر او الزينة من وشى *
والزبردج	الزبرجد *

Next, she—that is the woman—while contemplating these jewels, will lose no time in dividing the entire population of the cosmopolis into five work groups: 2.16.8

Work Group 1: For the Preparation of Gems and Precious Metals

including *tijāb*,	"what is extracted from silver-bearing rock at a single smelting"
and *mashkhalabah*,	"white beads in the form of pearls or jewelry made from fiber and beads; also a name that may be applied to a girl because of the beads she has on; there is no other word of this pattern"; I declare, I seem to remember that Ibn al-Athīr cites it as *makhshalab*
and *ḍi'b*,	"seed pearls"
and *qaṣab*,	"any elongated gemstones . . . pearls of the first water or peridot of the first water studded with rubies"
and *yashab*,	["jasper"] "a stone too well known to require definition"
and *baht*,	["aetites, eagle stone"] "a stone too well known to require definition"
and *kibrīt*,	"red rubies, or gold, or gemstones whose source is beyond al-Tubbat, in the Valley of the Ants"; under *t-b-t* [in the *Qāmūs*], "Tubbat [*sic*] is a land in the east from which comes the finest musk"
and *yāqūt*,	["rubies"] "too well known to require definition"
and *dahnaj*,	"a gemstone like emerald"
and *zibrij*,	gems, or an ornament with figures
and *zabardaj*,	"the same as *zabarjad* ('peridot')"

والصَلِيجة سبيكة الفضة المصفّاة * ٩،١٦،٢

والمُرْجان م وتعريفه في القاموس انه صغار اللولو *

والخَرايد الخريدة اللولوة لم تثقب *

والفَرِيد الشَذْر يفصّل بين اللولو والذهب ج فرائد والجوهرة النفيسة والدرّ *

والجُذاذ حجارة الذهب *

والبَلّور جوهر معروف *

والتِبْر الذهب والفضة او فتاتهما قبل ان يصاغا فاذا صيغا فهما ذهب وفضة او ما استخرج من المعدن قبل ان يصاغ ومكسر الزجاج وكل جوهر يستعمل من النحاس والصفر *

والسِيَرآ الذهب الخالص *

والشَذْر قطع من الذهب تلقط من معدنه بلا اذابة او خرز يفصّل بها النظم او هو اللولو الصغار *

والشَمُّور الماس *

والعَمْرة الشذرة من خرز يفصل بها النظم * ١٠،١٦،٢

والنُضار الجوهر الخالص من التبر *

والخَرَز الجوهر وما يُنظم *

والفِلِزّ نحاس ابيض — او جواهر الارض كلها او ما ينفيه الكير من كل ما يذاب منها *

والهِبْرِزِيّ الذهب الخالص *

والتَرامِس الجمان *

and *ṣalījah*,	"a purified silver ingot"	2.16.9
and *murjān*,	["coral"] too well known to require definition; defined in the *Qāmūs* as meaning "small pearls"	
and *kharāʾid*,	"the *kharīdah* is the pearl, unbored"	
and *farīd*,	"a bead made as a spacer between pearls and gold [on a necklace], plural *farāʾid*; also any precious stone, or pearls"	
and *judhādh*,	"gold nuggets"	
and *ballawr*,	["crystal"] "a gemstone too well known to require definition"	
and *tibr*,	"gold and silver, or small pieces of either before being worked; once worked, they are known as *dhahab* ('gold') and *fiḍḍah* ('silver'); or what is extracted from the rock before being worked, or broken glass, or any decorative beads of copper or brass that may be used"	
and *sayrāʾ*,	"pure gold"	
and *shadhr*,	"pieces of gold extracted from ore without smelting, or beads used as spacers on necklaces, or small pearls"	
and *shammūr*,	"diamonds"	
and *ʿamrah*,	"beads used as spacers on necklaces"	2.16.10
and *nuḍār*,	"gemstones free of impurities"	
and *kharaz*,	"gemstones, or anything that is strung as a necklace"	
and *filizz*,	"white copper . . . any of the gemstones of the earth, or anything that the bellows extracts from any such minerals as have been smelted"	
and *hibrizī*,	"pure gold"	
and *tarāmis*,	"pearls"	

والحُصّ	اللولوة ونحوها الخُوَضة *
والخِلاص	ما اخلصته من الذهب والفضة *
والدِّلِيص	مآ الذهب *
والخَضَض	خرز بيض صغار يلبسها الصغار*
والثَّعْثع	اللولو والصدف * ١١،١٦،٢
والجَزَع	الخرز اليمانى الصينى *
والزِّلع	ضرب من الودع *
واليَنَع	ضرب من العقيق *
والزُخْرف	الذهب وكمال حسن الشى *
والصَرِيف	الفضة الخالصة *
والسفائق	السفيقة الضربة الدقيقة الطويلة من الذهب والفضة ونحوهما *
والعقيق	معروف *
والخَضَل	اللولو والدر الصافى وخرز معروف
الحُوَمة	البلّور
الجُمان	اللولو او هنوات اشكال اللولو من فضة او خرز بيّض بمآ الفضة *
والمِينا	جوهر الزجاج *
والمَهو	اللولو وحصى ابيض والمَهاة البلورة *
والنِهآ	الزجاج ويقصر او القوارير وحجر ابيض ارخى من الرخام — وضرب من الخرز *

and *ḥuṣṣ*,	“pearl”; synonym *khūḍah*
and *khilāṣ*,	“whatever gold or silver one may have purified”
and *dalīṣ*,	“gold lacquer”
and *khaḍaḍ*,	“small white beads worn by children”
and *thaʿthaʿ*,	“pearls, or mother-of-pearl” **2.16.11**
and *jazaʿ*,	“Chinese beads from Yemen”
and *zaylaʿ*,	“a kind of seashell”
and *yanaʿ*,	“a kind of carnelian”
and *zukhruf*,	“gold, or the perfection of the beauty of something”
and *ṣarīf*,	“pure silver”
and *safāʾiq*,	“the *safīqah* [singular] is a long thin spill of gold and silver or the like”
and *ʿaqīq*,	[“carnelian”] “too well known to require definition”
and *khaḍl*,	“pearls, or pure pearls, or a certain kind of bead, too well known to require definition”
and *ḥūmah*,	“crystal”
and *jumān*,	“pearls, or little things with the appearance of pearls made of silver, or beads made white with silver lacquer”
and *mīnāʾ*,	“pure glass”
and *mahw*,	“pearls, or white pebbles”; also “*mahāh* means crystal”
and *nihāʾ*.	“glass (also occurs as *nihā*), or glass vessels, or a white stone softer than marble . . . or a kind of bead”

القسم الثانى فى عمل الحلىّ ١٢،١٦،٢

من البؤبؤ	راس المكحلة *
والأُرْبة	القلادة *
والأَرْنب	حلى *
والمِعْقب	القُرط ومثله الرَعْثة ج رِعاث *
والجِبّة	خرزة او لولوة تعلق فى الاذن *
والدُملج	معروف *
واليارَج	القُلْب او السوار*
والجانِح	الجانح من الدر نظم يعرّض اوكل ما جعلته فى نظام *
والداح	سوار ذو قوى *
والسَنيح	الدر اوخيطه قبل ان ينظم فيه والحلى *
والوِشاح	كِرْسان من لولو وجوهر منظومان يخالف بينهما معطوف احدهما على الآخر واديم عريض يرصع بالجوهر تشده المراة بين عاتقيها وكشحيها * ١٣،١٦،٢
والوَضَح	حلى من الفصة *
والفتخة	خاتم كبير فى اليد او الرجل وحلقة من فضة كالخاتم *
والخَلَدة	السِوار والقُرْط *
والزِراد	المِخْنقة *
والعِضاد	الدملج كالمعضاد *
والعِقْد	معروف *
والقِلادة	ما جعل فى العنق *

Work Group 2: For the Making of Jewelry and Ornaments 2.16.12

including the *bu'bu'*,	"lid of a kohl-pot"
and the *urbah*,	"a necklace"
and *arnab*,	"ornaments"
and the *mi'qab*,	"earrings"; synonym *ra'thah*, plural *ri'āth*
and the *ḥijjah*,	"a bead or pearl hung in the ear"
and the *dumluj*,	["beaded armlet"] "too well known to require definition"
and *yāraj*,	"women's bracelets"
and the *jāniḥ*,	"the *jāniḥ* is made of pearls, strung to be displayed, or anything one arranges in order"
and *dāḥ*,	"a bracelet with multiple strands"
and *sanīḥ*,	"pearls, or the thread before they are strung on it, or any jewelry"
and *wishāḥ*,	"two strings of alternating pearls and gemstones with a spacer between each and one string above the other, or a broad piece of leather studded with gems that a woman hangs over her shoulders and that falls to her hips" 2.16.13
and *waḍaḥ*,	"jewelry made of silver"
and the *fatkhah*,	"a large ring worn on the hand or foot, or a circle of silver like a ring"
and the *khaladah*,	"a bracelet, or earring"
and the *zirād*,	"a *mikhnaqah*"
and the *'iḍād*,	"the *dumluj*; synonym *mi'ḍād*"
and the *'iqd*,	["necklace"] "too well known to require definition"
and the *qilādah*,	"whatever is placed around the neck"

والِمنْجد	حلى مكلل بالفصوص وهو من لولو وذهب او قرنفل . . . . ياخذ من العنق الى اسفل الثديين يقع على موضع النجاد *
والمَسْجور	من اللولو المنظوم المسترسل *
والسَّفِيرة	قلادة بعرى من ذهب وفضة * ١٤،١٦،٢
والشعيرة	هَنَة تصاغ من فضة او حديد على شكل الشعيرة الخ *
والعِتْرة	قلادة تعجن بالمسك والافاويه *
والعَمْر	الشنف *
التِقْصار	القلادة ج تقاصير*
والكُسْبر	المَسَك من العاج كالسوار*
والقُفّاز	— او ضرب من الحلى لليدين والرجلين *
والجِبْس	سوار من فضة يجعل فى وسط القِرام *
والسَلْس	— او القُرْط من الحلى *
والشَمْس	ضرب من القلائد *
والقُداس	شى يعمل كالجمان من الفضة * ١٥،١٦،٢
والكَبِيس	حَلْى مجوف محشوّ طيبا *
والقلادة المكرَّسة	وهى ان ينظم اللولو والخرز فى خيط ثم يضمّا بفصول بخرز كبار*
والنِقْرس	شى يتخذ على صنعة الورد تغرزه المراة فى راسها *
والخَرْبَصِيص	القرط والحبة من الحلى *
والخُرْص	حلقة الذهب والفضة او حلقة القرط او الحلقة الصغيرة من الحلى *

and the *minjad,*	"a piece of jewelry edged with bezels consisting of pearls and gold or cloves . . . that occupies the space from the neck to the base of the breasts, worn like a sword belt"	
and the *masjūr,*	"[a piece of jewelry] made of strung, sagging pearls"	
and the *safīrah,*	"a neck collar with loops of gold and silver"	2.16.14
and the *shaʿīrah,*	"a trinket fashioned from silver or iron in the shape of a barleycorn," etc.	
and the *ʿitrah,*	"a neck collar rubbed with musk and other perfumes"	
and the *ʿamr,*	"the *shanf*"	
and the *tiqṣār,*	"a neck collar, plural *taqāṣīr*"	
and the *kusbur,*	"a bracelet of ivory"; synonym *siwār*	
and *quffāz,*	". . . or a kind of ornament for the hands or the feet"[249]	
and the *ḥibs,*	"a silver eyelet placed in the center of a curtain"	
and the *sals,*	". . . or decorative earrings"[250]	
and the *shams,*	"a kind of neck collar"	
and the *qudās,*	"something made like silver *jumān*"	2.16.15
and the *kabīs,*	"a piece of jewelry that has been hollowed out and filled with perfume"	
and the *qilādah mukarrasah,*	"pearls and beads are strung on a thread and then joined into segments with large beads"	
and the *niqris,*	"something made in the shape of a rose that a woman sticks in her head covering"	
and the *kharbaṣīṣ,*	"a pair of earrings, or something grain-shaped worn as jewelry"	
and the *khurṣ,*	"a hoop of gold or of silver, or the hoop of an earring, or a small hoop worn as decoration"	

والحَوْط خيط مفتول من لونين اسود واحمر فيه خرزات وهلال من فضة تشده المراة فى وسطها لئلاّ تصيبها العين *

والسِمْط قلادة اطول من المخنقة *

والعُلْطة القلادة *

والقُرْط الشنف او المعلّق فى شحمة الاذن *

واللّط القلادة من حب الحنظل المصبّغ * ١٦،١٦،٢

والاَنْواط المعاليق *

والرَصيعة حلية السيف المستديرة اوكل حلقة مستديرة فى سيف او سرج او غيرهما *

والشَنْف القرط الاعلى او معلاق فى قوف الاذن او ما علّق فى اعلاها *

والنُطْفة القرط واللولوة *

والوَقْف سوار من عاج *

والخِزاق السوار الغليظ *

والحِلْق خاتم من فضة بلا فصّ وهو ايضا خاتم المُلْك *

والمِخْنَقة القلادة وكذا المزنقة والمعنقة *

والخَوْق حلقة القُرط والشنف *

والدَيْسق كل حلى من فضة بيضآ خالصة * ١٧،١٦،٢

والزُناق كل رباط تحت الحنك *

والسَوْذق السوار والقُلْب *

والطارقيّة قلادة *

and the *ḥawṭ*,	"a twisted black and red thread on which are beads, or a silver crescent that a woman wears on her waist so that the evil eye will do her no harm"
and the *simṭ*,	"a neck collar longer than the *mikhnaqah*"
and the *ʿulṭah*,	"a neck collar"
and the *qurṭ*,	"the *shanf*, or an earring hung from the earlobe"
and the *laṭṭ*,	"a neck collar made of dyed colocynth seeds" **2.16.16**
and the *anwāṭ*,	"pendant earrings"
and the *raṣīʿah*,	"a round ornament on a sword, or any round ring on a sword, a saddle, or elsewhere"
and the *shanf*,	"a top earring, or a pendant earring in the upper edge of the ear, or anything suspended from its upper part"
and the *nuṭafah*,	"an earring, or pearl"
and the *waqf*,	"an ivory bracelet"
and the *ḥizāq*,	"a thick bracelet"
and the *ḥilq*,	"a silver finger ring without bezel, or 'the Ring of Power'[251]"
and the *mikhnaqah*,	"a necklace"; synonyms *minzaqah* and *miʿnaqah*
and the *khawq*,	"the ring of the *qurṭ* or the *shanf*"
and the *daysaq*,	"any ornament made of pure white silver" **2.16.17**
and the *zunāq*,	"anything tied under the chin"
and the *sawdhaq*,	"a bracelet, or a woman's bracelet"
and the *ṭāriqiyyah*,	"a necklace"

والطَوق معروف *

والقَلَقِيّ ضرب من القلائد *

والمَسَك الاسورة والخلاخيل *

والجَدِيل الوشاح *

والحُلْبة ضرب من الحلى *

والحِجْل الخلخال *

والمُرْسَلة قلادة طويلة تقع على الصدر او القلادة فيها الخرز * ١٨،١٦،٢

والسِدْل السمط من الدر يطول الى الصدر *

والاَشْكال حلى من لولوا وفضة يشبه بعضه بعضاً يقرَّط به النسآ الواحد شَكْل *

والطِمْل القلادة كالطِميل لانها تُطمَل اى تلطخ بالطيب *

والقبَل شى من عاج مستدير يتلالو يعلّق فى صدر المراة *

والقِرْمِل ما تشدّه المراة فى راسها *

والإكليل شبه عصابة تزيّن بالجوهر*

والمَحال ضرب من الحلى *

والنَخَل ضرب من الحلى *

والتهاويل الالوان المختلفة وزينة التصاوير والنقوش الخ *

والبَرِيم حبل للمراة فيه لونان مزيّن بجوهر* ١٩،١٦،٢

والتّوائم توائم اللولو ما تشابك منها *

والتُوْمة اللولوة والقرط فيه حبة كبيرة *

والخاتَم معروف *

and the *ṭawq*, ["decorative collar"] "too well known to require definition"
and the *qalaqī*, "a kind of necklace"
and *masak*, "bracelets or anklets"
and the *jadīl*, "a jeweled sash"
and *ḥulbah*, "a kind of jewelry"
and the *ḥijl*, "an anklet"
and the *mursalah*, "a long necklace draped over the breast, or a necklace containing beads" 2.16.18
and the *sidl*, "a *simṭ* of pearls that reaches the breast"
and *ashkāl*, "jewelry made of pearls and silver, each element resembling the next, which women wear as earrings; singular *shakl*"
and the *ṭiml*, "a necklace (synonym *ṭimīl*), because it is 'impregnated (*tuṭmalu*),' i.e., smeared with perfume"
and the *qabal*, "a round thing of ivory that shines and is hung on a woman's breast"
and the *qirmil*, "something a woman ties around her head"
and the *iklīl*, "something resembling a headband that is decorated with gems"
and *maḥāl*, "a kind of jewelry"
and *nakhl*, "a kind of jewelry"
and *tahāwīl*, "different colors, or decoration in the form of drawn figures and engravings"
and the *barīm*, "a woman's cord in which there are two colors and which is decorated with gems" 2.16.19
and *tawā'im*, "*tawā'im* pearls are those that are joined together"
and the *tūmah*, "a pearl, or an earring containing a large drop"
and the *khātam*, ["finger ring"] "too well known to require definition"

والعِصْمة	القلادة *
والكَرْم	القلادة ونوع من الصياغة فى المخانق او بنات كرم حلى كان يتخذ فى الجاهلية *
والاَنْظام	كل خيط نظم خرزا *
والثُكْنة	القلادة *
والجُمان	سفيفة من اَدَم ينسج وفيها خرز من كل لون تتوشحه المراة *
والبُرة	الخلخال *
والرِىّ	القلادة او التى توضع في عنق الغلام *
والوَنِيّة	العقد من الدر او اللولوة *
الى الخَشَل	روس الاسورة والخلاخيل *

القسم الثالث فى عمل الطيب واتخاذ المشموم ٢٠،١٦،٢

من الاَناب	المسك او عطر يضاهيه *
والجُلّاب	مآ الورد *
والزَرْنب	طيب او شجر طيّب الرائحة *
والكُرُكب	نبات طيب الرائحة *
والمَلاب	عطر او الزعفران *
والشَثّ	نبت طيب الريح يُدبَغ به *
واليَلَنْجوج	عود البخور*
والرَّباحىّ	جنس من الكافور*
والمُرَنَّخ	اجود عود البخور*

and the *ʿiṣmah,*	"a necklace"
and the *karm,*	"a necklace, or a kind of work on a *mikhnaqah*, or 'the Daughters of Karm'—ornaments that were made during the Days of Barbarism"
and the *anẓām,*	"any thread on which beads are strung"
and the *thuknah,*	"a necklace"
and the *jumān,*	"a plaited strip of hide with beads of all colors on it that women wear as a sash"
and the *burrah,*	"an anklet"
and the *riyy,*	"a necklace, or the thing placed round the neck of a boy"
and the *waniyyah,*	"a necklace of pearls"
and *khashal.*	"the terminals on bracelets or anklets"

Work Group 3: For Making Perfume and Concocting Fragrant Pastes **2.16.20**

including *anāb,*	"musk, or an aromatic substance resembling it"
and *jullāb,*	"rosewater"
and *zarnab,*	"a perfume, or a sweet-smelling tree"
and *kurkub,*	"a sweet-smelling plant"
and *malāb,*	"an aromatic substance, or saffron"
and *shathth,*	"sweet-smelling plants used in tanning"
and *yalanjūj,*	"aloe wood"
and *rabāḥī,*	"a kind of camphor"
and *murannaḥ,*	"best-quality aloe wood"

والرَيحان	نبت طيب الرائحة اوكل نبت كذلك *
والشِيح	نبت طيب الرائحة * ٢,١٦,٢١
والصَيّاح	عطر او غِسْل *
والنَضُوح	طيب *
والسَلِيخة	عطر كانه قشر منسلخ ودهن ثمر البان قبل ان يربَّب *
واللَّبِيخة	نافجة المسك *
واللَخْلَخة	طيب م *
والسُعْد	طيب م *
والرَنْد	شجر طيب الرائحة والعود والآس *
والزَبّاد	م ويسمى الزُهْم *
والعَبْد	نبات طيب الرائحة *
والقِنْديد	العنبر والكافور والمسك وطيب يعمل بالزعفران * ٢,١٦,٢٢
والنَدّ	طيب م *
والخَنِيذ	دهن والغسل المطيب *
والكاذى	شجر له ورد يطيب به الدهن *
والبَهار	نبت طيب الريح *
والخَطّار	دهن يتخذ من الزيت بافاويه الطيب *
والخُمْرة	الوَرْس واشياً من الطيب *
والذَرِيرة	عطر *
والزَبْعر	نبت طيب الرائحة *
والإِذْخِر	حشيش طيب الرائحة *

and *rayḥān*,	"a [particular] sweet-smelling plant [i.e., 'basil'] or any plant of that nature"
and *shīḥ*,	"a sweet-smelling plant" 2.16.21
and *ṣayyāḥ*,	"an aromatic substance, or a perfume for washing with"
and *naḍūḥ*,	"perfume"
and *salīkhah*,	"an aromatic substance like peeled bark, or the fat from the fruit of the ben tree before it is pulped"
and *labīkhah*,	"a vesica of musk"
and *lakhlakhah*,	"a perfume, too well known to require definition"
and *suʿd*,	"a perfume, too well known to require definition"
and *rand*,	"a sweet-smelling tree, or aloe, or myrtle"
and *zabād*,	["civet"] "too well known to require definition"; synonym *zuhm*
and *ʿabd*,	"a sweet-smelling plant"
and *qindīd*,	"amber, or camphor, or musk, or a perfume made from saffron" 2.16.22
and *nadd*,	["ambergris"] "a perfume, too well known to require definition"
and *ḥanīdh*,	"an ointment, or a scented wash"
and *kādhī*,	"a tree bearing flowers with which ointment is perfumed"
and *bahār*,	"a sweet-smelling plant"
and *khaṭṭār*,	"an ointment made from oil with aromatic perfume"
and *khumrah*,	"Indian yellow, or various kinds of perfume"
and *dharīrah*,	"an aromatic substance"
and *zabʿar*,	"a sweet-smelling plant"
and *idhkhir*,	"sweet-smelling grasses"

والسَّاهريّة عطر* ٢٣،١٦،٢

والضَيمُران الريحان الفارسى *

والمُطيَّر العود او المُطرّى منه *

والظَفار شى من العطر كانه ظفر مقتلف من اصله *

والعَبِير الزعفران او اخلاط من الطيب *

والعَبهر النرجس والياسمين ونبت آخر*

والعِطر الطيب *

والعَمار الريحان يزين به مجلس الشراب *

والعنبر روث دابة بحرية او نبع عين فيه *

والغرآ نبت طيب او هو الغُرَيرآ *

والفاغِرة طيب او الكبابة * ٢٤،١٦،٢

والقُطر العود الذى يتبخّر به *

والكافور نبت طيب نَوره كنور الاقحوان والطلع او وعآوه وطيب م يكون من شجر بجبال بحر الهند والصين الخ *

والنِسرين ورد م *

والعَجُوز ضرب من الطيب *

والبَلَسان شجر صغار كشجر الحنآ لا ينبت الّا بعين شمس ظاهر القاهرة يتنافس فى دهنها *

والقَلَسان نبات طيب الرائحة *

والقَنَس نبات طيب الرائحة ويسمى ايضا الراسَن *

والهَبَس الخِيَرىّ ويقال له المنثور والنمام *

and *sāhiriyyah,*	"an aromatic substance"	2.16.23
and *ḍaymurān,*	"Persian basil"	
and *muṭayyar,*	"aloe, or moistened aloe"	
and *ẓafār,*	"a sort of incense, so named because it resembles a fingernail (*ẓufr*) pulled from its root"	
and *ʿabīr,*	"saffron, or a mixture of perfumes"	
and *ʿabhar,*	"narcissus, or jasmine, or other plants"	
and *ʿiṭr,*	"an aromatic substance"	
and *ʿamār,*	"the sweet-smelling plants with which the place where men meet to drink is decorated"	
and *ʿanbar,*	"the dung of a sea creature, or a substance thrown up by a spring in the sea"	
and *gharrāʾ,*	"a scented plant, or it may be that the correct form is *ghurayrāʾ*"	
and *fāghirah,*	"a perfume, or cubeb"	2.16.24
and *quṭr,*	"aloe used for censing"	
and *kāfūr,*	"a scented plant whose flowers are like camomile and palm blossom, or the spadix of the latter, or a perfume too well known to require definition; it comes from trees in the mountains of the Sea of India and from China"	
and *nisrīn,*	["eglantine"] "a flower too well known to require definition"	
and *ʿajūz,*	"a sort of perfume"	
and *balasān,*	"small trees like those of henna that grow only in ʿAyn Shams, the Cairo suburb, and whose oil is much in demand"	
and *qalasān,*	"a sweet-smelling plant"	
and *qanas,*	"a sweet-smelling plant, also called *rāsan*"	
and *habas,*	"gillyflower, also called *manthūr* and *nammām*"	

والمَرْدَقوش طيب تجعله المراة فى مشطها *

والحُصّ الوَرْس والزعفران *

والسَعِيط البان ودهن الخردل * ٢٥,١٦,٢

والقُسْط عود هندى وعربى *

والضَياع ضرب من الطيب *

والمَيْعة عطر كالمائعة *

والنَقُوع صبغ فيه من افواه الطيب *

والعَوْف نبات طيب الرائحة *

والخِلاق ضرب من الطيب *

والرَّحِيق ضرب من الطيب *

والبُنْك طيب م *

والسُكّ طيب يتخذ من الرامك *

والمسك المشموع اى المخلوط بالعنبر* ٢٦,١٦,٢

والتَتْل ضرب من الطيب *

والرُعْلة اكليل من ريحان وآس *

والسُنْبل نبات طيب الرائحة *

والقُنْدُول شجر بالشام لزهره دهن شريف *

والمَنْدَل العود او اجوده كالمندلىّ *

والبَشام شجر عطر الرائحة *

والبَهْرمان العصفر والحنآ *

والثِوَمة شجرة اطيب رائحة من الآس*

and *mardaqūsh*,	"a perfume a woman puts on her comb"
and *ḥuṣṣ*,	"Indian yellow, or saffron"
and *saʿīṭ*,	"the ben tree, or mustard oil" **2.16.25**
and *qusṭ*,	"Indian or Arabian aloe"
and *ḍiyāʿ*,	"a kind of perfume"
and *mayʿah*,	"an aromatic substance; synonym *māʾiʿah*"
and *naqūʿ*,	"a dye containing sweet-smelling aromatics"
and *ʿawf*,	"a sweet-smelling plant"
and *khilāq*,	"a kind of perfume"
and *raḥīq*,	"a kind of perfume"
and *bunk*,	"a perfume too well known to require definition"
and *sukk*,	"a perfume made from *rāmik*[252]"
and *misk mashmūʿ*,	[literally, "waxed musk"] i.e., "mixed with amber" **2.16.26**
and *tatl*,	"a kind of perfume"
and *ruʿlah*,	"umbels of basil and myrtle"
and *sunbul*,	"a sweet-smelling plant"
and *qundūl*,	"a tree found in the Levant, whose flowers have an oil of excellent quality"
and *mandal*,	"aloe, or the best kind thereof; synonym *mandalī*"
and *bashām*,	"a fragrantly scented tree"
and *bahramān*,	"safflower, or henna"
and *thiwamah*,	"a tree more sweet-smelling than myrtle"

والجَيْهُمان الزعفران وكذا الرَيْهُقان *

والخُزامَى خِيرِىّ البرّ* ٢٧،١٦،٢

والضُرَم شجر طيب الريح *

والمَكْتُومة دهن يجعل فيه الزعفران او الكَتَم *

واللَطِيمة المسك *

والمَنْشَم عطر شاقّ الدقّ او قرون السنبل *

والنمّام نبت طيب *

والمَهْضُومة طيب يخلط بالمسك والبان *

والأُشْنة عطر ابيض مما يلتف على شجر البلوط والصنوبر*

والبان شجر لحب ثمرة دهن طيب *

والجَفْن شجر طيب الرائحة *

والحُنُون الفاغية او نَور كل شجر* ٢٨،١٦،٢

والرَقُون الحِنّا والزعفران *

والكُثْنة شى يتخذ من آس واغصان خلاف تبسط وينضد عليها الرياحين اصله كُثْنا او هى نَوَرْدجة من القصب والاغصان الرطبة الوريقة تحزم ويجعل جوفها النور قلت ونحوها الكُثْنة *

والمَيْسُوسَن شى تجعله النسآ فى الغِسْلة لروسهن *

والغالية طيب م *

والفاعِيَة النمامة وزهر الحنآ والافعآ الروائح الطيبة *

and *jayhumān*, “saffron; synonym *rayhuqān*”

and *khuzāmā*, “wild gillyflower” 2.16.27

and *ḍurm*, “a sweet-smelling tree”

and *maktūmah*, “an ointment containing saffron or *katam* (‘boxwood’)”

and *laṭīmah*, “musk”

and *mansham*, “an aromatic substance that is hard work to pound, or *sunbul* pods”

and *nammām*, “a sweet-smelling plant”

and *mahḍūmah*, “a perfume that is mixed with musk and ben”

and *ushnah*, “a white aromatic substance that wraps itself around oak and pine trees”

and *bān*, “a tree the seeds of whose fruits yield a sweet-smelling oil”

and *jafn*, “a sweet-smelling tree”

and *ḥannūn*, “Egyptian privet flower, or the blossoms of any tree” 2.16.28

and *raqūn*, “henna, or saffron”

and *kuthnah*, “something made from myrtle and branches of Egyptian willow, which are spread out and on which sweet-smelling herbs are layered, originally *kuthnā*; or it is something plaited from reeds and supple, leafy boughs bound together inside which a light is placed”; to which I would add that it has a synonym, *kunthah*

and *maysūsan*, “something women put in the wash they use on their heads”

and *ghāliya*, [“galia moschata”] “a perfume too well known to require definition”

and *fāʿiya*, “mint, or henna flowers, or pleasant, sweet odors”

في ذلك الموضع بعينه

والفاغية	نور الحنّا او يغرس غصن الحنّا مقلوبا فيثمر زهرا اطيب من الحنآ فذلك الفاغية *
والكِبآ	عود البخور او ضرب منه *
والكاذى	دهن ونبت طيب الرائحة *
واللُوّة	العود يتبخر به *
الى النّدا	شى يتطيّب به كالبخور*

القسم الرابع فى عمل الآنية والادوات والمتاع والفرش ٢٩،١٦،٢

من الغَرَب	جام من الفضة *
والشُفارِج	الطبق فيه الفيخات والسكرجات *
والصُراحيّة	آنية للخمر*
والمطافح	المغارف *
والبُهار	اناء كالابريق *
والطِرَجهارة	شبه كاس يشرب فيه ونحوه الطِرَجهالة والفنجانة ويقال للفنجانة الصغيرة سَوَمَلة *
والشَوارِف	وعآ الخمر من خابية ونحوها *

والاكواب والاباريق والقوارير والكؤس والاقداح والطاس والصحون والعُتُد والخروس والصيعان والدنان والصحاف والقِصاع والزُلَح والقوارى والجِفان والعِلاب والبواطى والماكل والقِعاب والنواجيد[١] والعِساس والعُسُس والفِدام والعُسوف *

والجَهمة	القدر الضخمة * ٣٠،١٦،٢
والهَيطلة	القدر من صفر*

١ ١٨٥٥: النواجيذ.

and *fāghiya*, "henna blossoms, or when a henna branch is planted upside down and then produces a flower sweeter smelling than henna itself, this being the *fāghiya*"
and *kibā'*, "aloe used for incense, or a kind thereof"
and *kādhī*, "an ointment, and a sweet-smelling plant"
and *luwwah*, "aloe used in censing"
and *nadā*. "something used for perfuming in the same way as incense"

Work Group 4: For Making Vessels, Tools, Household Articles, and Furnishings 2.16.29

including the *gharab*, "a silver basin"
and the *shufārij*, "a tray on which small dishes are placed"
and the *ṣurāḥiyyah*, "a vessel for wine"
and *maṭāfiḥ*, "ladles"
and the *buhār*, "a vessel resembling a pitcher"
and the *ṭirjahārah*, something like a drinking cup, synonyms *ṭirjahālah* and *finjānah*; a small *finjānah* is called a *sawmalah*
and *shawārif*, "a vessel for wine such as a jar or the like"
and cups, and pitchers, and bottles, and goblets, and bowls, and drinking scoops, and plates, and utensils, and wine-jars, and crocks, and tuns, and platters, and trenchers, and food trays, and troughs, and tureens, and milk pails, and decanters, and casseroles, and drinking horns, and wine vessels, and beakers, and kettles, and strainers, and jeroboams,
and the *jahmah*, "a huge cooking pot" 2.16.30
and the *hayṭalah*, "a brass cooking pot"

والمِرْجل القدر من الحجارة والنحاس *

والكَفْت القدر الصغيرة *

والهِلْجاب القدر العظيمة وكذا البِساط *

والتأمورة الابريق والحقة والتميمة المشدودة الراس *

والقَعْن الجفنة يعجن فيها *

والجام م ونحوه الصاع *

والمكّوك طاس يشرب به *

والعَيْزار ضرب من اقداح الزجاج *

والسُعُوف الاقداح الكبار وامتعة البيت وكل شى جاد وبلغ من مملوك ٢،١٦،٣١

او علق او دار فهو سَعَف وبالتسكين السلعة *

والوَرْسىّ من اجود اقداح النُضار*

والزَوْرآ انآء من فضة *

والفاثور الطست او الخوان من رخام او فضة والناجود والباطية *

والقُذْمور الخوان من فضة *

والدَيْسق خوان من فضة *

والقَرْقار انآء *

المِثْبَنة كيس تضع فيه المراة مرآتها واداتها *

والعِكْم نَمَط تجعل فيه المراة ذخيرتها *

والقَشْوة قفة من خوص لعطر المراة *

والجُوْنة سَفَط مغشّى بجلد ظرف للطيب * ٢،١٦،٣٢

and the *mirjal*, “a cooking pot of stone or copper”
and the *kaft*, “a small cooking pot”
and *hiljāb*, “a large cooking pot”; synonym *bisāṭ*
and the *ta’mūrah*, “a pitcher, or a kind of wine receptacle, or a *thamīmah*[253] with a narrow top”
and the *qaʿn*, “a kneading bowl”
and the *jām*, [“silver vessel”] “too well known to require definition”; synonym *ṣāʿ*
and the *makkūk*, “a drinking scoop”
and the *ʿayzār*, “a kind of glass drinking bowl”
and *suʿūf*, “large drinking bowls, or household goods, or anything, be it a slave, or a valued possession, or a house, that is of quality and value; singular *saʿaf* . . . and spelled *saʿf* it means ‘. . . an item of goods’” 2.16.31
and the *warsī*, “a drinking bowl of the best wood”
and the *zawrā’*, “a silver vessel”
and the *fāthūr*, “a basin, or dining table made of marble or silver, or a wine vessel, or a decanter”
and the *qudhmūr*, “a silver dining table”
and the *daysaq*, “a silver dining table”
and the *qarqār*, “a vessel”
and the *mathbanah*, “a purse in which a woman puts her mirror and its accessories”
and the *ʿikm*, “a piece of carpet in which a woman wraps her supplies”
and the *qashwah*, “a palm-leaf basket for a woman’s perfumes”
and the *ju’nah*, “a basket lined with hide”; a container for perfume 2.16.32

والعَتِيدة — الطبلة او الحقّة يكون فيها طيب الرجل والعروس وكذا الشريط *

والدُرْج — حِفش النسآء الواحدة بهآ *

والصِوان — ما يصان فيه الثوب *

والتَخْت — وعآ تصان فيه الثياب ونحوه العَيْبة والمَبْناة *

والاَسْطان — آنية الصفر*

والاَبْزَن — حوض يغتسل فيه وقد يتخذ من نحاس *

والشِجاب — خشبات منصوبة توضع عليها الثياب *

والغُدُن — الغِدان القضيب تعلق عليه الثياب *

والقَفَدانة — غلاف المكحلة وخريطة من اَدَم للعطر وغيره *

والحناجيد — الحُنْجود قارورة طويلة للذريرة ووعآ كالسفط الصغير ونحوه الحُنْجور* ٣٣،١٦،٢

والبَزّ — الثياب او متاع البيت من الثياب ونحوها *

والعَقار — متاع البيت ونضده الذى لا يبتذل الّا فى الاعياد *

والثَقَل — كل شى نفيس مصون *

والبَتات — الجهاز ومتاع البيت ونحوه المَحاش والاَثَلة والشَذَب والزَلْزَل والاَهَرة والرِهاط والسُفاطة ويقال لقماش البيت خاشِ ماشِ وقاش ماش وقَرَنْشُوش *

والنَجْد — ما ينجّد به البيت من بُسط وفرش *

والنَضَد — السرير ينضّد عليه *

والنَضِيدة — الوسادة وما حشى من المتاع *

and the *ʿatīdah*,	“a drum, or a casket containing a man’s or a bridegroom’s perfume”; synonym *sharīṭ*	
and *durj*,	“small containers used by women”; singular *durjah*	
and the *ṣiwān*,	“the thing in which clothes are kept”	
and the *takht*,	“a container in which clothes and the like are kept”; synonyms *ʿaybah* and *mabnāh*	
and *asṭān*,	“brass vessels”	
and the *abzan*,	“a basin for ablution, sometimes made of copper”	
and *shijāb*,	“upright pieces of wood on which clothes are placed”	
and the *ghudun*,	“*ghidān* [plural] are bars from which clothes are hung”	
and the *qafadānah*,	“an outer covering for a kohl pot, or a leather pouch for solid perfumes and so on”	
and *ḥanājīd*,	“the *ḥunjūd* [singular] is a tall bottle for *dharīrah* , or a receptacle like a small *safaṭ*”; synonym *ḥunjūr*	**2.16.33**
and *bazz*,	“clothes, or household goods such as clothes and the like”	
and *ʿaqār*,	“household goods, or the most prized of these that are only used on feast days”	
and *thaqal*,	“anything precious and cared for”	
and *batāt*,	“furniture, or household goods”; synonyms *maḥāsh*, *athalah*, *shadhab*, *zalzal*, *aharah*, *rihāṭ*, and *sufāṭah*; the cloth for a tent is called *khāshi māshi*, *qāsh māsh*, and *qarbashūsh*	
and *najd*,	“the carpets and spreads with which a house is upholstered”	
and the *naḍad*,	“a bed frame on which household goods are placed in layers”	
and the *naḍīdah*,	“a cushion, or any other stuffed household item”	

والبُوريّة	الحصير المنسوج *
والمِسْوَر	متكا من ادم *
والعَبْقرىّ	ضرب من البسط * ٣٤،١٦،٢
والرَفْرف	ثياب خضر تتخذ منها المحابس وتبسط — والفراش والوسادة والبسط *
والزِلّيّة	البساط *
والنَمَط	ضرب من البسط *
والمِسْخيّة	نوع من البسط *
والاِراض	بساط ضخم من صوف او وبر*
والنُسُج	السجادات *
والزّرابىّ	النّمارق والبسط اوكل ما اتّكى عليه الواحد زِرْبىّ *
والرِحال	الطنافس الحيرية *
والنمارق	الوسادة والميثرة والطنفسة *
والدُرْنوك	ضرب من البسط * ٣٥،١٦،٢
والوِراك	ثوب يزيّن به المَوْرِك وهو الموضع الذى يجعل عليه الراكب رجله *
والبَراطِل	البُرْطلة المظلة الضيقة *
والظُلَل	الظُلّة الغاشية وشى يستتر به من الحرّ والبرد *
والمماطر	المِمْطر ثوب صوف يتوقى به من المطر كالممطرة *
والاَزْفان	الزِفْن ظلة يتخذونها فوق سطوحهم تقيهم من حر البحر ونداه *

and the *būriyyah*, "a woven mat"
and the *miswar*, "a rest made of hide"
and the *ʿabqarī*, "a kind of carpet" 2.16.34
and *rafraf*, "green lengths of cloth from which bedspreads are made and which are spread out; . . . or bedding, or cushions, or carpets"
and the *zilliyyah*, "a carpet"
and the *namaṭ*, "a kind of carpet"
and the *miskhiyyah*, "a kind of carpet"
and the *irāḍ*, "a huge carpet of wool or camel hair"
and *nusuj*, "mats"
and *zarābī*, "small cushions, or carpets, or anything that is used to rest one's body on"; singular *zirbī*
and *riḥāl*, "saddlecloths of the kind called *ṭanāfis*, made of cloth from al-Ḥīrah"
and *namāriq*, "small cushions, or silk saddlecloths, or saddlecloths of the kind called *ṭanāfis*"
and the *durnūk*, "a kind of carpet" 2.16.35
and the *wirāk*, "a cloth with which the place where the rider puts his leg is decorated"
and *barāṭil*, "a *barṭalah* is a narrow sunshade"
and *ẓulal*, "a *ẓullah* [singular] is a covering, or anything used as protection from heat or cold"
and *mamāṭir*, "a *mimṭar* is a woolen cloth used to provide shelter from the rain"; synonym *mimṭarah*
and *azfān*, "a *zifn* is a protective covering that they make over their tents to guard them from the heat of the sea and its dampness"

والسُرادقات السرادق الذى يمد فوق صحن البيت والبيت من الكرسف

ولا بد كذلك من اتخاذ النَسِيفَة للحّمام وهى حجارة سود ذات نخاريب يحك بها الرجل * ثم تزين تلك الدار السعيدة *

بالفُسَيفَسآ والسَرنْج * الفسيفساء الوان من الخرز تركّب فى حيطان البيوت من داخل* والسَرنْج شى من الصنعة كالفسيفسآء *

وبسُرَر مرمَّلة اى مزينة بالجواهر ونحوها وبِحَجَلات ومِنَصّات وبارائك وعروش وكراسى وطوارق من

العاج عظم الفيل * ٣٦،١٦،٢

والساج شجر*

والشِيْزَى خشب اسود للقصاع او هو الابنوس او الساسَم او خشب الجوز *

والسَمُر شجر معروف *

والنُضار خشب للاوانى *

والعَيْزار شجر*

والضُبار شجر البلّوط *

والساسَم شجر اسود او الابنوس *

والثُوَع شجر جبلى يسمو *

والشَوحَط شجر تتخذ منه القسىّ او ضرب من النبع *

والضَبْر شجر جوز البر * ٣٧،١٦،٢

والصَوْمَر شجر الباذروج *

والصِنار الدُلب *

and *surādiqāt*. “the *surādiq* is what is stretched over the forecourt of the tent, or a tent made of cotton”

Likewise, *nasīfah* (which are “pitted black stones with which the feet are scraped”) must be obtained for the bathhouse. Next, that happy home must be made attractive with

fusayfusā’ and *saranj*, “*fusayfusā’* are colored beads mounted on the inner walls of houses,” and *saranj* are “something crafted like *fusayfusā’*”

and with beds that are *murammalah*, meaning they have been “decorated with gems and so on,” and with curtained bridal alcoves, bridal thrones, couches, trellises, chairs, and small beds made from

‘āj, “ivory” **2.16.36**
and *sāj*, “a certain tree”
and *shīzā*, “a black wood used for trenchers, or it may be the same as ebony, or *sa’sam*, or walnut wood”
and *samur*, “a certain tree too well known to require definition” [“gum acacia”]
and *nuḍār*, “wood for containers”
and *‘ayzār*, “a certain tree”
and *ḍubār*, “oak”
and *sa’sam*, “a certain black tree, or ebony”
and *thuwa‘*, “a certain lofty mountain tree”
and *shawḥaṭ*, “a certain tree from which bows are made, or a species of jujube”
and *ḍabr*, “wild walnut trees” **2.16.37**
and *ṣawmar*, “grand basil trees”
and *ṣinār*, “plane trees”

والسَّلام	شجر* قيل لاعرابى السلام عليك قال الجثجاث عليك قيل ما هذا جواب قال هما شجران مرّان وانت جعلت علىّ واحدا فجعلت عليك الآخر*
والكَنَهْبَل	شجر عظام *
والبَقْس	شجر كالاس ورقا وحبا او هو الشِمْشاذ *
والنَشَم	شجر للقسى *
والضّال	السِدْر البرى وشجر آخر*
والبَقْش	شجر يقال له بالفارسية خوش ساى *
والنِبْش	شجر كالصنوبر ارزن من الابنوس *
والشَحْس	شجر صلب * ٣٨،١٦،٢
والمَيْس	شجر عظام *
والوَعْس	شجر يعمل منه البرابط والاعواد *
والقَطَف	شجر جبلى خشبه متين *

ثم تزين بقوارير من البلّور*

والقِطْر	ضرب من النحاس *
والقِلِزّ	النحاس الذى لا يعمل فيه الحديد *
والفِلِزّ	نحاس ابيض تجعل منه القدور المفرغة او— *
والبَلَنْط	شى كالرخام الا انه دونه فى اللين *
والبَلَق	حجارة باليمن تضى ما ورآها كالزجاج *
والحَكَك	حجر ابيض كالرخام *
والنِهآء	حجر ابيض ارخى من الرخام *

and *salām*, “a certain tree; someone once said to a Bedouin, ‘*Salām* (“peace”) be upon you,’ to which the Bedouin replied, ‘And *jathjāth* upon you!’ ‘What kind of a reply is that?’ he was asked, and he said, ‘They are both trees with bitter fruits. You wished one on me, so I wished the other on you!’”

and *kanahbal*, “a certain large tree”

and *baqs*, “a tree with leaves and berries like the myrtle, or it may be that it is the same as the *shimshādh* (‘common box’)”

and *nasham*, “a certain tree used to make bows”

and *ḍāl*, “the wild lote tree, or a certain other tree”

and *baqsh*, “a tree, called *khūsh sāy* in Persian”

and *nibsh*, “a certain tree like the pine, harder than ebony”

and *shaḥṣ*, “a certain hard tree” 2.16.38

and *mays*, “a certain large tree”

and *waʿs*, “a certain tree from which lutes and ouds are made”

and *qaṭaf*. “a certain mountain tree with long-lasting wood”

Next, it must be made attractive with crystal bottles and with

qiṭr, “a kind of copper”

and *qilizz*, “copper to which iron has been added”

and *filizz*, “white copper from which hollow pots are made, or . . .”[254]

and *balnaṭ*, “a thing like marble but harder”

and *balaq*, “stones in Yemen that illuminate whatever is behind them like glass”

and *ḥakak*, “a white stone like marble”

and *nihāʾ*, “a white stone softer than marble”

والمُهَل اسم يجمع مدعنيات الجواهر كالفضة والحديد ونحوهما *

والهَيْصَم ضرب من الحجارة املس *

ثم تمام زينة هذا المكان الشريف وِثاب محشوّ بالعُشَر والحُرَيملة * الوثاب السرير والفراش * والعُشَر شجر يحشى فى المخاد ويخرج من زهره وشُعَبه سكّر * والحريملة شجرة تنشقّ جراوها عن الين قطن ويُحشَى به مخاد الملوك * غير انى ارتكبت هنا غلطا فاحشا فى تاخيرى ذكر الفراش وهو اول ما يخطر ببال المراة عند دخولها بلدا * وهنا تمّ اثاث الدار * وفكرك لم يزل مشغولا بالحمار *

القسم الخامس فى عمل الثياب ٢،١٦،٣٩

الثُرَقِيَّة وهى ثياب بيض من كتّان مصر *

والجِلْباب القميص وثوب واسع للمراة *

والسَكْب ضرب من الثياب *

والسِلاب الثياب السود *

والقَصَب ثياب ناعمة من كتّان *

واللِّبيبة ثوب كالبقيرة *

والنُقْبة ثوب كالازار *

والبِظْماج ما كان احد طرفيه مخملا او وسطه مخمل وطرفاه مغيّران *

والمعرَّجة المخططة فى التوآ *

والموثوجة ثياب رخوة الغزل والنسج *

والهبْرَج الموشى من الثياب * ٢،١٦،٤٠

والمترّحة المترّح من الثياب ما صبغ صبغا مشبعا *

and *muhl,*	"a name that embraces the precious metals such as silver, iron [sic], and others"
and *hayṣam.*	"a kind of stones, smooth"

Next, the finishing touch to this noble place are *withāb* stuffed with *ʿushar* and *ḥuraymilāt* (*withāb* are "beds and bedding," *ʿushar* is "a plant used as a stuffing for pillows and from whose flowers and twigs sugar is extracted," and *ḥuraymilāt* are trees "whose pericarps open to reveal the softest cotton, with which the pillows of kings are stuffed"), though I have committed a grave error here in keeping mention of bedding to the end, the latter being the first thing to enter a woman's mind when she arrives in a country. The furnishings for the house are now *amassed* (and you're still worrying about the *ass*).

Work Group 5: For the Making of Clothes 2.16.39

The *thurqubiyyah,*	"White garments made from the linen of Egypt"	
the *jilbāb,*	"the shirt, or a wide garment for a woman"	
the *sakb,*	"a certain garment"	
silāb,	"black garments"	
qaṣab,	"soft garments of linen"	
the *labībah,*	"a garment like the *baqīrah*"	
the *nuqbah,*	"a garment like the *izār*"	
the *bizmāj,*	"any garment one of whose ends is of velvet, or whose middle is of velvet and whose two ends are of a different weave"	
the *muʿarrajah,*	"[a garment] with a wavy stripe"	
the *mawthūjah,*	"loosely spun and woven garments"	
habraj,	"embroidered garments"	2.16.40
the *mutarraḥah,*	"*mutarraḥ* garments are garments that have been well steeped in dye"	

والوَصِيح الصفيق من الثياب *
والخَوخة ضرب من الثياب اخضر*
والوَلِيخ ثوب من كتّان *
والثفافيد ضرب من الثياب *
والجِماد ضرب من الثياب *
والمعضَّدة المعضد ثوب له علم فى موضع العضد *
والفِرنْد ثوب م *
والمُقَرمَدة ثوب مقرمد مطلى بشبه الزعفران *
والمجسَّدة المصبوغة بالزعفران * ٢،١٦،٤١
والمَقَدِيّة ثياب م *
والهُرديّة المصبوغة بعروق الهُرد *
واللاّذة ثوب حرير صينى *
والبُقْطرية الثياب البيض الواسعة *
والحَصِير ثوب مزخرف موشى اذا نشر اخذت القلوب مآخذه لحسنه *
والخُسْروانية نوع من الثياب *
والدِثار ما فوق الشِعار من الثياب *
والسّابريّة الثياب الرقيقة الجيدة *
والمُسيَّرة المسيَّر ثوب فيه خطوط *
والصُدْرة ثوب م * ٢،١٦،٤٢
والصِدار ثوب راسه كالمقنعة واسفله يغشى الصدر*

wajiḥ,	"tightly woven garments"
the *khawkhah*,	"a kind of garment, green"
walīkh,	"garments of linen"
the *thafāfīd*,	"a kind of garment"
the *jimād*,	"a kind of garment"
the *muʿaḍḍadah*,	"the *muʿaḍḍad* are certain garments with a mark on the upper arm"
the *firind*,	"a garment, too well known to require definition"
the *muqarmadah*,	"a garment that is *muqarmad* is coated with a substance like saffron"
the *mujassadah*,	"[a garment] dyed with saffron" 2.16.41
the *maqadiyyah*,	"a garment, too well known to require definition"
the *hurdiyyah*,	"[a garment] dyed with *hurd* roots"
the *lādhah*,	"a garment of Chinese silk"
the *buqṭuriyyah*,	"a certain wide, white garment"
the *ḥaṣīr*,	"an embroidered, decorated garment that, spread out, is so beautiful that it captures the heart"
the *khusrawāniyyah*,	"a kind of garment"
the *dithār*,	"any item of apparel worn over the *shiʿār*[255]"
the *sābiriyyah*,	"a delicate, high-quality garment"
the *musayyarah*,	"a striped garment"
the *ṣudrah*,	"a certain garment, too well known to require definition" ["waistcoat"] 2.16.42
the *ṣidār*,	"a certain garment whose upper part is like a women's head scarf and whose lower part covers the breast"

في ذلك الموضع بعينه

والعَبقَرية	عبقر بلدة ثيابها فى غاية الحسن *	
والمِعْجر	ثوب تعتجر به المراة وثوب يمانى *	
والعُشاريّة	ثوب عشارىّ طوله عشرة اذرع *	
والعُقار	ضرب من الثياب احمر*	
والقُبْطرية	ثياب كتّان بيض *	
والمرَمّر	ضرب من تقطيع ثياب النسآ *	
والمنيَّرة	المنسوجة على نيرين *	
والباغِزيّة	ثياب من الخزاو كالحرير *	
والتوَّزية	منسوبة *	٤٣,١٦,٢
والمُمرْعَزة	المِرعزّى الزغب الذى تحت شعر العنز *	
والمطرَّزة	المعلَمة *	
والمفروزة	ثوب مفروز له تطاريف *	
والقرمزية	المصبوغة بالقرمز *	
والقَهز	ثياب من صوف احمر كالمرعزى وربما يخالطها الحرير*	
والتِنّيسيّة	تنّيس د تنسب اليه الثياب الفاخرة *	
والمُدمقسة	الدِمَقّس الابرِيسم اوالقزّاو الديباج اوالكتّان *	
والقَسّية	منسوبة الى قسّ من ارض مصر*	
والكِرْباس	ثوب من القطن الابيض *	
المُسَلسلة	الموشّاة المخطّطة *	٤٤,١٦,٢
والنَرْسيّة	نرس ة بالعراق *	
والمورَّسة	المصبوغة بالورس *	

the *ʿabqariyyah*,	"ʿAbqar is a town whose clothes are extremely attractive"	
the *miʿjar*,	"a certain item of apparel that a woman winds around her head and over which she then dons her *jilbāb*, or a Yemeni garment"	
the *ʿushāriyyah*,	"a certain garment ten cubits in length"	
the *ʿuqār*,	"a kind of garment, red"	
the *qubṭuriyyah*,	"a certain white linen garment"	
marmar,	"a style of tailoring women's clothes"	
munayyarah,	"[cloth] that is woven on two looms"	
bāghiziyyah,	"garments of silk-wool, or resembling silk"	
the *tawwaziyyah*,	"eponymous" [from Tawwaz, in Persia]	**2.16.43**
the *mumarʿazah*,	"*mirʿizzā* is the downy fur that is under a goat's hair"	
the *muṭarrazah*,	a garment with decorated borders	
the *mafrūzah*,	"a garment that is *mafrūz* has marks like fingerprints"	
the *qirmiziyyah*,	"a garment dyed with cochineal"	
the *qahz*,	"garments of red wool resembling the *mirʿizzā* and sometimes mixed with silk"	
the *tinnīsiyyah*,	"Tinnīs is a town from which fine garments are said to come"	
the *mudamqasah*,	"*dimqis* is loosely woven cloth, or raw silk, or silk brocade, or linen"	
the *qassiyyah*,	"from eponymous Qass, an area of Egypt"	
kirbās,	"garments of white cotton"	
the *mulaslasah*,	"a garment that is embroidered and striped"	**2.16.44**
the *narsiyyah*,	"[from] Nars, a village in Iraq"	
the *muwarrasah*,	"any garment dyed with Indian yellow"	

والاكياش الثوب الذى اعيد غزله مثل الخز والصوف *
والماجُشون الثياب المصبّغة *
والمقفّصة المخططة كهيئة القفص *
والمحرّضة المصبوغة بالاِحْريض للعصفر *
والعَرْضىّ جنس من الثياب *
والمِعْرَض ثوب تجلى فيه الجارية *
والرَيْطة كل مُلآة غير ذات لفقين كلها نسج واحد وقطعة واحدة
اوكل ثوب ليّن رقيق *
والسِجِلّاط ثياب كتّان موشية وكانّ وشيه خاتم * ٤٥،١٦،٢
والسُمُط ثوب من صوف وبالكسر الثوب ليست له بطانة طيلسان *
والمقطّعات القصار من الثياب — او برود عليها وشى *
والمردّعة التى فيها اثر طيب *
والصَدِيع ثوب يلبس تحت الدرع *
والمضلّعة المسيرة المخططة وما جعل وشيها على هيئة الاضلاع *
والنِصْع ثوب ابيض *
والموشّعة المعلَمة *
والشُرافىّ ثياب بيض *
والشَفّ ويكسر الثوب الرقيق * ٤٦،١٦،٢
والبُنْدقية ثياب كتّان رفيعة *
والمحقّقة المحكمة النسج *
والخُزانق الثياب البيض *

akyāsh, "fabrics that are re-spun, such as silk-wool and wool"
mājushūn, "dyed garments"
the *muqaffaṣah,* "a garment with stripes in the shape of a cage"
the *muḥarraḍah,* "a garment dyed with safflower grains"
the *ʿarḍī,* "a class of garment"
the *miʿraḍ,* "a garment in which a girl is displayed"
the *rayṭah,* "any piece of cloth that is not sewn to another but is all of one weaving and one piece, or any fine, soft garment"
sijillāṭ, "linen garments embroidered with ornamentations that look like rings" **2.16.45**
the *sumṭ,* "a certain garment of wool; spelled *simṭ* it means an unlined garment, or a *ṭaylasān* ('net shawl')"
muqaṭṭaʿāt, "short garments . . . or embroidered wraps"
the *muraddaʿah,* "[a garment] on which are traces of perfume"
the *ṣadīʿ,* "a certain garment worn beneath a coat of mail"
the *muḍallaʿah,* "a striped *musayyarah,* or one whose ornamentation takes the form of ribs"
the *niṣʿ,* "a certain white garment"
the *muwashshaʿah,* "a garment with decorated borders"
the *shurāfī,* "a certain white garment"
the *shaff,* "also *shiff*: a delicate garment" **2.16.46**
the *bunduqiyyah,* "a certain garment of fine linen"
the *muḥaqqaqah,* "any tightly woven garment"
khuzrāniq, "white garments"

الدَّبيقية	ديبق د بمصر *
والرِتاق	ثوبان يرتقان بحواشيهما
والرازقية	ثياب كتّان بيض *
والمزبرقة	المصبوغة بحمرة او صفرة *
والعِلقة	ثوب بلا كمّين — او الثوب النفيس *
واللِفاق	ثوبان يلفق احدهما بالاخر*
والمحبّكة	الموثقة المخططة * ٢،١٦،٤٧
والمِجوَل	ثوب للنسآ *
والخملة	الثوب المخمل كالكساء ونحوه كالخميل *
والخال	الثوب الناعم وبرد يمنى *
والدِرقل	ثياب كالارمنية *
والمُمَرجِل	ثياب فيها صور المراجل *
والممرجَل	ضرب من ثياب الوشى (اورد صاحب القاموس التى بكسر الجيم فى رج ل والتى بفتحها فى مادة على حدتها) *
والمرمّلة	المرققة *
والسَحل	ثوب ابيض من قطن ونحوه المِسحَل *
والمُسَلسَلة	ثوب مسلسل فيه وشى مخطط *
والعقَل	الثوب الاحمر* ٢،١٦،٤٨
والمفلفلة	الموشاة كالفلفل *
والقَسطلانية	ثياب منسوبة الى عامل *
والوَصيلة	ثوب مخطط يمان *

the *dabīqiyyah,*	"Dabīq is a town in Egypt"
the *ritāq,*	"two garments whose edges have been sewn together"
rāziqiyyah,	"white linen garments"
the *muzabraqah,*	[a garment] dyed red or yellow
the *ʿilqah,*	"a certain sleeveless garment . . . or a precious garment"
the *lifāq,*	"two garments that have been sewn together"
the *muḥabbakah,*	"a garment that is tightly sewn and striped" **2.16.47**
the *mijwal,*	"a women's garment"
the *khamlah,*	"a certain garment with a nap like the *kisāʾ* ('a kind of cloak') and so on"; synonym *khamīl*
khāl,	"smooth garments, or a striped garment of Yemen"
the *diraql,*	"a garment resembling the *armaniyyah*[256]"
the *mumarjil,*	"a garment with images of men on it"
the *mumarjal,*	"a kind of embroidered garment" (the author of the *Qāmūs* lists the preceding word under *r-j-l* and the present word in an entry of its own)[257]
the *murammalah,*	"a thin garment"
the *saḥl,*	"a certain white cotton garment"; synonym *misḥal*
the *musalsalah,*	"a *musalsal* garment is one with striped decoration"
the *ʿaql,*	"a red garment" **2.16.48**
the *mufalfalah,*	[a garment] "decorated as though with peppercorns"
the *qasṭalāniyyah,*	"[a garment] that derives its name from a certain governor"[258]
the *waṣīlah,*	"a striped Yemeni garment"

والمهلَهلة الرقيقة *

والآمِيّة منسوبة *

والمُبرَم جنس من الثياب والثوب المفتول الغزل طاقين *

والجَهْرَميّة ثياب منسوبة من نحو البسط اوهى من الكتّان *

والمرسَّمة المخططة *

والمرقَّمة المخططة والرقم ضرب من الوشى او الخزاو البرود *

والعَقْم المرط الاحمر اوكل ثوب احمر* ٢,١٦,٤٩

والقَدْم ثوب احمر*

والقِرام ثوب ملون من صوف فيه رقم ونقوش او ستر رقيق كالمِقْرَم *

وابى قَلَمون ثوب رومى يتلون الوانا *

والملحَم جنس من الثياب *

والنِيم كل ليّن من عيش او ثوب *

والآخِنىّ الثوب المخطط *

والدَفَنىّ ثوب مخطط *

والأُرْجوان ثياب حمر*

والسَّبَنِيّة ثياب من حرير فيها امثال الاترجّ * ٢,١٦,٥٠

والشَّتُون اللينة من الثياب *

والشاذكونة ثياب غلاظ مضربة تعمل باليمن *

والمُعرجَنة المصوّر فيها اشكال العرجون *

والمعينَّة ماكان فى وشيها ترابيع صغار كعيون الوحش *

the *muhalhalah,*	"a delicately woven garment"	
the *āmmiyyah,*	eponymous[259]	
the *mubram,*	"a class of garments, or a garment whose yarn is double-twisted"	
the *jahramiyyah,*	"eponymously named [after Jahram, a town in Persia] garments similar to carpeting or made of linen"	
the *murassamah,*	"a striped garment"	
the *muraqqamah,*	"a striped garment (*raqm* being a kind of decoration), or silk-wool, or wraps"	
the *ʿaqm,*	"a red tunic, or any red garment"	2.16.49
the *qadm,*	"a red garment"	
the *qirām,*	"a colored garment of wool with *raqm*-decoration and designs, or a delicate veil; synonym *miqram*"	
the *abū qalamūn,*	"a Greek garment of many colors"	
the *milḥam,*	"a class of garment"	
the *nīm,*	"any bread or garment that is supple"	
the *ākhinī,*	"a striped garment"	
the *dafanī,*	"a striped garment"	
urjuwān,	"red garments"	
the *sabaniyyah,*	"a silk garment on which are the likenesses of citrons"	2.16.50
shatūn,	"supple garments"	
the *shādhakūnah,*	"a thick quilted garment made in Yemen"	
the *muʿarjanah,*	"a gament on which palm racemes are pictured"	
the *muʿayyanah,*	"a garment whose decoration includes small squares resembling the eyes of a wild beast"	

والمفنّنة ثوب مفنّن فيه طرائق ليست من جنسه *

والمفوّهة المصبوغة بالفوّه (عبارة القاموس فى ف و هـ والفوّه كسكر عروق رقاق طوال حمر يصبغ بها الخ وفى ف و ى الفوّة كالقوّة عروق يصبغ بها) *

والقُوهِىّ ثياب بيض *

والنَهْنه الثوب الرقيق النسج *

والمُلَهْلهة الملهله من الثياب كالمهلهل *

والموجَّهة ما كان لها وجهان * ٢،١٦،٥١

والمِحْشأ كسآ غليظ او ابيض صغير يتّرز به او ازار يشتمل به *

والسَّبيجة كسآ اسود *

والخَسِيج كسآ من صوف *

والإِضْرِيج كسآ اصفر و الخز الاحمر *

والمسبَّح الكسآ القوى الشديد ونحوه المشبّح *

والسَيِّح الكسآ المخطط كالمسيّح *

والبِجاد كسآ مخطط *

والبُرْجُد كسآ غليظ *

والجُودِيآ الكسآ *

والاَغْثَر ما كثر صوفه من الاكسية * ٢،١٦،٥٢

والخَمِيصة كسآ اسود مربّع له علمان *

والمِرْط كسآ من صوف او خز ج مروط *

والشَمْلة كسآ دون القطيفة *

the *mufannanah*,	“a garment of diversified design containing strips made of a different cloth”	
the *mufawwahah*,	“[a garment] dyed with madder” (see in the *Qāmūs* under *f-w-h*: “*fuwwah*, on the pattern of *sukkar*, are long thin red roots used in dyeing” etc. and under *f-w-y*: “*fuwwah*, on the pattern of *quwwah*, are roots used in dyeing”)	
the *qūhī*,	“a certain white garment”	
the *nahnah*,	“a delicately woven garment”	
the *mulahlahah*,	garments described as *mulahlah* are those that are delicately woven; synonym *muhalhal*	
muwajjahah,	“double-sided fabrics”	**2.16.51**
the *miḥsha’*,	“a thick wrap, or a short white wrap which one wraps around one’s waist, or a waist wrap in which one envelops oneself”	
the *sabīḥah*,	“a black wrap”	
the *khasīj*,	“a wrap of wool”	
the *iḍrīj*,	“a yellow wrap, or red silk-wool”	
the *musabbaḥ*,	“a tough, strong wrap”; synonym *mushabbaḥ*	
the *sayḥ*,	“a striped wrap” synonym *musayyaḥ*	
the *bijād*,	“a striped wrap”	
the *burjud*,	“a thick wrap”	
the *jūdiyā’*,	“a wrap”	
the *aghthar*,	“wraps made with large quantities of wool”	**2.16.52**
the *khamīṣah*,	“a rectangular black wrap with two decorated borders”	
the *mirṭ*,	“a wrap of wool or silk-wool; plural *murūṭ*”	
the *shamlah*,	“a wrap [similar to but] less [valuable] than the *qaṭīfah*”	

والطِمل الكسآ الاسود والثوب المشبع صبغا *

والمارِىّ كسآ صغير له خطوط مرسلة *

والشَرْعَبىّ ضرب من البرود *

والعَصْب ضرب من البرود *

والمكعَّب الموشى من البرود والاثواب والثوب المطوى الشديد الادراج *

والخِلاج ضرب من البرود المخططة *

والشِيَح برد يمنى * ٥٣،١٦،٢

والقُرْدح ضرب من البرود *

والسَّعِيدية ضرب من برود اليمن *

والسَنَد ضرب من البرود *

والبَقير برد يشقّ فيلبس بلا كمين كالبقيرة *

والحِبَر ضرب من برود اليمن مفرده حِبَرة كعنبة *

والحَبير البرد المرشى والثوب الجديد *

والسِيَرآ نوع من البرود فيه خطوط صفر او يخالطه صفر او يخالطه حرير*

والمطيَّر ضرب من البرود *

والقِطْر ضرب منها *

والمشيَّز المخطط بحمرة * ٥٤،١٦،٢

والمرَيَّش البرد الموشى *

the *ṭiml*,	"a black wrap, or a garment thoroughly dyed"
the *mārī*,	"a small wrap with hanging threads"
the *sharʿabī*,	"a kind of mantle"
the *ʿaṣb*,	"a kind of mantle"
mukaʿʿab,	"embroidered mantles, or a garment folded into stiff pleats"
the *khilāj*,	"a kind of striped mantle"
the *shīḥ*,	"a Yemeni mantle" 2.16.53
the *qurduḥ*,	"a kind of mantle"
the *saʿīdiyyah*,	"a kind of Yemeni mantle"
the *sanad*,	"a kind of mantle"
the *baqīr*,	"a mantle that is divided in half and worn without sleeves; synonym *baqīrah*"
ḥibar,	"a kind of Yemeni mantle; singular *ḥibarah*, on the pattern of *ʿinabah*"
the *ḥabīr*,	"a decorated mantle, or new clothes"
the *sīrāʾ*,	"a kind of yellow-striped mantle, or one mixed with silk"
the *muṭayyar*,	"a kind of mantle"
the *qiṭr*,	"another kind [of mantle]"
the *mushayyaz*,	"any red-striped garment" 2.16.54
the *murayyash*,	"an embroidered mantle"

والفُوف ضرب من برود اليمن وبرد مفوَّف رقيق او فيه خطوط بيض *

والنَصِيف الخِمار ومن البرد ما له لونان *

والبِرَكة برد يمنى *

والمَرْجَل برد يمنى *

والمرحَّل ما فيه تصاوير رحل *

والتَحَمة البرود المخططة بالصفرة *

والاَتْحمىّ برد معروف *

والمسهَّم البرد المخطط *

والقَطيفة ردآ مخمل * ٥٥،١٦،٢

والمُطرَف ردآء من خز مربع له اعلام *

والجَنِيَّة ردآ من خز *

والجِيم الديباج *

والسُندس ضرب من البزيون او ضرب من رقيق الديباج *

والاسْتَبْرَق الديباج الغليظ[١] او ديباج يعمل بالذهب او ثياب حرير صفاق *

والمشجّر المشجّر من الديباج ما كان فيه نقش كهيئة الشجر *

والسِبّ شقة رقيقة كالسبيبة *

والطَرِيدة شقة مستطيلة من الحرير *

والسَرَق شقق الحرير الابيض او عامة *

---

١ ١٨٥٥: الغليط.

the *fūf*,	"a kind of Yemeni mantle; the *mufawwaf* mantle is a delicate mantle, or one with white stripes"
the *naṣīf*,	"a woman's head wrap, or a bi-colored mantle"
the *birkah*,	"a Yemeni mantle"
the *marjal*,	"a Yemeni mantle"
the *muraḥḥal*,	"[a garment] with camel's saddle designs"
the *taḥamah*,	"mantles striped with yellow"
the *atḥamī*,	"a mantle too well known to require definition"
musahham,	"striped mantles"
the *qaṭīfah*,	"a velvet cloak" **2.16.55**
the *muṭraf*,	"a cloak of silk-wool, rectangular, with decorated borders"
the *janiyyah*,	"a cloak of silk-wool"
jīm,	"silk brocade"
sundus,	"a kind of *bizyawn*,[260] or a kind of fine silk brocade"
istabraq,	"thick silk brocade, or silk brocade worked with gold, or tightly woven silk garments"
mushajjar,	"silk brocade that is *mushajjar* is that which has on it designs in the form of trees (*shajar*)"
the *sibb*,	"a length of fine cloth; synonym *sabībah*"
the *ṭarīdah*,	"an oblong length of silk cloth"
saraq,	"oblong lengths of white silk, or of silk generally"

والبَتّ الطيلسان من خز ونحوه * ٥٦،١٦،٢

والسُدُوس الطيلسان الاخضر*

والطِلْس الطيلسان الاسود *

والطاق الطيلسان او الاخضر*

والساج الطيلسان الاخضر والاسود *

والصُتَيّة الملحفة او ثوب يمنى *

والشَوْذر الملحفة والإتْب *

والدُواج اللحاف الذى يلبس *

والمِشْمال ملحفة *

واللِفاع الملحفة او الكسآ او النطع او الردآ وكل ما تتلفع به المراة *

والمُرجَّل ازار خز فيه عَلَم * ٥٧،١٦،٢

والمُدارة الازار الموشى *

والحَقْو الازار ومثلة الخِصار*

والصِداد ما اصطدّت به المراة وهو الستر*

والفُوَط ثياب تجلب من السند ومآزر مخططة *

والدِثار ما فوق الشعار من الثياب *

والحُلَل واحدتها حُلّة وهى ازار ورداء وبرد او غيره ولا تكون حلة الا من ثوبين او ثوب له بطانة *

والسِرْبال القميص او الدرع او كل ما لبس*

والقُرْطَق لبس م *

واليَلْمَق القبآ معرب يلمه *

the *batt*, "a *taylasān* of silk-wool or the like" 2.16.56
the *sundūs*, "a green *taylasān*"
the *ṭils*, "a black *taylasān*"
the *ṭāq*, "a *taylasān*, or a green *taylasān*"
the *sāj*, "a green and black *taylasān*"
the *ṣuttiyyah*, "an enveloping over-robe, or a certain Yemeni garment"
the *shawdhar*, "an enveloping over-robe, or a mid-leg shift"
the *duwāj*, "a sheet of cloth worn as a garment"
the *mishmāl*, "an enveloping over-robe"
the *lifāʿ*, "an enveloping over-robe, or a wrap, or a mat of hide, or a mantle, or anything that a woman wraps around herself"
the *murajjal*, "a waist wrap of silk-wool with a decorated border" 2.16.57
the *mudārah*, "an embroidered waist wrap"
the *ḥaqw*, "a waist wrap"; synonym *khiṣār*
the *ṣidād*, "anything a woman veils herself with; synonym *sitr*"
fuwaṭ, "garments imported from Sind, or striped waist wraps"
the *dithār*, "any cloth worn over the *shiʿār*"
ḥulal, "singular *ḥullah*, meaning a waist wrap, or a robe, or a mantle, or anything else of the same sort; a *ḥullah* always consists of two pieces of cloth or a single piece with a lining"
the *sirbāl*, "a shirt, or a chemise, or anything that is worn"
the *qurṭaq*, "a garment, too well known to require definition"
the *yalmaq*, "a tunic" (Arabized from *yalmah*)

والقَرقَر لباس المراة * ٢،١٦،٥٨

والقُرزح لباس كان لنسآئهم *

والمِفضل المفضل والمفضلة والفُضُل الثوب الذى تفضل فيه المراة اى توشح *

والحِقاب شى تعلق به المراة الحَلْى وتشده فى وسطها كالحَقَب *

والنِطاق شقة تلبسها المراة وتشد وسطها فترسل الاعلى على الاسفل الى الارض والاسفل ينجر على الارض الخ *

والمِجَنّ الوشاح وقد تقدم فى باب الحلى *

والاِتْب برد يشقّ فتلبسه المراة من غير جيب ولا كمين والبقيرة ودرع المراة *

والجَوْب درع المراة اى قميصها *

والأُصدَة قميص يلبس تحت الثوب *

والخَيْلَع القميص بلاكمّ *

والرادعة قميص قد لُمِّع بالزعفران او بالطيب * ٢،١٦،٥٩

والقُمُص السنبلانية اى السابغة الطول او منسوبة الى بلد بالروم *

والشِعار ما تحت الدثار من اللباس وهو يلى شعر الجسد ويفتح *

والقِدْعة المِجْوَل وهى الدُرّاعة الصغيرة *

والجِيْد المدرعة الصغيرة *

والغِلالة شعار تحت الثوب كالغُلّة *

والهَفّاف الهفّاف من القميص الرقيق الشفاف كالهَفْهاف *

والشَلِيل الغلالة تلبس تحت الدرع *

qarqar,	"women's garments"	2.16.58
the *qurzaḥ,*	"a garment that their women used to wear"	
the *mifḍal,*	"the *mifḍal,* the *mifḍalah,* and the *fuḍul* are garments which women wear long, so that they trail on the ground, or which they wrap themselves in"	
the *ḥiqāb,*	"a thing onto which women hang ornaments and which they tie around their waists; synonym *ḥaqab*"	
the *niṭāq,*	"a length of cloth that a woman wears and ties around her middle in such a way that the upper part hangs down over the lower, reaching the ground, and the lower trails on the ground," etc.	
the *mijann,*	"the *wishāḥ*" (already mentioined under the rubric of ornaments)	
the *itb,*	"a woman's collarless sleeveless mantle split down the sides, or a *baqīrah,* or a woman's shirt"	
the *jawb,*	"a woman's *dirʿ* or shirt"	
the *uṣdah,*	"a shirt worn under a garment"	
the *khaylaʿ,*	"a sleeveless shirt"	
the *rādiʿah,*	"a shirt that has been splashed with saffron or with perfume"	2.16.59
qumuṣ sunbulāniyyah,	"long loose-fitting shirts, or those named after a town in Anatolia"	
the *shiʿār,*	"what is worn next to the hair of the body under the *dithār*; also *shaʿār*"	
the *qidʿah,*	"the *mijwal,* which is the small tunic split in front"	
the *jīd,*	"a small woolen open-fronted tunic"	
the *ghilālah,*	"any undergarment; synonym *ghullah*"	
haffāf,	"*haffāf* shirts are those that are fine and diaphanous, synonym *hafhāf*"	
the *shalīl,*	"the undergarment that is worn under the chemise"	

والقَرْقل قميص للنسآ او ثوب لا كمّ له *

والغِطاية ما تغطت به المراة من حشو الثياب كغلالة ونحوها *

والفَرْوة معروف * ٦٠،١٦،٢

والسَبَنْجُونة فروة من الثعالب *

والشَعْرآ الفروة *

والمُسْتُقة فروة طويلة الكم *

والخَيْعل الفرو او ثوب غير مخيط الفرجين او درع يخاط الخ *

والمِعْقَب الخمار للمراة *

والنِقاب ما تنتقب به المراة *

والخِمار النصيف وهو العمامة وكل ما غطّى الراس *

والوَصاوِص البراقع الصغار *

والمِقْنعة ما تقنّع به المراة راسها والقِناع اوسع منها *

والعِصابة ما عُصب به والعمامة * ٦١،١٦،٢

والسِيْدارة الوقاية تحت المقنعة والعصابة *

والعَمارة كل شى على الراس *

والعَمْر منديل تغطى به الحرة راسها *

والخُنُبْعة مقنعة صغيرة للمراة *

والبُخْنَق خرقة تتقنع بها الجارية فتشد طرفيها تحت حنكيها لتقى الخِمار من الدهن والدهن من الغبار والبرقع والبرنس الصغيران *

والصِقاع البرقع — وخرقة تقى الخِمار من الدهن كالصوقعة ونحوها الغِفارة *

the *qarqal*,	"a woman's shirt, or a sleeveless garment"	
the *ghiṭāyah*,	"undergarments that a woman covers herself with, such as the *ghilālah* and the like"	
the *farwah*,	"too well known to require definition" ["fur-edged coat"]	2.16.60
the *sabanjūnah*,	"a coat edged with fox fur"	
the *sha'rā'*,	"a fur-edged coat"	
the *mustuqah*,	"a fur-edged coat with long sleeves"	
the *khay'al*,	"a fur, or a piece of cloth with unsewn edges, or a shift . . ." etc.	
the *mi'qab*,	"a woman's head covering"	
the *niqāb*,	"anything with which a woman covers her face"	
the *khimār*,	"a *naṣīf*, which is a turban, or anything with which the head is covered"	
waṣāwiṣ,	"small face-veils that reveal the eyes"	
the *miqna'ah*,	"anything with which a woman veils her head; the *qinā'* . . . is wider"	
the *'iṣābah*,	"anything tied around the head, or a turban"	2.16.61
the *sīdārah*,	"a protective covering under the *miqna'ah* and the *miqna'* and the *'iṣābah*"	
the *'amārah*,	"anything worn on the head"	
the *'amar*,	"a kerchief with which a free-born woman covers her head"	
the *khunbu'ah*,	"a small *miqna'ah* for a woman"	
the *bukhnaq*,	"a piece of cloth that a girl covers her face with, tying the two ends under her chin to protect the *khimār* from moisture and the moisture from dust, or a small face-veil that reveals the eyes, or a small cloak"	
the *ṣiqā'*,	"a small face-veil that reveals the eyes . . . and a piece of cloth that protects the *khimār* from moisture; synonym *ṣawqa'ah*"	

والقُنْبع خرقة تخاط شبيهة بالبرنس والخنبعة او شبهها *

والقُنْزعة التى تتخذها المراة على راسها كالقنذعة *

والهُنُبع شبه مقنعة للجوارى وقد خيط مقدّمها *

والقُرْزل الشى تتخذه المراة فوق راسها كالقنزعة * ٦٢،١٦،٢

والجُنّة خرقة تلبسها المراة تغطّى راسها ما قَبَل ودبر غير وسطه وتغطى الوجه وجنبى الصدر وفيه عينان مجوبتان كالبرقع *

والتَّساخين الخِفاف وشى كالطيالس *

والجَراميق الجرموق الذى يلبس فوق الخف *

والكَوْث القَفْش الذى يلبس في الرجل اى الخف القصير *

والران كالخف الا انه لا قدم له وهو اطول من الخف *

الجَورب لفافة الرجل وجوربته البسته اياه *

والقُفّاز شى يعمل لليدين يحشى بقطن تلبسهما المراة للبرد او ضرب من الحلىّ الخ *

وتمام هذا كله ثلثمائة وخمسة وستون حِبْسا ومثلها مقارم * الحِبس سوار من فضة يجعل فى وسط القِرام * والمقرمة مَحْبس الفراش ومثلها سراويل من

الاَرْبانىّ الخزّ الادكن * ٦٣،١٦،٢

والسَّنا ضرب من الحرير *

والاَرْدن ضرب من الخز *

والطارُونى ضرب منه والطُرْن الخز *

والقَتِين الخز المطبوخ الابيض *

والبِرْس القطن او شبيه به او قطن البَرْدىّ *

the *qunbuʿ*, “a piece of sewn cloth resembling the *burnus*, or a *khunbuʿah* or something resembling it”

the *qunzuʿah*, “what a woman puts on her head, synonym *qundhuʿah*”

the *hunbuʿ*, “something like a *miqnaʿah* for girls, the front of which is sewn”

the *qurzul*, “the thing a woman puts on her head; synonym *qunzuʿah*” 2.16.62

the *junnah*, “a piece of cloth a woman wears to cover her head in front and behind but not from the sides and which covers her face and the two sides of her chest; it has two eyeholes cut in it, like the *burquʿ*”

tasākhīn, “boots, or things like a *ṭaylasān*”

jarāmīq, “the *jurmūq* [singular] is the thing worn above the boot”

kawth, “the *qafsh*, meaning short boots, that are worn on the feet”

the *rān*, “a thing like a boot but with no foot and taller than a boot”

jawrab, “a wrapping for the feet; one says *jawrabtuhu* meaning ‘I put his stockings on for him’”

quffāz, “things stuffed with cotton made for the hands that a woman wears against the cold, or a kind of ornament, etc.”

and, to round this out, three hundred and sixty-five *aḥbās* and a similar number of *maqārim* (the *ḥibs* [singular] being a silver eyelet made in the middle of a red curtain, while the *miqramah* [singular] is a bedspread), plus the same number of pairs of underdrawers made of

arnabānī, “blackish silk-wool” 2.16.63

and *sinnā*, “a kind of silk”

and *ardan*, “a kind of silk-wool”

and *ṭārūnī*, another kind of silk-wool; *ṭurn* is silk-wool

and *qaṭīn*, “bleached white silk-wool”

and *birs*, “cotton or something similar to it, or papyrus flock”

والشَريع   الكتّان الجيد *

والقَز   الابريسم وهو الدِمَقْس ويقال ايضا الدِقَمْس والمدقس *

وقد زل بى القلم ايضا زلة ثانية فان السراويل يجب تقديمها على جميع ما سواها ليطابق الذكرُ الفكر* ثم انك اذا اخذتها الى ساحات المدينة واسواقها حيث تزدحم ٦٤،١٦،٢
الناس * فاول ما تلمح فرهدا غَسّانيّا غيسانيا تقول هذا يصلح لان يكون زير نسآء ولان يركب الجياد ويتقلد السيف ويعتقل الرمح ويطعن به * او غلاما مترعرعا قالت هذا يصلح لان يربى فى المدرسة الزيريّة حتى ينبغ * او كهلاً قالت وهذا جدير بان يقعد فى بيته ويتعاطى الغزل والنسيب ليجهّز ما يلزم لتلاميذ المدرسة منه * او شيخا همّا هِرَما قالت وهذا قمِين بان يكون مشيرا فى الامور التى تعسر على الاغرار من الخِرّيجين فيكفيهم النصب فى ايشائها * فان لم يلفَ عنده الراى السديد فليدرج فى كفن ويرمس * هذا وفكرك لم يزل مشغولا بالحمار او بالآكاف * فامّا وجه كون مشاعرتها انفع فلانّه قد جرت عادة من شاخ من ٦٥،١٦،٢
ذوى الامر والنهى انه اذا جفّ دمهم وضوى لحمهم حتى لم يَعُد التدثر بالثياب يدفئهم * شاعروا واحدة من هولآ النواعم فاستغنوا بحرها عن حرارة الدثار والنار والابازير * والاحسن فى ذلك ان تكون جارية عذرآ * وقد اختلفوا فى علة الحرارة ومأتاها * فبعضهم على ان نفسها من فيها هو الذى يدفئ المقرور* واعتُرض بان هذا النفس لا بدّ وان يختلط بالشنب فيبرد * وغيرهم على ان منفذ الحرارة انما هو من المسامّ التى ينبت فيها الشعر* فان المراة لما كانت مفتوحة المسامّ كان صعود الحرارة منها ابلغ * بخلاف الرجل فان مسامّه مسدودة بما له من الشعر* وردّ بان الامرد مثل المراة فى كونه مفتوحها ولم يقل احد بان مشاعرته تدفى * ٦٦،١٦،٢

and *sharīʿ*, "high-quality linen"
and *qazz*, "that is, *ibrīsam* ('a kind of silk'), which is the same as *dimaqs* (also pronounced *diqams* and *midaqs*)"

though once more the pen has carried me away: underdrawers ought to have come first, so as to give them a place in the *list* appropriate to the underlying *gist*.[261]

Next, if you take her off to the city's open spaces and marketplaces, where people gather, as soon as she claps eyes on some handsome well-built young whelp, she'll say, "That one would make a ladies' man and be good for riding fine steeds, buckling on a sword, bracing a spear between leg and stirrup, and thrusting"; or if she sees a blooming boy, she'll say, "That one ought to go to lady-killers school, to realize his potential"; or if an older man, "That one ought to stay at home and take up the composition of love lyrics and saucy songs to prepare for the needs of the pupils of the aforementioned school"; or an old man, decrepit and decomposing, "And that one is fit to give counsel on those matters that perplex its still green graduates; let him exert himself to the utmost in setting them straight, and if no pertinent opinion is to be had from him, let him be rolled up in a shroud and buried." All this, and your thoughts are still preoccupied with the donkey, or its saddle. 2.16.64

As for the argument that sleeping with her inside her slip is more fortifying, this is because it has become the custom for any of those whose commands and prohibitions must be obeyed, who is growing old, and whose blood had dried and flesh shriveled to the point that he can no longer get warm by cloaking himself in his clothes, to sleep with one of these smooth-skinned beauties inside her slip, thus substituting her warmth for that of cloak, fire, and hot spices, the best for such purposes being a virgin. There are differences of opinion over the cause and point of origin of this warmth. Some claim that it is the breath from her mouth that warms the chilled, while others object that that same breath must inevitably become embroiled with his mustache and thus cool down. Others would have it that the outlet is obviously the pores, from which sprouts the hair; thus the rising of warmth from a woman, whose pores are open, must be less impeded, in contrast to the situation with a man, whose pores are blocked by his hair. 2.16.65

To this, response was made that the beardless boy is like the woman in terms of his pores being open, but no one has ever claimed that to sleep with one of them inside his slip is more fortifying. Some believe that the breath 2.16.66

وذهب بعض الى ان الحرارة انما هى من النفس من انفها * وقال قوم من المتهافتين
على الجناس انها من موضع آخر * قال فى القاموس تكوّى الرجل بامراته تدفّا
واصطلى بحر جسدها * قلت ومع حرص المولف على جمع الالفاظ الغريبة النادرة
لم يذكر فعلا يدل على اصطلا المراة بحرارة جسد الرجل * ولهذا اى لاجل ان فى
جسم المراة من الحرارة ما لا يوجد فى جسم الرجل كان اخف ما يكون من الدثار
يدفئها ولو فى الصِرّ * والرجل اذ ذاك يُكْهى ويقفقف ويقرعبّ ويتقرقف *
ومثله غرابةً ان اكلها يكون اقلّ من اكل الرجل ولحمها اكثر من لحمه * قال المتكلمون ٦٧،١٦،٢
ووافقهم على ذلك الاطبآ النطاسيّون * ان مما فضل الله سبحانه المراة به ان
جعل فيها قوة حج الخصم وهداية الضالّ الى الدين القويم * واوردوا على ذلك
شاهدا ما جرى لذلك المعتزلى مع امراته * وذلك ان بعض المشاهير من علمآ
المعتزلة الذين يزعمون ان افعال العبد ليست مخلوقة لله كان يجادل اهل السنّة
ويورد لهم من الادلة والبراهين على تايد مذهبه ما يربكهم به * فانبرت له امراة
لبيبة سُنّية وقالت لقومها زوجونى به فاخصمه فى ليلة واحدة ان شآ الله فبات
معها تلك الليلة على الحاده * حتى اذا قضى لها الفرض ثم تنفّل بعده وتطوّع وظن
انه استحق الثواب وخَلُق بالاغتماض * قالت له واين الرابع والخامس والعاشر
يا شِرْواض * فتجلّد لآخر ثم قال قد نفد ما فى الوطاب * فلا ملام ولا عتاب *
قالت امثلك من يبدى هذا الاعتذار * وانت تقول ان الافعال غير مخلوقة
للواحد القهار * قال قد نبّهت من كان غافلا * وهديت من كان ضالا * انى
عدّيت عن مذهبى القديم * وقد هدانى الله الى الصراط المستقيم * قلت ويعلم ٦٨،١٦،٢
من كتب التاريخ ان المراة لها اعظم مدخل فى دخول النصرانية فى بلاد الافرنج *

must come from her nose, while a certain paronomasia-obsessed school claims that it comes from some other place, saying that in the *Qāmūs* it states that "'the man *takawwā* ("cuddled") with his wife' means that he sought comfort in the *ḥarr/ḥirr*[262] of her body." I have to point out that, despite the care the author has taken to collect rare and strange vocabulary items, he fails to mention a verb that means "the *woman* sought comfort in the warmth of a *man's* body." It is for this reason—i.e., because the woman's body possesses a warmth not to be be found in the man's—that the lightest of coverings is enough to warm her even in the coldest weather, while at the same time the man is blowing on his fingers and shivering and shrinking, his teeth chattering. Equally strange is the fact that she eats less than a man but has more flesh than he.

Schoolmen have claimed—and skilled physicians agree—that among the gifts that God, glory be to Him, has bestowed on women is the power to persuade their opponents to their way of thinking and lead the misguided to His true religion. As testimony to this, they advance the story of the Muʿtazilī and his wife, when a certain celebrated scholar of this group, who claim that the acts of mortal men are not of God's creation, was debating with certain Sunnis and put to them such arguments and proofs in support of his view that they were at a loss to respond. At this point a sharp-witted Sunni woman upped and said to her co-believers, "Marry me to him and I'll defeat him in a single night, God willing." He spent that night with her as a free-thinker, until such time as he had performed his marital duty, after which he performed a further, supererogatory act, and then an additonal, voluntary, good deed, believing that by so doing he'd earned heavenly reward and deserved a wink of sleep. "And what," said the woman, "of the fourth, fifth, and tenth, you flaccid *poof*?" so he pulled himself together for one more go, after which he said, "There's no more milk left in the milk-skin now, so no blame and no *reproof*." "Such an excuse is *very poor, sir*," replied the woman, "when you claim a mortal's acts are not the creation of the One, the *Enforcer*!" Said the man, "You have brought a fool to his senses, guided one misled to the proper *path*. I hereby relinquish my former way of thinking; God has guided me to the road that averts His *wrath*." 2.16.67

For my part, I declare that a reading of the history books teaches that to women should go the lion's share of the credit for the introduction of Christianity into the lands of the Franks. A certain witty litterateur once said, 2.16.68

قال بعض الظرفآ من الادبآ ان المراة اذا رامت ان تشترى حاجة او تستقضى احدا
شيا لم يلزمها ان تنقد البائع او القاضى مالاً * وانما تنقده العين من العين * قال
ولذلك جآ هذا الحرف بالمعنيين * بخلاف الرجل فانه اذا اراد قضآ شى ايا كان
ولا سيما النشنشة فلا بد وان يحل عقدته بنفاثات الدرهم او الدينار* وانها ايضا ٦٩،١٦،٢
اذا توحّمت على شى تحبه وهى حبلى ظهر ذلك الشى المتوحّم عليه فى الولد *
فينبغى للاب ان يتفقد ولده ليعلم اى شكل من الاشكال بدا فى اجسامهم *
وما انكره منها فليكتمه * قال وان القدرة الخالقية قد اوجدت لها من النبات
وغيره اشكالا كثيرة تقرّ بها عينها وينشرح صدرها اذا نظرتها او لمستها * وليس
للرجل شى من هذه الخصائص * وان امراة واحدة اذا كانت فى مجلس قد اجتمع ٧٠،١٦،٢
فيه عشرون رجلا امكن لها ان تهندهم كلهم اجمعين * فتصبىّ هذا بلفظة *
وذلك بلحظة * وذا بغمزة * وذاك بهجلة * وآخر بخزرة * وغيره بتحشيفة *
وآخر باسجادة * غيره بزفرة * واخر بالتفاتة * وغيره بليّة جيد * وآخر بشمّة *
وغيره بنزنزة * واخر بعضّة على لسانها * وغيره باخراجه ونضنضته * وآخر
بضم شفتيها وانفاصهما * وغيره بعَرض عارضها * وآخر بتفيئ شعرها * وغيره
بابتسامة * واخر بضحكة * وغيره بقهقهة * فيقوم الجميع عنها راضين * وابرع ما
تكون المراة ما اذا جلست بين زمرة من الفتيان يغازلونها ويداعبونها ويتملقونها *
قال ومن خصائصها ايضا انها تعرف ما فى قلوب الرجال * فلذلك تفتنهم بوكوكتها ٧١،١٦،٢
وحركتها وتعمُدهم وتُصَبيهم * وتتبلهم وتشجيهم * وتحسّرهم وتبلبلهم * وتطربهم
وتشغلهم * وتعبّدهم وتهنّدهم * وتتيّمهم وتهيّمهم * وتشوقهم وتروعهم *
وتعوقهم وتلوعهم * وتؤرّقهم وتسبيهم * وتشرقهم وتشبيهم * وتخلبهم وتسحرهم *

"If a woman wants to buy something or requires a service, she has no need to pay the seller or the provider in cash. She can just pay him in kind with a look that's kind, which is why this word has meanings of two kinds."[263] It's a different case with the man: if he wants to get anything, no matter what but especially if it involves any untying of drawstrings, he has to dissolve the knots with puffs[264] of silver and gold.

A further peculiarity of women is that, if one of them craves something she likes when she's pregnant, the image of what she craves will appear on the child, and a father must therefore inspect his offspring to find out what particular shape appears on their bodies, though if he finds something unacceptable, he'll just have to hold his tongue over it. Further, the woman's creative power is so great that it confers on plants and many other forms qualities that please her eye and bring her comfort if she sees or touches them. Men have none of these peculiarities. **2.16.69**

Another is that a single woman in a gathering of twenty men can bewitch each and every one of them, charming this with a word, that with a look, this with a wink, that with a blink, this with a squint, that with a look through narrowed eyes, this with a nod, that with a sigh, this with a turn, that with a twisting of the neck, this with a sniff, that with a cocking of the head, this by biting her tongue, that by sticking it out, this by moving it back and forth, that by pressing together or parting her lips, this by showing off her profile, that by loosening her hair, this with a smile, that with a laugh, and this with a guffaw, so that all leave well disposed toward her; a woman is at her most brilliant when seated amongst a company of young men who are flirting with her, joking with her, and flattering her. **2.16.70**

Another of her peculiarities is that she knows what is in men's hearts, which allows her to bewitch them with her rolling gait and her movements, grieving them and driving them wild, making them sick with love and filling them with anxiety, saddening them and confusing them, sending them into ecstasy and taking over their thoughts, enslaving them and enchanting them, making them love-lorn and distracted, filling them with longing and with terror, occupying their thoughts and putting them through agony, keeping them awake and taking them captive, choking them and setting them on fire, rending their livers and binding them with their spells, plundering them and working them till they can do no more, selling them and buying them, starving them and making them thirst, striking them in their hearts and souls, **2.16.71**

وتحربهم وتبهرهم * وتبيعهم وتشتريهم * وتجيعهم وتصديهم * وتقلُبهم وتفأدهم * وترآهم وتصدرهم * وتكبدهم وتطحلهم * وتمعدهم وتخذهم * وتبطنهم وتستهم * فاما ما قيل فى خصائص فرنستها من انها تحسن اعمال البيت ٧٢،١٦،٢
كالخياطة والتطريز وغيره فمذكور في كثير من الكتب فعليك بمراجعتها * انتهى الكلام الان على المراة بغير مرآ على ان عندى منه ما عند الفرآ من حتى * قال بعض معاتيه العلمآ المراة كلها شرّ * وشر ما فيها انه لا بد منها *

قلت وهو حكم جحي نصفه صدق ونصفه كذب *

فالصادق منه قوله انه

لا بد

منها

*

afflicting them in their lungs and breasts, tearing up their livers and spleens, hurting them in their stomachs and thighs, and beating them on their bellies and bottoms.

Concerning the claims that have been made as to her possessing peculiar skills in terms of the excellent management of such household tasks as sewing, embroidery, and the like, these are mentioned in many a book, and you'll have to look them up yourselves. This concludes our discussion of women for the time being, though let none doubt that I have as much more to say on the subject as al-Farrā' has on *ḥattā*.[265] Some idiot of a scholar has said, "Women are pure evil, and the most evil thing about them is that there's no doing without them." **2.16.72**

I declare: this, like Juḥā's[266] dream,
is half true and half untrue,
and the half that's true
is that
there's no doing
without them.

الفصل السابع عشر

في رثا حمار

١،١٧،٢ اهلاً بك يافارياق اين انت وفيمَ كنت هذه المدة الطويلة — فى نظم الابيات السريّة —ولكن هذا معلوم عندى ولم اسالك الّا عن امرحديث — قد فجعت بالامس بحمار لى وسالت عنه الجيران فلم يقل احد منهم انه سرقه * فاكتريت مناديا بدرهم فجعل ينادى فى الاسواق اَلا قد فرّ اليوم حمار الفارياق وخلّى قيده فى الوتد فهل منكم من رآه * فلم يجبه احد الّا بقوله ما اكثر الحمير الآبقة اليوم من بيوت مواليها * فلما عاد الىّ بهذه البشرى بلغ منى الغيظ كل مبلغ * وآليت ان لا انظر بعدها فى وجه حمار سواكان حقيقيا او مجازيا * فقد قال بعض ائمّة اللغة ان من خصائص لغتنا هذه الشريفة دون غيرها ان يقال للرجل الجاهل حمار * ثم اخذت ارثيه بهذه الابيات وهى

٢،١٧،٢
راح الحمار وخلّى القيد في الوتدِ ... وما راى اثره فى الناس من احدِ
فهل انا راكب من بعده وتداً ... ام مجزئى قيده لوكان من مَسَد
ام كيف ادخل داراكان لى سكنًا ... فيها وأُنزِل عندى مُنزَل الولد
سرهدته بيدى كالطفل من شَفَق ... كالطفل من شفق سرهدته بيدى
وجئته بشعير لا يخالطه ... ماسٌ ولا عسجد خوفا من الدَرَد

Chapter 17

Elegy for a Donkey

"Hello there, Fāriyāq! Where have you been and what have you been up to this long while?"—"Writing poems for princes."—"I already knew that. I'm asking you for something new."—"Yesterday I was shocked to lose a donkey of mine. I asked the neighbors about him, but none of them admitted to stealing him, so, for a dirham, I hired a crier who set about crying in the markets, 'Oyez! Today the Fāriyāq's donkey ran away, leaving his shackle on its peg. Has any of you seen him?' but the only response he got was 'How many a donkey has fled from its master's house today!' When he came back to me with this good news, my choler reached its zenith and I swore that from that day forth I'd never again look into the face of a donkey, real or figurative (a leading scholar of the language having said that one of the characteristics that distinguishes our noble tongue from all others is that in it an ignoramus may be called an ass).[267] Then I set to elegizing him in the following lines: 2.17.1

The donkey's gone, leaving the shackle on the peg, 2.17.2
And of it not one soul has seen a trace.
Am I now to ride a peg,
Or is the shackle, though of palm fiber made, supposed to take its place?
How, too, can I return to a house where was once my home
And where he once dwelt as though we shared a familial bond?
I was that fond of him, I fed him, like a child, with mine own hand—
With mine own hand, I say, just like a child I fed him, of him I was that fond.
Barley I brought him, unmixed with diamonds, or even gold,
So concerned was I that he his teeth should keep.

وكان يوقطنى منه النهاق اذا استثقلت نوما بصوت مطرب غَرِد

كم حادبى عن مَضيق حين ابصرمن حولى الجمال تبلّ الارض بالزبد

وسار بى فى طريق بلّ جانبها اهل الجَمال بمآ الورد وهو ندى

وكم جرى فارها اذ لاح عن بعد زفاف خود اليها بالغ الامد

واذ تبيّن نعشا للجنازة لم يمرر به مع اليم النخس في الكَتَد

٣،١٧،٢ ما ضل يوما عن استقرآ معلفه اكان فى روضة غنّآ ام جَرَد

قد رابنى حذقه حتى ظننت به مَسْخيّة مثل بعض الخلق عن احد

وما شكا قط من وخز ولا ضعفت رجلاه عن جوب وَعْث طال او جَدَد

شُلّت يدا مَن به ولَّى وغادرنى امشى وانشب فى اوحال ذا البلد

اعالمٌ اننى من بعده جَزِع وان فرقته نار على كبدى

وان صوت المنادى اليوم يزعق اَن البسْ اِكافك فى جنح الدجى وعُد

لا يَغْرُرَنَّك رَغْد انت واجده عند الحرامىّ خصمى فيك من حسد

فانما ذا لحِينْ انت تعلمه ما دام شهرا على طِرْف ولا عَتَد

يفديك كل حمار ندّ من بطَر اوضجّ من لَغَب او خار من جَهَد

اوحار من شَبَق قلّاب جحفلة كرّاف بول قديم جف كالقِدَد

مصنبع الراس ممشوق القوائم لم يحرن اذا سُمته خَسْفا ولم يَحِد

آليّةً انه بالطرق اَعْرَف من مولاه ان لم يَعُقْه القيد ذو العقد

If I o'erslept, his braying would wake me,
Like the voice of a sweetly trilling songbird, from sleep.
How oft did he divert me from some narrow defile
Where, as he saw, the camels on the ground around me their froth did spew
And take me on a road whose sides had been wetted
By the Beauteous with water-of-roses, otherwise known as dew!
How oft did he swiftly run, when some pretty maid's wedding parade
Appeared in the distance, and go flat out!
And, if e'er he spied a funeral bier, he'd ne'er o'ertake it,
No matter how often between his shoulders I gave him a painful clout.
Not a day passed but he closely examined his manger,
Whether he was in a rich meadow or a prairie stripped of vegetation. 2.17.3
His wit was so human, I even thought
He must be the product, as some beasts are, of transmutation.
Ne'er did he complain at a goading, nor did his legs, to take a tour,
However long and whate'er the terrain, e'er tire.
Paralyzed be the hands of him who took him and left me
To slog through this town on foot and sink into the mire!
Doth he know that since he went I've been on tenterhooks,
That separation from him like a fire my liver doth rack,
And that the voice of the crier cries out today,
'Under cover of darkness, put on your saddle and come back!'?
Let not any pampering you may get from the thief, my rival, seduce you.
He does it only out of envy.
Even for the noble or well-trained steed such things don't last,
As you well know—they're never lengthy.
May every donkey that from willfulness skedaddled,
From exhaustion vociferated,
From effort balked, or whose mind by must was addled,
Every lip-twisting sniffer of old she-donkey pee
Gone dry as jerky, your ransom be!
Long-headed, slender-leggèd, ne'er refusing
When pushed to the limit nor turning off the track,
I swear, a better guide to the roads he'd be
Than his master, were he not curbed by his knotted tack!

يا ليت لى خصلة من ذيله اثرًا   ارنو اليها كما يُرنَى الى الخُرُد

٤،١٧،٢ قال فقلت له لقد ضاع شعرك فى الحمار العادى * كما ضاع الدرهم فى المنادى * قال اما الدرهم فقد ضاع حقا واما الحمار فلا * قلت كيف ذلك والدار منه بلقع * قال من عادتى انى اذا فقدت شيا وذكرته فى الشعر خيّل لى انى عُوّضت عنه * فان لم اذكره بقيت متحسّرا على فقده * قلت او يقوم النثر مقام النظم * قال ربما يقوم عند بعض الناس * فقد بلغنى ان كثيرا من المولفين كانوا يحاولون ادراك اوطار حرمهم منها قلّة ذات اليد فالفوا فيها كتبا واستغنوا بها عنها * قلت من قال ذلك * قال هم قائلوه * قلت هذا محض كذب فانى الّفت فى النسآ كذا وكذا رسالة وما خطر ببالى قط انى عُوّضت عن واحدة ممن وصفت * قال ولِمَ الّفتها اذًا * قلت لم يكن لى من شغل ولا حركة * ووجدت الزمان علىّ طويلا ولا سيما الليالى من دون مباشرة شى ما فلفقت ما كان يخطر

٥،١٧،٢ ببالى * قال وهلاّ تفرح الان بتاليفك اذا قراته او اذا سمعت ان الناس يقراونه * قلت بل اضحك من سخف عقلى وقتئذ * فانى قد عرّضت عرضى لالسن القادحين فضلا عن كونى اضعت اوقاتى عبثا فيما لم يجدنى نفعا * وقد بلغنى ان كثيرا من المتزوجين سآهم ما قلته فى النسآ وذكر مكايدهن فاستظهروا علىّ بجماعة من العلمآ عابوا علىّ تبويب كتبى وخطّاونى فى عبارتها * وكنت ايضا حكيت كلاما عن بعض النسآ بلفظه فقالوا لا ينبغى ان يحكى الكلام بلفظه فى الكتب وغير ذلك مما ندّمنى كثيرا * قال قد سمعت ان الناس لا يزالون يعادون المولف حال حياته * فاذا مات حرصوا على كلمة ياثرونها عنه كما قال الشاعر

ترى الفتى ينكر فضل الفتى   ما دام حيّا فاذا ما ذهب
لجّ به الحرص على نكتة   يكتبها عنه بماء الذهب

Would I had a tress from his tail that his mem'ry ne'er might fade—
I'd gaze upon it as one does upon a cloistered, unwed maid!"

I told him, "Your poetry was as much wasted on that ordinary donkey as your money on the crier." He replied, "The money is truly lost but not the donkey." "How can that be?" I asked, "when the house is devoid of his presence?" "It's my custom," he answered, "if I lose something and then memorialize it in verse, to imagine I've been compensated for it. If I don't do so, I continue to grieve its loss." "And can prose play the same role as verse?" I asked. "Possibly," he replied, "with some people, for I hear that many writers, having tried to achieve pressing goals for which they lacked the wherewithal, wrote books about them and in that way were able to do without them." "Who says so?" I asked. "They themselves," he replied. "It's a pack of lies," I said. "I've written vast numbers of treatises on women and never for a moment felt I'd gained a replacement for one of those I was describing." "Why, then, did you write them?" he asked. "I had no work and no business to attend to," I said, "and found that time lay heavy on my hands, especially at night, when I had nothing to do. So I jotted down whatever came to mind." 2.17.4

"And," he asked, "do you not find pleasure in your writings when you read them now, or hear that others are reading them?" "On the contrary," I replied, "I laugh at how stupid I was in those days, for I exposed my honor to the tongues of those who would vilify me, not to mention that I wasted my time in vain on things that could gain me nothing. I hear that many a married man was upset by what I said about women and my recounting of their wiles, so they tried to defeat me by using a company of scholars, who reproached me for the way my books were organized and found fault with the way they were written. I'd also quoted some of the things that had been said about women verbatim, and they claimed one shouldn't quote things verbatim in books, plus other matters that gave me great cause for regret." "I have heard," he said, "that people never cease attacking a writer as long as he's alive, but when he dies, will go to great lengths to find some saying of his they can pass down. As the poet says, 2.17.5

You'll find one lad denies all merit to another
While he's alive, but once the man's gone cold
Looks everywhere for a pleasant anecdote
On him to inscribe in lines of gold."

٦،١٧،٢ قلت وما نفع هذا الحرص لمن مات * قال لا نفع منه غير انى ارى ان فى النظم للذة عظيمة * ولا بدّ وان يكون النثر ايضا مثله فانهما كليهما يخرجان من مخرج واحد * افلا تقول بصحة ذلك * قلت انى اقول باللذّة فى التاليف من جهة ان المولف يعرف شيا جهله غيره * ولا شك ان فى معرفة الحقائق لذة * غير انه يقابلها من الالم ما يرجحها * وذلك ان المولف اذا عرفت مثلاً حقيقة واراد ان يعرّف غيره

٧،١٧،٢ اياها وجد اكثر الناس قد صمّوا عن سماعها * ومَثَل ذلك مثل طبيب نصوح راى اهل بلده يستحمّون بالمآ البارد فى حال كونهم محمومين * فنصح لهم ان لا يفعلوا ذلك فأبَوا وقالوا ان هذه البرودة تزيل الحرارة * فهو من جهة انّه عارف بالحقيقة مسرور * ومن جهة انه يرى غيره فى ضلال عنها محزون * وسروره لنفسه لا يوازن حزنه على غيره * الا ترى ان اهل العلم كلهم ضعاف ضاوون قليلو الكلام والنوم والاكل والضحك * وان الجهال سمان تارّون اصحا كثيروا الاكل والنوم وغيره مما جُعل لتقويم الطبيعة * قال فما بال الاطبآ سمان ايضا وهم بمنزلة العلمآ فى كونهم يعلمون من المنافع ما يجهله غيرهم * قلت ان الطبيب لا يرى الناس حين ياكلون ويشربون ويباعلون * وانما يراهم حين يمرضون فلا تحزنه افعالهم * فاما العالم فانه فى كل وقت ومكان يرى من العامة ما يدل على ضلالهم وجهلهم * فلا يمكنه والحالة هذه الا ان يتاسّف على ما هم فيه من الغباوة والغفلة * قال افتقول

٨،١٧،٢ اذا بالجهل * قلت هنيئا لمن رضى به * قال وما قولك فى الشعر * قلت ان كان هو لمصلحة اى لشى يعود الى القيام بأَوَدك فنِعمَ هو * وان يكن عن مجرد هوس وميل الى التجنيس والترصيع ايان رايت امراة جميلة او وردة او روضة كما هو داب اكثر الشعرآ يتكلفون للنظم فى كل ما لاح لهم * او كرثائك الحمار الآن فتركه اولى *

"What good does such solicitude do one who's dead?" I said. "None," he replied, "except that writing verse provides, in my opinion, great pleasure. No doubt prose is the same, for both emerge from the same source, wouldn't you agree?" I said, "Concerning the pleasures of writing, I'd say that on the one hand the writer knows something others do not, and there can be no doubt that knowledge of true things is a source of pleasure. Opposed to this, however, is a pain that outweighs it, namely, that if the writer is aware of a certain fact and wants to communicate it to others, he'll find that most people turn a deaf ear to it. 2.17.6

"For example, a wise physician who sees the people of his country bathing in cold water when they have a fever may advise them against so doing, only for them to refuse and say, 'The cold gets rid of the heat.' He is happy then from the perspective that he knows the truth but sad from the perspective that he sees that everyone else is misled, and his personal happiness does not outweigh his sadness on behalf of others. Have you not observed that scholars are, without exception, weak and scrawny, and speak, sleep, eat, and laugh little, while the ignorant are fat, soft, and healthy and get plenty of food, sleep, and everything else that exists to keep the constitution balanced?" "How come, in that case," he said, "that physicians are also fat, when they're the equivalent of scholars in terms of possessing useful knowledge unknown to others?" I said, "The physician doesn't see people when they're eating, drinking, and lying with their spouses. He sees them only when they get sick and, as a result, doesn't grieve over what they get up to. The scholar, on the other hand, observes, at all times and in all places, things that point to the errors and ignorance of the common people. Thus he has no alternative but to sorrow over the stupidity and naïveté from which they suffer." "Do you mean," he said, "that you're in favor of ignorance?" "Good luck," said I, "to those who are resigned to it." 2.17.7

"What do you think of poetry, then?" he asked. I replied, "If it serves some interest of yours, meaning that it will help you survive, it's an excellent thing. But if it's just the product of some obsession and a fondness for the production of paronomasia and other forms of word play at the sight of a beautiful woman, a rose, or a garden, after the manner of most poets, who go to great efforts to compose poetry about everything that crosses their paths, 2.17.8

قال ولكن احسن الشعر ما جآء عن هوس اى عن السليقة لا بالتكلف * فانى حين امدح السرىّ اجد فى ضم لفظة الى اخرى ما يجده المُعانى لضم نقيضين مختلفين * وليس كذلك ما نظمته فى الحمار * فانى نظمت فيه هذه المرثية فى ساعة من الزمن * قلت ولكن الناس لا ينظرون الّا الى الظاهر * فقصيدتك
فى الحمار يسمونها حمارية * وابياتك فى السرىّ سريّة * قال ان كان الامر كما ٩،١٧،٢
ذكرت فلم رغبت عن التاليف ولكن لا فى النسآ فان ذلك امر مستفيض * قلت اما اوّلا فلان المولف يوقع نفسه فى كلاليب السنة الناس فيمزقون عرضه وجلده كما ذكرت لك انفا * والثانى فان حقيقة اسم المولف غير محمود * فهو عند من يعلم حقيقة معناه بمعنى الملفّق واكثر الناس يضحكون من هذا الحرف * فيحسبون انه من التاليف بين شخصين * وانما يقولون لمن تعاطى ذلك شيخ * وهو ايضا
مكروه عند بعض الناس وخصوصا عند النسآء * واحسن الالقاب هنا فيما ١٠،١٧،٢
ارى عند النصارى قسيس وعند المسلمين بيك * اما القسيس فلاَنّ كل الناس تلثم يده وتتبرك بذلك * وان المراة من القبط لتغسل رجلى القسيس بيديها بمآ الزهر ثم توعى مآهما فى زجاجة * وانه متى جاع حمل امعآه الى دار احد من معارفه فاستقبلته زوجته بالبشاشة والاكرام فزعبها اى زعب * واذا شآ ان يبقى فى بيته لعارض من العوارض بعث غلامه بعلامة الى احد البيوت فجآه منها بغدآء ينظم فيه شعرآ عصرنا قصائد * فاما البيك فانه وان يكن مقامه بين الناس كريما الا انه لا يمكنه ان يبلغ من البيوت ما يبلغه القسيس * اذ لا يتاتّى له ان يمشى وحده * فلا بدّ وان يمشى معه اثنان عن اليمين والشمال وهما وان اظهرا له الخضوع والاحترام ففى قلوبهما منه حزازات تبعثهما على مراقبته والتعنّت عليه * اللهم الّا اذا تزيّا بزى خادم له و ﺣ فظاهر اللباس يجبئ عنه العين *

or like your elegy for the donkey just now, then you're better off without it." "But," he said, "the best poetry is the kind that's born of an obsession, meaning spontaneously and not artificially. Thus, when I write a panegyric to the prince, I suffer as must anyone who has to reconcile two opposites, but what I wrote about the donkey wasn't like that: I wrote what I did about him in an hour flat." "On the other hand," I said, "people look only at the outside, so your ode on the ass they'll call asinine, while your lines on the prince they'll call princely."

"If things are as you say," he said, "why have you foresworn writing in general but not about women, which is something that's in abundant supply?"[268] "First," I replied, "because the writer casts himself into the pincers of people's jaws and they proceed to rip his honor and his patience to pieces, as noted above. Secondly, the true meaning of the word *mu'allif* ('author, composer') is dishonorable, for it has the same sense, according to those who know, as *mulaffiq* ('concocter'). Also, most people laugh at the former, believing that it refers to *ta'līf* ('making peace') between two persons,[269] the proper term for one who practices such things being 'shaykh,' which is itself repugnant to some people, especially women.[270] **2.17.9**

"The best titles to have here, as far as I can see, are, among the Christians, *qissīs* ('priest') and, among the Muslims, *bayk* ('bey'). *Qissīs* is good because people kiss the priest's hand for blessing. A Coptic woman will go so far as to wash the priest's feet in orange-blossom water with her own hands and then preserve the water in a bottle; and when the priest gets hungry, he lugs his guts over to the house of one of his acquaintances, whose wife receives him with beaming face and does him honor, and how he stuffs them then![271] If he prefers to stay at home because of something that's cropped up, he sends with a note to one of their houses a boy, who returns with a luncheon such as the poets of our day write odes to. As to *bayk*, the bey, even though honored among the people, cannot get the same from their houses as does the priest. This is because it is not easy for him to walk alone. He has to have with him, when walking out, two men, one on his right and one on his left, and these, though they show him deference and respect, harbor grudges in their hearts that impel them to watch his every move and do him harm. The exception is when they wear the costume of a servant, at which time the sight of their dress causes men to look away in awe." **2.17.10**

١١،١٧،٢ قال هيهات ان اصير قسيسا * هيهات ان اصير بيكا * اما حرفة القسيس فانها لا تصلح لى لانى لا احبّ الركاكة * واما صفة البيك فانى لا اصلح لها فان القدرة الازلية لم ترتض لى منذ الازل بالبوكية للبيكية * وما بقى امامى الا الشيخية * قد توكلت على الله * قلت انى مفارقك

على ان تخبرنى بما سيحدث لك فى شيختك *

قال سافعل ذلك

ان شا

الله

*

"How unlikely," said the Fāriyāq, "that I'll ever be a *qissīs*! How unlikely that I'll ever be a *bayk*! The profession of priest won't do for me because I don't like bad writing, and I'm not fit for the title of *bayk,* because Eternal Providence has not been pleased to grant me, from before the beginning of time, any possibility of bungling my way into a bey-ship. 2.17.11
The only thing left for me then is a shaykh-ship. I'm off!"
I told him, "I will let you go only on condition you tell me
what happens to you when you get your shaykh-ship."
"And so I shall," replied he,
"if God
wills."

الفصل الثامن عشر

في الوان مختلفة من المرض

١٫١٨٫٢ ثم لازمَ الفارياق نظم الابيات وهو حريص على الاتّسام بسمة شيخ * فعنّ له ان
يقرا النحو على بعض المشايخ لما انه راى ان القدر الذى كان تعلمه منه فى بلاده لا
يكفى لممدح السرىّ * وفى ذلك الشهر الذى نوى فيه القرآة أُصيب برمد اليم *
فلما افاق شرع فى العلم فقرا على الشيخ مصطفى كتبا صغيرة فى النحو والصرف * ثم
اشتد به دآ الديدان الذى سببه فيما قيل اكل اللحم نَيّئا * وتلك عادة مشهورة عند
اهل الشام * فكان يتمعّص منه وقت القرآة والشيخ يظن ان ذلك من اختلاف
المسائل وكثرة التعليل * حتى قال له مرة سبحان الله ما احد قرا علىّ هذا الفن الّا
وتمعّص * فقال له ليس التمعّص كله ياسيدى الشيخ من زيد وعمرو * فان لجماعة
الديدان ايضا مدخلا * فانى لا اكل شيا الّا وسبقوا معدتى اليه * قال لا باس
٢٫١٨٫٢ عليك عسى ان يخف عنك ببركة العلم * واتفق للفارياق وقتئذ ان ساله احد
معارفه ان يقرا على الشيخ المذكور ذلك الكتاب الذى تقراه النصارى فى الجبل *
وهو كتاب بحث المطالب * فلما ختمه التمس من الشيخ ان يكتب له اجازة اقرائه فى
بلاده * فكتب له اجازة وعرضها على الفارياق * فحين تصفحها راى فيها خطأً فى
اللغة والاعراب * فاستاذن من شيخه ان يوقفه على الغلط * فلما وقف عليه قال

Chapter 18

Various Forms of Sickness

Thenceforth the Fāriyāq, being anxious to become known by the title of "Shaykh," devoted himself to writing verse. To that end it occurred to him to study grammar under certain Egyptian shaykhs, for he'd made up his mind that what he'd acquired in his own country wasn't enough for the prince's Panegyricon. In the same month, however, that he declared his intent to study, he was afflicted with a painful case of ophthalmia. When he recovered, he made his first foray into scholarship and studied with Shaykh Muṣṭafā[272] a few small books on morphology and syntax. Then he got a bad case of worms, caused, he was told, by eating raw meat, a well-known custom among Levantines. Whenever his stomach hurt him during the classes, the shaykh would put it down to the wide range of topics and the intensiveness of the analysis. Once he even said to him, "Glory be to God, no one has studied this science at my hands without getting a stomach ache!" to which the Fāriyāq replied, "The stomach ache isn't all from Zayd and ʿAmr,[273] Master Shaykh. The worms have a role to play in it too, for there's nothing I eat that they haven't got to before my stomach does." "Never mind," replied the shaykh, "Perhaps the blessings of scholarship will provide some relief." 2.18.1

Around this time, the Fāriyāq happened to be asked by an acquaintance if he could study[274] with the aforementioned shaykh the book the Christians study on the Mountain, namely the *Baḥth al-maṭālib*.[275] When this acquaintance had gone through it all, he asked the shaykh to write him a certificate allowing him to teach the book in his own country,[276] which the shaykh did, showing the result to the Fāriyāq. When the latter examined it, he found mistakes in the language and the inflections, and he asked his shaykh if he might point the errors out to him. On examining them, the shaykh said, 2.18.2

ساكتب له غدا اخرى * ثم كتب له اجازة غيرها فلما امعن الفارياق فيها النظر اذا بها كالاولى * فنبّه شيخه على ما فيها * فقال له اكتب له انت عنى ما شئت * فكتب له ما اعجب به * على ان الشيخ كان مضطلعا بفن النحو غاية ما يكون * فكان يقضى ساعة تامة فى شرح جملة غير تامة * الا انه لم يكن يزاول الانشآ والتاليف فكان علمه كله فى صدره وعلى لسانه ولا يكاد يخرج منه الى القلم شى * ثم بعد ٣،١٨،٢

قراة النحو على النسق المذكور راجع الفارياق وجع العينين * فلما افاق راى ان يقرا شرح التلخيص فى المعانى * فشرع فيه مع الشيخ احمد * فلم يسِرْ فيه قليلا حتى اصابته الحكة ولم يكن قد عرفها فى مبادئها فلهذا استمرّ على القرآء * حتى اذا كان الشيخ آخذاً مرة فى شرح مسألة معضلة ثارت الحكة فى بدن الفارياق فجعل يحكّ بكلتا يديه * فالتفت اليه الشيخ فرآه منهمكا فى الحك * فقال له ما بالك تحك وانت على ما يظهر لى غير منتبه لقيل واجيب * هل نحن الان فى محاكة الالفاظ او فى محاكة الاعضآ * قال لا تؤاخذنى ياسيدى فانى ارى لذة الحك مانعة لى من التنبّه لغيره * قال اَوَ بك الحكة * قال لعلها هى * فنظر الشيخ الى يديه فقال هى والله فينبغى ان تقتصر فى بيتك وتطلى جسمك بخرء الكلاب فليس لها من علاج سواه * فلزم الفارياق بيته وجعل يطلى بدنه كل يوم بالخرء المشار اليه ويقعد فى الشمس ساعات حتى لقى من ذلك عذاب الهون * ثم لما افاق رجع الى القرآة *

٤،١٨،٢ وبعد ان ختم الكتاب عاودته ضرينة الرمد * ثم نقر فى راسه ان يقرا شرح السلّم للاخضرى فى المنطق * فشرع فى قرآته على الشيخ محمود فاصابته الهيضة وهى الدآء المسمى فى مصر بالهوآ الاصفر * فبقى ثلثة ايام لا يعى ولا يعقل من الدنيا شيا ولا يقدر على النطق * سوى انه سمعه خادمه مرة يهذى ويقول كلّية موجبة كبرى *

"Tomorrow I shall write him another" and he wrote him another certificate. When the Fāriyāq took a close look at this, he found that it was as bad as the first. He alerted his shaykh to the mistakes, but the latter told him, "You write him whatever you want." This was despite the fact that the shaykh was as well versed in the science of grammar as anyone could be and was capable of devoting a whole hour to the analysis of just part of a sentence. He did not, however, practice prose or verse composition, and, as a result, all his knowledge was in his heart and on his tongue, and he was almost incapable of getting any of it out and into his pen.

After studying grammar in the manner mentioned, the Fāriyāq had a recurrence of eye pain. When he recovered, he decided to study *Al-Talkhīṣ fī l-maʿānī* (*The Epitome on Tropes*).[277] He started on it with Shaykh Aḥmad but had not got far into it before he was struck by pruritis, which he failed to recognize at the onset, which explains why he went on studying. Once, as the shaykh embarked on the explanation of some complex issue, the Fāriyāq's body started itching all over, so he started scratching with both hands. The shaykh turned and, seeing him absorbed in scratching, asked him, "Why are you scratching and, as far as I can see, paying no attention to the 'if-it-be-saids' and the 'answer-may-be-mades'? Are we here to scratch limbs or words?" "Please forgive me," replied the Fāriyāq, "but the relief provided by scratching distracts me from everything else." "You have pruritis?" the other asked. "It may be so," he replied. The shaykh looked at his hands and said, "It is, by God. You must keep to your house and smear your body with dogs' feces, for that is the only treatment." So the Fāriyāq stayed at home and took to smearing his body every day with the aforementioned dogs' feces and sitting in the sun for hours, until he found relief from that torment. Then, when he was cured, he returned to his studies. 2.18.3

After he finished going through that book, he suffered another attack of ophthalmia. Then he conceived the notion of studying al-Akhḍarī's *Sharḥ al-Sullam* (*The Commentary on the Ladder*)[278] on logic, so he started reading it under the direction of Shaykh Maḥmūd and was struck down by the *hayḍah*, which is the disease Egyptians call "the yellow air,"[279] and spent three days oblivious to everything going on around him and incapable of uttering a sound, except that once his servant heard him raving about "the greater affirmative universal"[280] and, thinking he was complaining of the severity of his state, replied that it was indeed "one of the greaters." No one else had then 2.18.4

فظن انه يستعظم مصيبته فيقول انها كبرى * ولم يكن احد اصيب بهذا الدآ فى مصر * فلما مضت ثلثون يوما انتشر فى البلد وعمّ بلاوه والعياذ بالله فكان يموت به كل يوم الوف * ووقتئذ عرف الفارياق انه كان المقدّم فى هذه البليّة وغيره التالى ٢،١٨،٥
كما تقول المناطقة * وان الديدان التى كان يقاسى منها هى التى عجلت له بهذا الدآء فجل هو بها *فجعل اى الفارياق يركب حماره ويطوف فى الاسواق وكانّه اَمِن من المقدور * (حاشية لم يكن هذا الحمار ذلك الذى استحق الرثآ والتابين بل كان ممّن يحقّ له التقريظ) * فسار الى قرية فى الريف ومعه خادمه وخادمته * فعلم به بعض ولاة البلاد فاستدعى به وبالخادم والخادمة * وقال له اَىْ لبيب هل هذا وقت الموت او وقت الايلاد حتى جئت بهذه الجارية هنا * قال انا مدّاح السرىّ وقد اتيت لاسرّح ناظرى فى نظرة الريف فاجيد مدحه بعد موت من يموت * فقد ضقت بالمدينة ذرعا وخشيت على قريحتى العقم * قال ما هذه واشار الى الخادمة * قال هى اخت هذا يعنى الخادم * قال وما هذا * قال خولىّ هذا يعنى الحمار* فالتفت الامير الى الخادم فراى عليه طلاوة * فقال له من حيث انك شاعر السرىّ او شعروره فلا تثريب عليك * وانما ينبغى ان تترك الخادم هنا فانه يصلح لخدمتى * قال لك علىّ الِامرة فخذه * فاستبد به الامير تلك الليلة وساله عن الفارياق مليًّا * فقال له الخادم والله ياسيدى انه رجل طيب غير انى اظن انه
اعجمى فانى لا اكاد افهمه حين يتكلم بلغتنا * فلما اصبح الصباح تاهب الفارياق ٢،١٨،٦
للرجوع فلم يجد الحمار* فظن انه لحق بالاول *فجعل يبحث عنه فوجده قد خرج مع حمار آخر من حمر الامير الى سهل وهو تحته يرقع وينخر* فلما ان راه على حالة المفعولية غلبه الضحك فقال * قد ورد فى الحديث ان الناس على دين ملوكهم *

contracted the disease in Egypt but by the time thirty days had passed it had spread throughout the country and become a general affliction, God save us, with thousands dying of it every day.

At this point, the Fāriyāq realized that he had been, to use the language of the logicians, the first term in this disaster, the others the second, and that it was the worms from which he suffered that had expedited his early subjection to this illness. Because of them, then, he moved quickly too and took—the Fāriyāq, that is—to mounting his donkey and touring the markets as though Fate could no longer touch him (note: this wasn't the donkey that merited an elegy and a funeral oration; this one, being still alive, merited a eulogy), and went to a village in the countryside, accompanied by his male and female servant. A local governor, hearing of his presence, summoned him and his servants, the male and the female, and said to him, "Hey, wise guy! Is this a time for dying or a time for knocking people up? What are you doing bringing a girl like this here?" He replied, "I am the prince's panegyrist, and I have come to let my eyes wander over the greenery of the countryside so I can praise it well, after the death of so many, for I have grown tired of the city and was afraid my creative powers would dry up." "So who's she?" he then said, pointing to the girl servant. "His sister," said the Fāriyāq, indicating the male servant. "And who's he?" he said. "His keeper," he replied, indicating the donkey. The emir turned to the male servant and, finding him comely, said, "Since you're the prince's poet, or his poetaster, you cannot be sanctioned. But you will have to leave this servant with me, for he has the right qualifications to enter my service." "You're the boss," said the Fāriyāq. "Take him!" That night the emir, having had his way with the boy, asked him insistently about the Fāriyāq and the servant told him, "Honestly, my lord, he's a good man, but I think he may not be an Arab because I can hardly understand him when he speaks to me in our language." 2.18.5

When morning came, the Fāriyāq made his preparations for the return journey but couldn't find the donkey, so he decided he must have run off to join the first. He went looking for him and found that he'd gone off with another of the emir's donkeys to an empty patch of ground, where he was bellowing and snorting beneath him. When the Fāriyāq saw him taking the passive role, he couldn't contain his laughter and said, "It says in the hadith, 'People follow the religion of their kings' but no one ever said donkeys should follow the sect of their owners. Anyway, better the ass's ass than the 2.18.6

الا انه لم يقل احد قط ان الحمير على مذهب اصحابها * ولكن بالعير ولا بالمُعِير *
ثم رجع الى الدار فوجد خادمه وخادمته ينتظرانه * وقال له الخادم قد سرّحنى
الامير فانه لم يرنى اهلا لخدمته الّا ليلة واحدة وها انا الآن حرّ* ثم ان الفارياق ٧،١٨،٢
بعد ان هنّا الامير ومرّأه رجع الى مصر وكان البلآ قد خفّ * فسال عن شيخه
المنطق فقيل له انه حىّ لم يقضِ من القضايا * فرجع اليه واتمّ ما كان ابتدا به * فلما
بلغ آخر درجة من السلّم عاودته ضريبة الرمد فلزم بيته * فلما افاق راى ان يتعلم
شيا من الفقه وعلم الكلام * فبدا بالكنز وبالرسالة السنوسيّة فمرض— فراه بعض
معارفه من الفرنساوية فساله عن سبب ضعفه فاخبر الخبر* فقال له انا اشفيك منه
باذن الله ولكن على شرط ان تعلم ابنى العربية * فقال حبا وكرامة * فشرع مذ ذلك
الوقت فى تعليمه وفى تعاطى الدوآ من عند ابيه * ولكن لا بدّ لتفصيل ذلك من فصل
على حدته

ass's lender's ass!" Then he returned to the house, where he found his serving boy and girl waiting for him. The boy told him, "The emir has released me from his service, because he found my qualifications were good for one night only, so now I'm free."

Then the Fāriyāq, after having paid his respects to the emir and wished 2.18.7
him good health, returned to Cairo, where the affliction had died down. He asked after his logic teacher and was told that he was alive and not numbered among the dead,[281] so he went back to him and completed with him what he'd started. When he reached the last step on the *Ladder*, he suffered another attack of ophthalmia and stayed at home. When he recovered, he decided to learn something of jurisprudence and the science of theology, so he started on the *Kanz* (*The Treasure*)[282] and the *Risālah al-Sanūsiyyah* (*The Senoussi Treatise*)[283] and fell ill. A French acquaintance asked why he was so weak, and he told him the story. "I shall cure you," the other said, "God willing, but on condition you teach my son Arabic." "With the greatest of pleasure," he returned, and immediately he started teaching him and taking the medication from his father. This, however, will have to be set out in detail in another chapter,

on its own.

الفصل التاسع عشر

في دائرة هذا الكون ومركز هذا الكتاب

كان هذا الرجل طبيبا مشهورا بمصر * ولكن شهرته فى دائه اكثر منها فى دوآئه * ١،١٩،٢
وذلك انه كان قد تزوج جارية تارّة على كبر سنّه فاولدها بنتا وصبيا * ثم عجز عن
ادآ حقها فجعل دابه الملاطفة لها والتملق * وتلك عادة الرجل مع المراة من انه كلما
قصّر فى اعتابها وارضائها فى الحقوق الزوجية زاد حرصه عليها وكلفه وتردّبه لها *
توهّم ان هذا يسدّ عند المراة مسدّ ذلك * وكذا حالته معها اذا كان يخونها ويرأم
اخرى * كما ان داب المراة ان تزيد هشهشتها وعروبيّتها لزوجها بزيادة اشباعه
اياها واطفاف الكيل لها * او تملقها له اذا كانت تخونه * وبنا على ذلك قال الطبيب ٢،١٩،٢
لزوجته يوما من الايام * ياهذى انى ارى ان قد صدئ مفتاحى عن قفلك * وان
سنّك وترارتك تقتضيان ان تتخذى لك آلة رصاعية لتتلهّى بها حتى يحين حَيْنى
فتتزوجى بآخر * والّا انى اخاف ان تفركينى وتطيرى من عندى كما يطير الحمام *
وقد يهون علىّ ان اخسر منك شيا واحدا ولا اخسرك بجملتك * فانك ام ولدى *
ومحل سرّى من كبدى * فلا اطيق فراقك * فاختارى لنفسك من شئت آتك به
بقرنيه * فضحكت المراة عند ذلك * ثم قال ومن حيث انى معروف فى هذا البلد
بانى طبيب فاذا راى الجيران رجلا قادما الىّ بل رجالا فلا يكون عليك شبهة *
فضحكت المراة ايضا لقوله رجالا * قال فان الناس يقرعون باب الطبيب ولو

Chapter 19

The Circle of the Universe and the Center of This Book[284]

This man was a famous doctor in Egypt, but his reputation for causing decease was greater than that for curing it, the reason being that, at an advanced age, he'd married a fresh young girl and fathered on her a daughter and a son. Thereafter he'd ceased to be able to give her her marital rights, so he made it his habit to humor her and flatter her, which is how men usually treat their wives in such cases—falling short of pleasing and satisfying her in this area, he increases his attentions, his demonstrations of affection, and his loving treatment of her, imagining that these will make up in the woman's eyes for the other, and he does the same when he's unfaithful to her and falls in love with another. Likewise, the wife likewise usually increases her demonstrations of love and passion for her husband by giving herself to him to the point that he becomes sated with her and his cup runs over, or she flatters him, if it's she who's being unfaithful. 2.19.1

In keeping with this logic, the doctor told his wife one day, "Good woman, I observe that my key has become too rusty for use in your lock and that your age and blooming good health require you find yourself a copulative instrument to amuse yourself with until my time is done and you marry another. If you don't, I'm afraid you'll come to hate me and fly away and leave me as does the dove. It would be easier for me to lose one part of you than to lose you altogether, for you are the mother of my children and the closest thing to my heart, and I could not bear to be separated from you. Choose whomever you'd like and I'll drag him to you by his horns." (The woman laughed at this.) Then he added, "And given that I am well known in this town to be a doctor, if the neighbors see a man, or even men, coming to me 2.19.2

فى نصف الليل * وهنا ضحكت ايضا * ثم تمادى فى الكلام معها الى ان قال
ولا تظنى انى انا وحدى تفردت بهذه العادة * فان امثالى من اهل بلادى يفعلون
كذلك وهنا قهقهت * فلما فرغ من بقية خطبته على هذا النسق ظنت زوجته ٣،١٩،٢
اوّلا انه قصد بذلك ان يستطلع سرّها ويتصيّدها بزلّة * فبكت من شدة الغيظ
وقالت له ازعمتنى بغيّا حتى تقابلنى بمثل هذا الكلام وتسيىء بى الظن * قال حاشا
لله من ذلك * وانما تكلمت معك بمقتضى الطبع فتدبّرى قولى بعد حين وردّى علىّ
الجواب * فانصرفت المراة من حضرته وهى واجمة مرتابة * ثم مضت عليهما ايام
غير قليلة والرجل لا يهارش ولا يعاظل * ولا يلاعب ولا يباعل * فقلقت جدّا
لهذه الحال * وضاق صدرها عن صبر الاعتزال * واخذت تفكر فيما قاله لها
زوجها * فتبعّلت له يوما من الايام وتبرّجت وتعطرت وقصدت غرفته وهى تقول
فى نفسها * اليوم يكون برزخ الحالتين * وفيصل الحدّين * فان لم تكن منه مباعلة
ذكّرته بما قال * فتلقاها بالبشر والبشاشة واجلسها بجانبه وعرف انها كَرِعت * اذ ٤،١٩،٢
راى قدعلت عينيها حمرة وهما ترارئان وفى صوتها تهدّج اى رعشة واضطراب *
فلما استقرت بادرها بالكلام بان قال هل تبصّرت ما قلته لك منذ ايام * قالت نعم
ولكن اما عندك فضلة تغنينى عن هذا الامر * قال ما عندى والله من وَشَل ولا
فضلة * ولا ثَمَد ولا ثُمْلة * ولم يبق لى امل لاصلاح شانى فى ناعوظ ما لا فى
لحم السقنقور ولا فى شحم الوَرَل دَلْكا ولا فى الزنجبيل ولا الفلفل ولا التامول ولا
القاقلة ولا الراسن ولا الفوفل ولا القرنفل ولا السنبل ولا المصطكى ولا الجوزبوّا
ولا الهال ولا الرازيانج ولا فى عاقرقرحا ولا فى حب الصنوبر ولا الحمص ولا
الكابلى ولا البليلج ولا دارفلفل ولا السمسم ولا الخولنجان ولا البسباسة ولا دهن
البلسان ولا خصى الثعلب ولا فى بيض العصافير ولا فى دهن السوسن ولا فى

no one will suspect you" (the woman laughed too at his mention of "men") "for people knock on a doctor's door at night—even at midnight" (and here she laughed again). Having talked to her at length in this vein, he ended by saying, "Don't think that I'm the only one who practices this custom. In my country, people like me do the same" (at which, she let out a great whoop of laughter).

His wife's first thought, once he'd finished the rest of his speech along these lines, was that he was trying by this means to discover her inmost feelings and trap her into making a slip, so she wept with rage and said to him, "You must believe I'm a whore to confront me with such words and hold such a low opinion of me." "God forbid!" said he. "I spoke to you simply of what nature requires. Think over what I said in a little while and let me know your answer." The woman left him, scowling and suspicious. A good few days passed and the man neither fondled her nor mounted her nor played with her nor performed his husbandly duties with her. She, becoming worried when the situation promised to *persist*, was too annoyed to have the patience to *desist*, and started thinking about what her husband had said to her. One day, then, she dressed herself in the clothes that pleased him best, made up her face, put on perfume, and set off for his room, telling herself, "Today will be the *watershed*, the dividing line between what's past and what lies *ahead*. If he doesn't treat me like a wife, I'll remind him of his words." 2.19.3

He received her with joy and a beaming face and sat her down at his side, noting that she was aroused, for a redness had suffused her eyes, which glistened, while her voice had a tremolosity, which is to say a shake and a shiver, to it. When she'd settled herself, he started off by asking her if she had thought over what he'd said a few days before. "Yes," she said. "But don't you have a bit left that would relieve me of this matter?" He replied, "I swear I don't have a drop or a *pottle*, the dregs of a puddle or the lees of a *bottle*, and I've no hope left of improving the situation with any aphrodisiac—not by the rubbing on of flesh of skink or fat of varan, nor by use of ginger or pepper or pan-leaf or saltwort or elecampane or betel-nut or cloves or spikenard or mastic or nutmeg or fennel, or of Spanish pelletory or pinenuts or chickpea or emblic or myrobalans or long pepper or sesame or alpinia or mace or balm-tree oil or ragwort, or in birds' eggs or in iris oil or in colocassia or in narcissus root steeped two nights in milk or in celery whose seeds have 2.19.4

القلقاس ولا فى اصل النرجس منقوعا فى الحليب ليلتين ولا فى الكرفس مدقوقا بزره بالسكر والسمن ولا فى لبس الثوب المورَّس ولا فى اكل اصل اللُوف ولا فى الضَجْع معصورا ماوه فى اللبن الرائب ولا فى البورق مدوفا بالعسل او فى دهن الزنبق ولا فى البندق الهندى ولا فى الهَمْقاق مقلوّا ولا فى علك البطم والينبوت ولا فى المسك مدوفا بدهن الخِيرىّ ولا فى البَهْمَن ولا فى الجزَر ولا فى الهليون ولا فى الاملج ولا فى البَسفارذانَج ولا فى اخضر الباقلّى بالزنجبيل ولا فى القلقل مدقوقا بالسمسم معجونا بالعسل ولا فى صمغ الكَنْدَلَى ولا فى المُقل ولا فى ثمر البطم ولا فى التيجير بخفيف لحم الرخم مخلوطا بخردل سبع مرات ولا فى حب الزَلَم ولا فى لبّ القرطم ولا فى معك الغَنَم ولا فى الموز ولا فى مسح دماغ الخفاش بالاخمصين ولا فى لحم الحمام ولا فى قرفة القرنفل والّا لما ضننت عليك بشى لما تعلمين من فرط محبتى لك * فقالت له اذا كان الامر ياسيدى كما ذكرت فانى اختار قسيسا * قال ٥،١٩،٢
اى وسواس وسوس اليك هذا الاختيار الذى ليس من الخير فى شى * قالت اما اولا فلانّ الناس لا يسيئون به الظن اذا راوه داخلا الىّ كل يوم * والثانى انه يقال ان مادة القسيس متوفرة فيه * قال قد غويت ومع ذلك فانى اخشى منه على ولدىّ فانه ربما يغريهما بخلافى حالة كونى مخالفا له فى معتقده فالاولى ان تختارى آخر * قالت انت طبيب تعرف الصحيح من العليل والقوى من الضعيف فاختر لى ما تشآ فانى ارضى بكل ما ترضى به انت * قال بارك الله فيك * ثم قبّلها من فرحه ووعدها بانجاز عدته فى اليوم القابل * وما كاد يسفر الفجر الا وهو فوق حماره يقصد ٦،١٩،٢
بعض اصحابه * فلما اجتمع به قال له ان لى عندك حاجة جئت التمسها منك * قال قل ما بدا لك * قال على شرط ان لا تخيّبنى * قال سابذل مجهودى كله ان شاء الله فى قضآئها * فاخذ يده ع توثيقا للعهد ثم قال له انى اريد ان تكون خليفتى فى

been crushed with sugar and clarified butter or in wearing clothes dyed with Indian yellow or in eating mandrake root or in glasswort juice squeezed into fermented milk or in borax mixed with honey or in oil of jasmine or in Indian hazelnut or in fried *hamqāq*[285] or in terebinth or in burdock resin or in musk blended with gillyflower oil or in salvia root or in carrots or in asparagus or in Indian gooseberry or in *mughāth*[286] fruit or in fava-bean greens with ginger or in cassia ground with sesame and kneaded with honey or in mangrove gum or in bdellium or in terebinth fruits or in being censed seven times with lean meat of the Egyptian vulture mixed with mustard seed or in tigernut sedge or in safflower kernels or in rubbed red sand worms or in bananas or in wiping the soles of my feet with bats' brains or in pigeon flesh or in cassia bark; otherwise I would have spurned no possibility of making you happy, for the excessive affection that you know I bear you."

She replied, "If things stand as you say, sir, I choose a priest." "And what wicked tempter has whispered this utterly evil choice into your ear?" he asked. "Firstly," she answered, "it's so that people won't think badly of me when they see him entering my house every day, and secondly because they say that the priest has vital juices in abundance." "You err. Also, I fear what effect he may have on my children, for he may try to seduce them into disobeying me, given that I follow a different creed than he. You had better choose someone else." "You," she replied, "are a doctor and know the sound from the sick, the strong from the weak. Choose me whomever you please, and with whatever contents you I shall be content." "God bless you!" he responded. Then he kissed her, so joyful was he, and promised that he would do as he had promised the following day. 2.19.5

Dawn had hardly broken before he was on his donkey and making his way to one of his friends. When he met with him, he told him, "I have a request to make of you." "Ask away," said the other. "On condition that you don't refuse me," he said. When the other replied, "I shall devote all my effort, God willing, to fulfilling it," he took his hand to seal their agreement. Then he told him, "I want you to succeed me with regard to my wife." "Have you decided to quit Egypt and leave your wife behind?" the man asked him. "No," he said. "You'll succeed me while I'm still here." Offended, the man asked, "Has some doubt got into you as to whether I am truly your friend, making you seek covertly to uncover my innermost thoughts and private affairs?" 2.19.6

زوجتى * فقال له الرجل هل بدا لك سفرعن مصر وان تترك زوجتك هنا * قال لا وانما تكون خلافتك عنى فى حضورى * فاستآ الرجل وقال او خامرك ريب فى صداقتى لك حتى اضمرت استطلاع سرّى * وخفى امرى * فعند ذلك صرّح له بالقضية والحّ عليه فى القدوم معه * ولما ان قدما انعقد البيع بحضرة كلّ من الزوج والزوجة وتم التراضى * وصار الرجل مذ ذلك الوقت يتردد على دار الخلافة وبقى كذلك مدة * ثم ان الزوجة لما ملّته كما هى عادة النسآ وظهر له ذلك من قلة ٧،١٩،٢
احتفالها به مرة ومن اعتذارها اليه اخرى * جرى هو ايضا على عادة الرجال من انه افشى سرّها لصاحب له * فجرى هذا ايضا على جَدَد امثاله وجعل يتودد اليها وقام عنده مقام الاول * ثم ملّته فافشى سرها * ثم جاها آخر فقبلته * ثم آخر وآخرحتى صاروا جماعة عظيمة * ثم تراجع اليها احبّاوها الاوّلون وانهمكت فى التبديل والتغيير حتى صارت دار الطبيب كالمشرعة * ولم تكن هذه القضية قد شهرت فى مبادئها عند الجيران اذ كانوا يظنون القوم ياتون ليتداووا من علل بهم * ولكنها علمت بعد ذلك * وكان سببه ان الطبيب اتخذ له دارا اخرى خارج البلد ليصيف فيها وترك امراته فى الدار الاولى والزائرون على ما كانوا عليه من الورود والصدور * فتنبّه ح الناس لذلك * وفى هذا الوقت اى ورود ٨،١٩،٢
الخلق الى هذا المغنم البارد كان الفارياق المسكين يتردد على منزل الطبيب ليعلم ابنه ويتداوى * فظن الناس انه من جملة الزائرين * وتقلدوا اثمه فى اعناقهم الى يوم الدين * فانه كان معطّلا وفعله مُلغًى عن العمل * وبقى على تلك الحالة مدة من دون ان يرى فائدة من العلاج * فكأنّ الطبيب اراد ان تطول المدة عليه الى غاية تعليم ابنه * فمن ثم اقتصر الفارياق عن التردد اليه وتداوى عند غيره وشفى * وفى ٩،١٩،٢
خلال ذلك سافر الى الاسكندرية لمصلحة ما * فاجتمع فيها بواحد من الخرجيين

At this, the man made a clean breast of the matter and urged him to go with him. When they arrived, the deal was contracted in the presence of both husband and wife, and everyone was content, the man calling in daily from that time on at "the caliphal palace."[287]

Things went on this way for a while. Then, when the wife grew bored with the man, the way women do—a situation made apparent to him through her showing a lack of enthusiasm at the sight of him on one occasion and making of excuses on another—he in turn divulged her secret to a friend, the way men do. The latter followed the well-beaten path of others of his ilk, started playing court to her, and took the place of the first. Then she grew bored with him, and he told on her, and another came along, and she accepted him, and then another and another, until they'd become a mighty company. At this, her first lovers returned to her too, and she busied herself changing and exchanging until the doctor's house came to resemble nothing so much as a watering hole. In the beginning, the affair acquired no notoriety with the neighbors because they thought that all those people were coming to be treated for some illness. Later, however, it got out, because the doctor took a second home outside the country in which to spend the summer and left his wife in the first, where the visitors continued to come and go just as before, so people caught on. 2.19.7

Now, at the very time when all these good folk had been turning up to avail themselves of that cold feast, the poor Fāriyāq had been frequenting the doctor's house to give his son lessons and receive treatment, and, as a result, everyone suspected that he was one of those visitors, a sin they will carry round their necks till the Day of Judgment,[288] for he was hors de combat and wasn't up to doing anything anyway.[289] He went on like that for a while without seeing any improvement from the treatment, as though the doctor wanted to drag out the time till he'd finished teaching his son. Consequently, the Fāriyāq cut short his visits, sought treatment with another, and was cured. 2.19.8

While this was going on, he traveled to Alexandria on some business and there met with a righteous Bag-man, who asked him to go back to Cairo with him to teach some pupils in his house, and this he did, though he was interested only because the Bag-men are prompt in paying those who work for them. During this period too, it occurred to him to study prosody, so he embarked 2.19.9

الصالحين * فساله هذا ان يرجع معه الى مصر ليعلم عنده بعض تلاميذ فاجابه الى ذلك * وانما رغب فيه لكون الخرجيّين لا يوخرون اجرة من يعمل لهم * وفى اثنآء هذا عنّ له ان يقرا علم العروض * فاخذ فى قراة شرح الكافى على الشيخ محمد * فما كاد يختمه حتى فشا الطاعون بمصر * فاشتد بالمولى الخرجى الحرص على حياته ابقآءً للمصلحة الخرجية كما زعم * فمن ثم راى ان يتباعد عن وهدة الفخ قليلا لكيلا ينطبق عليه فيفجع الخرجيون امثاله بفقده فيكون فقده سببا فى فقد غيره * اذ قد تقرر عندهم ان شدة الحزن تميت * فجعل الفارياقَ مع الخِرّيجين الخُرَيْجيين ومع رجل لبيب ذى خبرة بالعلاج المانع من عدوى الطاعون * ثم استصحب ما لزم له وفرّ الى الصعيد وتفصيل ذلك فى الفصل الاتى *

on a reading of *Sharḥ al-Kāfī* (*The Commentary on the Kāfī*)[290] under Shaykh Muḥammad. He barely had time to finish the book before plague broke out in Cairo. At this the Lord caused the Bag-man to feel extreme concern for his own life—out of a desire to ensure the preservation of the Bag-men's interests, as he claimed—and he decided, as a result, to put a little distance between him and the trap that had been dug so he wouldn't find himself buried inside it, thus resulting in a loss that would have inflicted on other Bag-men like him intolerable grief, which would in turn have led to the loss of yet others, for they hold it as a firm belief that extreme sorrow leads to death. He therefore put the Fāriyāq with the graduate Baguettes plus a clever man who had experience in preventive treatment of the bubonic infection, and then gathered to him his own and fled to Upper Egypt,
details to follow in the next chapter.

الفصل العشرون

في معجزات وكرامات

كان عند الخرجى المذكور خادمة رعبوبة من اهل بلاده * فلما عزم على الفرار راى ١,٢٠,٢
ان يغادرها فى منزله لتصون حاجته فيه * وانما ابَى ان يستصحبها معه لانه كان متزوجا بامراة هى دونها فى الحسن * كما جرت العادة فى بلاد الافرنج من ان الخادمة غالبا تكون فوق مخدومتها فى القسامة والجمال ودونها فى الدراية والمعارف * فوقع فى خاطر زوجته انه اذا نشبت فيها عوالق الخ اوّلا ربما اتخذ زوجها تلك الخويدمة فى فراشها وطاب عنها نفسا * وان اوّل شى تتعلمه البنت من امها قبل زواجها هو منع الاسباب التى تبعث زوجها على الاستغناء عن شخصها او عن ذكرها * ولذلك كان من عادة نسآ الافرنج ان يهدين الى بعولتهن صورهن وان كانت شنيعة
ليجعلوها فى قمصهم * او خصلا من شعورهن وان تكن حمرآ ليتختموا بها * ثم بدا ٢,٢٠,٢
مشكل آخر * وهو ان الخادمة اذا بقيت وحدها فى الدار لم تامن من ان يتسّور عليها احد فى الليل فيقع المحذور * ويحمى التنّور * ويكسر المجبور * ويمّد المجزور * ويطم المحفور * ويذال المذخور * ويحرث البور * وتفك الطلاسم عن المسحور * ويفتق المشصور * ويسمد الصُعْبور * ويوسع الصُنبور * ويبعثر المطمور * وتذلّل العبسور * ويصدع الفاثور * ويخرب القهقور * وينقر فى الناقور * فتتلّم شوكة الزنبور * فارتاى بعد ان رفع يديه بالابتهال الى الله تعالى ان يضمّ اليها رجلا من اهل بلاده

Chapter 20

Miracles and Supernatural Acts

The aforementioned Bag-man had living with him a fresh-faced, comely serving girl from his own country. When he resolved to flee, he decided to leave her in his house to look after his things, refusing to take her with him because he was married to a woman less beautiful than she, it being the custom in the lands of the Franks for maids to be, for the most part, superior to their mistresses in form and beauty, though inferior in knowledge and education. It therefore occurred to the wife that, should she fall into the trap before he did, her husband might take the little maid into his bed and find her more to his liking. She recalled too that the first thing a girl learns from her mother before she gets married is how to prevent anything that might lead her husband to do without her, in her presence or in her absence, which is why most Frankish women give their husbands their pictures, even if they be ugly, to wear inside their shirts, or locks of their hair, even if it be red, to wear in a ring. 2.20.1

Then another issue arose, to wit, that if the maid stayed on in the house alone, she would be exposed to the danger of someone climbing the wall to get at her by night, in which case the unthinkable would come to pass, and the once cold oven be *heated*, broken would be the bone that once was set and turned again the tide that had *retreated*, the well once dug would be choked with silt, and what had been stored would be *depleted*, the fallow would be turned, the spells that had protected *deleted*, the seam that had been sewn would be *unpicked*, the pinhead stand *erect*, the pipe once narrow be *rebored*, the grain spilt from the silo where it once was *stored*, the swift, headstrong she-camel be broken to the *rein*, the golden table cleft in *twain*, the cairn *o'erthrown*, the trumpet *blown*, and, as a result, the hornet's stinger 2.20.2

نحيفا قشعوما * اعتقاد انه لا يقدر على ارتكاب شى من الافعال التى جرّت هذه القوافى المتعددة * وذلك من جملة الاغلاط الفاضحة التى اشتهرت بين الناس * اعنى انهم يظنون فى الغالب من دون مراجعة النسآ والاستشهاد بقولهن ان النحيف لا يقدر على ما يقدر عليه السمين * وكان الاولى ان لا يستبدّوا برايهم

فى ذلك * فمكث القشعوم مع الخادمة فى اهنا عيش * اما ماكان من الخُرُنجيين ٣,٢٠,٢
فان مخرّجهم اى مربّيهم وكّل بهم ذلك الرجل اللبيب * واوعز اليه فى ان يحظرهن عن الخروج * وان لا يدع احدا من اقاربهم يدخل اليهم * وان يستخدم رجلا ليشترى لهم ما يلزم من الخارج * ولا يستلم منه شيا الا بعد ان يغمسه فى الخلّ او يبخّره بالشيح * وغير ذلك مما عرف فى اصطلاح الافرنج لمنع اسباب الوباء * وكان هذا الوكيل من مشاهير علمآ ملّته * وكان فى مبدا امره كافرا لا يعتقد بدين من الاديان * لكنه كان حميد الخصال حسن الاخلاق * غير ان كفره حال بينه وبين رزقه فاضطر الى ان ينحاز الى الخرجيين من اهل بلاده * ففرحوا بهدايته كثيرا * واحسنوا اليه احسانا وفيرا * فانقلب هزله جدّا وتمكنت منه الوساوس والاوهام حتى اعتقد اخيرا انه اهل للكرامات والمعجزات * فكان يتمنّى ان تسنح له

فرصة لذلك * واتفق فى هذا الاوان ان مات بالطاعون ذلك الخادم الذى كان ٤,٢٠,٢
يشترى لوازم الدار * فلما جآء الدفّانون ليحملوه اعترضهم الوكيل من داخل الدار * فخافوا ان يخالفوه لكونه من الافرنج فان لهم عند اهل مصر حرمة زائدة * ثم انه مضى الى موضع منفرد وجثا على ركبتيه وهو يدعو الله سبحانه وتعالى لان يحقّق له صدق عقيدته * ثم فتح الباب وخرج والقى نفسه على جثة الميت وجعل فمه فى اذنه وهو يناديه قائلا * ياعبد الجليل (اسم الميت) انى ادعوك باسم المسيح ابن الله لان تعود من ظلمة الموت الى نور الحياة * ثم اصغى ليستمع الجواب فلم يجبه احد * فاشار الى الدفانين اَنِ اصبروا * ثم سار الى ذلك الموضع الذى صلّى

torn. He therefore saw fit, after first raising his hands to the Almighty in prayerful invocation, to add to her as reinforcement a thin little chit of a man of his country, in the belief that he'd be incapable of performing any of the acts that have drawn in their wake the preceding plethora of rhymes. This is one of a number of scandalous misconceptions that have become widespread, namely that people generally think, without first checking with women or taking their testimony into account, that the thin man isn't up to what the fat man can do; they'd be well advised not to be so opinionated.

The thin man thus stayed with the maid in the utmost felicity. As for the 2.20.3
Baguettes, the one who'd bagged them up (i.e., the one who'd raised them) entrusted their care to that clever man and instructed him to forbid them to leave the house and not to let any of their relatives enter to see them and to employ a man to buy them what they needed from the outside and to accept nothing from him until he had washed it in vinegar, censed it with wormwood, and done the other things that Franks conventionally do to keep away whatever may bring the plague. This agent was a famous scholar of his nation who had, at the beginning of his life, been an infidel, without belief in any religion, despite which he was of noble character and excellent morals. His unbelief, however, had stood in the way of his making a living, and he'd been forced to join sides with the Bag-men of his country, who, delighted at his having found his *Saviour*, bestowed upon him every *favor*. His light-hearted spirit now turned somber and became prey to devilish insinuations and delusions to the point that, in the end, he believed himself capable of performing extraordinary acts and miracles, for a chance to practice which he was always on the lookout.

It now happened that the servant who bought the supplies for the house 2.20.4
died of the plague. When the gravediggers came to carry him away, the agent prevented them from entering, and they were afraid to oppose him because he was a Frank, the Franks being regarded by the Egyptians with excessive respect. The man then proceeded to a place where he could be on his own and went down on his knees, praying to the Mighty and Glorious to give him evidence of the truth of his belief. Then he opened the door, came out, threw himself on top of the body of the deceased and put his mouth to his ear, crying, "'Abd al-Jalīl"—the dead man's name—"I call on you in the name of Christ the son of God to return from the darkness of death to the light of life!"

فيه اوّلا * وغيّر رِكعته بان جعل فمه بين فخذيه وهو يجمجم فى الدعآ وذلك على منوال الياس النبى حين صلّى لانزال المطر بعد ان قتل انبيآ بعل * وكان عددهم اربعمائة وخمسين نبيّا على ما ذكر فى الفصل الثامن عشر من سفر الملوك الاول * الا انّ بين الداعييَن فرقا * وهو ان النبى صلى هكذا بعد القتل وصاحبنا هذا قبل الاِحيآ * وكان الاولى ان يرفع عبد الجليل الى غرفة كما فعل النبى المذكور بابن الارملة التى كانت تعوله * وكان دعآوه الى الله لاحيائه ان قال ايها الرب
٢،٢٠،٥ الهى اجلبتَ الشرّ ايضا على هذه المراة بقتل ابنها الخ * ثم انه شبح يديه حتى صارت جثته على شكل صليب * ثم قام ناشطا مسرورا واسرع فى ان القى جثته على الميت واعاد فى اذنيه كلامه الاول * فلما لم يجبه احد وراى الميت لم يزل مفتوح الفم مطبق الجفنين ولم يمش مرة هنا ومرة هناك ولم يعطس سبع عطسات كما عطس ابن المراة الذى احياه النبى اليشع على ما ذكر فى الفصل الرابع من سفر الملوك الثانى * ذهب الى المطبخ وامر الطباخ بان يصنع له مرقة على الفور * فلما صبّت المرقة اقبل بها الى عبد الجليل وجعل يفرغ منها فى حلقه وذاك مشغول عنه بناكر ونكير * فلما اعياه امره امر الدفانين ان يحملوه وقال ما علىّ ذنب فى كونى لم ارد ان ابعثه وانما الذنب عليه * ثم اقبل الى حجرة الفارياق وقال له لا تواخذنى ياخليلي بعجزى عن احيآء الخادم فان زمن الانشار لمّا يبلغ * ولكنى لا اتراخى فى عقيدتى بان افعل ذلك المرة الآتية ان شاء الله * فلما سمع الفارياق ذلك اضطرب باله وثار دمه غيظا وحزنا * فاصابه فى ذلك اليوم الدآء الفاشى * فخرج تحت ابطه سلعة كالاترجة وحمّ واخذه صداع اليم * فاما الوكيل فلم يصبه شى * وذلك من
٢،٢٠،٦ الاسرار التى يعجز عن ادراكها الحكمآ * ثم ان الفارياق كان حال مرضه يفكّر فيما جرى عليه وهو وحيد غريب لا مونس عنده يسليه * ولا طبيب يداويه * وكان يقول فى نفسه اذا مت على هذه الحالة فمن عساه يتمتع بكتبى هذه التى سهرت

He cocked an ear to hear the reply, but no one answered, so he gestured to the gravediggers to be patient and went back to the same place in which he'd prayed the first time and changed his kneeling posture so that his mouth was now between his legs while he mumbled his prayers, after the manner of the Prophet Ilyās when he prayed for the rain to descend after killing the prophets of Baal (who were four hundred and fifty in number, according to 1 Kings 17). There was, however, a difference between the two praying persons, in that the prophet prayed thus after a killing, whereas our man prayed before a resurrection. It would have been more appropriate if he'd carried ʿAbd al-Jalīl up into a loft as the aforementioned prophet did with the son of the widow who had been sustaining him, his prayer to God to resurrect the man being, "O Lord my God, hast thou also brought evil upon the widow with whom I sojourn, by slaying her son?"[291] etc.

Next, the man spread out the arms of the corpse to make a cross, sprang happily to his feet, and made haste to throw his body onto that of the deceased, repeating his earlier words in its ear. When no one answered him and he saw that the dead man was still lying there with his mouth open and his eyelids closed and hadn't got up and walked around and about and hadn't sneezed seven times as did the widow's son raised by the Prophet al-Yashuʿ as mentioned in 2 Kings 4, he went to the kitchen and ordered the cook to make him some broth on the double. When the broth was poured, he took it to ʿAbd al-Jalīl and started emptying it down his throat, though the latter was too busy to pay attention as he was talking to Nākir and Nakīr. When all his efforts failed, he ordered the gravediggers to take him away, saying, "It's not my fault I didn't manage to resurrect him, it's his." Then he went to the Fāriyāq's room and said to him, "Excuse me, friend, for failing to resurrect the servant, but the time of resurrection is not yet come. Still, I shall not weaken in my faith that I shall do it next time, God willing." When the Fāriyāq heard this, he lost his composure and his blood rose in fury and sorrow, and on that same day the disease that was making the rounds afflicted him, a ganglion the size of a citron appeared in his armpit, he became feverish, and he got a painful headache. The agent, though, was unaffected, which is one of those mysteries that physicians cannot understand. 2.20.5

During his illness, the Fāriyāq pondered his situation, as a lone stranger with no companion to bring him *cheer*, no doctor to give him *care*. He said 2.20.6

الليالى على نسخها * نعم ان الموت على كل حال صعب مكروه غير ان موت الفتى مثلى غريبا اصعب * وانى قد ابتليت والحمد لله فى هذه المدينة بجميع انواع الادوآ المصبوغة بلون الحِمام * فاذا فسح الله الآن فى اجلى فلا افارق هذه الدنيا الا قرير العين بنجل يرثنى * وان لم يكن عندى من حطام الدنيا غير الكتب * كيف لا وقد جآء عن ابيشلوم ولد سيدنا داود انه بنى له جدارا ليذكر به بعد موته اذ لم يكن له خلف * فلاتزوجنّ فان لم ياتنى خلف فالطوب بمصر كثير * اللهم يسّر * غوثك
٧,٢٠,٢ ياكريم * يارحمان يارحيم * ثم لما كان يمعن النظر فى حال الزواج ويتصوّر مشاقّه وشدائده التى كان يرى اودّآءه ومعارفه يقاسونها وينّئون من باهظ حملها * يرجع عن عزمه ويسخر من استحالة عقله وضعف فهمه لضعف جسمه * ثم يعتذر لنفسه بان كل انسان اذا عاش مدة حياته على راى لم يوافق راى الجماعة * وكان يعتقد وهو حىّ صحيح الجسم معافى انهم كلهم على ضلال وانه هو وحده على هدى * فاذا ادركه ضعف جسم لم يلبث ان يتغير عقله فيميل عن مذهبه الاول * كما جرى لبيون الفيلسوف ولكثير غيره من الحكمآ والفلاسفة * ثم ان الله تعالى تدارك الفارياق برحمته * ومنّ عليه بالشفآء من علته * فقام من فراشه كانما قام من جَدَثه واقبل على الطنبور يعزف به ويغنى * فدعه الان على هذه الحالة ولا تنغص عليه عيشته * وشمر اذيالك معى

لنطفر فوق هذا الاجيج المتاجج

امامنا فيما

يلى

هذا

*

تم الكتاب الثانى

to himself, "If I should die now, who will benefit from these books of mine that I have spent so many nights in copying? True, death is hard and hateful under any circumstances, but for a young man like me to die in a strange land is harder still to bear. I have been afflicted in this city, praise God, with every kind of sickness that bears the tint of death. If God should now grant me a reprieve before my time is up, let me not leave this world without the solace of a son and heir, even if my worldly relics consist of nothing but my books. How can it be otherwise when Abīshalūm, son of Our Master Dā'ūd, built himself a wall[292] to be remembered by after his death because he had no children. Let me then marry; if I have no children, there are plenty of bricks in Egypt. God make smooth the path! Your aid, O Generous One, O Compassionate, O Merciful!"

Every time, however, he thought carefully about the married state and pictured the troubles and hardships from the devastating heaviness of whose load he'd seen his friends and acquaintances suffer and moan, he'd go back on his decision and laugh at how puerile his mind was and at the weakness of its ability to understand the weakness of his body. Then he'd exuse himself on the basis that anybody who had spent his whole life with opinions opposed to everyone else's and believing, when in good spirits, sound of body, and in good health, that all of them were in the wrong and he alone in the right, must inevitably quickly change his mind and reject his former way of thinking when afflicted by some bodily weakness. This is what happened to the philosopher Bion[293] and many other sages and philosophers. Then the Almighty made amends to the Fāriyāq with His *mercy* and granted him relief from *adversity*, and he rose from his bed like one rising from the tomb, went straight to his tambour, and played on it and sang. Leave him now in this state and do nothing to spoil his mood, 2.20.7

but gird instead your loins,
along with me,
and make ready to leap
the blazing bonfire that awaits us
in Book Three.

*

End of Book Two

Notes

1 "the Five Stars" (*al-nujūm al-khamsah*): the planets known to Islamic astronomy (Saturn, Jupiter, Mars, Venus, Mercury), called *khunnas* because they return (*takhnusu*) in their courses.

2 "the *Mijarrah*—'the gateway of the sky, or its anus'" (*mijarratuhā—bāb al-samāʾi aw sharajuhā*): the *Lisān* explains the first part of the gloss by the resemblance of the Milky Way to an arch.

3 "the *rujum*—'the stars used for stoning'" (*rujumuhā—al-nujūmu llatī yurmā bihā*): the stars with which God stones Satan, who is commonly referred to as *al-rajīm* for this reason; in popular belief, shooting stars (see, for Egypt, Lane, *Manners*, 223).

4 "the Two Calves" (*al-farqadayn*): stars γ and β in Ursa Minor (the Little Dipper); also known as Pherkad and Kochab (*al-kawkab*).

5 "all those gazettes" (*fī hādhihi l-waqāʾiʿ al-ikhbāriyyah*): no doubt a reference to *Al-Waqāʾiʿ al-Miṣriyyah*, on which see further n. 132 to 2.11.5 below.

6 "Friends of God" (*awliyāʾ Allāh*): individuals believed to be chosen by God for special favor; sometimes they manifest unusual spiritual powers.

7 "to bring about divorces" (*li-l-taṭlīq*): a reference, perhaps, to the notary (*maʾdhūn*) who gives formal recognition to a divorce.

8 "as a legitimizer" (*li-l-taḥlīl*): if a Muslim man divorces his wife three times—thus irrevocably—and then regrets his act, he may hire a man (known as a *muḥallil*, approx. "legitimizer") to marry her and then divorce her, rendering remarriage legally possible.

9 Though the references in the following passage are, in some cases, at least, to recognized rhetorical figures, their precise meaning is less important than the impression of erudite obfuscation that they convey.

10 "the method of the sage" (*uslūb al-ḥakīm*): taking advantage of an inappropriate or unanswerable question to open a more important discussion.

11 "person-switching" (*iltifāt*): a rhetorical figure consisting of an "abrupt change of grammatical person from second to third and from third to second," as in the words of the poet Jarīr "When were the tents at Dhū Ṭulūḥ? O tents, may you be watered by ample rain!" (Meisami and Starkey, *Encyclopedia*, 2:657).

12 "tight weaving" (*iḥtibāk*): a rhetorical figure defined, in a widely taught formulation (http://www.alfaseeh.com/vb/showthread.php?t=9355), as "the omission from the

earlier part of the utterance of something whose equal or equivalent comes in the later, and the omission from the later of something whose equal or equivalent comes in the earlier"; an example is the Qur'ānic verse "a company that fights for God and a disbelieving company" (Q Āl 'Imrān 3:13), meaning "a [believing] company that fights for God and a disbelieving company [that fights for the Devil]."

13 "an Arabized word": via Latin, from Greek *manganon.*

14 "like common caltrops" (*'alā mithāl al-ḥasak al-ma'rūf*): i.e., like starweed (*Centaurea calcitrapa*), whose spiked seed-cases pierce sandals and feet when stepped on.

15 "a padded outer garment . . . a weapon . . . thick shields": the confusion as to the word's meaning seems to stem from its foreign, probably Persian, origin.

16 "a device for war worn by horse and man alike": cataphract armor.

17 *al-'adhrā'*: literally, "the virgin"—"a kind of collar by means of which the hands, or arms, are confined together with the neck" (Lane, *Lexicon*).

18 Jadīs and Ṭasm: related tribes of 'Ād, a pre-Islamic people destroyed, according to the Qur'an, for their ungodliness.

19 al-'Abbās ibn Mirdās: an early Meccan convert to Islam who burned al-Dimār, the idol of his clan.

20 'Amr ibn Luḥayy: a leader of Mecca in the Days of Barbarism, and supposedly the first to introduce the worship of idols into the Arabian Peninsula.

21 "Ilyās, peace be upon him": Ilyās (Elias) is regarded in Islam as a prophet.

22 "'Urwah's hadith 'al-Rabbah'" (*ḥadīth 'Urwatin al-Rabbah*): the tradition recounts that a recent convert to Islam, 'Urwah ibn Mas'ūd, was refused entry to his home unless he first visited "al-Rabbah" (literally, "the Mistress"), "meaning al-Lāt, which is the rock that [the tribe of] Thaqīf used to worship at al-Ṭā'if" (see Ibn al-Athīr, *Al-Nihāyah,* 1:56).

23 Dhāt 'Irq: a place, 92 kilometers north of Mecca.

24 "*Furdūd*, Pherkad . . . *Kuwayy*": names of stars in this list that have accepted English names (all but one of which in fact derive from Arabic) are printed in regular font, while those impossible to identify from the extensive list provided by the Wikipedia article "List of Arabic Star Names" are transcribed in italics.

25 "instruments that . . .": see the Translator's Afterword (Volume Four) on the choice of synonyms in this passage; note that, while the Arabic list contains forty-eight items, only forty-five are represented in the translation, because three (*daghz*, *zazz*, and *waqz*) could not be found in the dictionaries.

26 "headgear of a generic nature" (*'imārāt*): *'imārah* is defined in the *Qāmūs* as "anything worn on the head, be it a turban (*'imāmah*), a cap (*qalansuwah*), a crown (*tāj*), or anything else."

27 "watermelon-shaped . . . cantaloupe-shaped . . . caps" (*bi-arāṣīṣ . . . bi-arāsīs*): while the author, in this footnote, specifies the shape of the former, the dictionaries say of the latter merely that it is "a cap" (*qalansuwah*); however, it seems to be a variant of the first.

28 "judges' tun-caps" (*danniyyāt*): so called from their resemblance to a *dann* or large wine barrel.

29 "antimacassars" (*ṣawāqiʿ*): cloths worn by a woman on her head to protect her veil from grease (*Qāmūs*).

30 "pass their hands over what is in front of the latter" (*yatamassaḥūna bi-mā amāmahu*): the significance is unclear; the *Qāmūs* cites the usage *yutamassaḥu bi-hi* ("people pass their hands over him/it,") and says that it means *yutabarraku bi-hi li-faḍlihi* ("blessing is derived from him because of his/its virtue"). This brings to mind the habit of visitors to certain mosques of passing their hands over the grills enclosing saints' tombs in the belief that they will thus obtain *barakah* ("grace").

31 "*underwear*" (*andarward*): the English word is probably intended; *andarward* may be due to a mishearing by the author or possibly a joke (*andar-ward* "under-roses").

32 i.e., must never stop calling out pious phrases to warn those around him of his presence or that he is "coming through."

33 "As God wills! . . . O God!" (*mā shāʾa llāh . . . Allāh*): typical expressions of delight, pleasure, and appreciation, all of which invoke God's name to protect the one praised from the possible effects of envy.

34 "her peepings through her fingers against the sun to see . . . , her shading of her eyes against the sun to see and her peering through her fingers against the sun to see" (*istikfāfihā . . . wa-stīḍāḥihā wa-stishfāfihā*): all defined in the *Qāmūs* as synonyms.

35 "a fourth way of walking, with further letters changed" (*wa-qahbalatihā*): again, defined in the *Qamūs* as "a way of walking."

36 "a fifth way of walking, with further letters changed" (*hayqalatihā*): again, defined in the *Qamūs* as "a way of walking."

37 "her walking with tiny steps" (*khadhʿalatihā*): the *Qāmūs* defines again as "a way of walking"; however, a second sense given is "cutting a watermelon etc. into small pieces."

38 "her marching proudly (spelled two ways)" (*tabahrusihā wa-tahabrusihā*): synonyms, meaning *tabakhtur* ("strutting"), according to the *Lisān* (s.v. *tabahrasa*).

39 "the same said another way" (*wa-unufihā*): synonym of the preceding item, according to the *Qāmūs*.

40 "two lines": four hemistichs, each hemistich starting here on a new line.

41 The word *muʿqanafishan* has not been found in any dictionary, but cf. *ʿaqanfas*, variant of *ʿafanqas* "ill-tempered, base" (*ʿasir al-akhlāq laʾīm*).

42 "*bardhaʿah*s . . . *ikāf*s . . . *qitbah*s . . . *bāṣar*s": all types of saddle.

43 "with a thread of paper" (*bi-khayṭin min al-kāghid*): perhaps referring to the domination of the bureaucracy by Turks.

44 "leading . . . 'leading' him" (*yaqūdu . . . yaqūdūna lahu*): the author plays with two senses of the verb, *qāda* "to lead" and *qāda li-* "to pimp for."

45 "*bakalım kapalım* ('let's see-bee')": the phrase is constructed by adding a non-existent word *kapalım* to the genuine word *bakalım* ("let's see") thus mimicking such genuine Turkish rhyming couplets as the preceding.

46 "*Ghaṭāliq* . . . ": most of the supposed Turkish of the following lines is in fact nonsense, though it does contain distinctive Turkish features, such as the ending *-lik/lıq*; the first hemistich of the last line does make sense in Turkish ("They're like donkeys too, by God!"), and the second hemistich of the same line can be read as near-meaningless Arabic ("Their troubles are their confusions").

47 "head . . . tail": by "head" the author may mean the promontory of Raʾs al-Tīn ("the Head(land) of the Figs") and by "tail" the land end of that promontory, where the popular quarter of Anfūshī, home to the city's fish market, is situated.

48 Qayʿar Qayʿār: an invented name that may be translated as something like "Plummy Pompous," from the literal senses of *qayʿar* and *qayʿār*, both of which mean one who "speaks affectedly and from the back of his mouth" (*tashaddaqa wa-takallama bi-aqṣā famihi*). If we follow the clues offered by the similarly coded name Baʿīr Bayʿar (= al-Amīr Ḥaydar (1.5.2)), we may suppose that the first name of this individual may have been Ḥaydar, while the second may have been Bayṭār or another name of the same pattern. However, it is also possible that a European was intended (see next endnote).

49 "the Himyaritic lands" (*al-bilād al-Ḥimyariyyah*): i.e., southern Arabia, though the orthography also allows the reading *al-bilād al-ḥamīriyyah*, meaning "the lands of the donkeys," and it is unclear whether the Fāriyāq is referring to an Arab or a "Frank"; some phrases and topoi in the passage that follows are reminiscent of those used when Franks are lampooned for their bad Arabic, as in the following chapter.

50 "the science of 'subjects' and 'objects'" (*ʿilm al-fāʿil wa-l-mafʿūl*): i.e., Arabic grammar.

51 "chronograms" (*ʿilm al-jummal*): each letter of the Arabic alphabet has a conventionally assigned numerical value under a system known as *hisāb al-jummal*. The construction of chronograms capable of being read both as words and as dates became a common feature of congratulatory poetry starting in the ninth/fifteenth century. For examples, see Volume Four, section 4.20.13.

52 *ʿĪsā*: a proper name, cognate with "Jesus."

53 "within this p'tcher" (*fī hādhā l-kuzz*): *kuzz* appears to be a nonce-word derived from the common word *kūz* by shortening the vowel and doubling the second consonant, the charlatan teacher's idea being that the word needs to contain a doubled consonant (*shadda*, a word conveying the idea of "tightening") to fit with something that is "confined"; the same logic might apply to *zanbīl/zabbīl* below, though both forms in this case are genuine.

54 "*khams daqāʾiq* . . . and not *khamsah daqāʾiq*": the humor lies in the author's attribution of an irrelevant cause to a grammatical rule, the rule in this case being that a feminine noun (here the implied *daqīqah*, singular of *daqāʾiq*) is preceded by the shorter, masculine, number form when counted.

55 "because each is a 'congregator of fineness' (*jāmiʿ al-nuʿūmah*)": the language is that of rhetorical theory, which would claim that the words for "flour" and "minutes" share the same consonantal root (*d-q-q*) because flour consists of finely ground grain while minutes are fine divisions of hours, and the phrase might more accurately be rendered "because they share the common factor of fineness"; however, the wording is primarily a set-up for the play on words that follows a little later.

56 "The first six have 'parts' at either end" (*al-sitt al-ʾūlā fī-hā farq*): i.e., "have distinct beginnings and endings"; however, *sitt* ("six") also means in the Egyptian dialect "lady, mistress" (from *sayyidah*), while *farq* ("dividing, partitioning") also means a "parting" as a way of dressing the hair; thus, the words are a set-up to allow the joke that follows.

57 "Nuʿūmah Mosque" (*jāmiʿ al-nuʿūmah*): while *jāmiʿ* is, as the shaykh will explain, an active participle, of the verb *jamaʿa, yajmaʿu* ("to gather together, collect, congregate"), it is also used in common parlance as a substantive meaning "mosque."

58 "ʿUdhrah . . . Virgin . . . must be stretched out" (*ʿUdhrah . . . ʿadhrāʾ . . . yajibu madduhā*): the learned monk wrote of a tribe famous for the celebration by its poets of passionate but unconsummated love; however, the ignorant Qayʿar Qayʿār, seeing *ʿUdhrah*, thinks that the monk intended *ʿadhrāʾ* ("virgin"), which should be pronounced with a long vowel at the end (*madd*), though in the colloquial it is pronounced with a short vowel. Thus, while stating a correct grammatical rule (the word for "virgin" should be written with *–āʾ* at the end), he demonstrates that "a little learning is a dangerous thing."

59 "*daʿawtu ʿalayh . . . ṣallaytu ʿalayh*": the use of a preposition after a verb in Arabic, as in other languages, may modify the sense of the verb. Thus plain *daʿawtu* and *ṣallaytu* both mean "I prayed," but *daʿawtu ʿalayh* means "I cursed him" whereas *ṣallaytu ʿalayh* means "I prayed for him."

60 "*tashīl... ishāl*": verbs with the consonant-vowel patterns CVCCVCV (verbal noun form $taC_1C_2\bar{i}C_3$) and VCCVCV (verbal noun form $iC_1C_2\bar{a}C_3$) may have causative or declarative sense relative to the semantic area of the three-consonant root. Thus, from the root *s-h-l*, associated with "ease," are created the verbs *sahhala* (*tashīl*) and *ashala* (*ishāl*). Each, however, has a different denotation. Thus, *sahhala* means "to make easy, facilitate," while *ashala* means "to be struck with diarrhea."

61 Many of the words used in the letter are double entendres or malapropisms, as follows: "sodomitical"—*ibnī* "filial" may be read as *ubnī* (from *ubnah* ("passive sodomy")); "penetrated it"—*awlajtu* should mean "I caused to enter" and is often used in connection with sexual intercourse, but here is used intransitively; "the shittiest part"—*ukhrāh* "its end" is both a deformation of *ākhiratihi* and also may be read *akhra'ihi* (from *kharā'* ("excrement")); "excrements"—*al-fuḍūl* may mean either "(bodily) wastes" or "merits, favors"; "creator of pestilence"—*al-fuṣūl* may mean either "chapters" or "plagues"; "a 'congregator' of both the branches of knowledge and its roots"—the word *jāmiʿ* appears to be used here simply to maintain the running joke relating to "congregator/mosque," which is resumed in the immediately following passage; "long of tongue"—*ṭawīl al-lisān* may intend "eloquent" but idiomatically means "impertinent"; "with 'ands too short to"—*qaṣīr al-yadāni ʿan* commits, for the sake of the rhyme, the gross grammatical error of *al-yadāni* for *al-yadayni*; "of broad little brow"—reading *wāsiʿ al-jubayn* (counterintuitively in the diminutive) for the expected *wāsiʿ al-jabīn* ("broad of brow"); "wide waistcoated"— reading *ʿarīḍ al-ṣudar* (from *ṣudrah* "waistcoat") for the expected *ʿarīḍ al-ṣadr* ("wide of breast, magnanimous"); "deeply in debt"—reading *ʿamīq al-dayn* for the expected *ʿamīq al-dīn* ("deeply religious"); and "of ideas bereft"—reading *mujawwaf al-fikar* for *mujawwif al-fikr* ("pentrating of thought"), itself probably a spurious locution.

62 "The Extraction of the Fāriyāq from Alexandria, by Sail" (*Fī-nqilāʿ al-Fāriyāq min al-Iskandariyyah*): the base sense of *inqilāʿ* is "to pull up by the roots," but the references to sailing in the first paragraph indicate that the author is simultaneously implying the concoction of a humorous new sense derived from *qilʿ* "sail," which has the same root as *inqilāʿ*.

63 al-Ṣāḥib ibn al-ʿAbbād : 326–85/938–95, vizier to the Būyid rulers of Iran; the verses evoke such Qur'anic passages as "And unto Solomon (We subdued) the wind and its raging" (Q Anbiyā' 21:81).

64 The priest substitutes letters he can pronounce for those he cannot. Thus he says *hā'* (*h*) for *ḥ* (*ḥā'*) as in *al-rahmān* for *al-raḥmān* ("the merciful"), for *ʿayn* (ʿ) as in *hitābukum* for *ʿitābukum* ("censuring you"), for *khā'* (*kh*) as in *al-mihaddah* for *al-mikhaddah* ("the

bolster"), and for the glottal stop (ʾ) as in *rahzan* for *raʾsan* ("resolutely"); *hamzah* (ʾ) for *ʿayn* (ʿ) as in *al-ʾālam* for *al-ʿālam* ("the world"); *kāf* (*k*) for *qāf* (*q*) as in *akūl* for *aqūl* ("I say"), for *khāʾ* (*kh*) as in *akshā* for *akhshā* ("I fear"), and for *ghayn* (*gh*) as in *mashkūl* for *mashghūl* ("busy"); *sīn* (*s*) for *ṣād* (*ṣ*) as in *nasārā* for *naṣārā* ("Christians") and for *thāʾ* (*th*) as in *akassir* for *akaththir* ("I repeat often") ; *dāl* (*d*) for *ḍād* (*ḍ*) as in *al-hādirīn* for *al-ḥāḍirīn* ("those present"); *tāʾ* (*t*) for *ṭāʾ* (*ṭ*) as in *tūlihi* for *ṭūlihi* ("its length"); and *zayn* (*z*) for *dhāl* (*dh*) as in *lazzāt* for *ladhdhāt* ("pleasures") and for *ẓāʾ* (*ẓ*) as in *mawhizatī* for *mawʿiẓatī* ("my counsel"); *s* for *th* and *z* for *dhāl* are also common "errors" of native speakers. Sometimes the same letter is used with different values in the same word as in *al-akdak* for *al-aghdaq* ("the most bountiful"), or all the letters in a words are changed, as in *al-sukh* for *al-ṣuqʿ* ("the region"). These changes sometimes result in the production of meaningful words (e.g., *kalbukum* ("your dog") for *qalbukum* ("your heart")) but more often in nonsense, e.g., *rahmān* and *rahīm*.

65 "the Arabic-language-challenged . . . Sponging . . . Aleppine" (*al-Ḥalabī al-Bushkānī . . . al-Immaʿī . . .*): names of prominent persons are often followed by a series of attributive adjectives ending in *-ī* (*nisbahs*) indicating pedigree, place of origin, place of residence, legal school, etc.; here only *al-Ḥalabī* ("of Aleppo") is a real *nisbah*; the rest are made by adding *-ī* to words associated with gluttony, parasitism, and ignorance of Arabic.

66 Metropolitan Atanāsiyūs al-Tutūnjī (or Athanāsiyūs al-Tūtunjī) (d. 1874), Melkite bishop of Tripoli from 1836, was dismissed for scandalous behavior and spent some time in England in the early 1840s seeking to promote union between the Anglican and Eastern churches. The author hated him because he denigrated the translation of the Book of Common Prayer on which the author was then engaged for the Society for the Propagation of Christian Knowledge (SPCK) and suggested that he could do better. He did in fact produce a specimen, which al-Shidyāq saw, whereupon he sent the SPCK (in March 1844) "an Arabic Poem expressing the ungenerous behaviours of the Society for Promotion of Christian Knowledge . . . in having employed in my stead an ignorant person [i.e., al-Tutūnjī]—not withstanding I have addressed them in two letters respecting the numerous grammatical mistakes he has committed" (letter in English in the Church Missionary Society; I am indebted to Geoffrey Roper for this information); subsequently, the SPCK changed its view and reinstated al-Shidyāq as their translator. The author alludes to this imbroglio and a further spat between him and al-Tutūnjī in Book Three (3.18.1).

67 *Al-Ḥakākah fī l-rakākah* (*The Leavings Pile Concerning Lame Style*): we have failed to identify the original of the work whose title is parodied here; according to Georg Graf, al-Tutūnjī wrote only on theological and ecclesiastical matters (see Graf, *Geschichte*,

3:278), but this and further references here (3.5.14, 3.18.1) imply that he was active in the teaching of language and translation.

68 "or . . .": the *Qāmūs* continues "to ʿAdawl, a man who used to make the ships, or to a people who used to camp in Hajar."

69 The verse is attributed to ʿAlī ibn al-Jahm (ca. 188–249/804–63).

70 "their cousins": i.e., the Roman Catholic Maltese.

71 Khalīl ibn Aybak al-Ṣafadī (d. 764/1363): a litterateur whose works include *Lawʿat al-shākī wa-damʿat al-bākī* (*The Plaint of the Lovelorn and Tears of the Disconsolate*), which describes the agonies of love.

72 "his 'stable management (of affairs),' his 'leadership qualities,' and his 'horse sense'" (*al-siyāsah wa-l-qiyādah wa-l-firāsah/farāsah*): the humor lies in the fact that each word has one meaning appropriate to the donkey-boy's supposed elevated state and another appropriate to his actual occupation; thus *siyāsah*, whose original sense is "the management of animals" also means "the management of men," and thence "rule," while *qiyādah* originally meant "the leading of horses, or caravans" and thence "command (e.g., of an army)"; *firāsah* means "horsemanship," while *farāsah* (the two forms being indistinguishable in unvowelled writing) means "intuitive perception."

73 *ʿanmī*: after the red fruit of the *ʿanam* (pomegranate) tree.

74 [?]: *ghurmah*, a word not found in the dictionaries.

75 Sūrat Nūn: i.e., Sūrat al-Qalam (sura 68), which begins with the initial *nūn* and is thus appropriate for a *nūnah* ("cleft in the chin").

76 "I am copying them from one who looked deeply into every veiled face(t)" (*nāqilan lahu ʿamman tabaṣṣara l-wajha l-maḥjūb*): meaning that definitions that the author provides above are those of the author the *Qāmūs*, who, as a lexicographer, has looked deeply into every facet of the meaning of each word just as, as a man, he has looked deeply into the veiled faces of women (*wajh* means both "face" and "facet").

77 "hasn't seen her as did Our Master Yaʿqūb": cf. Gen. 29:10–11 "Jacob saw Rachel . . . and Jacob kissed Rachel."

78 "Professors Amorato . . ." (*al-Ṣabābātī . . .*): given their form, it is clear that these fictitious but contextually appropriate names are intended to represent scholars, as are those a few lines below.

79 "the letter *ṣād* . . . the letter *mīm*" (*al-ṣādī wa-l-mīmī*): *ṣād* ( ) was used conventionally, because of its shape, as a coded reference to the vagina and *mīm* ( ) to the anus.

80 Cairo (*Miṣr*): the author uses the word, as Egyptians often do, to refer to the capital city rather than the country as a whole.

81 "answering to the needs of hot-humored men (contrary to what ʿAbd al-Laṭīf al-Baghdādī has said)": in his brief description of Cairo, al-Baghdādī (557–629/1162–1231), a scholar from Baghdad, writes that "you rarely find among them diseases exclusively of the bile; indeed, the most prevalent types are those of the sputum, even among the youth and the hot-humored (*al-shabāb wa-l-maḥrūrīn*)" (al-Baghdādī, *Ifādah,* 18), a comment to which the author gives an insinuating twist not intended by the original.

82 The precise meaning or historical referent of a number of these teasingly described "curiosities" is unclear, and most of interpretations offered in the following notes are tentative.

83 "on the ceiling or the walls": perhaps a reference to depictions of women (or goddesses or nymphs) on the walls and ceilings of buildings done in the European style.

84 "the treatment of the feminine as masculine and of the masculine as feminine" (*tadhakkur al-muʾannath wa-taʾannuth al-mudhakkar*): while the comment appears to refer to a linguistic practice, it is hard to know exactly which, as there is no whole-scale reversal of, for instance, noun gender in Egyptian Arabic vis-à-vis literary Arabic; perhaps the author has in mind the word *raʾs* ("head"), which is most often masculine in literary (and Levantine) Arabic but is feminine in its Egyptian form (*rās*), or the use of *ḥabībī* ("my dear," masculine) as a term of endearment among women or *bāsha* ("pasha") by men as a flirtatious term of address to a woman.

85 "in their bathhouses they constantly recite a sura or two of the Qurʾan that mention 'cups' and 'those who pass around with them,'" a reference to either Sūrat al-Zukhruf (Q Zukhruf 43:71 "*yuṭāfu ʿalayhim bi-ṣiḥāfin min dhahabin wa-akwāb*"—"There shall be passed among them platters of gold and cups") or similarly Sūrat al-Insān (Insān 76:15); the author may be implying that the presence in the bathhouses of young boys offering refreshment stimulates the patrons into uttering these verses. Lane, in fact, states that it is considered improper to recite the Qurʾan in a bathhouse, as such places are inhabited by jinn (Lane, *Manners,* 337).

86 "many of the city's men have no hearts" etc.: perhaps meaning that they prefer sex to love.

87 "they took to lopping off their fingers" (*fa-jaʿalū yashdhibūna aṣābiʿahum*): perhaps a reference to the chopping off of the index finger of the right hand by young men so as to render themselves incapable of pulling a trigger and hence unfit for military service, which was introduced by Egypt's ruler, Muḥammad ʿAlī, in the 1820s.

88 "veil their beards" (*yubarqiʿuna liḥāhum*): according to the *Qāmūs*, the expression means "to become a passive sodomite" (*ṣāra maʾbūnan*).

89 "Sons of Ḥannā": if the correction of the original from Ḥinnā is correct, this probably is a reference to Copts (Ḥannā is a common name among Christians).

90 "a way of writing that is known to none but themselves": Ottoman financial documents were written in a script known as *qirmah* (perhaps from Turkish *kırmak* "to break"), developed from the *ruqʿah* script, that was indecipherable to the uninitiated and so small that upward of thirty words and figures might be inscribed within an area of 1.5 square centimetres; it was not, in fact, peculiar to Egypt, but was introduced there by the Ottoman authorities (see El Mouelhy, "Le Qirmeh,").

91 "his family wail and keen over him in the hope that he will return to them": perhaps the author is implying jokingly that such excessive (as he sees it) mourning must be intended to ensure the return of the deceased with gifts from the next world.

92 "ignoble birds . . . may pretend to be mighty eagles" (*al-bughāth . . . yastansir*): a well-known idiom describing presumptuous behavior by the lowly.

93 "the exiguously monied one (meaning the owner of the money)" (*al-muflis ay ṣāḥib al-fulūs*): the author knows that the reader is likely to understand *muflis* in its common sense of "bankrupt," whereas he is using it in its original dictionary definition of "endowed with copper coins (after having owned silver coins)" (*Qāmūs*).

94 "the rise in her fortunes came from her setting herself down" (*ṭāliʿuhā min maḥallihā*): it is supposed that unmarried guests at weddings often to meet their own future spouses there.

95 "'a kind of joking back and forth that resembles mutual insult'" (*mufākahah tushbihu l-sibāb*): this definition of *mujārazah* is from the *Qāmūs*; from the description, *anqāṭ* resemble the twentieth-century pun-based *qāfiyah*, on which see Amīn, *Qāmūs*, 317–18.

96 "Its viceroy" (*wālīhā*): Muḥammad ʿAlī Pasha, who ruled as an autonomous viceroy on behalf of the Ottoman sultan from 1805 to 1848 and laid the foundations of the modern Egyptian state.

97 By the time of the publication of *Al-Sāq*, the author had attracted the favorable notice of the ruler of Tunis by writing odes in his praise and had twice visited the city, in 1841 and 1847 (see 3.18.3, 4.8.2). Later (1857–59), he would take up residence in Tunis and work for its government.

98 "a poet of great skill": identified by one scholar as Naṣr al-Dīn al-Ṭarābulsī (1770–1840), a Catholic from Aleppo who immigrated to Egypt in 1828 and came to direct the Arabic-language section of *Al-Waqāʾiʿ al-Miṣriyyah*, where the author was later employed (al-Maṭwī, *Aḥmad*, 1:76); elsewhere (2.10.1), the author refers to him as "Khawājā Yanṣur."

99 al-Āmidī: see 1.11.1. Al-Āmidī's detailed comparison of the poets al-Buḥturī and Abū l-Tammām distinguishes between the *maṣnūʿ* ("artificial") and *maṭbūʿ* ("natural") in poetry, but al-Āmidī's concern is style rather than, as here, the motivation of the poet.

100 Āmid: a city in southeastern Turkey, now called Diyarbakır.

101 al-Bustī: Abū l-Fatḥ al-Bustī (335–400/946–1009), poet and prose stylist.

102 Abū l-ʿAtāhiyah: a poet of Baghdad mainly known for his pious and censorious verse (131–211/748–826).

103 Abū Nuwās: one of the most famous poets of the Abbasid "Golden Age," especially in the fields of wine poetry and the love lyric (ca. 130–98/747–813).

104 al-Farazdaq: Tammām ibn Ghālib, known as al-Farazdaq ("the Lump of Dough"), a satirist and panegyrist (d. 110/728 or 112/730).

105 Jarīr: one of the greatest poets of the Umayyad period (ca. 33–111/653–729).

106 Abū Tammām: Abbasid poet and anthologist (ca. 189–232/805–45).

107 al-Mutanabbī: celebrated panegyrist and lampoonist (ca. 303–54/915–65).

108 "Our Master Sulaymān's ring": this magic signet ring, sometimes referred to as a seal, allowed Sulaymān to command demons and talk to animals.

109 "Zayd . . . ʿAmr": Zayd and ʿAmr are names used to demonstrate grammatical points in examples memorized by school children.

110 "a grave offense against him" (*mina l-mūbiqāti lahu*): perhaps because to do so might imply jealousy, or because both beauty and riches are regarded as gifts of God rather than qualities implying merit.

111 "flap of skin" (*zanamah*): the author appears to have in mind the following among a number of definitions of this word given in the *Qāmūs*: "something cut off the ear of a camel and left hanging, done to the best bred."

112 "it is incorrect to refer to the son of a marquis as a 'marquisito' or as being 'marquisate'" (*lā yaṣiḥḥu an yuqāla li-bni l-markīzi muraykīzun aw markīzī*): i.e., it is incorrect to refer to the son of a marquis with a diminutive noun or a relative adjective derived from "marquis," meaning, perhaps, that European titles—which are, unlike oriental titles, hereditary—can be applied to only one holder at a time.

113 On whom see 2.3.5: the Melkites of Tripoli numbered "barely ten" (Graf, *Geschichte,* 3:277).

114 The author's distinction recognizes the fact that such titles are informal terms of respect rather than titles awarded by an authority.

115 "Muʿallim . . . *muʿallim* or *muʿallam*": *muʿallim* means literally "teacher" and is used as a term of polite address to Christians and others; read as *muʿallam,* the same word means "taught."

116 "they apply the term Khawājā to others": i.e., to other Christians (from Persian *khōjā* ("teacher")).

117 "God relieve you (or shrive you or deceive you)," etc. (*maṣaḥa llāhu mā bi-ka . . . aw masaḥa aw mazaḥa . . .*): *sirāṭ* and *zirāṭ* are recognized variants of *ṣirāṭ* ("path"), as *busāq* and *buzāq* are of *buṣāq* ("the best camels"); but *masaḥa* ("to wipe") and *mazaḥa* ("to joke") are not variants of *maṣaḥa* and have unrelated, comically inappropriate, meanings.

118 ʿAzrāʾīl: the angel of death.

119 "*kubaybah . . . kubbah*": both are dishes made of cracked-wheat kernels, with meat, onions, etc., but the first form is Egyptian, the second Levantine ("kibbeh").

120 "*kubbah* . . . patootie . . . *kubbah* . . . pastries!" (*fī ʿijānak . . . kubbah . . . ʿajīnī*): a pair of puns as (1) *kubbah* means, as well as a certain dish, a "boil" or "bubo" and is used in curses, and (2) *ʿijān* ("anus") is from the same root as *ʿajīn* ("pastry"); the foreign doctor confuses the two meanings in the first case and mishears in the second.

121 "like a rugged boulder hurled from on high by the torrent" (*ka-julmūdi ṣakhrin ḥaṭṭahu l-saylu min ʿali*): a hemistich from the *muʿallaqah* of the pre-Islamic poet Imruʾ al-Qays (translation Arberry, *Seven Odes,* 64).

122 "One of these *giaours* (plural of *cure*)" (*aḥada hādhihi l-ʿulūj (jamiʿi ʿilāj)*): the plural of *ʿilāj* ("cure, treatment") is in fact *ʿilājāt*, whereas *ʿulūj*, though from the same root, is the plural of *ʿilj* ("infidel"); again the doctor confuses the words.

123 "Tell the emir that I am, thank God, a bachelor" etc.: a reference to the exchange at the end of 2.10.3.

124 "his consul's office": in Egypt, legal cases involving a foreigner and an Egyptian could be tried in the foreign plaintiff's consular court.

125 "his turban in Lebanon and its ill-fated fall": see Volume One (1.2).

126 *Baḥth al-maṭālib*: in full *Kitāb Baḥth al-maṭālib fī ʿilm al-ʿArabiyyah* (*The Book of the Discussion of Issues in the Science of Arabic*), by Jirmānūs Farḥāt, a grammar published for the first time under al-Shidyāq's supervision in Malta in 1836; on Farḥāt, see Volume One (n. 130 to 1.3.2).

127 "with no vowel on the rhyme consonant" (*sākinat al-rawī*): see Volume One (n. 24 to 1.11.8).

128 "*wa-ʿawlajtu fī-hā*": the metropolitan's solecism lies in his use of *awlajtu*, a Form IV, or *rubāʿī* (*mazīd*), verb, intransitively, i.e., to mean "I entered," when it should only be used to mean "I caused (something) to enter, I inserted (something)." For the original letter, see 2.2.15.

129 "from *habba* meaning 'to rise'" (*min habba idhā qāma*): the root *h-b-b* is used in two distinct semantic areas: "to rise," as in *habbat al-rīḥ* "the wind rose," and *hibāb*, "soot".

130 "Take heed" etc.: Matthew 24:4–5 in the King James Version, with a difference in the translation of the last clause between the Arabic, reflected above, and the English, though it would seem that the translators of the English were as much in error, from the author's perspective, as those of the Arabic.

131 "Let the deacons be the husbands of one wife": 1 Timothy 3:12: again, the English translators are as guilty as the Arab.

132 "Panegyricon" (*mamdaḥ*): an invented word, literally "a place for eulogizing," by which the author means the offices of the Egyptian government's official gazette and the first daily newspaper to be printed in Arabic, namely *Al-Waqā'i' al-Miṣriyyah*, which was issued for the first time in December 1828 and on which al-Shidyāq worked from January 1829; in its early years, the gazette contained material in both Turkish and Arabic.

133 "neglected" (*uhmilat*): a play on words, as undotted letters are known technically as *muhmalah*.

134 "how can the witness of the instrument itself—the reason for the discounting of its owner's witness—be valid": the speaker implies that musicians are not considered *'udūl* (men of probity) and that their testimony cannot be accepted in a court law.

135 "demolish the castles where you store your peddlers' goods, as well as any king's trumpet!": perhaps a reference to the destruction of the walls of Jericho by the trumpets blown at Joshua's command (Joshua 6:20).

136 *Allāh!*: see Volume One (n. 151 to 1.5.3).

137 "his ode known as *Al-Ghabab*": the reference is to a line in an ode in which al-Mutanabbī mocks his former patron, Sayf al-Dawlah, saying, "He who rides the bull after riding fine horses * Ignores its cloven hoofs and its wattle (*aẓlāfahu wa-l-ghabab*)" (Mutanabbī, *Dīwān*, 432).

138 "'nation' ought to have been put in the dual" (*ummatu ḥaqquhā an takūna ummatā*): because the "nation of men-and-jinn" could logically be considered two nations.

139 *al-thaqalayn . . . thaqīlah . . . thiqal*: the author plays with the root *th-q-l*, whose basic sense is of heaviness; *al-thaqalayn* is an idiom meaning "mankind and the jinn," an appellation explained as being "because, by the discrimination they possess, they excel other animate beings" (Lane, *Lexicon*).

140 "the rule of *taghlīb*": *taghlīb* ("awarding of precedence") is a stylistically elegant usage according to which the dual form of one noun is used to indicate both that noun and another with which it is closely associated, e.g., *al-qamarān* (literally, "the two moons"), meaning "the moon and the sun" and *al-aṣfarān* (literally, "the two yellow things"),

meaning "gold and silver"; the argument here, therefore, turns the convention upside down and claims that, since *māshiyayn* ("two persons walking on foot"), were it an example of *taghlīb*, would give precedence to the prince, the singular (*māshiyan*) may be assumed to mean "the prince and others."

141 "the body (singular) of each of the two" or "the bodies (plural) of each of the two," (*jismuhumā aw ajsāmuhumā*): i.e., the prince and the squadron should be regarded as consisting of either two entities with one body each or of two entities with a plurality of bodies. Objection may be made that it would be simpler and more natural to take *sariyyah* as the feminine singular equivalent of *sarī*, in which case the translation would run, "The prince repaired with *the princess*" etc. To this the riposte would be that, had the critics entertained this possibility, they would have proposed the dual form of the noun (*jismāhumā*) as being (along with the singular) the "more chaste" option, rather than the plural (*ajsāmuhumā*).

142 "the poet": ʿAdī ibn Zayd al-ʿIbādī (d. ca. AD 600).

143 "Objection was made that *aẓāfir* should not be inflected" (*fa-ʿuriḍa ʿalay-hi ṣarfu aẓāfir*): i.e., *aẓāfir* is normally diptote (i.e., should be read here as *aẓāfira*) but in these verses has to be read as triptote (*aẓāfirin*), a bending of the rules that is permitted, as the author says, for the sake of the meter (Wright, *Grammar*, 2:387) and which is determined by the form of the following word, (*ẓafirat*).

144 "for the sake of the paronomasia": i.e., because *aḥlas* and *malḥūs*, while having different meanings, share the same triliteral root (*ḥ-l-s*).

145 "Except for the words 'in glory'": *tanawwarā*, repeated at the end of each hemistich of the first line ("to reveal a brighter fate" and "was made depilate"), is an example of both "perfect paronomasia" (identicality of form with difference of meaning) and "antithesis" (the use of two contrasting ideas in one line); *al-shiʿr* ("poetry") and *al-shiʿrāʾ* ("pubic hair") are examples of near-perfect paronomasia and antithesis; *mafkharā* ("in glory") stands out as neither paronomasia nor antithesis.

146 "the word *qaḥaba*": this, in the unchaste or vernacular language, means "to whore."

147 "the repetitive form" (*al-takthīr*): i.e., *fassā* versus *fasā*, the former indicating repeated performance of the action indicated by the latter.

148 "*ẓallām li-l-ʿabīd*": the phrase occurs several times in the Qurʾan (e.g., Q Āl ʿImrān 3:182); *ẓallām*, from *ẓālim*, is the nominal equivalent of the verbal intensive.

149 This apparently irrelevant aside may perhaps be explained by the fact that the author contracted a venereal disease while in Malta.

150 "at this point": i.e., at the thirteenth chapter of each book.

151 "Hie ye to security!" (*ḥayya ilā l-falāḥ*): a phrase in the call to prayer.

152 "a turban of different fashion": in Egypt, men of different religious communities wore turbans of different colors and, sometimes, shapes (see Lane, *Manners*, 31).

153 "pilgrims from 'Arafāt": the gathering on Mount 'Arafāt outside of Mecca is the final rite of pilgrimage, after which the pilgrims disperse to their separate countries.

154 "You are to me as my mother's back!" (*anti 'alayya ka-ẓahri ummī*): i.e., "intercourse with you is as forbidden to me as it is with my mother," a pre-Islamic divorce formula; the "back" is specified rather than the belly because intercourse with a woman is likened to riding an animal (see Lane, *Lexicon*, s.v. *ẓāhara*).

155 "Your nose-rope is on the top of your hump!" (*ḥabluki 'alā ghāribiki*): meaning "Go wherever you want" because when a she-camel that is wearing a nose-rope is sent out to graze, the rope is thrown on top of her hump, for if she can see the rope, she will not want to eat anything (al-Maydānī, *Majma'*, 1:132); the expression is associated with divorce.

156 "Return to your covert!" (*'ūdī ilā kināsiki*): as though she were a gazelle or an oryx that had made itself a shelter against the heat.

157 "(un)buckle to her will and her every demand fulfil" (*yuwāṭi'ahā 'alay-hi wa-yujāmi'ahā*): the verbs *wāṭa'a* and *jāma'a* both mean both "to agree with" and "to copulate with."

158 "legal dalliance" (*al-mut'ah*): a marriage legally contracted for a set period, usually short.

159 "How many a heart has been tied to the rack . . . or gold coins expended" (*wa-la-kam taṣadda'at qulūb . . . wa-danānīra nuqidat*): evocative of Q Takwīr 81:1–14.

160 "Verily . . . it is a great woe" (*innahā la-iḥdā l-kubar*): Q Muddaththir 74:35.

161 "ill you answered though well you heard!" (*asa'ta jābatan ba'da an aṣabta sam'an*): a distortion of the proverb *asā'a sam'an fa-asā'a jābatan,* "he answered ill because he heard ill."

162 In fact, none of the obscure words explained in this chapter occur in the preceding.

163 The author uses the double entendres implicit in the terminology of grammar (*fā'il* "actor/subject of a verb"; *maf'ūl* "acted upon/object of a verb"; *fi'l* "act/verb"; *raf'*, literally "raising," i.e., the vowel ending *-u* when used to mark the nominative case; *naṣb*, literally "erecting,") i.e., the vowel ending *-a* when used to mark the accusative case to describe sexual acts (a common conceit). The thrust of the argument laid out below is that there is no word for marriage that does not derive from other words that originally refer to something else; thus, the rites and institutions that have developed around it are historically contingent and further (2.14.5), religion's, or the state's, interference in what is a private contract is without justification.

164 Abū l-Baqā': Ayyūb ibn Mūsā Abū l-Baqā' al-Kaffawī (ca. 1027/1618 to ca. 1093/1682); his *Kitāb al-Kulliyyāt* is a dictionary.

165 "noun *nikāḥ*" etc.: the issue here is that this word, which is the preferred legal term for sexual congress, is regarded by some as embarrassingly direct.

166 "mysterious letters" (*asrār*): letters of unknown signification that occur at the beginning of certain suras of the Qur'an (see Watt, *Bell's Introduction*, 61–65).

167 "*Nūn*. By the Pen and all that they write!" (*nūn wa-l-qalami wa-mā yasṭurūn*): Q Anfāl 8:1.

168 *kāf-hā'-yā'-ṣād*: letters occurring at the beginning of Sūrat Maryam (Q Maryam 19:1).

169 *alif-lām-fā'*: letters occurring at the beginning of Sūrat al-Baqarah (Q Baqarah 2:1).

170 *ḥā'-mīm*: letters occurring at the beginning of suras 40–46.

171 "an active participle of the verb *ḥ-y-y* . . . an imperative verb formed from *kāna*": i.e., if نكاح is written backwards the result, حاكِن, may be broken down (ignoring short vowels) into حا, to be understood according to the orthography used here as حايٍ ("alive, quick," an epithet of God) from حَيِيَ (or حَيَّ) and كُنْ ("Be!") from كان .

172 "the letter *nūn* followed by the letter *kāf*": i.e., *nik*, meaning "fuck!"

173 "the *alif* and the *ḥā'*": i.e., *āḥ*, which could also be understood as the exclamation "Ah!"

174 "by keeping only the end"(*bi-ḥaythu yaslamu l-ṭaraf*): i.e., by removing the initial syllable *nik-* from *nikāḥ*, leaving (by re-interpretation of the remaining ductus) *aḥḥ*, which is an "exclamation expressing . . . pleasure during sexual intercourse" peculiar to women (Hinds and Badawi, *Dictionary*).

175 "*mustaqbiḥah* and *mustafẓi'ah*": see 2.5.5 above; in fact, it is heads rather than bonnets that are so described.

176 On 'Ulayyān, see Volume One (n. 138 to 1.3.13); however, no anecdote involving a chicken occurs in al-Nīsābūrī.

177 "bag" (*haqībah*): literally, "a bag carried behind the saddle" and also, punningly, "posterior."

178 "well-known": the *Qāmūs* defines a girl who is *raṭbah* as being *rakhṣah* and defines *rakhṣ* as "smooth."

179 "mentioned under *burqu'*": there is no entry for *burqu'*; however, *shanab* ("lustrousness of the teeth") is referred to in the earlier passage describing the charms of *al-mutabarqi'āt* ("women who wear the *burqu'*") (2.4.5), as are *khanas* and *dhalaf*, which are likewise linked below to *burqu'*.

180 *'anaṭ* and *'ayaṭ* are synonyms.

181 "synonym *abārīq*": thus in the text, but, as the *Qāmūs* makes clear, *abārīq* is in fact the plural of *ibrīq*, which is synonymous with *barrāqah*.

182 "having a certain quality welcomed in a woman during copulation": this definition of *ḥārūq* is explained in the definition of *al-ḥāriqah* that precedes it in the *Qāmūs* and to which the author has referred earlier; see Volume 1 (n. 47 to 1.1.6).

183 Ṣāliḥ is a prophet referred to in the Qur'an (e.g., Q A'rāf 7:77); the People of the Cave (*ahl al-kahf*) are mentioned in the eponymous eighteenth sura of the Qur'an.

184 "or . . .": the entry in the *Qāmūs* continues "a house roofed with a single piece of wood, synonym *azaj*."

185 "or . . .": the entry in the *Qāmūs* continues "a place where people gather and sit for so long as they are gathered there."

186 "they": i.e., pastoralists of the Arabian peninsula.

187 "or . . .": other definitions given in the *Qāmūs* are "a village, or a granary, or flat land, or houses of the Persians in which are drink and entertainment."

188 "or . . .": the entry in the *Qāmūs* continues "for the harvester of truffles."

189 "a kind of building": according to the *Lisān*, "a house built in elongated form, called in Persian *ūsitān*."

190 "or . . .": the *Qāmūs* continues "a day on which they eat and drink."

191 al-Muqtadir: i.e., the Abbasid caliph Ja'far al-Muqtadir (ruled three times between 295/908 and 317/929).

192 "a pool of lead" (*birkatun mina l-raṣāṣ*): more often described as having been of mercury.

193 Al-Nu'mān: i.e., al-Nu'mān ibn Imru' al-Qays (r. AD 390–418), king of al-Ḥīrah, in the area of ancient Babylon in Iraq; the palace in question was named al-Khawarnaq.

194 Uḥayḥah: Uḥayḥah ibn al-Julāḥ was a pre-Islamic leader of the Aws tribe of Yathrib (now Medina).

195 al-Mutawakkil: an Abbasid caliph, r. 232–47/847–61.

196 Dawmat al-Jandal: a town in northwestern Arabia.

197 Khayzurān: mother of the caliph Hārūn al-Rashīd.

198 'Amr ibn al-'Āṣ: a leading general of the Muslim conquests in the time of the Prophet Muḥammad and after (b. before AD 573).

199 Wajj: a wadi east of Mecca and northeast of al-Ṭā'if.

200 "on which Adam . . . fell": i.e., after being cast out of heaven, the mountain being situated in modern Sri Lanka.

201 al-Jazīrah: the plain lying between the Tigris and the Euphrates, in Upper Mesopotamia.

202 "the lote-tree beyond which none may pass" (*sidrat al-muntahā*): see Q Najm 53:14; this tree "stands in the Seventh Heaven on the right hand of the throne of God; and is the utmost bounds beyond which the angels themselves must not pass; or . . . beyond which no creature's knowledge can extend" (Sale, *Koran*, 427 n. 1).

203 Ibn Hishām: ʿAbd al-Malik ibn Hishām (d. 218/833), an Egyptian scholar of South Arabian origin, who wrote, in addition to the authoritative *sīrah*, or biography, of the Prophet Muḥammad, for which he is best known, a collection of biblical and ancient Arabian lore entitled *Kitāb al-Tījān fī mulūk Ḥimyar* (*The Book of Crowns concerning the Kings of Ḥimyar*); this passage is quoted in the *Tāj* (s.v., *sh-f-r*) but not in the *Qāmūs*.

204 Ḥimyar: a kingdom of ancient Yemen that flourished between the first and fourth centuries AD.

205 "the battle of Badr": Ramaḍān 17, 2/March 13, 624, a victory for the Muslim forces of Medina over the pagans of Mecca.

206 ʿAlī: ʿAlī ibn Abī Ṭālib (d. 40/660), the Prophet Muḥammad's cousin, foster-brother, and son-in-law.

207 ʿĀd: an ancient people of Arabia, mentioned in the Qurʾan (Q Aʿrāf 7:65, Hūd 11:59, etc.).

208 "*nās, nasnās*, and *nasānis*": since *nās* ordinarily means "people" the implication is that there are three kinds of humanoid—(ordinary) people, *nasnās*, and *nasānis*.

209 Yākhūkh and Mākhūkh: Gog and Magog.

210 "or the remainder of the bearers of the Proof, which no part of the earth is without" (*wa-baqiyyatu ḥamalati l-ḥujjati lā takhlū l-arḍu minhum*): a Tradition mentioned by al-Jawharī (see *Lisān*, s.v. *r-b-ḍ*).

211 "an ant who spoke to Sulaymān" (*namlatun kallamat Sulaymān*): a reference to Q Naml 27:18 "when they came on the valley of the ants, an ant said . . . ."; since the ant did not in fact address Sulaymān directly, the verb has to be taken as meaning "spoke in the presence of."

212 "the ant mentioned in the Qurʾan": see Q Naml 27:18.

213 "Ibn Sīnā . . . the *Shifāʾ*": ʿAbdallāh ibn Sīnā (d. 428/1037), a philosopher of medieval Islam, known in the west as Avicenna.

214 "cup his ears with his hands": in the manner of a muezzin making the call to prayer.

215 "'Waḍḍāḥ's Bone'" (*ʿaẓmu Waḍḍāḥin*): "A certain game of the Arabs . . . in which they throw in the night . . . a white bone and he who lights upon it overcomes [sc. beats] his companions" (Lane, *Lexicon*).

216 "*ʿuqqah*": the dictionaries offer no further definition.

217 "on which one plays" (*yuḍrabu bihi*): i.e., not *ʿūd* in any of its other senses (such as "stick" or "a certain perfume").

218 "honey" (*ʿasal*): all references to "honey" (in its complete form *ʿasal abyaḍ* or "white honey") may be taken in the alternative sense of "molasses" (in its complete form *ʿasal aswad* or "black honey").

219 "*ḥays*": dates mixed with clarified butter and curd.

220 al-Maʾmūn: Abbasid caliph, r. 189–218/813–33.

221 "fatty dishes or . . .": the author appears to have misread the *Qāmūs*, which gives a different definition for *makhbūr* (*al-ṭayyib al-idām* or "good-tasting condiments") and in which *khubrah* is not a synonym of *makhbūr* but constitutes a new lemma, with *tharīdah ḍakhmah* as one of its definitions.

222 "*sikbājah*": not in the *Qāmūs* but presumably the same as *sikbāj*.

223 "*ruṭab* dates": i.e., dates that are fresh but soft and sugary (and neither fresh and astringent nor dried).

224 "*wars*": a plant, *Memecylon tinctorium*, grown in Yemen, from whose roots a yellow dye ("Indian yellow") is made.

225 al-Faḥfāḥ and al-Kawthar: rivers in Paradise.

226 "*tasnīm*": the beverage of the blessed in Paradise.

227 "among whom pass immortal youths . . . .": a collage of verses taken from three chapters of the Qur'an, namely al-Wāqiʿah, al-Raḥmān, and al-Insān (Q Wāqiʿah 56:17–18, 20–21, 28–34; Raḥmān 55:46, 48, 62, 64, 66, 68, 70, 11–12, 76, 54, 15 (note that here the author incorrectly writes *furushin* for *sururin*); Insān 76:17–19, 21); the translation is Arberry's, with minor adaptions.

228 "*zaqqūm*": see Volume One (n. 92 to 1.1.9).

229 "and shade from a smoking blaze" (*wa-ẓillin min yaḥmūmin*): Q Wāqiʿah 56:43.

230 "fire from a smokeless blaze" (*mārij mina l-nār*): Q Raḥmān 55:15.

231 "it was wholesome, healthy, and of beneficial effect" (*ṣāra marīʾan hanīʾan ḥandīda l-mighabbah*): the quotation is from the *Qāmūs*, though the designation of the verb as the etymon of the noun appears to be the author's.

232 "the glottal stop (*hamz*) in it is for purposes of elision (*waṣl*) and the elision (*waṣl*) in it is for purposes of compression (*hamz*)" (*hamzuhā li-l-waṣl wa-waṣluhā li-l-hamz*): the author plays with orthographic terminology, exploiting the fact that *imraʾah* begins (unusually for a concrete noun) with a glottal stop (*hamz*) that is elided when preceded by a word ending in a vowel and as such is distinguished from its non-elidable cousin by a sign called *waṣl*, while *hamz* also has the non-grammatical sense of "compression," here to be understood as "sexual intercourse."

233 "its plural" etc.: no plural is made from *imraʾah*; words for "women" are from the root *n-s-w* and have different forms (e.g., *niswah*, *nisāʾ*, *niswān*).

234 "in one language the word denotes 'man's woe' and in another 'pudendum'": i.e., in English, "woman" is a phonetic anagram of "man's woe" and in Ottoman Turkish the word for both "woman" and "pudendum" was عورت (realized in modern Turkish as *avrat* for the former, *avret* for the latter).

235 "*qarīnah* . . . whose etymology is well known": probably an allusion to *qarn* ("horn"), from the same root, and its figurative reference to cuckoldry.

236 "or vice versa": i.e., perhaps, when she returns to her parents' home in a fit of anger at her husband.

237 See 2.16.65 below.

238 "*ḥadādah*": a word whose semantic link to others with the same root is left unexplained by the lexicographers; thus *ḥadādatuka* means "your wife" (*Qāmūs*), but why it does so is not clear. The same is true of *niḍr*, *jathal*, and *ḥannah* below.

239 "*ʿirs*": from the verb *ʿarisa bi-* meaning "to cleave to."

240 "*shāʿah*": because, according to the *Qāmūs*, she takes her husband's part (*li-mushāyaʿatihā l-zawj*).

241 "the accession of women to the throne of England was an unalloyed blessing": perhaps because the reign of Elizabeth I witnessed the irreversibility of Protestantism as the national creed.

242 "the two queens of England": presumably, Mary and her successor Elizabeth I, the first queens regnant of England, the first of whom was Catholic, the second Protestant.

243 "Irene, wife of Leo IV, and Theodora, wife of Theophilus": Irene was Byzantine empress regnant from AD 797 to 802, while Theodora was regent for her son from AD 842 to 855. The significance of their being opposed here is not clear, since both, as anti-iconoclasts, took the same position with regard to the most important theological issue of their day.

244 Chapter 15: the dots seem to imply a silent dialogue between the author and his pen, in which the former tries to persuade the latter to move on to a new topic while the latter refuses, insisting that the renewed discussion, instead of taking place "at some other point" (*fī mawḍiʿin ākhar*) as promised at the end of the preceding chapter, should, in fact, take place "right there" (*fī dhālika l-mawḍiʿ*), as indicated by the hand, namely immediately, in the following chapter. The extreme shortness of the chapter, the dots, and the pointing hand have been noted by scholars as examples of the influence of Laurence Sterne's *Tristram Shandy* (see, e.g., Alwan, *Ahmad,* chap. 3, sect. 11).

245 "the mark of clemency" (*simat al-ḥilm*): a pun, in that the phrase may also be read as *simat al-ḥalam* ("the mark of the nipple").

246 Zubaydah daughter of Jaʿfar (d. 216/831) was cousin and wife of Hārūn al-Rashīd, fifth Abbasid caliph; this poem, which appears in many classical anthologies, is interpreted in those as illustrating (on the poet's side) the danger of misusing a rhetorical feature and (on Zubayda's) insight and generosity; thus, al-Nuwayrī (667–732/1279–1332) writes in his *Nihāyat al-arab fī funūn al-adab*, "When the poet recited the above, the slaves leapt up to beat him, but Zubayda said, 'Let him be! He must be rewarded well, for he who

means well and makes a mistake is better than he who means evil and is correct. He heard people saying, "Your nape is comelier than others' faces and your left hand more generous than others' right hands," so he supposed that what he had written was of the same sort. Give him what he hoped for and teach him what he did not know'" (http://www.alwaraq.net/, accessed 8 July 2012). The author's different interpretation ("his description was not wrong") implies that Zubaydah accepted the validity of the poet's comparison, in the sense, perhaps, that even with the tips of her toes she gave more than others gave with their whole hands.

247 "*ruḍāb*": literally, "saliva."

248 Genesis 36:20, "These are the sons of Seir the Horite, who inhabited the land; Lotan, and Shobal, and Zibeon, and Anah"; 36:24 "And these are the children of Zibeon; both Ajah, and Anah: this was that Anah that found the mules in the wilderness, as he fed the asses of Zibeon his father"; 36:29 "These are the dukes that came of the Horites; duke Lotan, duke Shobal, duke Zibeon, duke Anah."

249 "... or a kind of ornament for the hands or the feet": the entry in the *Qāmūs* reads "*quffāz* ...: something made for the hands that is stuffed with cotton and that women wear against the cold [sc. 'gloves'], or a kind of ornament for the hands or the feet," etc.

250 "... or decorative earrings": the entry in the *Qāmūs* reads "*sals* ...: the string on which the white beads worn by slave girls are strung, or decorative earrings."

251 "the Ring of Power" (*khātam al-mulk*): a magic ring by which jinn and other forces may be commanded.

252 "*rāmik*": described in the *Qāmūs* as being "something black that is mixed with musk."

253 "*thamīmah*": defined in the *Qāmūs* as synonymous with *ta'mūrah.*

254 "or. ...": the *Qāmūs* continues with further unrelated definitions.

255 "*shi'ār*": defined in the *Qāmūs* as "any item of apparel worn under the *dithār.*"

256 "*armaniyyah*": literally, "the Armenian [garment]. but not further defined."

257 "in an entry of its own": i.e., under *m-r-j-l*; in fact, available editions of the *Qāmūs* do not include *mumarjil* but read, under *r-j-l, al-mumarjal —thiyābun fīhā ṣuwaru l-marājil*; for more on the confusion around these and similar terms, see Lane, *Lexicon,* s.v. *mirjal.*

258 "from a certain governor": i.e., from a provincial governor whose name was al-Qasṭalānī ("the Castilian").

259 Cf. *Qāmūs* (s.v. *a-w-m*): "*Ām,* a town whose name is used to describe clothes."

260 "*bizyawn*": defined in the *Qāmūs* as "a kind of *sundus.*"

261 "so as to give them a place in the *list* appropriate to the underlying *gist*" (*li-yuṭābiqa l-dhikru l-fikr*): i.e., because they are put on before anything else.

262 "*ḥarr/ḥirr*": with the first vowelling, the word means "warmth," with the second, "vagina".

263 "in kind . . . kind . . . kinds" (*al-ʿayn . . . mina l-ʿayn . . . bi-l-maʿnayayn*): the author plays with two senses of *ʿayn*, namely "kind" (as opposed to "cash") and "eye," and rhymes the word with *maʿnayayn* ("two senses").

264 "he has to dissolve any knots with puffs" (*yaḥulla ʿuqdatahu bi-nafāthāt*): a reference to Q Falaq 113:1–4— *qul aʿūdhu bi-rabbi l-falaq min . . . sharri n-naffāthāti fī l-ʿuqad* ("Say, 'I seek refuge with the Lord of the daybreak . . . from the evil of those who blow on knots'"), the Qur'anic reference being to witches who performed magic using this method.

265 "as al-Farrā' has on *ḥattā*": Yaḥya ibn Ziyād al-Farrā' (144–207/761–822) was a leading grammarian; *ḥattā* is a conjunction and preposition with multiple functions.

266 "Juḥā's dream": Juḥā is the protagonist of jokes and anecdotes, in which he often plays the role of the "wise fool." A version of this story goes: "Juḥā told the following story: 'When sleeping I had a dream the first half of which was true, the second half untrue.' 'How can that be, O Abū Ghuṣn?' he was asked. He said, 'As I slept I seemed to behold myself come across a purse full of gold, silver, and golden coins, and when I picked it up, I defecated on myself from the effort of lifting it, it was so heavy. When I woke up, I found I was covered with filth and wetness, and the purse was no longer in my hands!'" (http://www.belkhechine07.com/joha.doc, accessed on 27 June 2012).

267 "a leading scholar of the language. . .": i.e., Jalāl al-Dīn al-Suyūṭī (see Volume One, 0.4.10).

268 "why have you foresworn writing [in general] but not [writing] about women": in what follows, the author answers that first part of the question but appears to forget the second.

269 "most people . . . [believe *mu'allif*] refers to *ta'līf* ('making peace') between two persons": *mu'allif* in the sense of "author" etc. was a nineteenth-century neologism.

270 "repugnant to some people, especially women": because "shaykh" also means "old man."

271 "and how he stuffs them then" (*fa-zaʿabahā ayya zaʿbin*): the phrase could also be understood "and how he stuffs her then!"

272 Shaykh Muṣṭafā: according to one scholar, a teacher at the mosque-university of al-Azhar but not further identified (al-Maṭwī, *Aḥmad*, 1:79), the same applying to the Shaykh Aḥmad, Shaykh Maḥmūd, and Shaykh Muḥammad mentioned later (2.18.3, 2.18.4, 2.19.9); however, it is possible that the author simply chose these common names to hide the identity of little-known scholars, as one might say "Tom, Dick, and Harry."

273 "Zayd and 'Amr": two characters used to illustrate points of grammar; for example, the sentence *ḍaraba Zaydun 'Amran* ("Zayd struck 'Amr") illustrates the typical verb-subject-object order of the Arabic sentence.

274 "happened to be asked . . . if he could study": presumably, the Fāriyāq's acquaintance asked him for an introduction to the shaykh.

275 "*Baḥth al-maṭālib*": see n. 126 to 2.11.3.

276 "to write him a license to teach the book" (*an yaktuba la-hu ijāzata iqrā'ihi*): traditionally, scholarly knowledge was acquired through the study of individual books at the hands of a shaykh, with the student reading the work out loud to the teacher, who corrected and commented. When the student had acquired full mastery of the text, the shaykh would write him a licence (*ijāzah*) to teach it in the same fashion to others, just as the shaykh had earlier received a licence from his teacher, and so on.

277 *Al-Talkhīṣ fī l-ma'ānī*: probably the commentary of Mas'ūd ibn 'Umar al-Taftazānī (d. between 791/1389 and 797/1395) on the *Talkhīṣ al-miftāḥ fī l-ma'ānī wal-l-bayān wa-l-badī'* by Jalāl al-Dīn Muḥammad ibn 'Abd al-Raḥmān al-Qazwīnī, known as Khaṭīb Dimashq (666–739/1268–1338), the "basic textbook for rhetorical studies in the *madrasas* of the later Middle Ages up to modern times" (Meisami and Starkey, *Encyclopedia,* 2:439).

278 "al-Akhḍarī's *Sharḥ al-Sullam*": 'Abd al-Raḥmān ibn Muḥammad al-Akhḍarī (920–83/1512–75) wrote this commentary on his own *Al-Sullam al-murawnaq fī l-manṭiq*.

279 "the yellow air" (*al-hawā' al-aṣfar*): summer cholera.

280 "greater affirmative universal" (*kulliyyah mūjibah kubrā*): presumably meaning, in the terms of Aristotelian logic, a "universal" statement of the form "all S are P."

281 "and not numbered among the dead" (*wa-lam yaqḍi mina l-qaḍāyā*); or, punningly, "and had not yet run out of syllogisms."

282 "the *Kanz*": probably the *Kanz al-daqā'iq* of 'Abdallāh ibn Aḥmad al-Nasafī (d. 710/1310).

283 "the *Risālah al-Sanūsiyyah*": probably the *Ḥāshiya* (marginal commentary) of Ibrāhīm ibn Muḥammad al-Bājūrī (or al-Bījūrī) (1189–1276/1784–1859) on the *Matn al-Sanūsiyyah* of Muḥammad ibn Yūsuf al-Sanūsī (after 830-95/1426-90).

284 "the Center of This Book": as the thirty-ninth chapter of a work consisting of eighty, this section is, in fact, slightly off-center.

285 "*hamqāq*": according to the *Qāmūs*, "seeds found in the mountains of Bal'amm that are fried and eaten to increase the capacity for intercourse."

286 *mughāth*: *Glossostemon bruguieri*, a plant with therapeutic and nutritional properties.

287 "the caliphal palace" (*dār al-khilāfah*): i.e., the place where, like the caliph, or successor to the Prophet Muḥammad, the man in question carries out his duties.

288 "everyone suspected . . . a sin that they would carry . . . till the Day of Judgment" (*fa-ẓanna l-nās . . . wa-taqalladū ithmahu . . . ilā yawmi l-dīn*): the passage evokes the words of the Quran *inna baʿḍa l-ẓanni ithm* ("Indeed some suspicion is a sin") (Q Ḥujurāt 49:12).

289 "for he was hors de combat and wasn't up to doing anything anyway" (*fa-innahu kāna muʿaṭṭalan wa-fiʿluhu mulghan ʿani l-ʿamal*): probably an allusion to the fact that he was receiving treatment for a venereal disease (see n. 149 to 2.12.18).

290 Probably *Al-Qawl al-wāfī fī sharḥ al-Kāfī fī ʿilmay al-ʿarūḍ wa-l-qawāfī*, a commentary by ʿAlī ibn ʿAbd al-Qādir al-Nabtītī (d. ca. 1065/1655) on a work by Yaḥyā ibn ʿAlī al-Tabrīzī (421–502/1030–1109).

291 "a loft . . .": see 1 Kings 17:19–20.

292 "a wall" (*judāran*): "Now Absalom in his lifetime had taken and reared up for himself a pillar, which is in the king's dale: for he said, I have no son to keep my name in remembrance: and he called the pillar after his own name: and it is called unto this day, Absalom's place" (2 Sam. 18:8).

293 Bion: Bion of Borysthenes (ca. 325–250), who is said to have attached himself to all the contemporary schools of philosophy in succession and to have attacked everyone and everything.

Glossary

Abīshalūm Absalom.

al-Andalus those parts of the Iberian Peninsula that were under Islamic rule from the seventh to the fifteenth centuries AD.

Bag-men (khurjiyyūn) the author's term for Protestant missionaries in the Middle East, whether the American Congregationalists of the Board of Commissioners of Foreign Missions, with whom he first came into contact in Beirut, or the British Anglicans of the Church Missionary Society, for whom he worked later in Malta, Egypt, and London. The Congregationalists established their first mission station in Beirut in 1823 (Makdisi, *Artillery*, 81, 83). In December 1823, when their intention to proselytize became clear, Maronite patriarch Yūsuf Ḥubaysh (1787–1845), who had initially received them cordially, ordered his flock to avoid all contact with what he referred to as "the Liberati" or "Biblemen" (Makdisi, *Artillery*, 95–97).

Bilqīs Queen of Saba' (Sheba) in Yemen, the story of whose visit to Sulaymān (Solomon) is told in the Quran (Q Naml 27:22–44).

cubit (dhirāʿ) 0.68 m.

Dā'ūd David.

Days of Barbarism (The) (al-Jāhiliyyah) the period in Arabia before the coming of Islam.

emir (amīr) a title (lit., "commander" or "prince") assumed by local leaders in the Arab world; as used in this work, the term refers most often to the emirs of the Shihābī dynasty of Mount Lebanon.

Fāriyāq (The) the hero of the events described in the book and the author's alter ego, the name itself being a contraction of Fāri(s al-Shid)yāq.

Himyar (Ḥimyar) a kingdom of ancient Yemen that flourished between the first and fourth centuries AD.

Ilyās Elias.

Khawājā a title of reference and address afforded Christians of substance.

maqāmah, plural maqāmāt "short independent prose narrations written in ornamented rhymed prose (*saj'*) with verse insertions which share a common plot-scheme and two constant protagonists: the narrator and the hero" (Meisami and Starkey, *Encyclopedia,* 2:507). The thirteenth chapter of each book of the present work is described by the author as a *maqāmah,* the plot-scheme in these *maqāmāt* being a debate. See further Zakharia, "Aḥmad Fāris al-Šidyāq."

Market Boss (The) (shaykh al-sūq) the author's term for the Maronite patriarch.

Market-men (sūqiyyūn) the author's term for the Maronite and Roman Catholic clergy, or the Maronite and Roman Catholic churches in general.

market trader (ḍawṭār, plural ḍawāṭirah) the author's term for a member of the Maronite upper clergy.

mawwāl a form of vernacular poetry, often involving complex rhyme schemes and word play.

Mountain (The) Mount Lebanon, a mountain range in Lebanon extending for 170 kilometers parallel to the Mediterranean coast and the historical homeland of both the Maronite and Druze Lebanese communities.

Mu'tazilite follower of a school of theology that appealed to reason as a basis for understanding the truths of Islam.

Nākir and Nakīr angels who question the deceased in the grave concerning his or her faith.

Nūḥ Noah.

Numrūdh Nimrod.

People of the Cave (ahl al-kahf) believing youths who, as recounted in the eighteenth *surah* (chapter) of the Qur'an (Q 18, Sūrat al-Kahf), were caused by God to fall asleep in a cave for many years and then revived and who had no knowledge of how many years they had passed there.

Qāmūs (al-) *Al-Qāmūs al-muḥīṭ* (*The Encompassing Ocean*), a dictionary compiled by Muḥammad ibn Ya'qūb al-Fīrūzābādī (d. 817/1415) that became so influential that *qāmūs* ("ocean") eventually came to mean simply "dictionary." The author later published a study of the *Qāmūs* entitled *Al-Jāsūs 'alā l-Qāmūs* (*The Spy on the Qāmūs*).

Qāyin Cain.

rhymed prose (saj') "artistic prose, subject to certain constraints of rhyme and rhythm. . . . Etymologically, the word referred to the cooing of pigeons" (Meisami and Starkey, *Encyclopedia,* 2:677). First used by pre-Islamic soothsayers, the form developed, often in combination with other types of parallelism, until it became virtually de rigueur by the tenth century AD, and it remained in use into the early twentieth century, "by which time, however, the modern revolt which has now largely swept away this sort of artifice was already growing strong" (idem). The author uses *sajʿ* in the title of the work and most of his chapter titles, in short scattered bursts in the midst of unrhymed prose (especially at moments of drama), and sometimes, as in the four preceding chapters, in sustained blocks. For further discussion of *sajʿ* in this work, see Jubran, "Function."

Sulaymān Solomon.

Surra Man Raʾā Samarra, a city in Iraq, capital of the Abbasid caliphate from 836 to 892; the name may be interpreted as "A Joy to All Who See It".

Waqāʾiʿ al-miṣriyyah (al-) the Egyptian official gazette (and the first newspaper issued, partially, in Arabic), established in December 1828.

Yashuʿ (al-) Elisha.

Yūnus Jonah.

Yūsuf Joseph.

Zabbāʾ (al-) Zenobia, queen of Tadmur in Syria during the third century AD.

Index

ʿAbd al-Jalīl, 405
ʿAbd al-Laṭīf al-Baghdādī, 105, 419n81
Abīshalūm (Absalom), 407
Abū ʿAtāhiyah, 127, 421n102
Abū l-Baqā, 187–89, 425n164
Abū Nuwās, 127, 421n103
Abū Tammām, 127, 421n106
Aḥmad, Shaykh, 385
al-Akhḍarī, 385
Alexandria, air in, 85; Arabs in, 45–49; Bag-man/Bag-men in, 59–61; Christians in, 51; dress in, 39–41; the Fāriyāq in, 9, 39, 59–61, 85; the Fāriyāq's voyage/travel to, 85, 397; food eaten in, 51; Franks in, 57; headwear in, 39; hospitality in, 57; Turks in, 45–49, 57–59; waters in, 49–51; women in, 41–45
ʿAlī, 191
al-Āmidī, 125, 421n99
ʿAmr ibn Luḥayy, 23, 25, 412n20
al-Andalus, 119
al-Anfūshī, 414n37
anqāṭ, 117
aphrodisiacs, 393–95
Arabic language, *Baḥth al-maṭālib* (*The Discussion of Issues*), 153; distinguishing feature of, 371; the Fāriyāq as teacher of, 389, 397; Frankish pronunciation of, 63–69, 414nn49; priest's pronunciation of, 63–69; Qur'an revealed in, 49; students from the Mountain and, 154; translations into, 155–57
Arabic literature, tropes, 15. *See also* rhymed prose
Arabic script, 239
Arabs, 45–49, 109, 119, 187
aromas/perfumes, words for, 315–25
asses, 87–89, 387–89
Atanāsiyūs al-Tutūnji, 69, 137, 417n66

the bag, Bag-man/Bag-men's preoccupation with, 61; the Fāriyāq's burden, 127, 155; point of, 81
bag, women's, 195, 426n177
Bag-man/Bag-men (Protestant missionaries), in Alexandria, 59–61; the bag, preoccupation with, 61; in Cairo, 85, 103; damage done by, 21; English queens, 291; the Fāriyāq and, 59–61, 73–75, 81–83, 85, 123, 161, 397–99; indifference to people's troubles, 31–33; language, 81; Market-man/Market-men, feuds with, 61, 77, 81; Market-woman/Market-women, 77–79; payment by, 397; pork-eating, 73–75; prototype of, 59; saddlebags of, 33; serving girl/maid, 401–3; tools of the trade, 15, 29; wife beating by, 59; wife of a, 401
Baguettes, 399, 403
Baḥth al-maṭālib (*The Discussion of Issues*), 153, 383, 422n126
bayk ("bey"), 379

beardless boys, 363
"Biblemen." *See* Bag-man/Bag-men
Bilqīs, 129, 229, 237
Bion, 407, 434n293
birds, words for, 241–43
bloodletting, 145–49
bread, words for, 273–75
the British, 79
buildings, words for, 229–31
burning, kinds of, 55
al-Bustī, 127, 421n101

Cairo, 105–23; air in, 109; Bag-man/Bag-men in, 85, 103; catamites in, 109; Christians in, 119, 123–25; curiosities of, 105–13, 111; Domestic Services Office, 107–9; the Fāriyāq in, 85–87, 103, 389, 397; girls in, 107–9, 175; hashish use, 113; hospitality in, 117; joking in, 117; lutes, 119; markets in, 105–7; men in, 105–7; nighttime lanterns, 109–11; people of, 105, 117–19; plague in, 399; poets in, 105, 107, 123–29; police chief, 109; prices in, 121; scholars in, 107, 117; singing in, 119; trees unique to ʻAyn Shams suburb, 319
carrying devices, words for, 47–49
castles, words for, 229–31
chambers, words for, 223–25
children, 29–31, 181
China, 107
Christ, 155
Christian religion, books of, 69
Christianity, introduction into Frankish lands, 365
Christians, in Alexandria, 51; best honorific for, 379; in Cairo, 119, 123–25; divorce, 177–79; in Egypt, 139; imitation of Muslims, 73, 119; monasteries, 137, 287–89; monks, 55, 155; polite address to, 421n115. *See also* priests
church books, 155
Church Missionary Society (CMS), 417n66
churches, 53, 77–79, 417n66
clothes/clothes making, words for, 337–63
confession, women during, 79
Copts, 59, 103, 119, 139, 379, 420n89
critics, 157, 163–73, 375, 424n141

Damascene territories, 51, 151
Damascus, 231
Days of Barbarism, 23, 187–89, 257, 315
the dead, praise of, 375–77
the Devil, 53–55, 83, 291
diversity of life, 9–15
divorce, 175–85; expression associated with, 425n155; the Fāriyāq's poem about, 185; *maqāmah* about, 175–85; Muslims, 411n8; pre-Islamic divorce formula, 425n154; scholars, 183–85
doctors/physicians, advice concerning women, 173; an impotent doctor, 391–93; fatness of, 377; goodness of, 31; scholars compared to, 377; treatment of the Fāriyāq, 143–49
Domestic Services Office, 107–9
donkey(s), elegy for, 371–75, 379; emirs and, 299, 387–89; the Fāriyāq's journey with a, 387–89; men's thoughts about, 299, 363
dress, 29, 39–41
drink(s), words for, 283–87
dwellings, words for, 223–25

Eastern churches, 417n66

ecclesiastical titles, 137

Egypt, Coptic Christians in, 139; the Fāriyāq's journey to, 83; *hayḍah* epidemic, 385–87; hospitality in, 151; Jews in, 119–21; mail delivery in, 129–31; people of, 157; scholars in, 139; as a state, 85–87, 119–21; Upper Egypt, 399. *See also* Alexandria, Cairo

Egyptians, 87, 403

emir(s), donkeys and, 299; the Fāriyāq's boy servant taken into service of, 387–89; poets, 143–47

England, 417n66

English notables, two, 73

English queens, 291

Europeans, 414n48

faces, words for, 89–101

al-Farazdaq, 127, 421n104

Farḥāt, Jirmānūs, 422n126

the Fāriyāq (protagonist of *Leg over Leg*), Aḥmad, Shaykh, 385; in Alexandria, 9, 39, 59–61, 85; Alexandria, voyage/travel to, 85, 397; bad luck of, 63; the bag, burden of, 127, 155; Bag-man/Bag-men, 59–63, 73–75, 81–83, 85, 123, 161, 397–99; in Cairo, 85–87, 103, 389, 397; countryside, travel in, 387–89; critics of, 375; doctor's treatment of, 143–47; donkey, journey by, 387–89; Egypt, journey to, 83; exile from his homeland, 61; Frankish dress worn by, 149; Maḥmūd, Shaykh, 385; on Malta, 73, 81–83; Malta, voyage to, 63, 69; marriage, consideration of, 407; Muhammad, Shaykh, 399; Muṣṭafā, Shaykh, 383–85; obscurity, preference for, 157; poetry by, 163–73, 185, 383; as a scholar, 157; scholarship, 383; servants of, 387–89; sicknesses, 383–89, 405–7; study of grammar, 383–85; study of jurisprudence, 389; study of *Kanz* (*The Treasure*), 389; study of prosody, 397–99; study of *al-Risālah al-Sanūsiyyah* (*The Senoussi Treatise*), 389; study of theology, 389; tambour, 103, 161, 407; as a teacher, 389, 397; title for, 379–81; writing, foreswearing of, 379; Yanṣur, letter to Khawājā, 123–33, 143; Yanṣur, visit with Khawājā, 151–57, 173

al-Farrā', 369, 432n265

fish, words for, 269–73

flowers, 11, 15

food, roundness and, 193

food, women as, 289

food eaten in Alexandria, 51

foods, words for, 257–87

Frankish countries, 193

Frankish dress, 149

Frankish headwear, 39, 57, 109–11

Frankish lands, Christianity in, 365

Frankish queens, 291

Frankish titles/honorifics, 135

Frankish women, 67, 77, 401

Franks, in Alexandria, 57; Egyptians' regard for, 403; hospitality, 151; letters of introduction, 151; limbs, 107; plague avoidance measures, 403; pronunciation of Arabic, 63–69, 414n49

fungi, words for, 267–69

games/diversions, words for, 243–53

garments, words for, 337–63

Genesis (book), 299, 431n248

al-Ghabab (*The Wattle*), 163, 423n137
girls, a Bag-man's serving girl, 401; beautiful serving girls, 139; in Cairo, 107–9, 175; a Copt's daughter, 103; a doctor's wife, 391–93, 391–95; faces of pretty girls, 91; the Fāriyāq's servant girl, 387–89; garments for, 343, 359, 361; Khayzurān, 229; milk for fattening, 267; veils, 45; words for, 195–97, 201–17, 301
Grand Panjandrum of the Panegyricon, 163

al-Ḥakākah fī l-rakākah (*The Leavings Pile Concerning Lame Style*) (Atanāsiyūs al-Tutūnji), 69, 137, 417–18n67
hashish, 113
headwear, in Alexandria, 39; Frankish, 39, 57, 109–11; market traders', 35–37; of Market-men of the Levant, 75–77; tarbush, 109
al-Hāwif ibn Hifām, 175, 183–85
heaven, words for, 233–35
Himyaritic lands, 51, 414n49
Hind, 187
horns, bulls', 163; dragging men by their, 391; husbands', 179; rams with and without, 139
hospitality, 57, 117, 151
household items, words for, 325–33
houses, words for, 227–29
humanity, common, 31
hunger, 29, 31, 75, 81, 85, 193

Ibn al-ʿAbbād, al-Ṣāḥib, 63, 416n63
Ibn al-Athīr, 301, 412n22
Ibn Aybak al-Ṣafadī, Khalīl, 85, 418n71
Ibn Hishām, 237, 428n203
Ibn Sīnā, 243
idols, words for, 21–27
the ignorant, scholars compared to, 377
Ilyās, 25, 405, 412n21
imra'ah, 289
Irene, 291
ʿĪsā, 51–53, 415n52
Islam, conversion to, 103, 412n19, 412n22
Islam, scholars of, 49
Islamic astronomy, 411n1
Islamic lands, 119
Islamic law, 139

jāmiʿ, 53
Jarīr, 127, 421n105
Jew(s), divorce, 181; in Egypt, 119–21; the Fāriyāq called a, 161; fish not eaten by, 269; *midrās* of, 229
jewelry, words for, 301–15
Juḥā, 369

Kaaba of Mecca, 21
Kanz (*The Treasure*), 389, 433n282
Khawājā (term of address), 129, 131, 137, 141, 143, 151–55, 173, 420, 421
Kitchen People, 65
kubaybah/kubbah, 145, 422n119
al-Kulliyyāt (*The Universals*), 187

lanterns, 109–11
Lebanon, 151, 422n125. *See also* Mountain, the
the Levant, 73, 75–77, 81, 117
Levantines, 145, 383
logic, 53
low matters, 9–11
lutes, 119, 255

Maḥmūd, Shaykh, 385

Malta, the Fāriyāq on, 71, 81–83; the Fāriyāq's voyage to, 63, 69; language spoken on, 79; priests on, 75–77; women on, 77–79

mantles, words for, 351–55

maqāmah, about marriage/divorce, 175–85

Market Boss, distress, his, 33; indifference to people's troubles, 37; market traders, disputes between, 35

market ledger, 37, 61

market traders, 35–37, 77

Market-man/Market-men, Bag-man/Bag-men, feuds with, 61, 77, 81; damage done by, 21; English queens, 291; indifference to people's troubles, 33–35; of the Levant, 75–77; tools of the trade, 15, 29

Market-woman/Market-women, 77–79

marriage, the Fāriyāq considers, 407

marriage, *maqāmah* about, 175–85

marriage, nature of, 191

mawwāl, 107, 119

meadows, words for, 221

meals, 193

Melkites, 421n113

men, beardless boys, 363; in Cairo, 105–7; erectile dysfunction, 289; impotent husbands, 391; poetry by, 299; thin men, 403; thoughts about donkeys, 299, 363; wise men, 31; women, knowledge of, 367–69; women compared to, 289, 295–99, 365, 367; women's thoughts about, 363

Messiah, 155

metropolitan (religious leader), 55–57, 155, 291

milk, words for kinds of, 275

monastery, 137, 287–89

monks, 55, 155

Mountain, the (Mount Lebanon), 153

Muʿallim (term of address), 137–39, 421n115

Muḥammad, Shaykh, 399

Muḥammad ʿAlī Pasha, 420n96

mujārazah, 117

musical instruments, words for, 255–57

Muslims, Christian imitation of, 73, 119; Copts and, 119; divorce, 177–81, 411n8; of the Levant, 117; titles (honorifics) for, 379

Muṣṭafā, Shaykh, 383–85, 432n272

al-Mutanabbī, 127, 163, 421n107

Muʿtazilite, 365

Nākir and Nakīr, 111, 405

New Testament, 155

Nile River, 107

non-Arabs, quick-witted woman on, 67

Nūh (Noah), 25, 221, 243

nūn, 187–89

nuns, 155

Nuʿūmah Mosque, 53, 415n57

Occidentals, 135

Panegyricon, 157, 161–63, 383, 423n132

panegyrics, 127, 167, 171, 379

panegyrist, a prince's, 387

paronomasia, al-Bustī, 127; in the Fāriyāq's poetry, 167–69; perfect paronomasia, 424n145; poets, 157; solecisms, 171

people, diversity of, 13–15

People of the Cave, 221, 427n183

perfumes/aromas, words for, 315–25

Persian(s), 59, 109

physicians/doctors. *See* doctors/physicians
pigs, 75
places, words for various, 231–33
plants, types of, 11
poetry, about divorce, 185; about veils, 45; elegy for a donkey, 371–75, 379; by the Fāriyāq, 163–73, 185, 383; *mawwāl*, 107, 119; by men, 299; for princes, 163–73; prose compared to, 375–77; as a means of survival, 377–79
by women, 299
poets, in Cairo, 105, 107, 123–29; celebrity, 157; characteristics, 123–25; diversity among, 13; drooling by, 97; emirs, 143–47; the manner of most, 377–79; need for critics, 157; paronomasia, 157; by trade vs. by nature, 125; women, 289
pork, 73–75, 81
priests, Arabic-language sermon by, 63–69; deference to, 379–81; doctor's wife's choice of, 395; as lovers, advantages of, 395; on Malta, 75–77
prose, by churchmen, 155–57; greetings and salutations, 129–31; long words, 189; *maqāmah*, 175–85; masters of, 87; Muṣṭafā, Shaykh, 385; quotations, use of, 375; verbs, proper use of, 55; verse compared to, 375–77
Protestant missionaries. *See* Bag-man/Bag-men

Qāmūs (al-Fīrūzābādī), 135, 365, 418n76
Qay'ar Qay'ār, 51, 59, 155, 414n48
qissīs ("priest"), 379
queens, 291
quotations, use in books, 375
Qur'an, 49, 189

Ra's al-Tīn, 414n47
resurrection, failed attempt at, 405
Revelation, 165, 187
rhymed prose (*saj'*), about Alexandria, 85–89; in the Fāriyāq's letter to Khawājā Yanṣur, 125–29; Khawājā Yanṣur on, 153–55; *maqāmah* in, 175–85
al-Risālah al-Sanūsiyyah (*The Senoussi Treatise*), 389, 433n283
saddlebags, 33, 59
St. Matthew, 155
St. Paul, 155
saj'. *See* rhymed prose
Ṣāliḥ (prophet), 221, 427n183
scholarly knowledge, 433n276
scholar(s), on a distinguishing feature of Arabic, 371; in Cairo, 107, 117; as critics of the Fāriyāq, 375; debate with a Mu'tazilite, 365; divorce, 183–85; doctors/physicians compared to, 377; in Egypt, 139; erudition, demonstrations of, 129; the Fāriyāq as a, 157; health of, 377; the ignorant compared to, 377; of Islam, 49; Islamic law, 139; market traders' hats, 37; physical weakness, 377; Qay'ar Qay'ār, 51; of religion, 189; women, 195, 295, 297, 369
scholarship, 107, 383
sciences, 53
sea-going vessels, words for, 69–73
second skins, 135–37, 141
senses, 11, 101
Sharḥ al-Kāfī (*The Commentary on the Kāfī*), 399
Sharḥ al-Sullam (*The Commentary on the Ladder*), study of, 385

Shaykh (term of address), 137–39, 379, 379, 383, 432n270
al-Shidyāq, [Aḥmad] Fāris, 417n66, 422n126, 423n132
Shifāʾ (*The Cure*) (Ibn Sīnā), 243
sickness, 383–85
skin flaps, 139
sleepers, 193
Society for Promoting Christian Knowledge (SPCK), 417n66
Sons of Ḥannā, 111, 420n89
stars, 11–13
Sterne, Laurence, 430n244
stones, words for, 335–37
Sulaymān (Solomon), 63, 129, 219
Sunnis, 365
al-Suyūṭī, 432n267
sweet things, words for, 275–83

taghlīb, 167, 423–24n140
al-Talkhīṣ fī l-maʿānī (*The Epitome on Tropes*), 385, 433n277
tambour, 103, 161, 257, 407
teacher, the Fāriyāq as, 389, 397
Theodora, 291
thirst, 193
time, 51–53
Timothy, 155
titles (honorific), 135–39, 379, 421n112
translators, 155–57, 423n130, 423n131
trees/woods, words for, 333–35
Tripoli, 137, 417n66, 421n113
Tristam Shandy (Sterne), 430n244
troopers, 57
tropes, 15
Tunis, 119, 420n97
Tunisia, 121
Turkish lady, 57–59
Turkish trooper, 57
Turks, 45–49, 103

Uḥayḥah, 229, 427n194
ʿUlayyān, 191
Upper Egypt, 399

veil-passion, 103
veils, catamites', 109; decent women's, 21; girls, 45; imagination, 89; poem about, 45; protection for, 413n29; sodomites, 419n88; ugliness concealed by, 41; words for, 359
verbs, proper use of, 55
viceroy of Egypt, 119–21, 420n96

al-Waqāʾiʿ al-Miṣriyyah, 423n132
wise men, 31
wives, unfaithful, 391
wives, words for, 291
women, 195–219; alcohol, 297; in Alexandria, 41–45; attention paid to, 191; backside, 295; bag, their, 195, 426n177; belly, 295; bewitching looks, 367; bodies and faces compared, 101–3; boldness, 219; in Cairo, 105–7; cheeks, 97–99; in China, 107; Christianity, 365; clemency, 295; clothed, fully, 101; coquettishness, 201, 207, 215; creation of, 191; doctor's advice concerning, 173; dreams of, 191–93; in Egypt, 87–89; essence, 101; European depictions, 419n83; evil, 369; eyes, 99; faces, 89–101; fantasies about, 219–21; fingers, 107; flirtatiousness, 41–45, 367; as food, 289; Frankish women, 67, 77, 401; generosity, 297;

women (cont.), great/good actions/ undertakings, 289, 291; heads of state, 291; household management, 369; *imra'ah*, 289; legs, 295; lips, 91–93; longevity, 297; on Malta, 77–79; Market-woman/Market-women, 77–79; men, knowledge of, 367–69; men, thoughts about, 363; men compared to, 289, 295–99, 365, 367; mouths, 97–99; naked, 101; necks, 99; nobility, 295; noses, 93–95; nuns, 155; payment in kind, 367; poetry by, 299; poets, 289; pregnant women, 367; presence of, 287–89; pretty ones, 41; quick-witted woman on non-Arabs, 67; scholars, 195, 295, 297, 369; seductiveness, 87, 195; sensuality, 201, 207, 215, 219; sharp-witted Sunni woman, 365; shaving by, 79; sleeping with, 363–65; teeth, 91; ugly ones, 41; unavailable women, 287–89; vanity, 41; virtue, 297; votive offerings, 79; warmth, bodily, 363–65; wives, unfaithful, 391; wives, words for, 291; words for, 195–219; *See also* girls

wonders, words for, 235–43

woods/trees, words for, 333–35

writers, attacks on, 375

writing, pleasures of, 377

Yanṣur, Khawājā, the Fāriyāq's letter to, 123–33, 143

Yanṣur, Khawājā, the Fāriyāq's visits to, 151–57, 173

Ya'qūb (Jacob), 101

Yūnus (Jonah), 221

Yūsuf (Joseph), 221

Zayd and 'Amr, 33, 129, 187, 383, 421n109, 433n273

Zubaydah, 297, 430n246

About the NYU Abu Dhabi Institute

NYU
ABU DHABI
INSTITUTE

The Library of Arabic Literature is supported by a grant from The NYU Abu Dhabi Institute, a major hub of intellectual and creative activity and advanced research. The Institute hosts academic conferences, workshops, lectures, film series, performances, and other public programs directed both to audiences within the UAE and to the worldwide academic and research community. It is a center of the scholarly community for Abu Dhabi, bringing together faculty and researchers from institutions of higher learning throughout the region.

NYU Abu Dhabi, through the NYU Abu Dhabi Institute, is a world-class center of cutting-edge research, scholarship, and cultural activity. The Institute creates singular opportunities for leading researchers from across the arts, humanities, social sciences, sciences, engineering, and the professions to carry out creative scholarship and conduct research on issues of major disciplinary, multidisciplinary, and global significance.

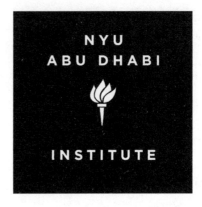

About the Typefaces

The Arabic body text is set in DecoType Naskh, designed by Thomas Milo and Mirjam Somers, based on an analysis of five centuries of Ottoman manuscript practice. The exceptionally legible result is the first and only typeface in a style that fully implements the principles of script grammar (*qawāʿid al-khaṭṭ*).

The Arabic text in the footnotes and margin notes is set in DecoType Emiri, drawn by Mirjam Somers, based on the metal typeface in the naskh style that was cut for the 1924 Cairo edition of the Qur'an.

Both Arabic typefaces in this series are controlled by a dedicated font layout engine. ACE, the Arabic Calligraphic Engine, invented by Peter Somers, Thomas Milo, and Mirjam Somers of DecoType, first operational in 1985, pioneered the principle followed by later smart font layout technologies such as OpenType, which is used for all other typefaces in this series.

The Arabic text was set with WinSoft Tasmeem, a sophisticated user interface for DecoType ACE inside Adobe InDesign. Tasmeem was conceived and created by Thomas Milo (DecoType) and Pascal Rubini (WinSoft) in 2005.

The English text is set in Adobe Text, a new and versatile text typeface family designed by Robert Slimbach for Western (Latin, Greek, Cyrillic) typesetting. Its workhorse qualities make it perfect for a wide variety of applications, especially for longer passages of text where legibility and economy are important. Adobe Text bridges the gap between calligraphic Renaissance types of the 15th and 16th centuries and high-contrast Modern styles of the 18th century, taking many of its design cues from early post-Renaissance Baroque transitional types cut by designers such as Christoffel van Dijck, Nicolaus Kis, and William Caslon. While grounded in classical form, Adobe Text is also a statement of contemporary utilitarian design, well suited to a wide variety of print and on-screen applications.

About the Editor-Translator

Humphrey Davies is an award-winning translator of some twenty works of modern Arabic literature, among them Alaa Al-Aswany's *The Yacoubian Building* and Elias Khoury's *The Gate of the Sun*. He has also made a critical edition, translation, and lexicon of the Ottoman-period *Hazz al-quḥūf bi-sharḥ Abī Shādūf* (*Brains Confounded by the Ode of Abū Shadūf Expounded*) by Yūsuf al-Shirbīnī and compiled with a colleague an anthology entitled *Al-ʿāmmiyyah al-miṣriyyah al-maktūbah: mukhtārāt min 1400 ilā 2009* (*Egyptian Colloquial Writing: selections from 1400 to 2009*). He read Arabic at the University of Cambridge, received his Ph.D. from the University of California at Berkeley, and, previous to undertaking his first translation in 2003, worked for social development and research organizations in Egypt, Tunisia, Palestine, and Sudan. He is affiliated with the American University in Cairo, where he lives.